F SM!

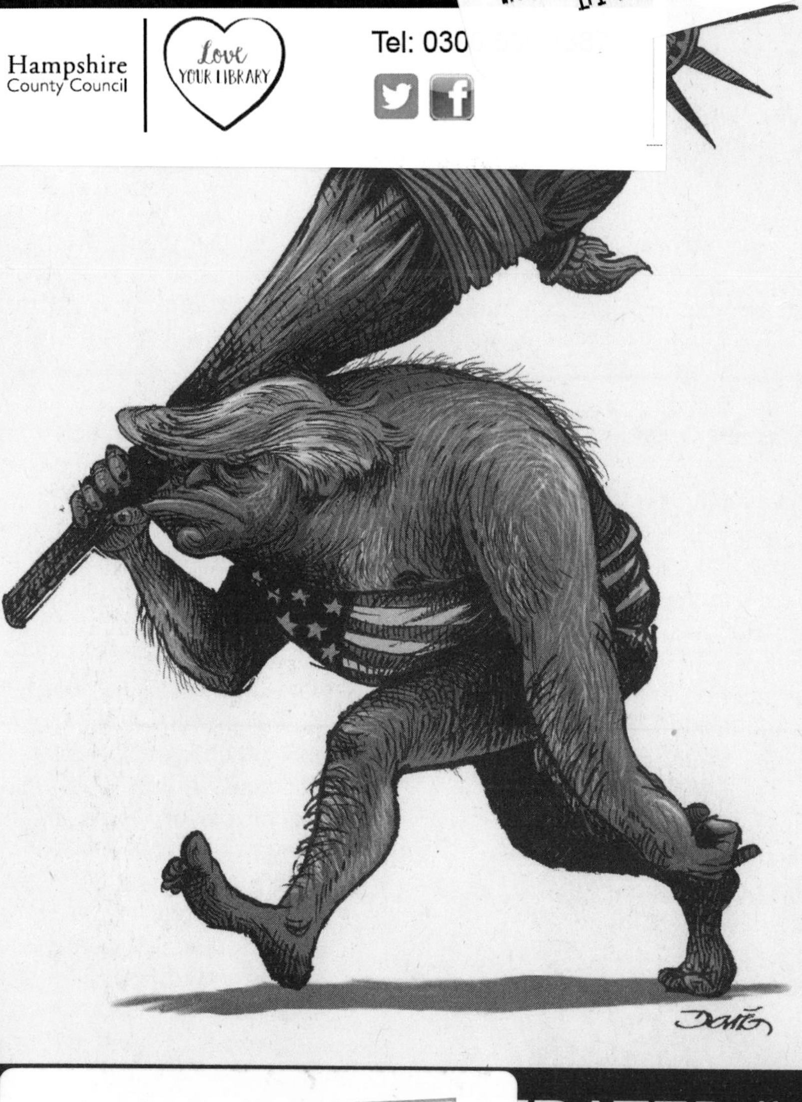

WOR TRATED # 48

FIGHT FASCISM!

This collection of comics and illustrations responds to the emergence of fascism in the United States in 2017. Fascism evident in the election of Donald Trump, and in the words and actions of his supporters and administration. But this book is also a tribute to the broad-based resistance we have seen this year.

This is the 48th issue of the magazine *World War 3 Illustrated.* Because of the collapse of magazine distribution in the U.S., we have transformed *World War 3 Illustrated* into an annual book, published as an imprint of AK Press.

World War 3 Illustrated was founded in 1979 to resist the rise of Ronald Reagan through art and comics. At that time we pointed out the danger of a fascist tendency on the Republican right. We also addressed police brutality, homelessness, gentrification and many other issues that unfortunately remain troublesome today. We have been consistent in our art and politics for nearly 40 years. Today the staff of the magazine includes original members as well as artists who were not yet born when we started.

This history affords us a unique perspective. There are many parallels between the days of Trump and the age of Reagan, and some differences. In many ways Trump is a crude parody of Reagan, down to the surreal exaggeration of a 1950s haircut.

Trump has plagiarized Reagan's signature rhetorical technique. Reagan would make public statements, that sounded like ignorant gaffs, but that also reflected widely held beliefs. Liberals would take the bait and ridicule him. The result would be that a large section of the population would come to the conclusion that the Democrats were elitist.

Both presidents are huge hypocrites when it comes to patriotism. Reagan had covert dealings with the government of Iran, and presided over the destruction of the U.S. economy, while Mr. "America First" is indeed the first American president to face credible charges of colluding with Russia to win an election.

Reagan, like Trump, had ties to the Klan, Nazis, etc. There is a long tradition of such ties within the American government and the financial elites. Men like Henry Ford and Prescott Bush had close relations with Adolf Hitler. But Trump is the first president since World War II to bring such alliances out in the open and seek respectability for American fascism.

There is one big difference. Ronald Reagan was the President of the United States, elected by the majority of the voters. Donald Trump would be nowhere without the electoral college, gerrymandering and voter suppression. Trump is a minority president, with extreme views which many Americans find obnoxious.

The opposition to Trump includes people from every walk of life. Not only artists, but football players. Not only students, but parents and teachers. Not only the poor and the dispossessed, but the middle class and even executives of some major corporations. If Reagan had faced this sort of opposition, the history of the last 30 years would have been much different and the world would probably be a happier and safer place today.

So this publication is not only a warning about the current administration, but a tribute to all of you who stand in resistance. It is not only an accusation directed against the American government but an expression of our belief in all of you and in what we can do together.

–The Editors

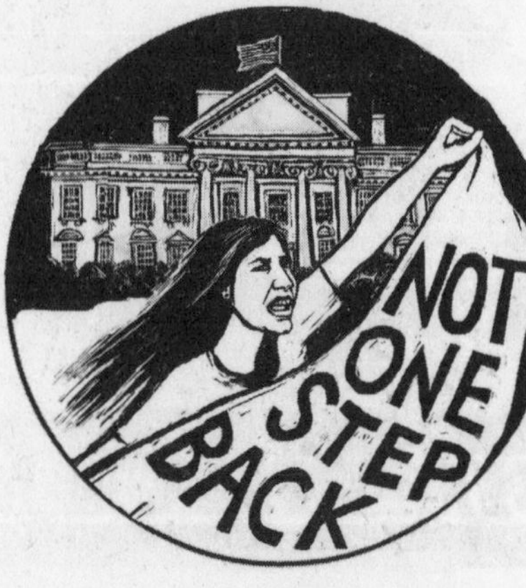
NOT ONE STEP BACK

Art: Susan Simensky Bietila

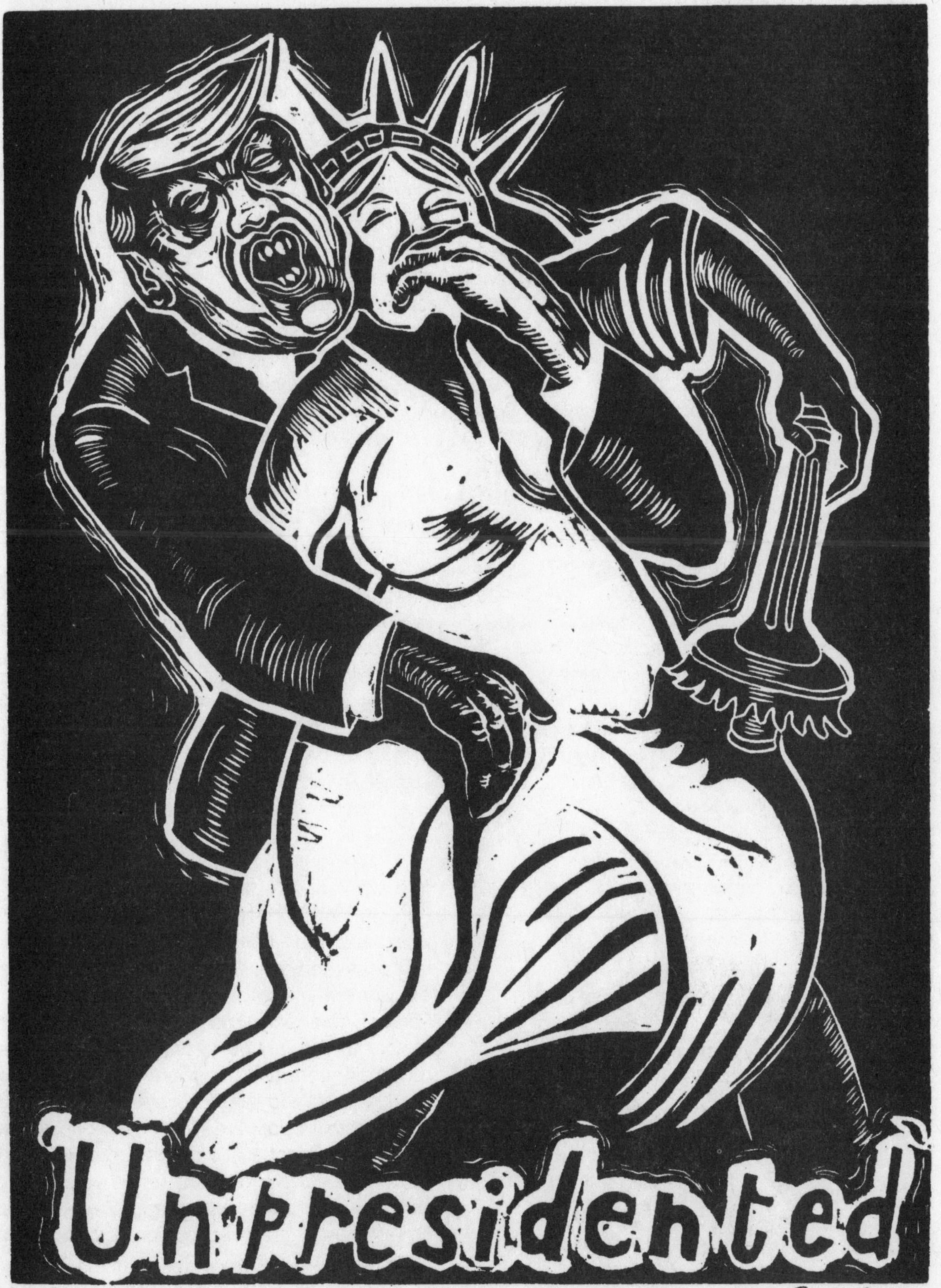
Unpresidented

Sue Coe 2017

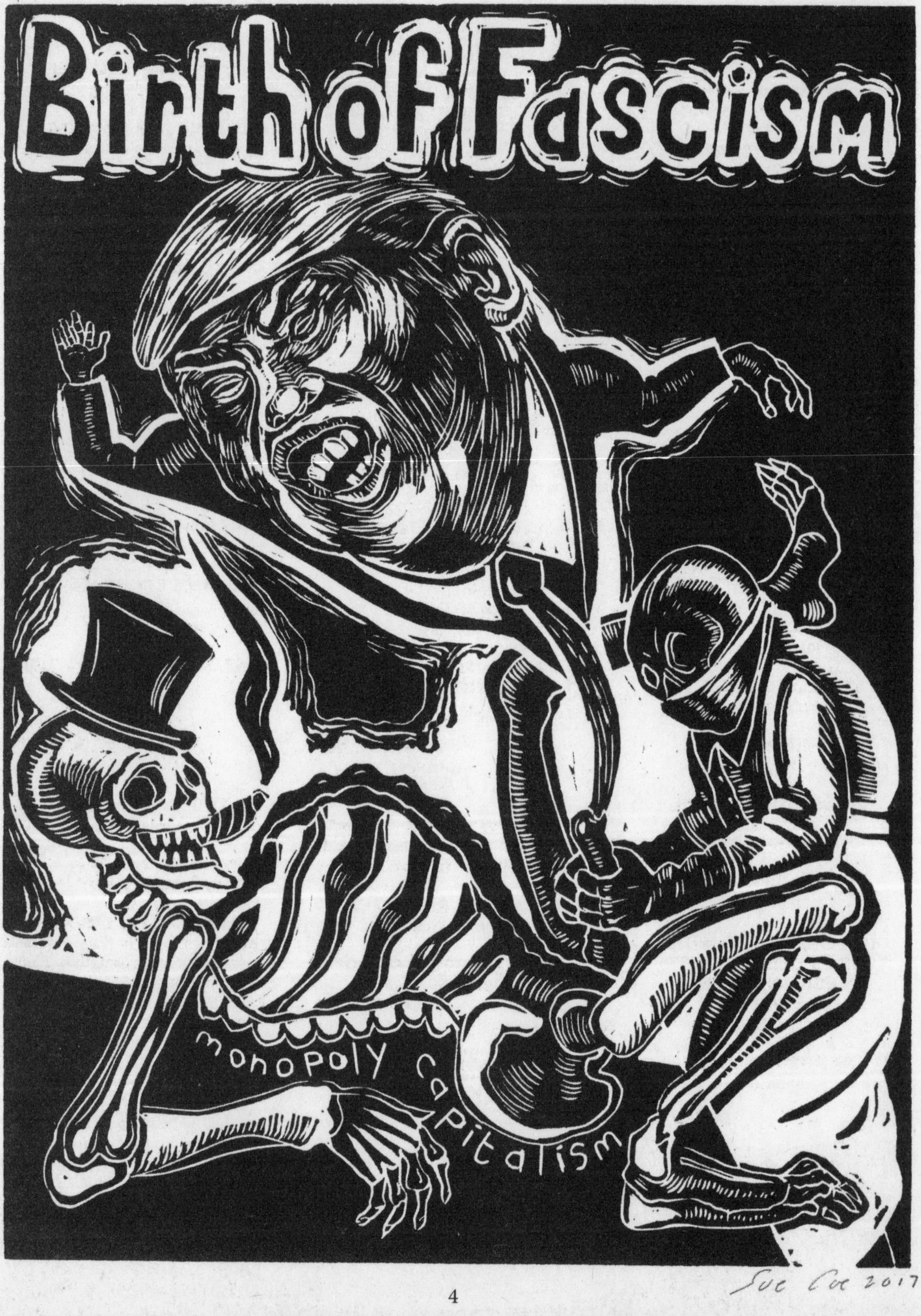
Birth of Fascism
monopoly capitalism
Sue Coe 2017

CONTENTS:

EDITORS THIS ISSUE:
Jordan Worley, Peter Kuper, Isabella
Bannerman, Susan Simensky Bietila,
Sandy Jimenez, and Seth Tobocman
World War 3 Illustrated is © 2017
to World War 3 Incorporated
All artwork is © the artist.

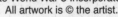

DEFINE FASCISM.

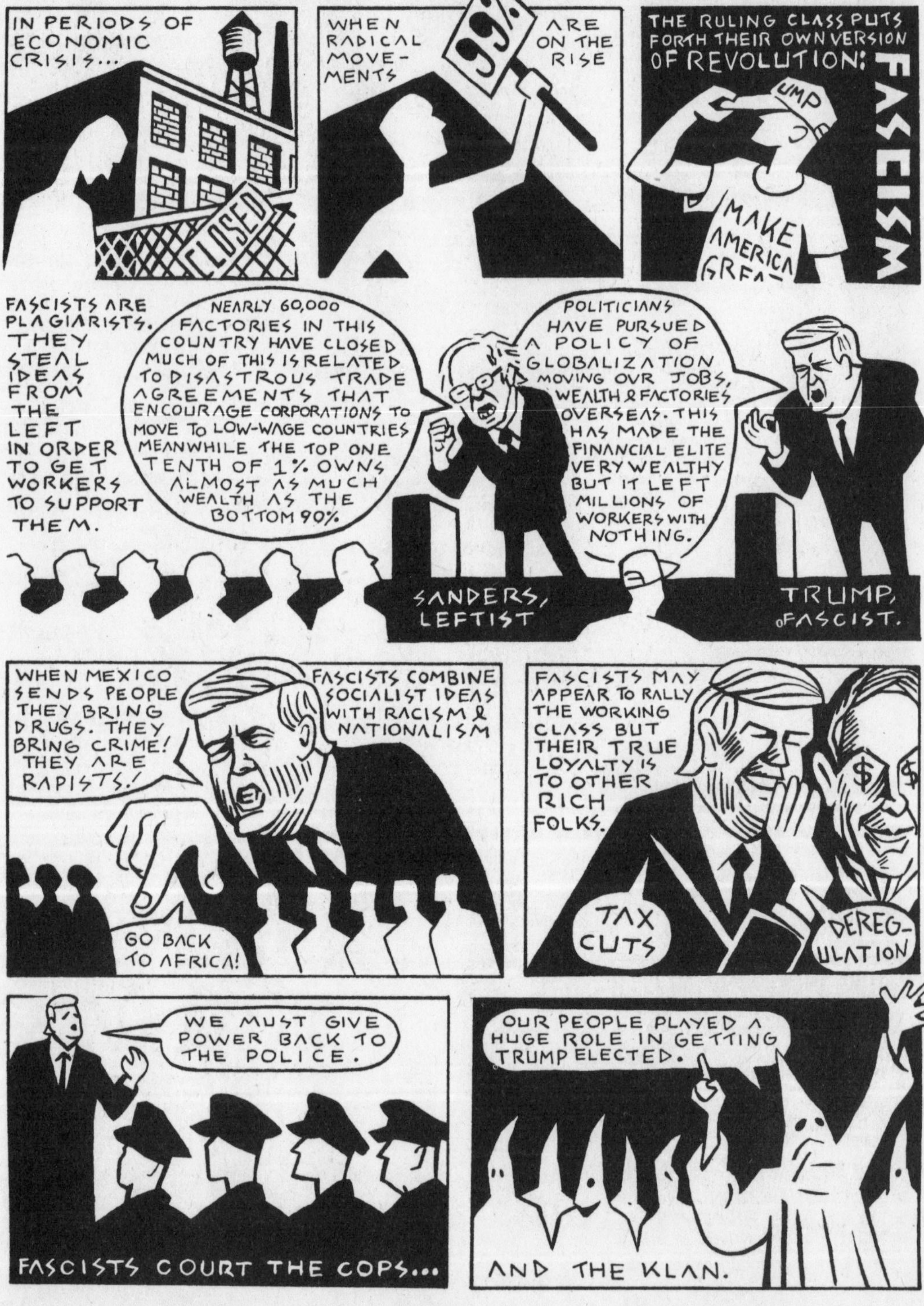

IN PERIODS OF ECONOMIC CRISIS...
CLOSED
WHEN RADICAL MOVEMENTS
99%
ARE ON THE RISE
THE RULING CLASS PUTS FORTH THEIR OWN VERSION OF REVOLUTION:
FASCISM
UMP
MAKE AMERICA GREA
FASCISTS ARE PLAGIARISTS. THEY STEAL IDEAS FROM THE LEFT IN ORDER TO GET WORKERS TO SUPPORT THEM.
NEARLY 60,000 FACTORIES IN THIS COUNTRY HAVE CLOSED MUCH OF THIS IS RELATED TO DISASTROUS TRADE AGREEMENTS THAT ENCOURAGE CORPORATIONS TO MOVE TO LOW-WAGE COUNTRIES MEANWHILE THE TOP ONE TENTH OF 1% OWNS ALMOST AS MUCH WEALTH AS THE BOTTOM 90%.
POLITICIANS HAVE PURSUED A POLICY OF GLOBALIZATION MOVING OUR JOBS, WEALTH & FACTORIES OVERSEAS. THIS HAS MADE THE FINANCIAL ELITE VERY WEALTHY BUT IT LEFT MILLIONS OF WORKERS WITH NOTHING.
SANDERS, LEFTIST
TRUMP, FASCIST.
WHEN MEXICO SENDS PEOPLE THEY BRING DRUGS. THEY BRING CRIME! THEY ARE RAPISTS!
FASCISTS COMBINE SOCIALIST IDEAS WITH RACISM & NATIONALISM
GO BACK TO AFRICA!
FASCISTS MAY APPEAR TO RALLY THE WORKING CLASS BUT THEIR TRUE LOYALTY IS TO OTHER RICH FOLKS.
TAX CUTS
DEREGULATION
WE MUST GIVE POWER BACK TO THE POLICE.
FASCISTS COURT THE COPS...
OUR PEOPLE PLAYED A HUGE ROLE IN GETTING TRUMP ELECTED.
AND THE KLAN.

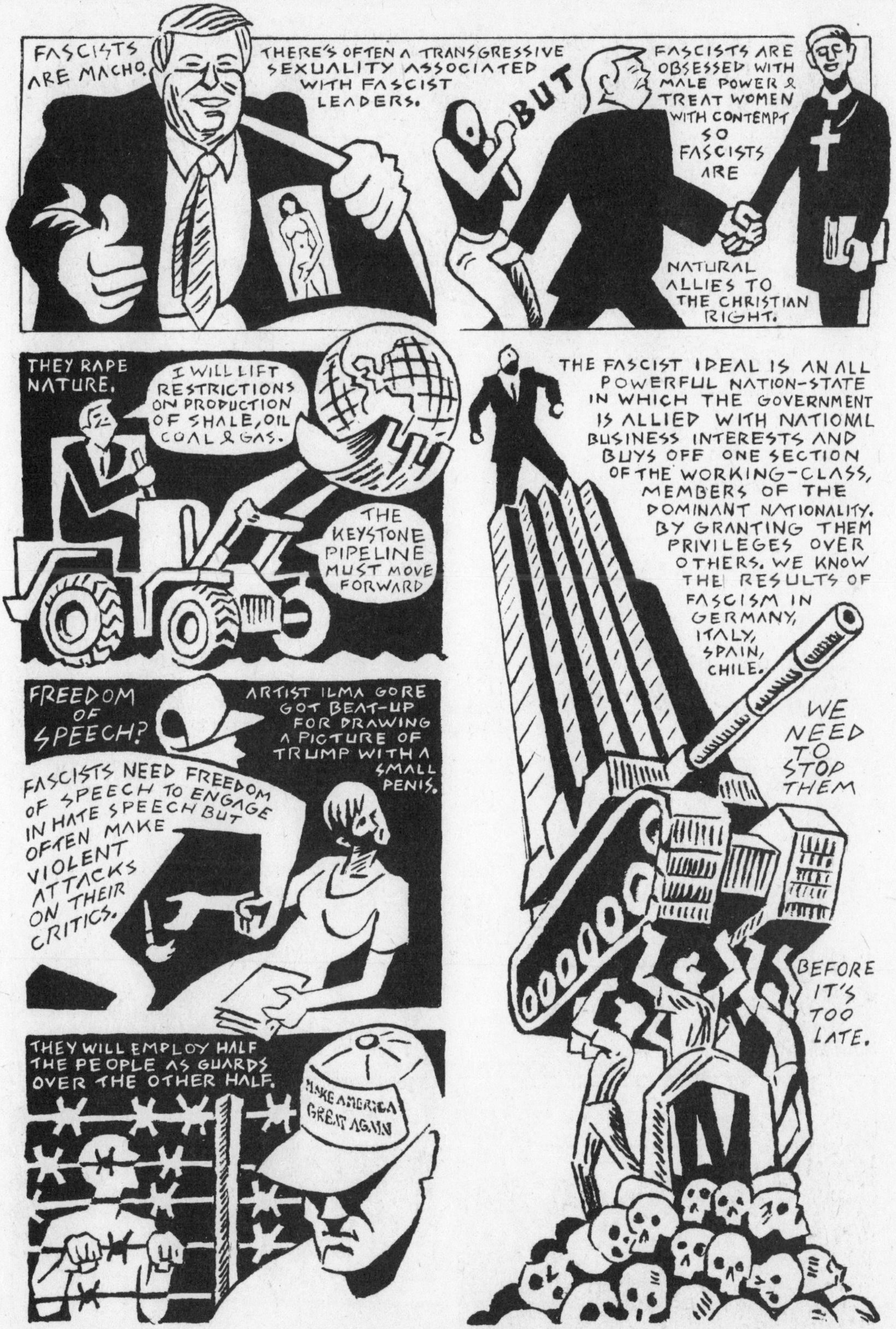

FASCISTS ARE MACHO.
THERE'S OFTEN A TRANSGRESSIVE SEXUALITY ASSOCIATED WITH FASCIST LEADERS.
BUT
FASCISTS ARE OBSESSED WITH MALE POWER & TREAT WOMEN WITH CONTEMPT SO FASCISTS ARE
NATURAL ALLIES TO THE CHRISTIAN RIGHT.
THEY RAPE NATURE.
I WILL LIFT RESTRICTIONS ON PRODUCTION OF SHALE, OIL COAL & GAS.
THE KEYSTONE PIPELINE MUST MOVE FORWARD
FREEDOM OF SPEECH?
ARTIST ILMA GORE GOT BEAT-UP FOR DRAWING A PICTURE OF TRUMP WITH A SMALL PENIS.
FASCISTS NEED FREEDOM OF SPEECH TO ENGAGE IN HATE SPEECH BUT OFTEN MAKE VIOLENT ATTACKS ON THEIR CRITICS.
THEY WILL EMPLOY HALF THE PEOPLE AS GUARDS OVER THE OTHER HALF.
MAKE AMERICA GREAT AGAIN
THE FASCIST IDEAL IS AN ALL POWERFUL NATION-STATE IN WHICH THE GOVERNMENT IS ALLIED WITH NATIONAL BUSINESS INTERESTS AND BUYS OFF ONE SECTION OF THE WORKING-CLASS, MEMBERS OF THE DOMINANT NATIONALITY. BY GRANTING THEM PRIVILEGES OVER OTHERS. WE KNOW THE RESULTS OF FASCISM IN GERMANY, ITALY, SPAIN, CHILE.
WE NEED TO STOP THEM
BEFORE IT'S TOO LATE.

STORY AND ART BY SETH TOBOCMAN, INKED BY JORDAN WORLEY

H
VOTE
feggo

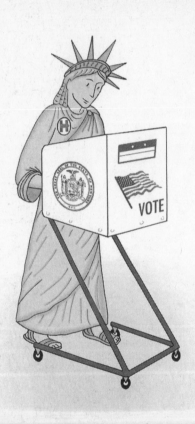

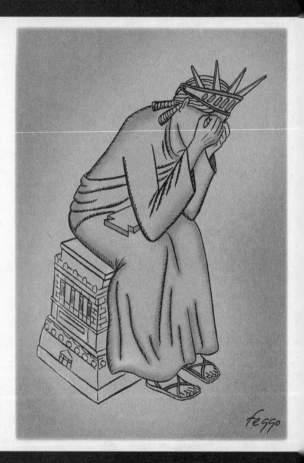

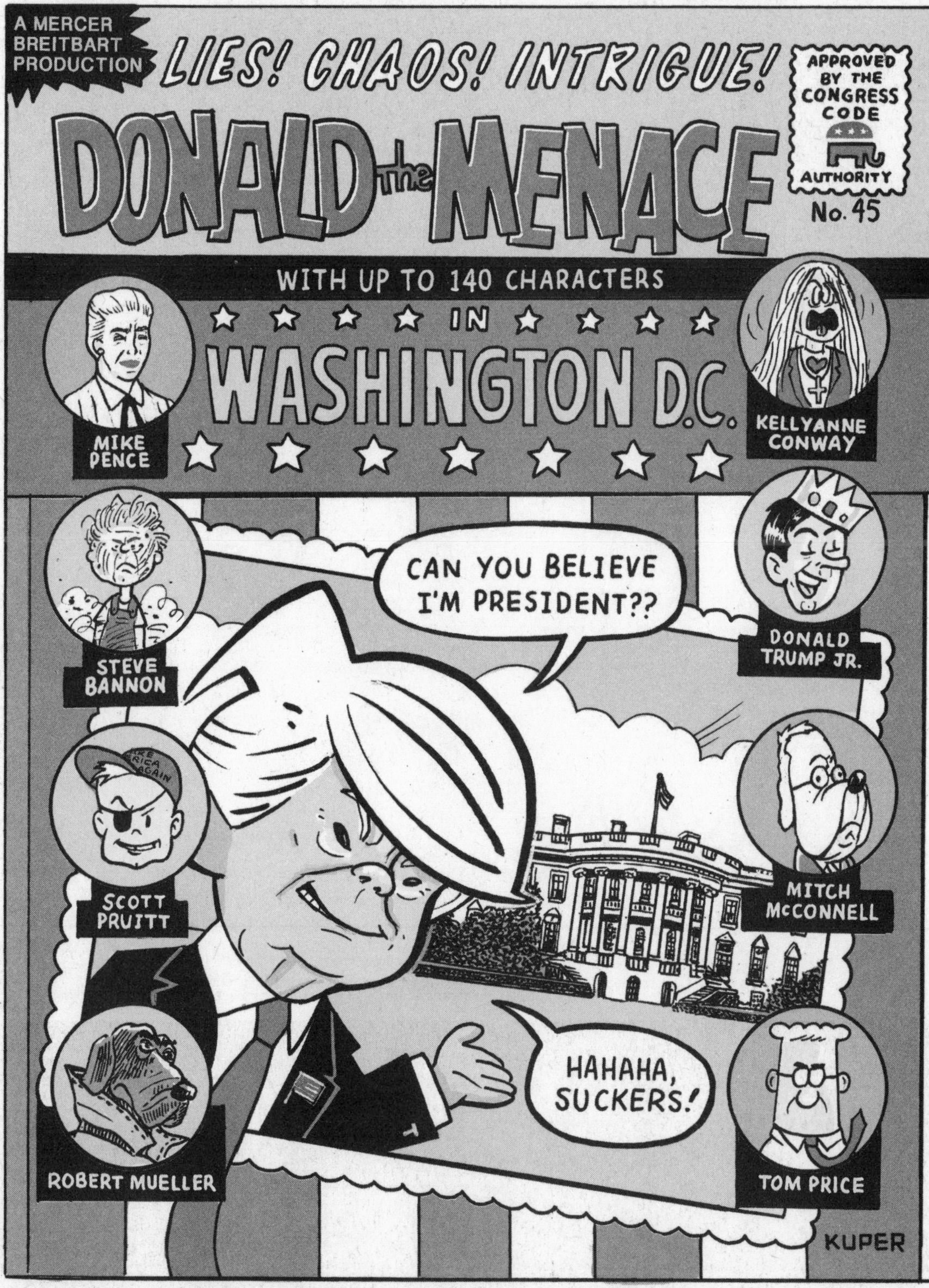

A MERCER BREITBART PRODUCTION
LIES! CHAOS! INTRIGUE!
APPROVED BY THE CONGRESS CODE AUTHORITY
DONALD the MENACE
No. 45
WITH UP TO 140 CHARACTERS
IN
WASHINGTON D.C.
MIKE PENCE
KELLYANNE CONWAY
STEVE BANNON
CAN YOU BELIEVE I'M PRESIDENT??
DONALD TRUMP JR.
SCOTT PRUITT
MITCH McCONNELL
HAHAHA, SUCKERS!
ROBERT MUELLER
TOM PRICE
KUPER

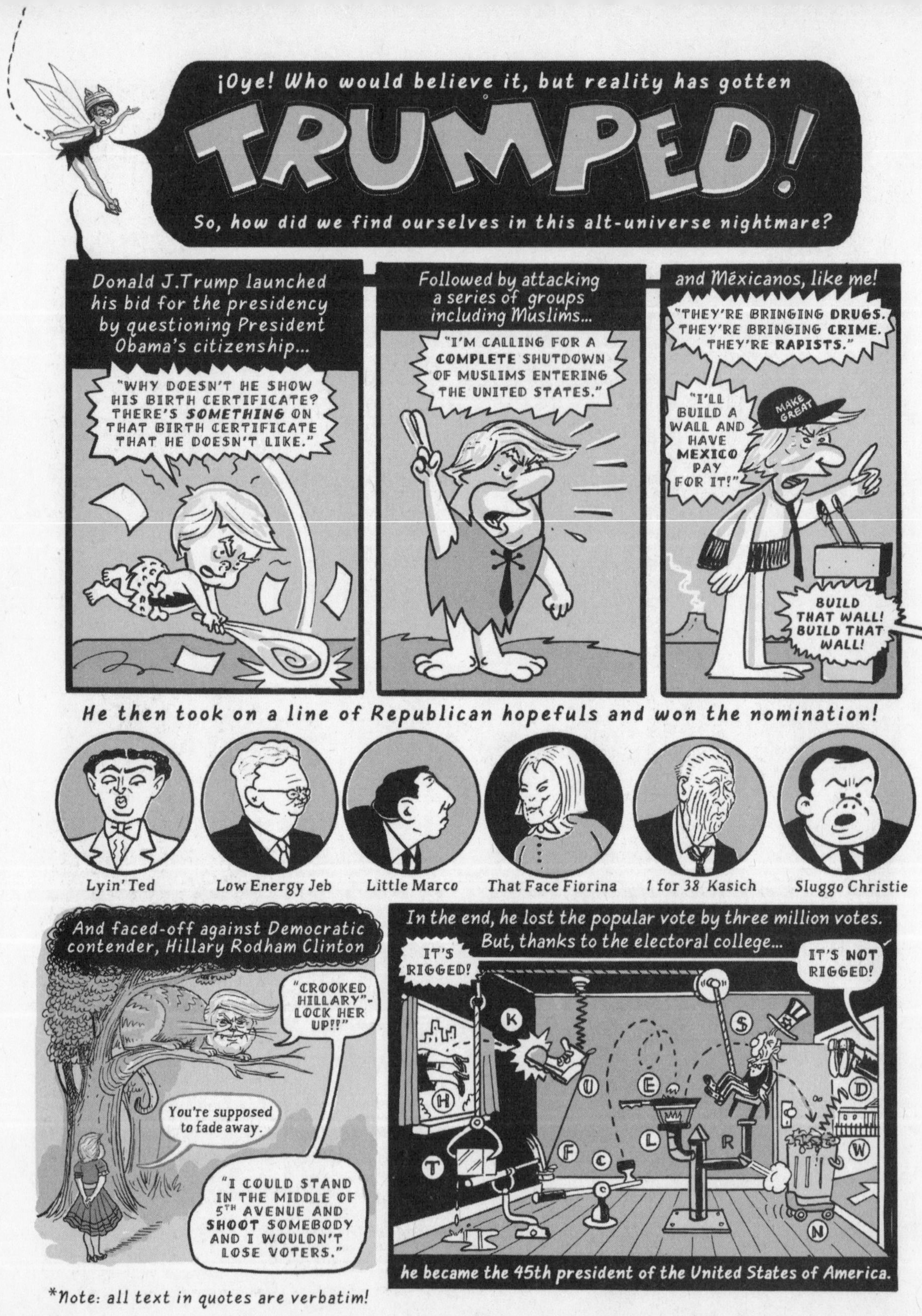

¡Oye! Who would believe it, but reality has gotten
TRUMPED!
So, how did we find ourselves in this alt-universe nightmare?
Donald J.Trump launched his bid for the presidency by questioning President Obama's citizenship...
"WHY DOESN'T HE SHOW HIS BIRTH CERTIFICATE? THERE'S SOMETHING ON THAT BIRTH CERTIFICATE THAT HE DOESN'T LIKE."
Followed by attacking a series of groups including Muslims...
"I'M CALLING FOR A COMPLETE SHUTDOWN OF MUSLIMS ENTERING THE UNITED STATES."
and Mëxicanos, like me!
"THEY'RE BRINGING DRUGS. THEY'RE BRINGING CRIME. THEY'RE RAPISTS."
MAKE GREAT
"I'LL BUILD A WALL AND HAVE MEXICO PAY FOR IT!"
BUILD THAT WALL! BUILD THAT WALL!
He then took on a line of Republican hopefuls and won the nomination!
Lyin' Ted
Low Energy Jeb
Little Marco
That Face Fiorina
1 for 38 Kasich
Sluggo Christie
And faced-off against Democratic contender, Hillary Rodham Clinton
"CROOKED HILLARY"- LOCK HER UP!!"
You're supposed to fade away.
"I COULD STAND IN THE MIDDLE OF 5TH AVENUE AND SHOOT SOMEBODY AND I WOULDN'T LOSE VOTERS."
In the end, he lost the popular vote by three million votes. But, thanks to the electoral college...
IT'S RIGGED!
IT'S NOT RIGGED!
he became the 45th president of the United States of America.

*Note: all text in quotes are verbatim!

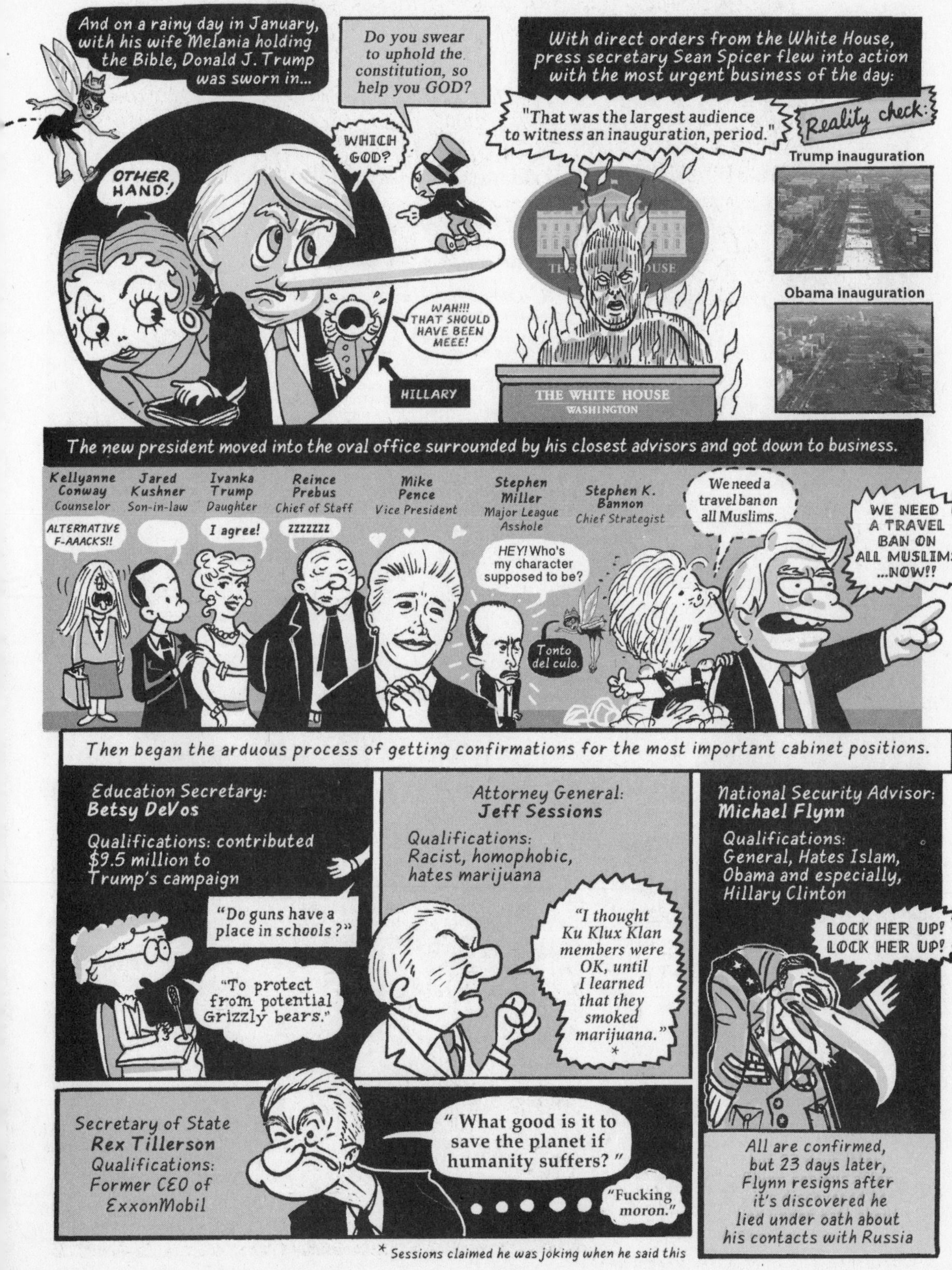

And on a rainy day in January, with his wife Melania holding the Bible, Donald J. Trump was sworn in...
Do you swear to uphold the constitution, so help you GOD?
WHICH GOD?
OTHER HAND!
WAH!!! THAT SHOULD HAVE BEEN MEEE!
HILLARY
With direct orders from the White House, press secretary Sean Spicer flew into action with the most urgent business of the day:
"That was the largest audience to witness an inauguration, period."
THE WHITE HOUSE WASHINGTON
Reality check:
Trump inauguration
Obama inauguration
The new president moved into the oval office surrounded by his closest advisors and got down to business.
Kellyanne Conway Counselor
Jared Kushner Son-in-law
Ivanka Trump Daughter
Reince Prebus Chief of Staff
Mike Pence Vice President
Stephen Miller Major League Asshole
Stephen K. Bannon Chief Strategist
ALTERNATIVE F-AAACKS!!
I agree!
ZZZZZZZ
HEY! Who's my character supposed to be?
Tonto del culo.
We need a travel ban on all Muslims.
WE NEED A TRAVEL BAN ON ALL MUSLIMS ...NOW!!
Then began the arduous process of getting confirmations for the most important cabinet positions.
Education Secretary: Betsy DeVos
Qualifications: contributed $9.5 million to Trump's campaign
"Do guns have a place in schools?"
"To protect from potential Grizzly bears."
Attorney General: Jeff Sessions
Qualifications: Racist, homophobic, hates marijuana
"I thought Ku Klux Klan members were OK, until I learned that they smoked marijuana." *
National Security Advisor: Michael Flynn
Qualifications: General, Hates Islam, Obama and especially, Hillary Clinton
LOCK HER UP! LOCK HER UP!
Secretary of State Rex Tillerson
Qualifications: Former CEO of ExxonMobil
"What good is it to save the planet if humanity suffers?"
"Fucking moron."
All are confirmed, but 23 days later, Flynn resigns after it's discovered he lied under oath about his contacts with Russia

* Sessions claimed he was joking when he said this

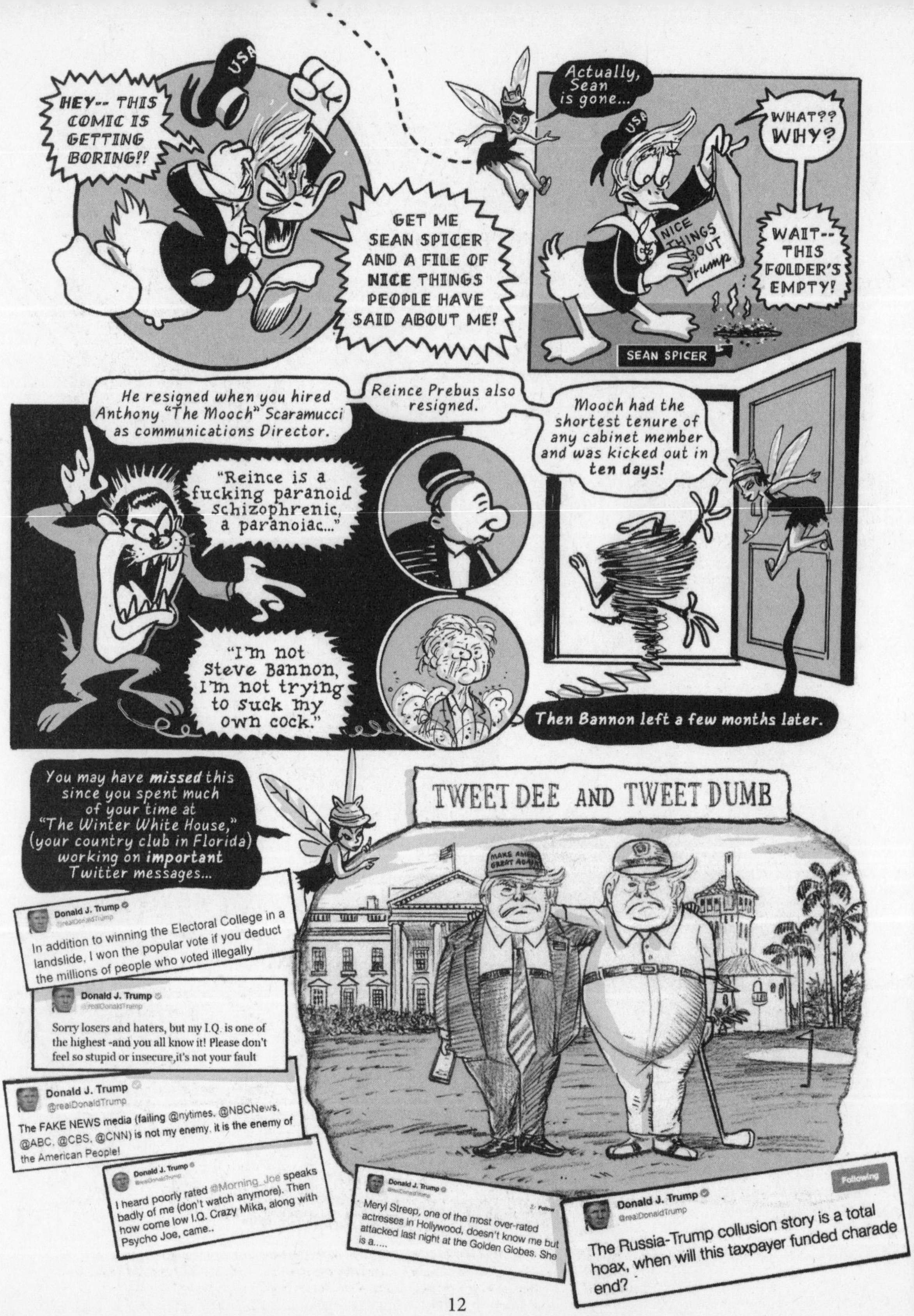
HEY-- THIS COMIC IS GETTING BORING!!
USA
GET ME SEAN SPICER AND A FILE OF NICE THINGS PEOPLE HAVE SAID ABOUT ME!
Actually, Sean is gone...
WHAT?? WHY?
NICE THINGS ABOUT Trump
WAIT-- THIS FOLDER'S EMPTY!
SEAN SPICER
He resigned when you hired Anthony "The Mooch" Scaramucci as communications Director.
Reince Prebus also resigned.
Mooch had the shortest tenure of any cabinet member and was kicked out in ten days!
"Reince is a fucking paranoid schizophrenic, a paranoiac..."
"I'm not Steve Bannon, I'm not trying to suck my own cock."
Then Bannon left a few months later.
You may have missed this since you spent much of your time at "The Winter White House," (your country club in Florida) working on important Twitter messages...
TWEET DEE AND TWEET DUMB
MAKE AMERICA GREAT AGAIN
Donald J. Trump @realDonaldTrump
In addition to winning the Electoral College in a landslide, I won the popular vote if you deduct the millions of people who voted illegally
Donald J. Trump @realDonaldTrump
Sorry losers and haters, but my I.Q. is one of the highest -and you all know it! Please don't feel so stupid or insecure,it's not your fault
Donald J. Trump @realDonaldTrump
The FAKE NEWS media (failing @nytimes, @NBCNews, @ABC, @CBS, @CNN) is not my enemy, it is the enemy of the American People!
Donald J. Trump @realDonaldTrump
I heard poorly rated @Morning_Joe speaks badly of me (don't watch anymore). Then how come low I.Q. Crazy Mika, along with Psycho Joe, came..
Donald J. Trump @realDonaldTrump
Follow
Meryl Streep, one of the most over-rated actresses in Hollywood, doesn't know me but attacked last night at the Golden Globes. She is a.....
Donald J. Trump @realDonaldTrump
Following
The Russia-Trump collusion story is a total hoax, when will this taxpayer funded charade end?

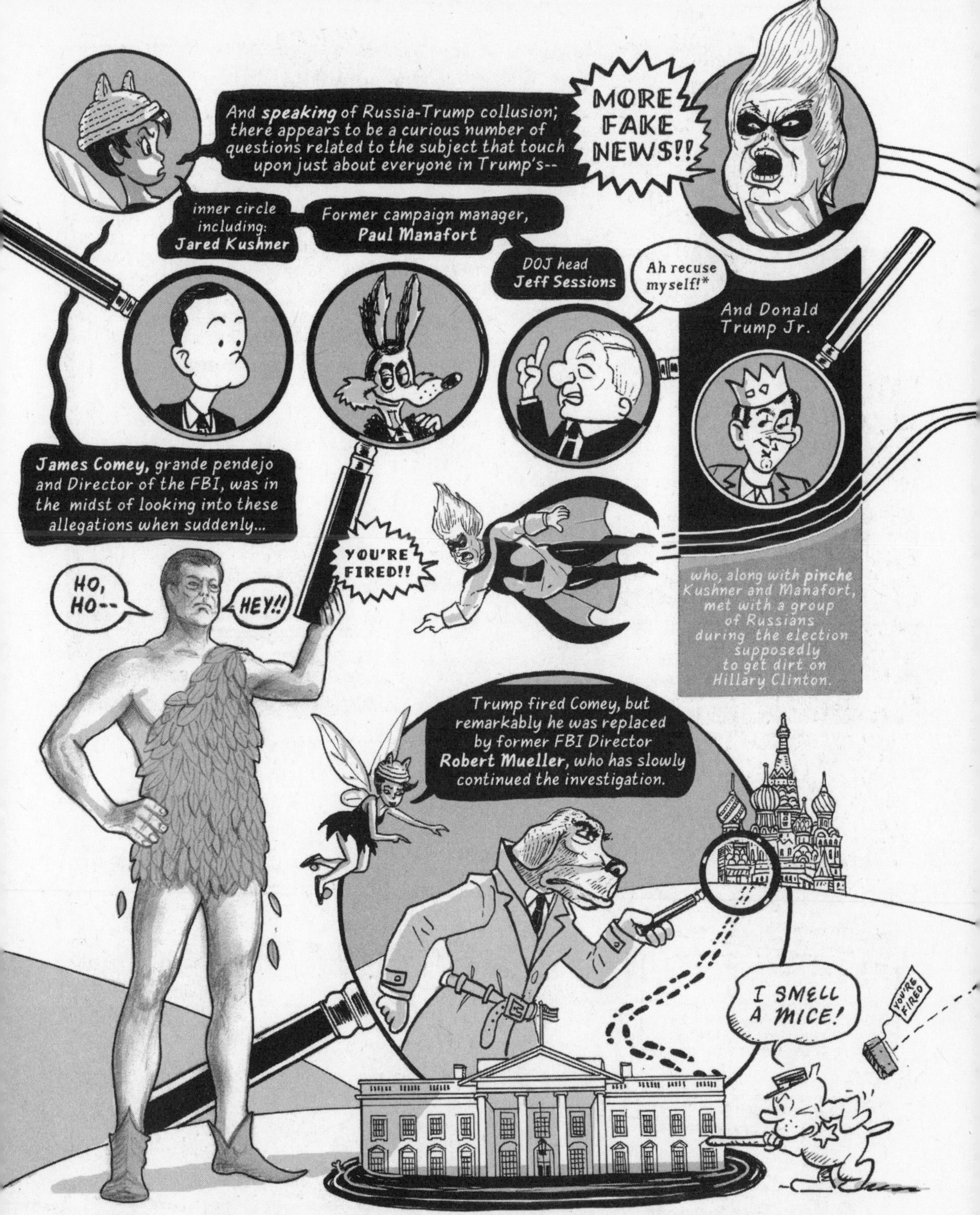
And speaking of Russia-Trump collusion; there appears to be a curious number of questions related to the subject that touch upon just about everyone in Trump's--
MORE FAKE NEWS!!
inner circle including: Jared Kushner
Former campaign manager, Paul Manafort
DOJ head Jeff Sessions
Ah recuse myself!*
And Donald Trump Jr.
James Comey, grande pendejo and Director of the FBI, was in the midst of looking into these allegations when suddenly...
YOU'RE FIRED!!
HO, HO--
HEY!!
who, along with pinche Kushner and Manafort, met with a group of Russians during the election supposedly to get dirt on Hillary Clinton.
Trump fired Comey, but remarkably he was replaced by former FBI Director Robert Mueller, who has slowly continued the investigation.
I SMELL A MICE!
YOU'RE FIRED

*Sessions was forced to recuse himself from the Russian investigation since after claiming during his confirmation hearing he'd had no previous contact with the Russians it was later revealed that he HAD met with Russian ambassador Sergey I. Kislyak while advising Trump during the election.

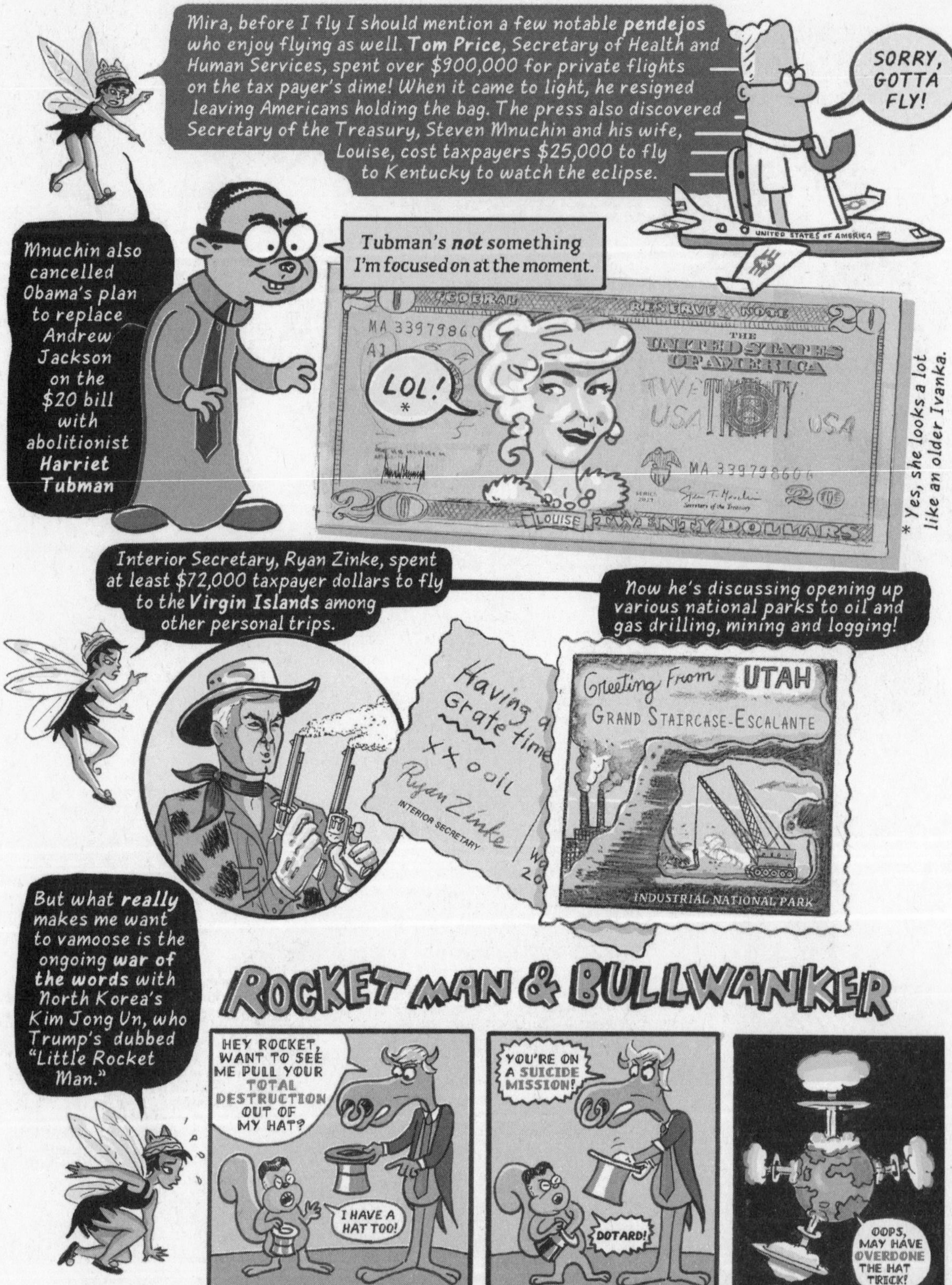

Mira, before I fly I should mention a few notable **pendejos** who enjoy flying as well. **Tom Price**, Secretary of Health and Human Services, spent over $900,000 for private flights on the tax payer's dime! When it came to light, he resigned leaving Americans holding the bag. The press also discovered Secretary of the Treasury, Steven Mnuchin and his wife, Louise, cost taxpayers $25,000 to fly to Kentucky to watch the eclipse.
SORRY, GOTTA FLY!
UNITED STATES OF AMERICA
Mnuchin also cancelled Obama's plan to replace Andrew Jackson on the $20 bill with abolitionist **Harriet Tubman**
Tubman's **not** something I'm focused on at the moment.
FEDERAL RESERVE NOTE
MA 33979860
A1
THE UNITED STATES OF AMERICA
TWENTY
USA
LOL! *
MA 33979860
LOUISE
TWENTY DOLLARS
* Yes, she looks a lot like an older Ivanka.
Interior Secretary, Ryan Zinke, spent at least $72,000 taxpayer dollars to fly to the **Virgin Islands** among other personal trips.
Now he's discussing opening up various national parks to oil and gas drilling, mining and logging!
Having a Grate time
xx ooil
Ryan Zinke
INTERIOR SECRETARY
Greeting From UTAH
GRAND STAIRCASE-ESCALANTE
INDUSTRIAL NATIONAL PARK
But what **really** makes me want to vamoose is the ongoing **war of the words** with North Korea's Kim Jong Un, who Trump's dubbed "Little Rocket Man."
ROCKET MAN & BULLWANKER
HEY ROCKET, WANT TO SEE ME PULL YOUR TOTAL DESTRUCTION OUT OF MY HAT?
I HAVE A HAT TOO!
YOU'RE ON A SUICIDE MISSION!
DOTARD!
OOPS, MAY HAVE OVERDONE THE HAT TRICK!

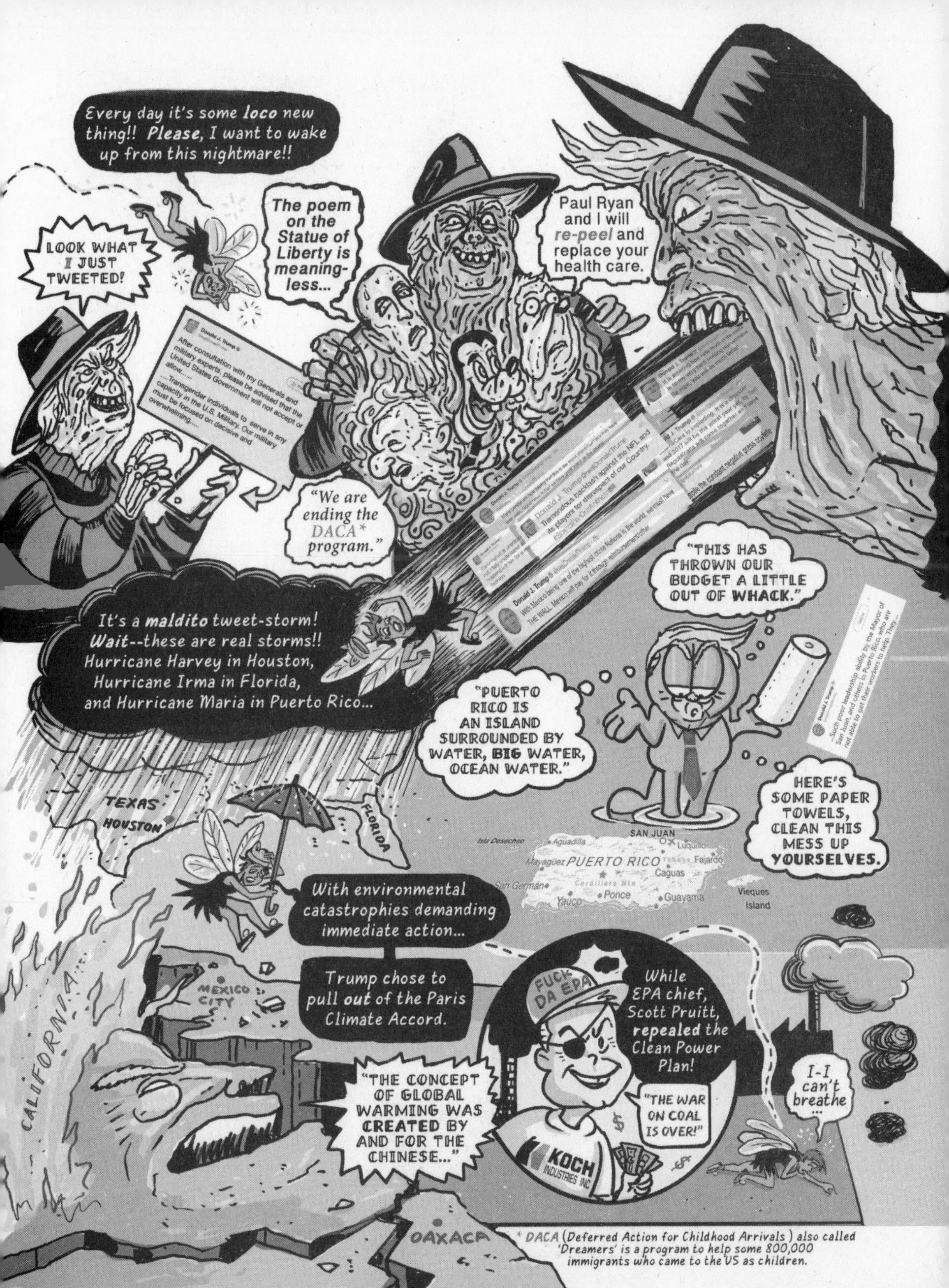
Every day it's some loco new thing!! Please, I want to wake up from this nightmare!!
LOOK WHAT I JUST TWEETED!
After consultation with my Generals and military experts, please be advised that the United States Government will not accept or allow......
....Transgender individuals to serve in any capacity in the U.S. Military. Our military must be focused on decisive and overwhelming.....
The poem on the Statue of Liberty is meaning-less...
Paul Ryan and I will re-peel and replace your health care.
"We are ending the DACA* program."
"THIS HAS THROWN OUR BUDGET A LITTLE OUT OF WHACK."
It's a maldito tweet-storm! Wait--these are real storms!! Hurricane Harvey in Houston, Hurricane Irma in Florida, and Hurricane Maria in Puerto Rico...
"PUERTO RICO IS AN ISLAND SURROUNDED BY WATER, BIG WATER, OCEAN WATER."
HERE'S SOME PAPER TOWELS, CLEAN THIS MESS UP YOURSELVES.
TEXAS
HOUSTON
FLORIDA
SAN JUAN
Isla Desecheo
Aguadilla
Luquillo
Fajardo
Mayagüez
PUERTO RICO
Caguas
San Germán
Cordillera Mtn
Ponce
Guayama
Yauco
Vieques Island
With environmental catastrophies demanding immediate action...
Trump chose to pull out of the Paris Climate Accord.
MEXICO CITY
CALIFORNIA
While EPA chief, Scott Pruitt, repealed the Clean Power Plan!
FUCK DA EPA
"THE WAR ON COAL IS OVER!"
KOCH INDUSTRIES INC
"THE CONCEPT OF GLOBAL WARMING WAS CREATED BY AND FOR THE CHINESE..."
I-I can't breathe...
OAXACA

* DACA (Deferred Action for Childhood Arrivals) also called 'Dreamers' is a program to help some 800,000 immigrants who came to the US as children.

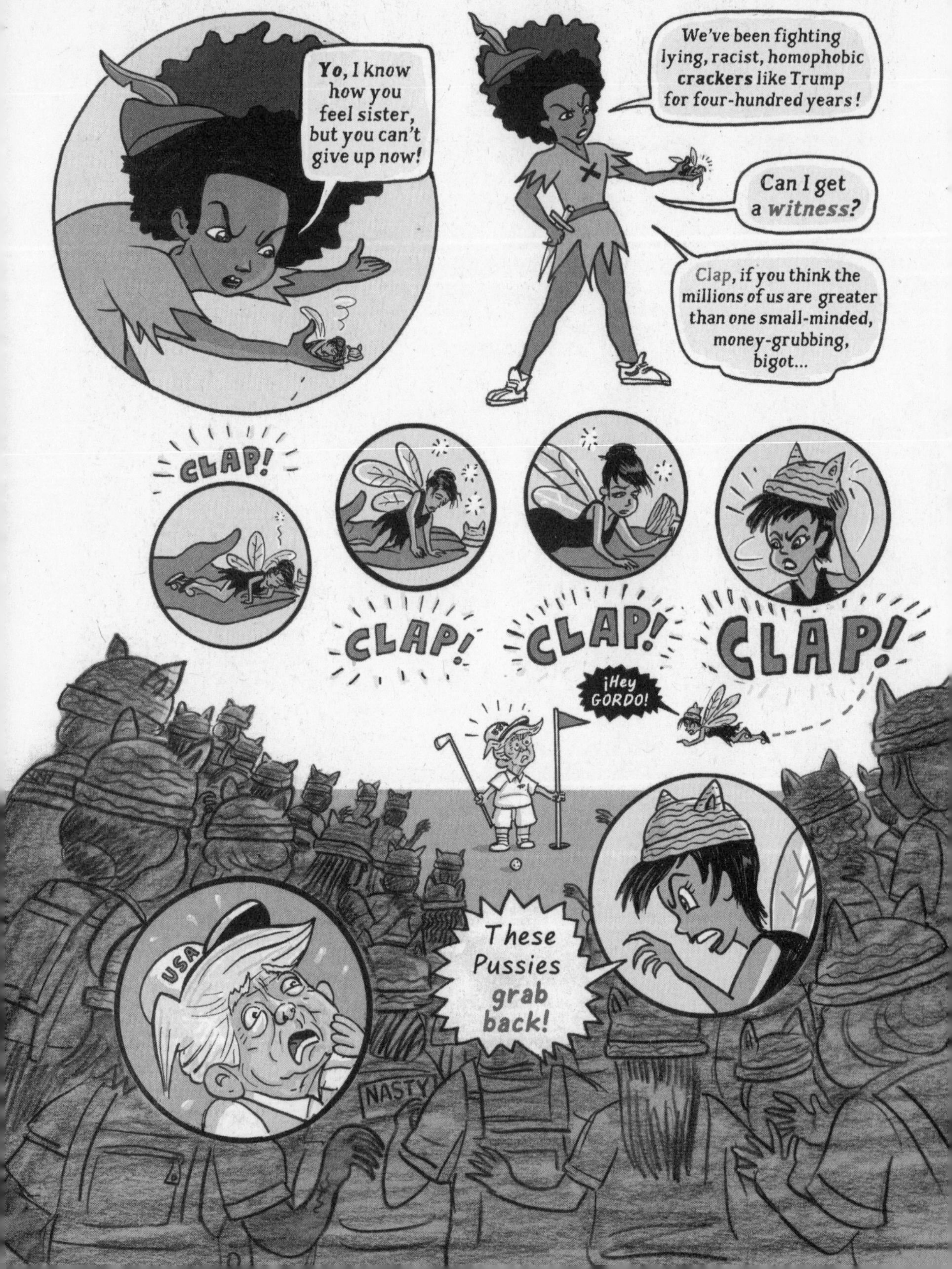
Yo, I know how you feel sister, but you can't give up now!
We've been fighting lying, racist, homophobic crackers like Trump for four-hundred years!
Can I get a witness?
Clap, if you think the millions of us are greater than one small-minded, money-grubbing, bigot...
CLAP!
CLAP!
CLAP!
CLAP!
¡Hey GORDO!
USA
These Pussies grab back!
NASTY

HAMMER

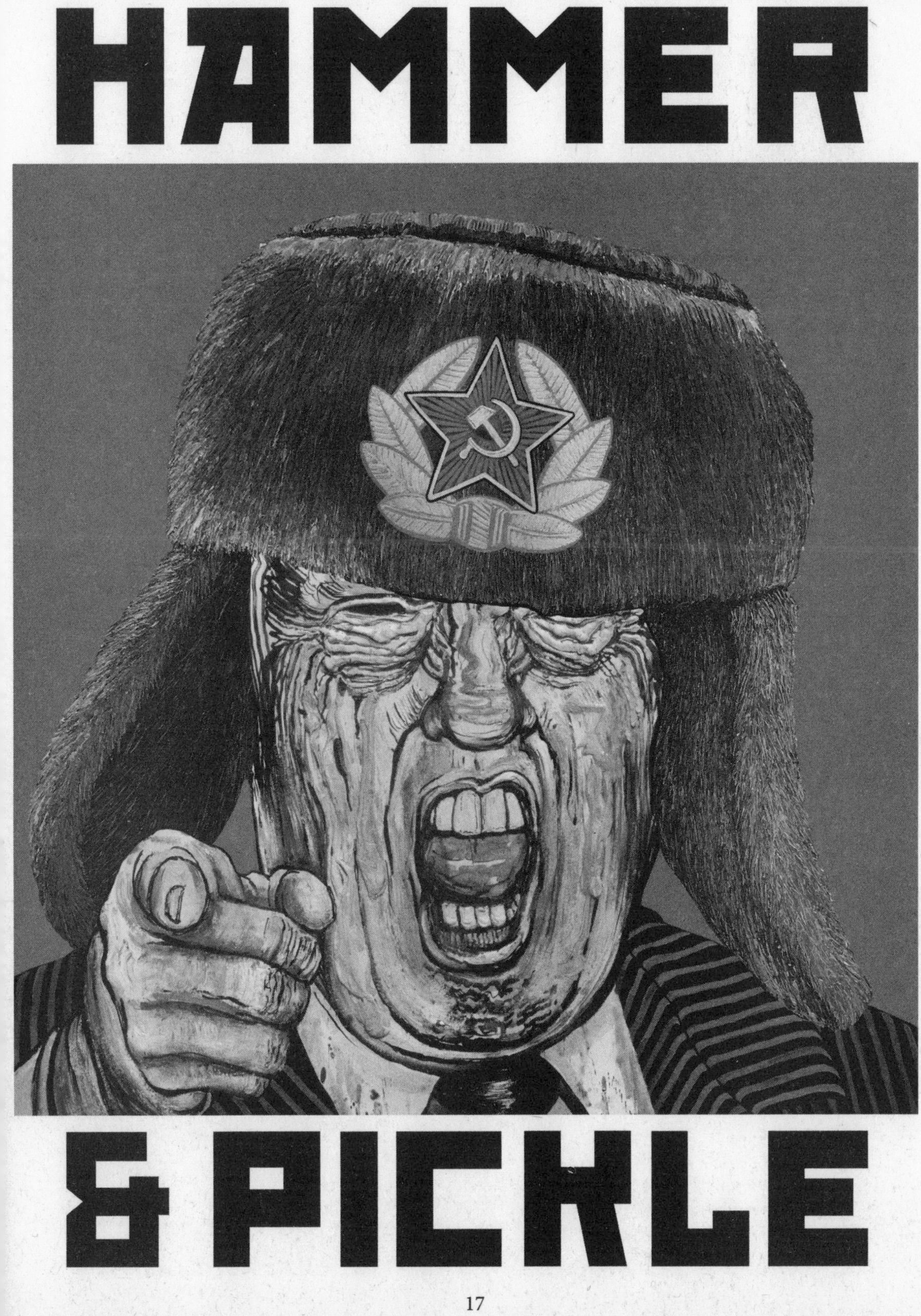

& PICKLE

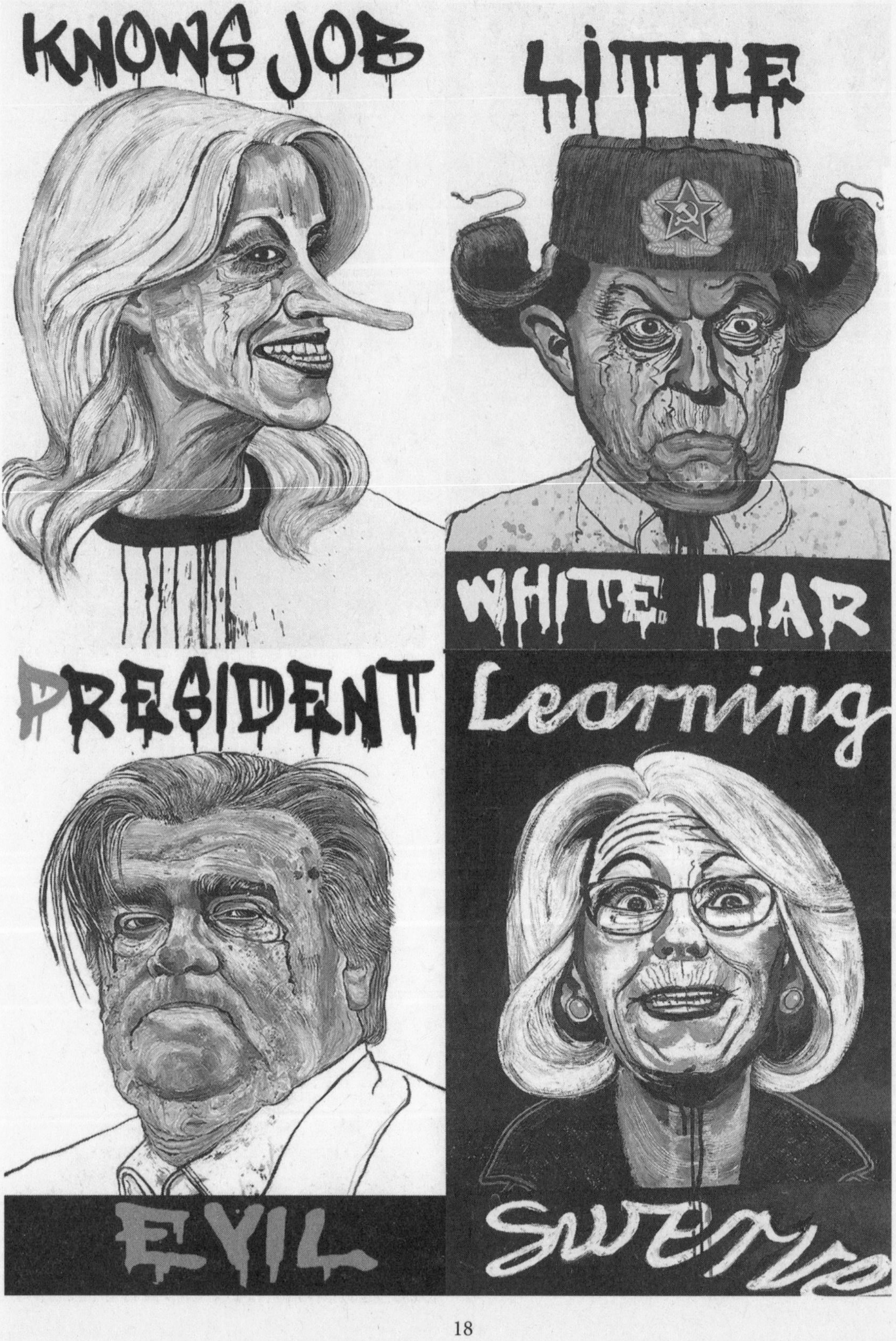
KNOWS JOB
LITTLE
WHITE LIAR
PRESIDENT
Learning
EVIL

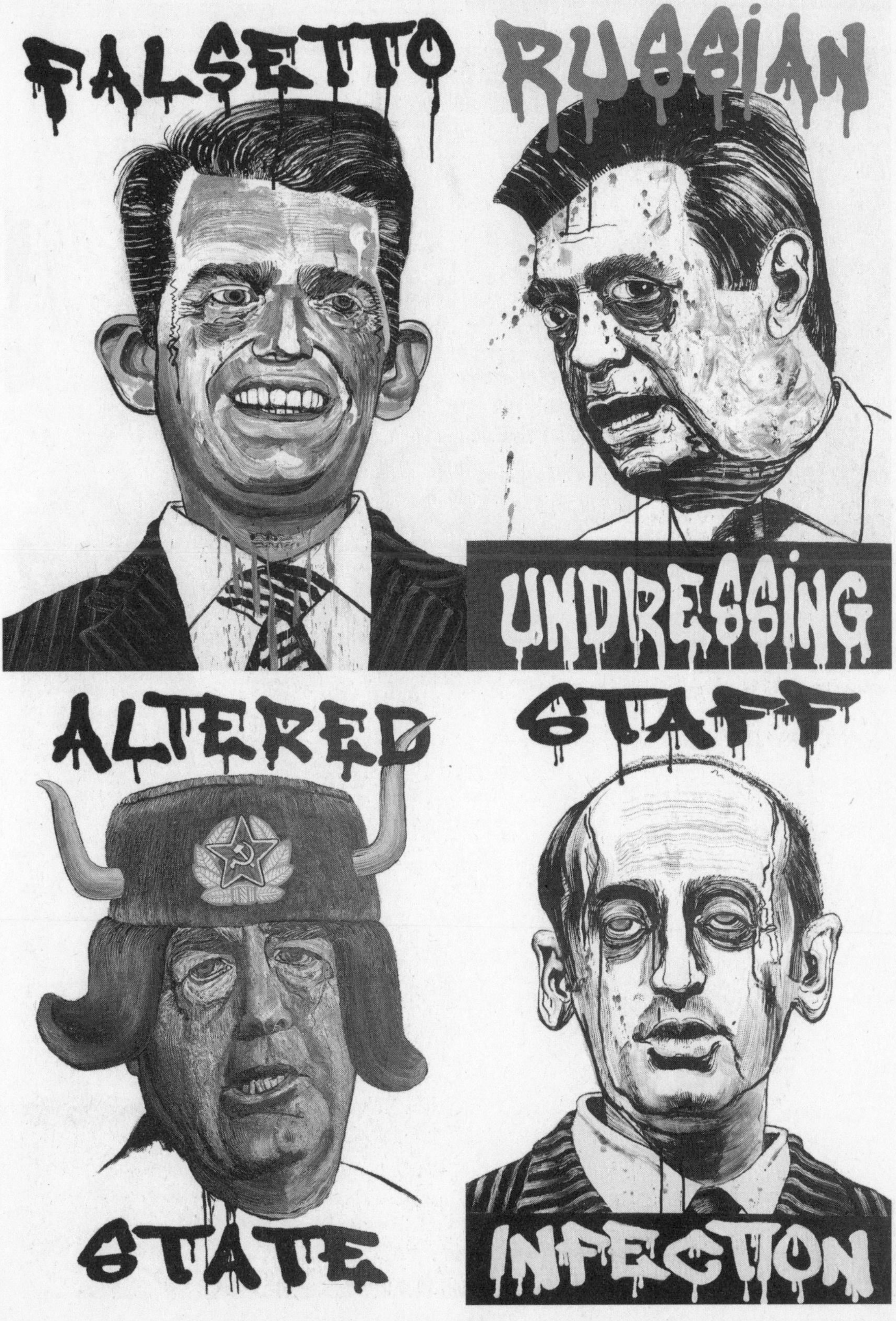
FALSETTO
RUSSIAN
UNDRESSING
ALTERED
STAFF
STATE
INFECTION

DRAW the figure year round seven days a week at MINERVA'S DRAWING STUDIO

293 Broome street New York, NY 10002

Minerva Durham, Director

springstudio@earthlink.net

Artist in Whiteland

Minah Kim

CHAPTER 1. Down to the Rabbit Hole

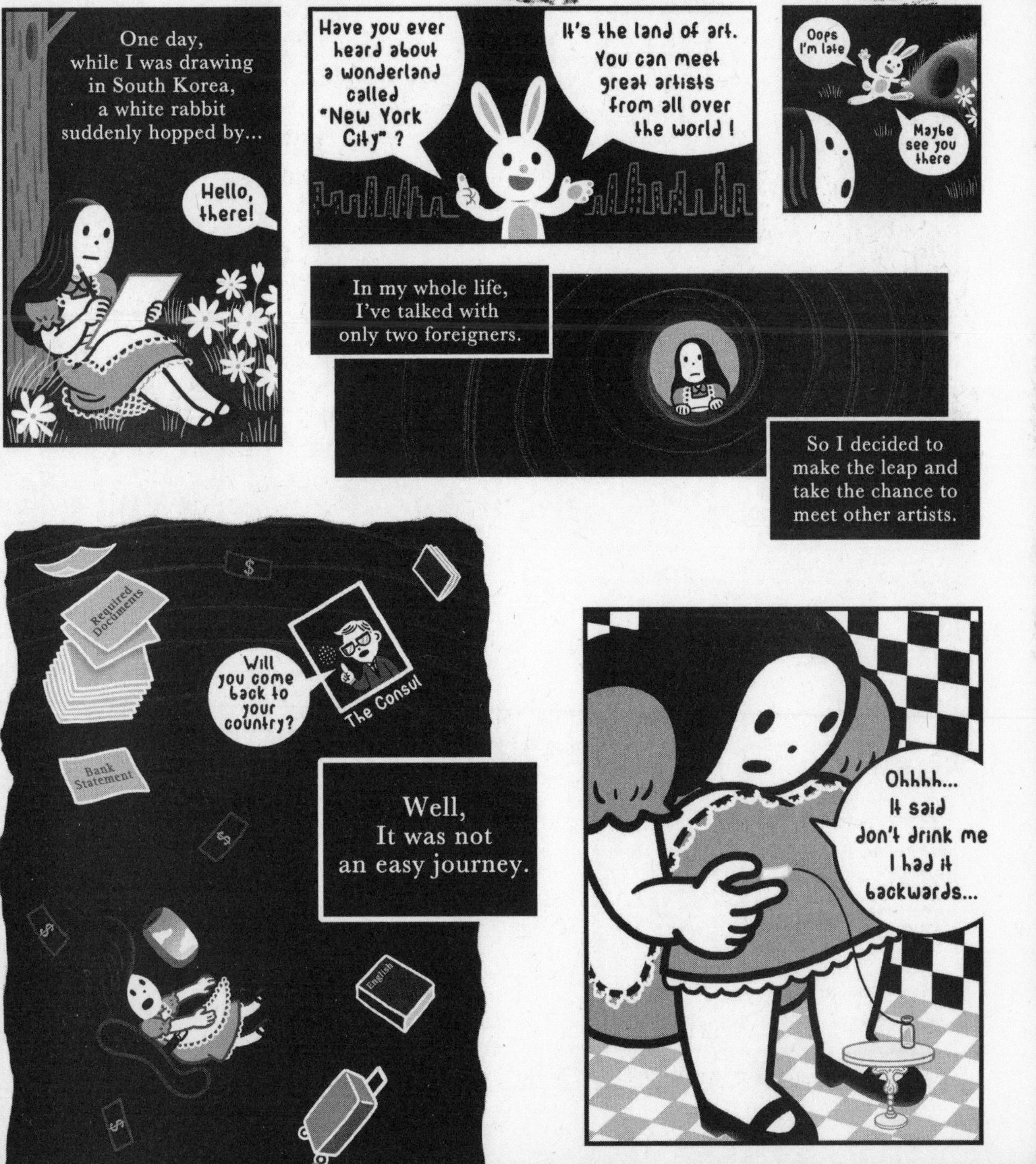
One day, while I was drawing in South Korea, a white rabbit suddenly hopped by...
Hello, there!
Have you ever heard about a wonderland called "New York City"?
It's the land of art. You can meet great artists from all over the world!
Oops I'm late
Maybe see you there
In my whole life, I've talked with only two foreigners.
So I decided to make the leap and take the chance to meet other artists.
Required Documents
$
Will you come back to your country?
The Consul
Bank Statement
Well, It was not an easy journey.
English
Ohhhh... It said don't drink me I had it backwards...

CHAPTER 2 . The Pool of Surprises

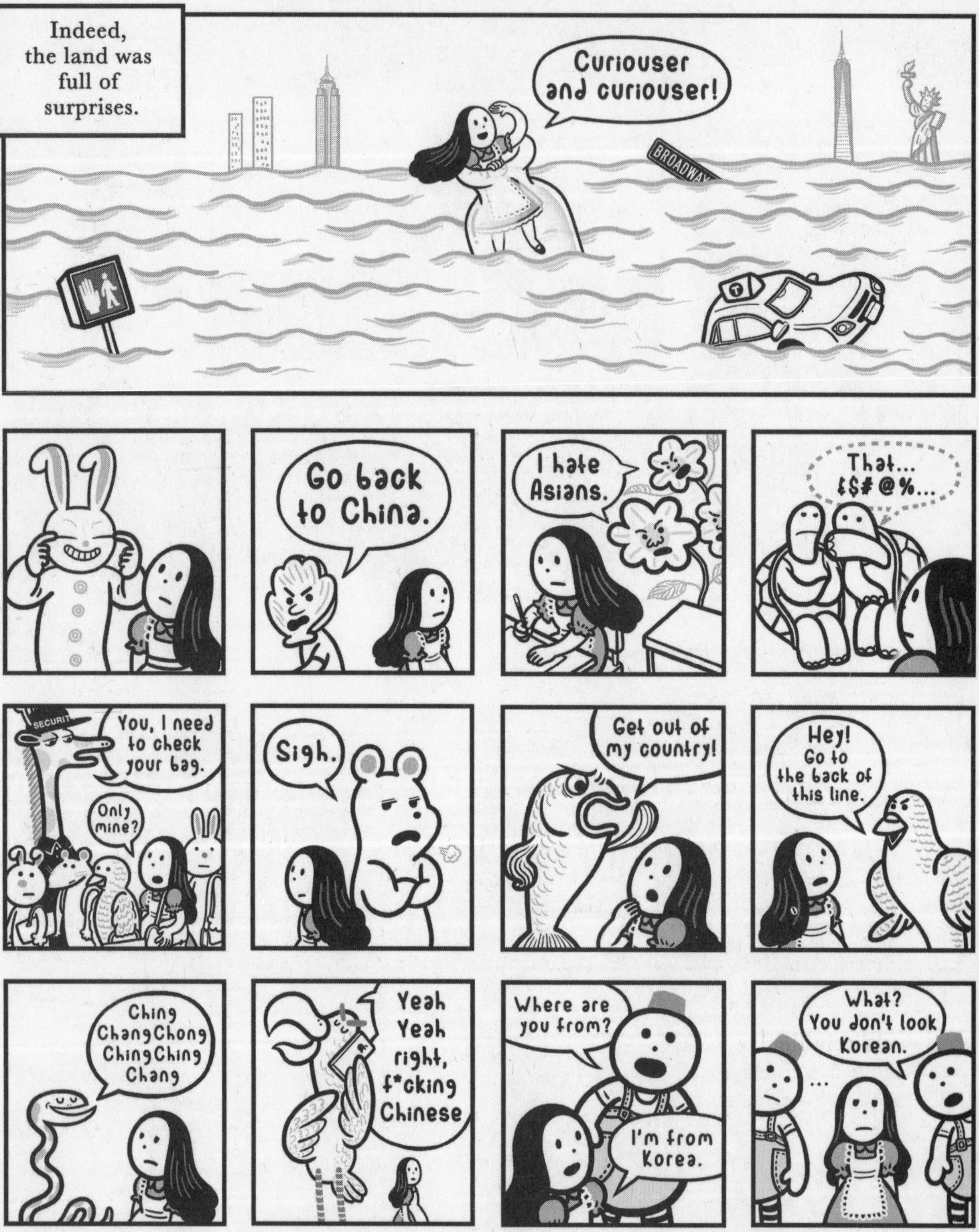

Indeed, the land was full of surprises.
Curiouser and curiouser!
BROADWAY
Go back to China.
I hate Asians.
That... £$# @%...
SECURIT
You, I need to check your bag.
Only mine?
Sigh.
Get out of my country!
Hey! Go to the back of this line.
Ching ChangChong ChingChing Chang
Yeah Yeah right, f*cking Chinese
Where are you from?
I'm from Korea.
What? You don't look Korean.
...

CHAPTER 3 . A MAD ART PARTY

Still, the land was a mad place.
I mean, in a good way.
Everything in the land was
artistic, creative and inspirational.
And I met countless art-lovers.

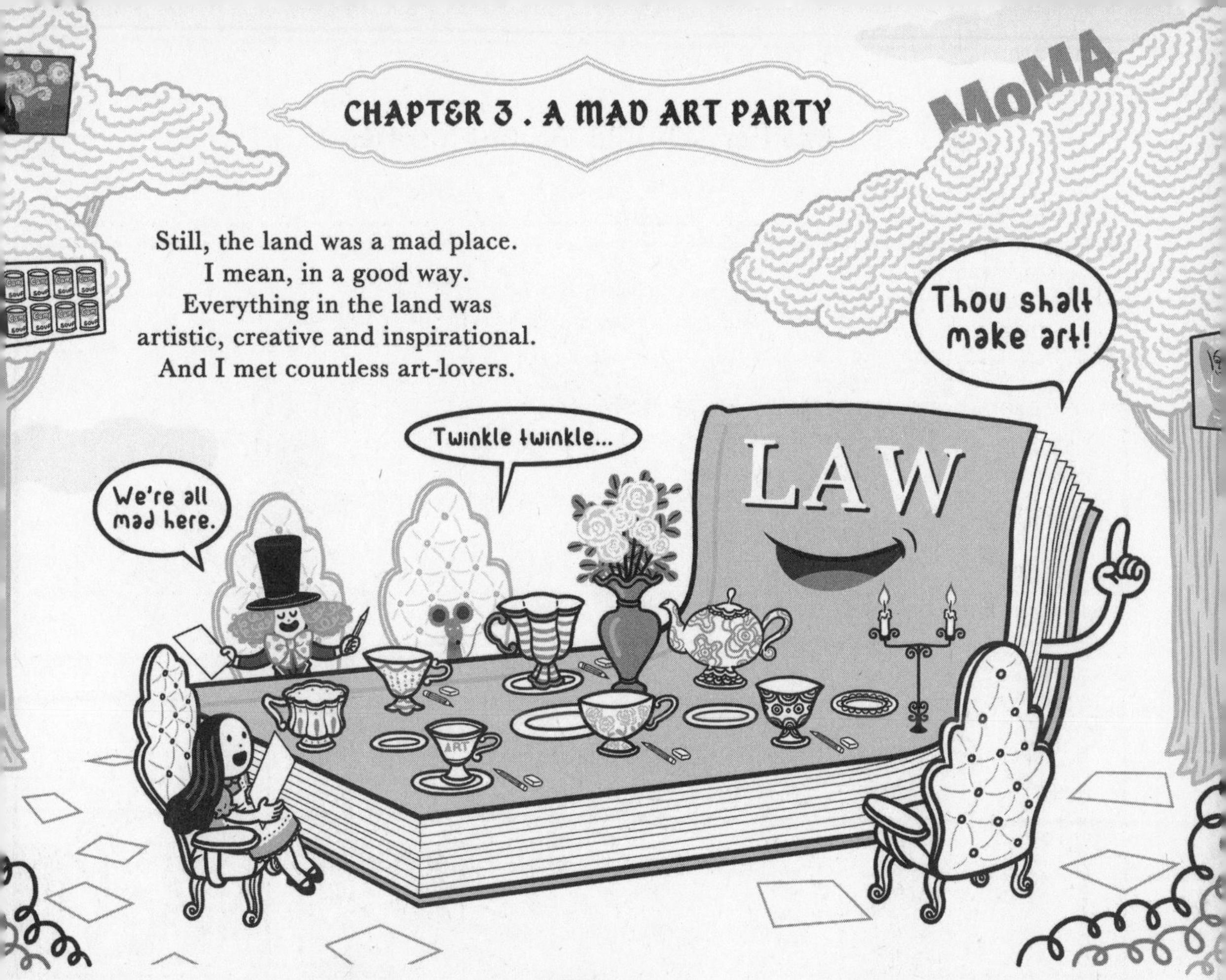
MoMA
Thou shalt make art!
Twinkle twinkle...
We're all mad here.
LAW
ART

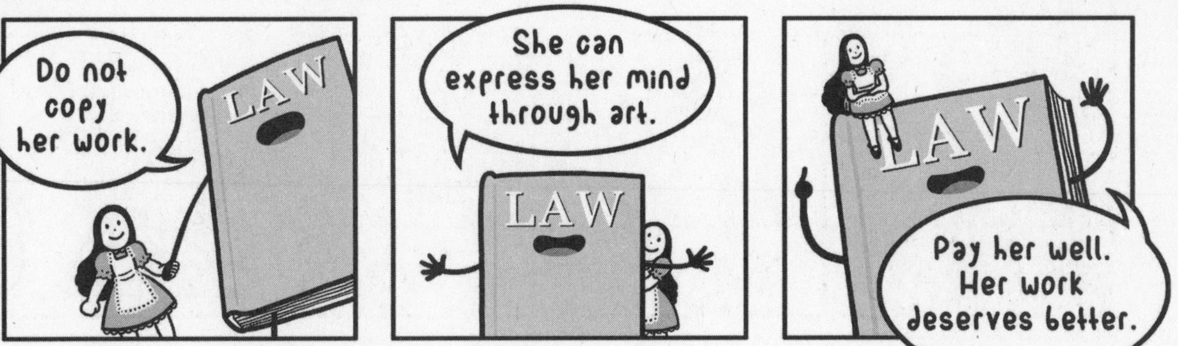
Do not copy her work.
LAW
She can express her mind through art.
LAW
LAW
Pay her well. Her work deserves better.

Within the law,
I could live freely and
make artwork safely.

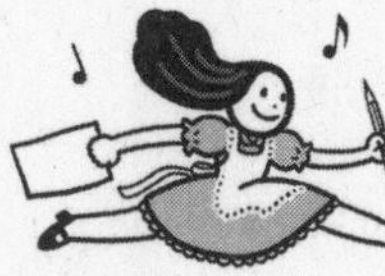

So I wanted to continue
living in this land
for as long as possible.

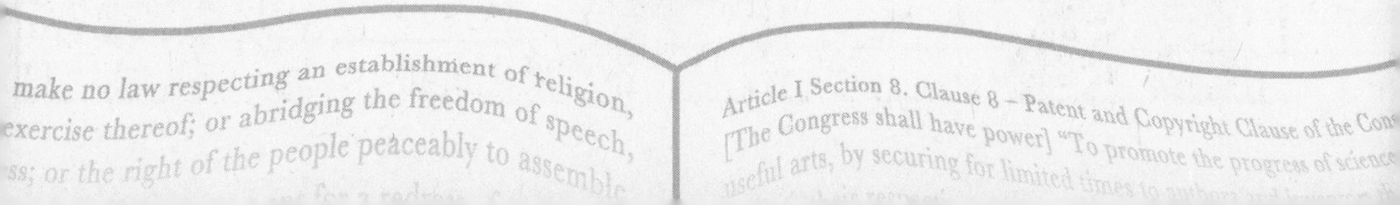
make no law respecting an establishment of religion,
exercise thereof; or abridging the freedom of speech,
ss; or the right of the people peaceably to assemble
Article I Section 8. Clause 8 – Patent and Copyright Clause of the Cons
[The Congress shall have power] "To promote the progress of science
useful arts, by securing for limited times to

CHAPTER 4 . ADVICE FROM A CLINTON CAT

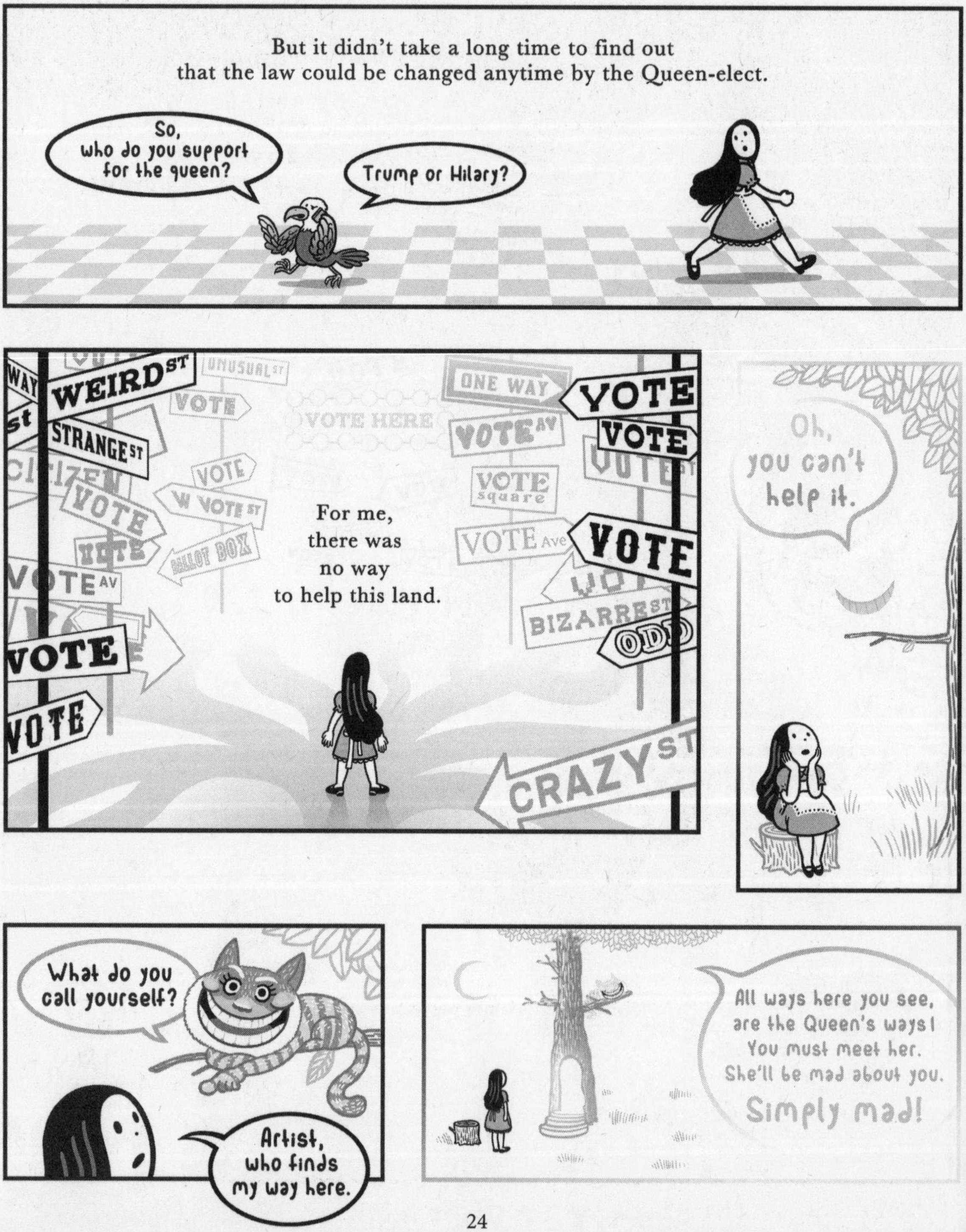

But it didn't take a long time to find out that the law could be changed anytime by the Queen-elect.
So, who do you support for the queen?
Trump or Hilary?
WEIRD ST
UNUSUAL ST
STRANGE ST
ONE WAY
VOTE HERE
VOTE AV
VOTE square
W VOTE ST
BALLOT BOX
VOTE Ave
BIZARRE ST
ODD
CRAZY ST
VOTE
For me, there was no way to help this land.
Oh, you can't help it.
What do you call yourself?
Artist, who finds my way here.
All ways here you see, are the Queen's ways! You must meet her. She'll be mad about you.
Simply mad!

CHAPTER 5 . The Queen's Arrival

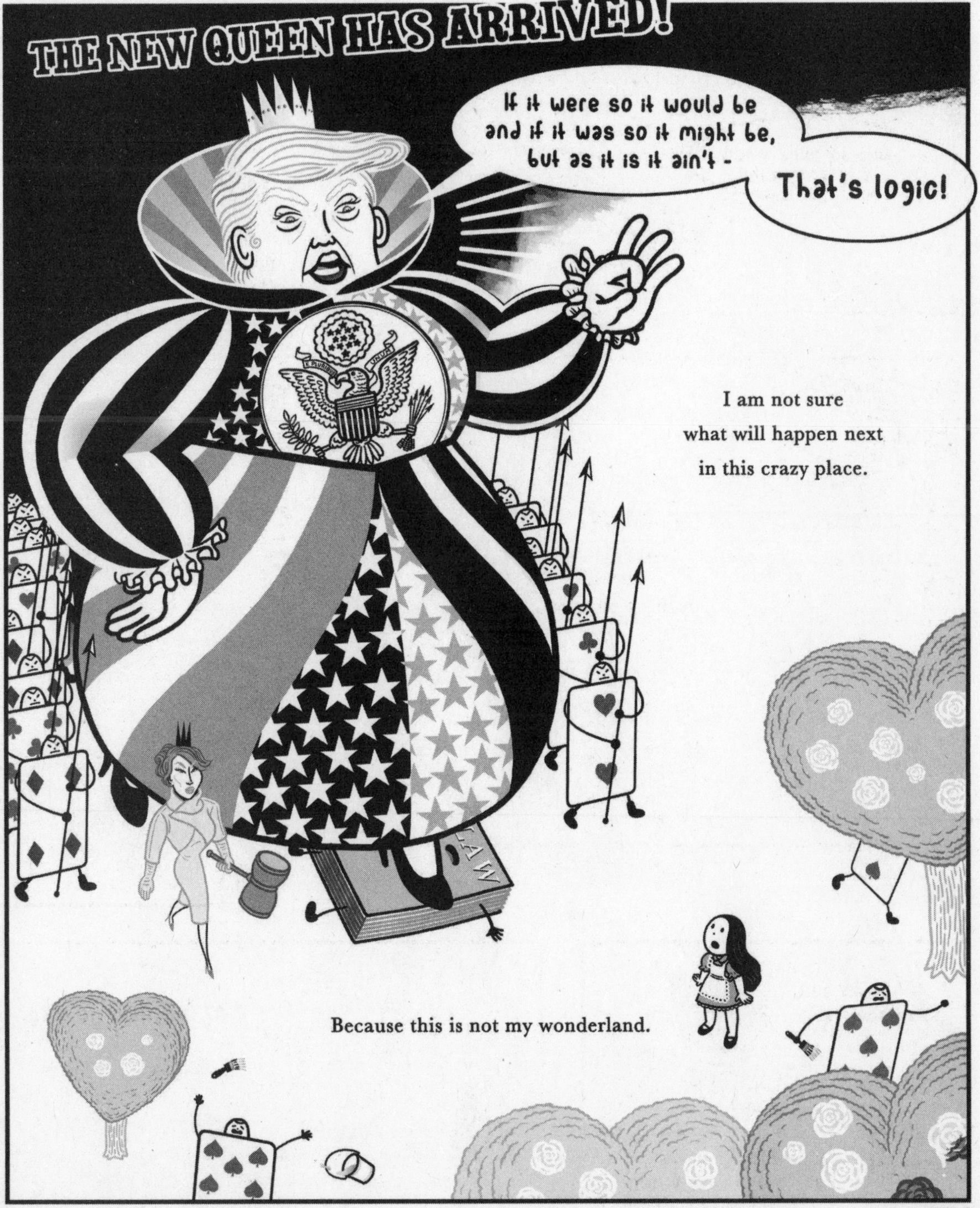

THE NEW QUEEN HAS ARRIVED!
If it were so it would be
and if it was so it might be,
but as it is it ain't -
That's logic!
I am not sure
what will happen next
in this crazy place.
LAW
Because this is not my wonderland.

END

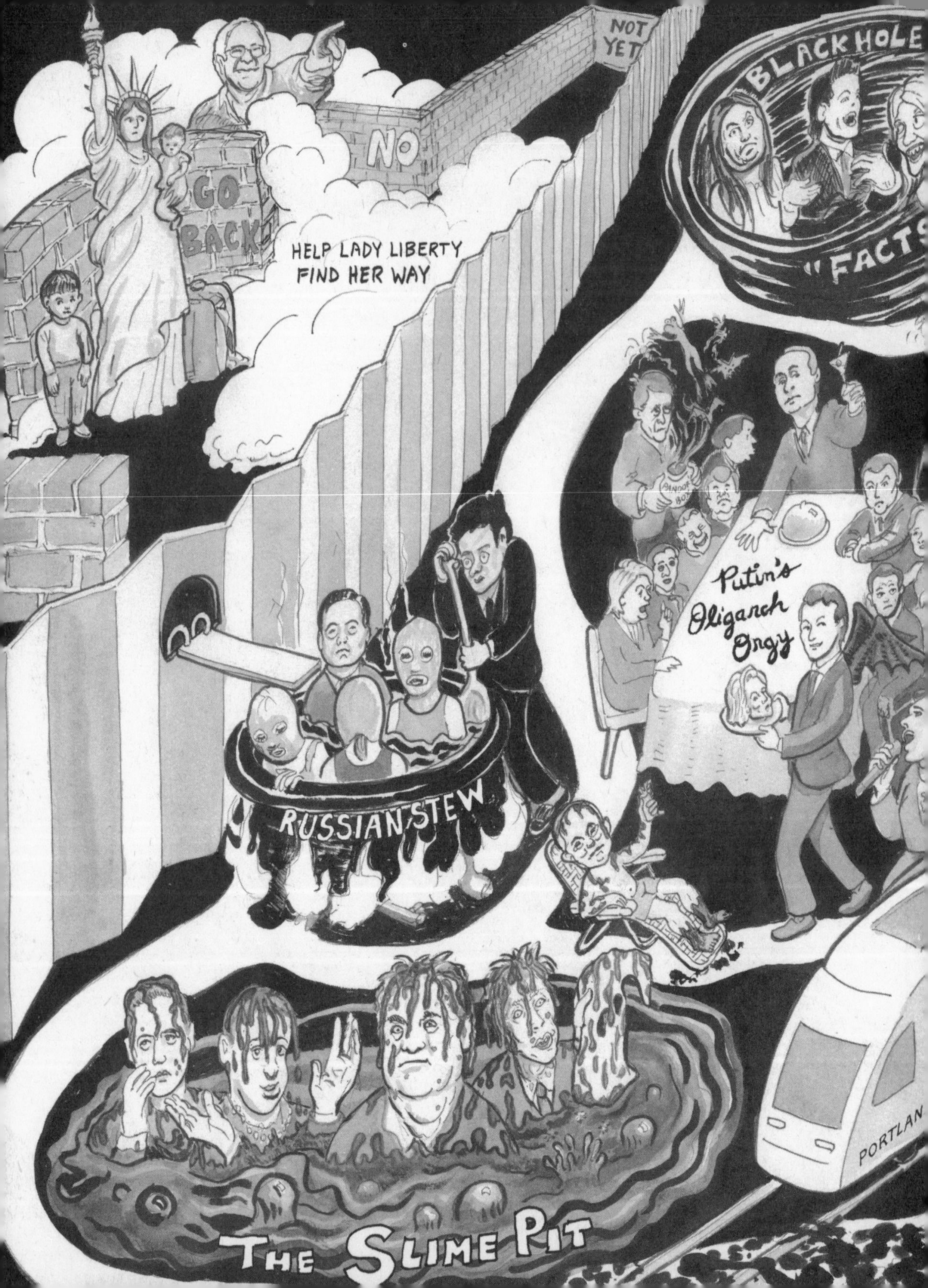
NOT YET
NO
GO BACK
HELP LADY LIBERTY FIND HER WAY
BLACK HOLE
"FACTS
Putin's Oligarch Orgy
RUSSIAN STEW
THE SLIME PIT

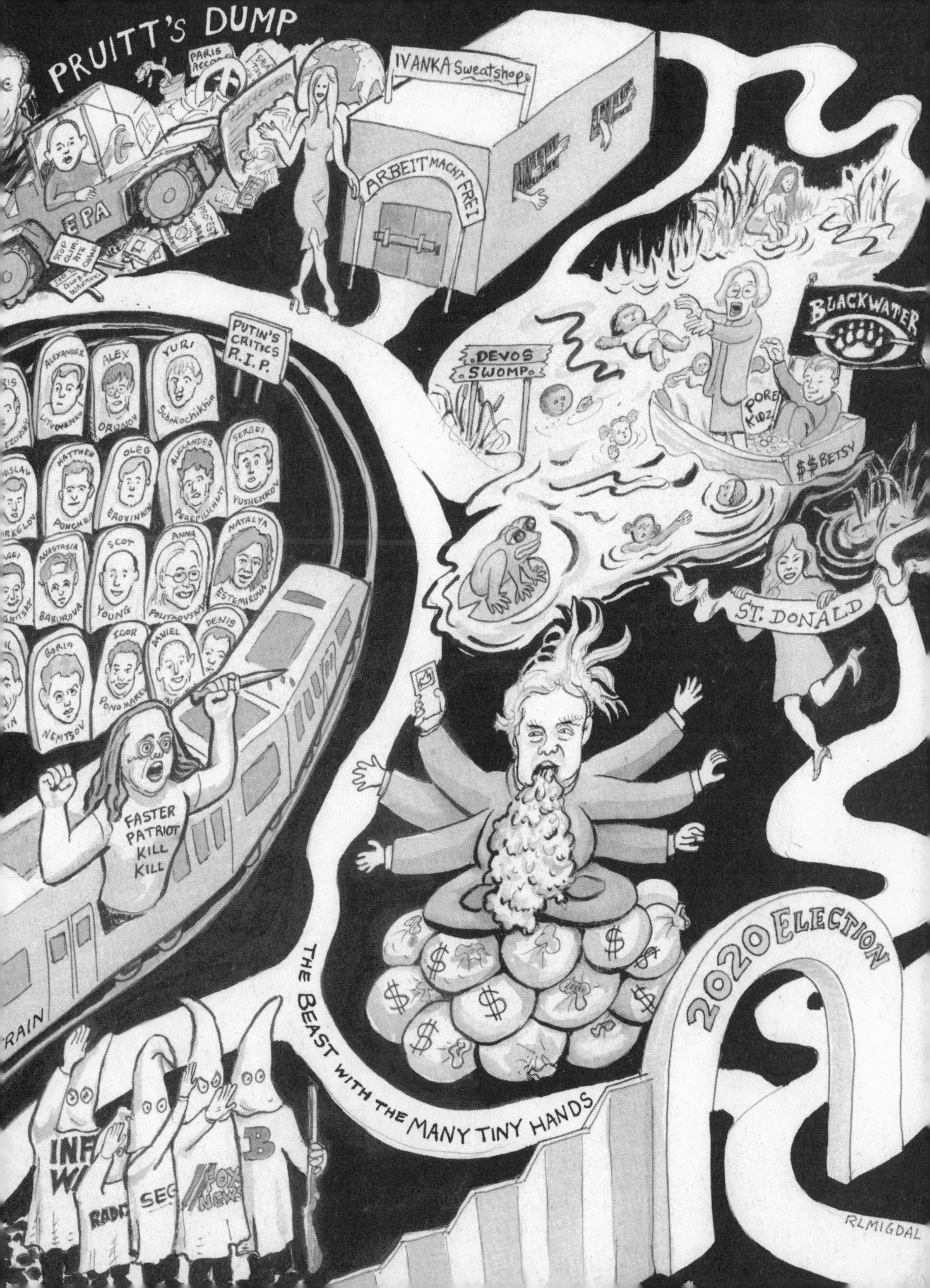

PRUITT'S DUMP
EPA
STOP CLIMATE CHANGE
IVANKA Sweatshop
ARBEIT MACHT FREI
BLACKWATER
DEVOS SWOMP
PORE KIDZ
$$BETSY
ST. DONALD
PUTIN'S CRITICS R.I.P.
ALEXANDER LITVINENKO
ALEX ORONOV
YURI Schekochikhin
MATTHEW PUNCHER
OLEG EROVINKIN
ALEXANDER PEREPILICHNYY
SERGEI YUSHENKOV
ANASTASIA BABUROVA
SCOT YOUNG
ANNA POLITKOVSKY
NATALYA ESTEMIROVA
BORIS NEMTSOV
IGOR PONOMAREV
DANIEL
DENIS
FASTER PATRIOT KILL KILL
TRAIN
THE BEAST WITH THE MANY TINY HANDS
2020 ELECTION
FOX NEWS
B
RLMIGDAL

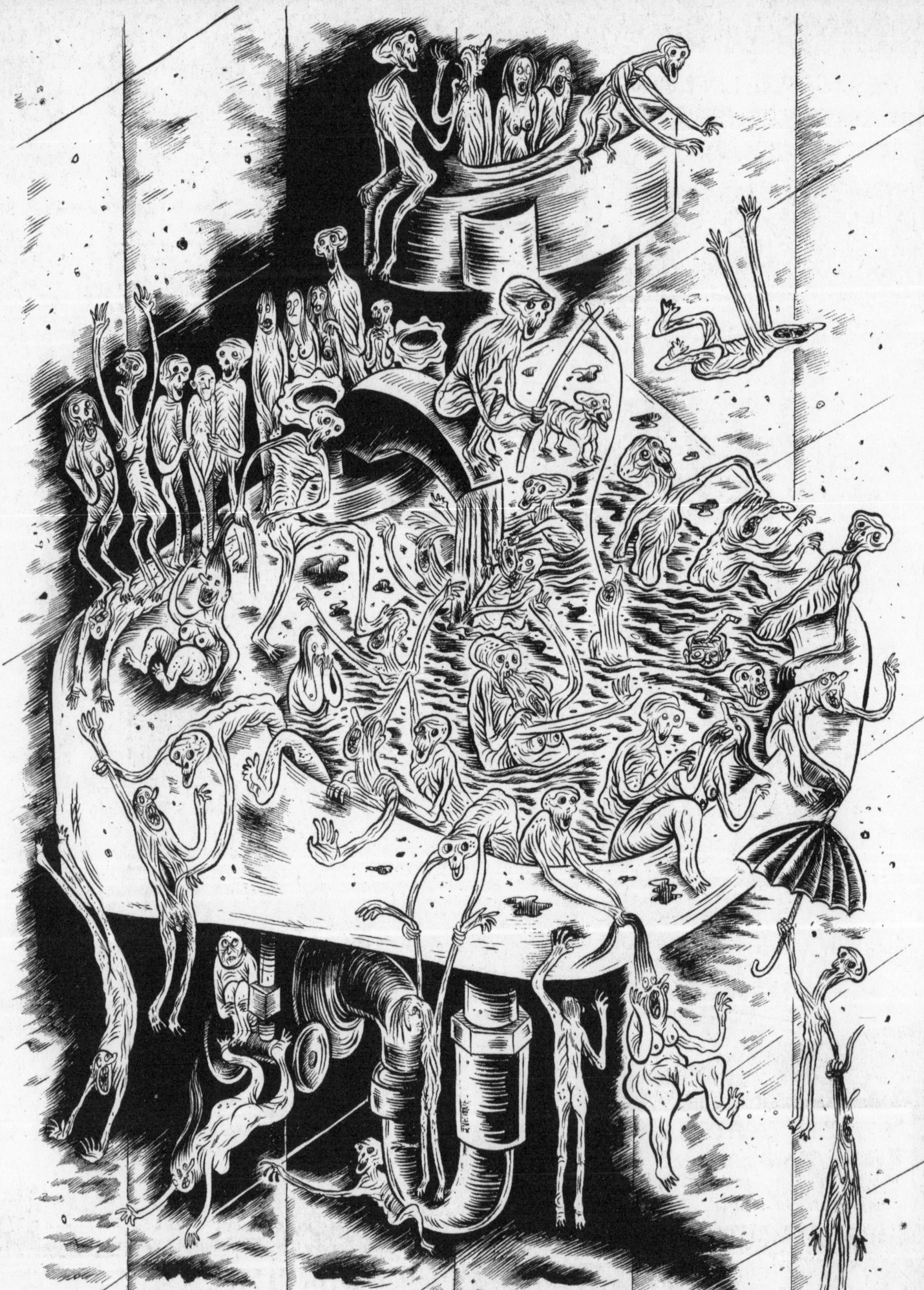

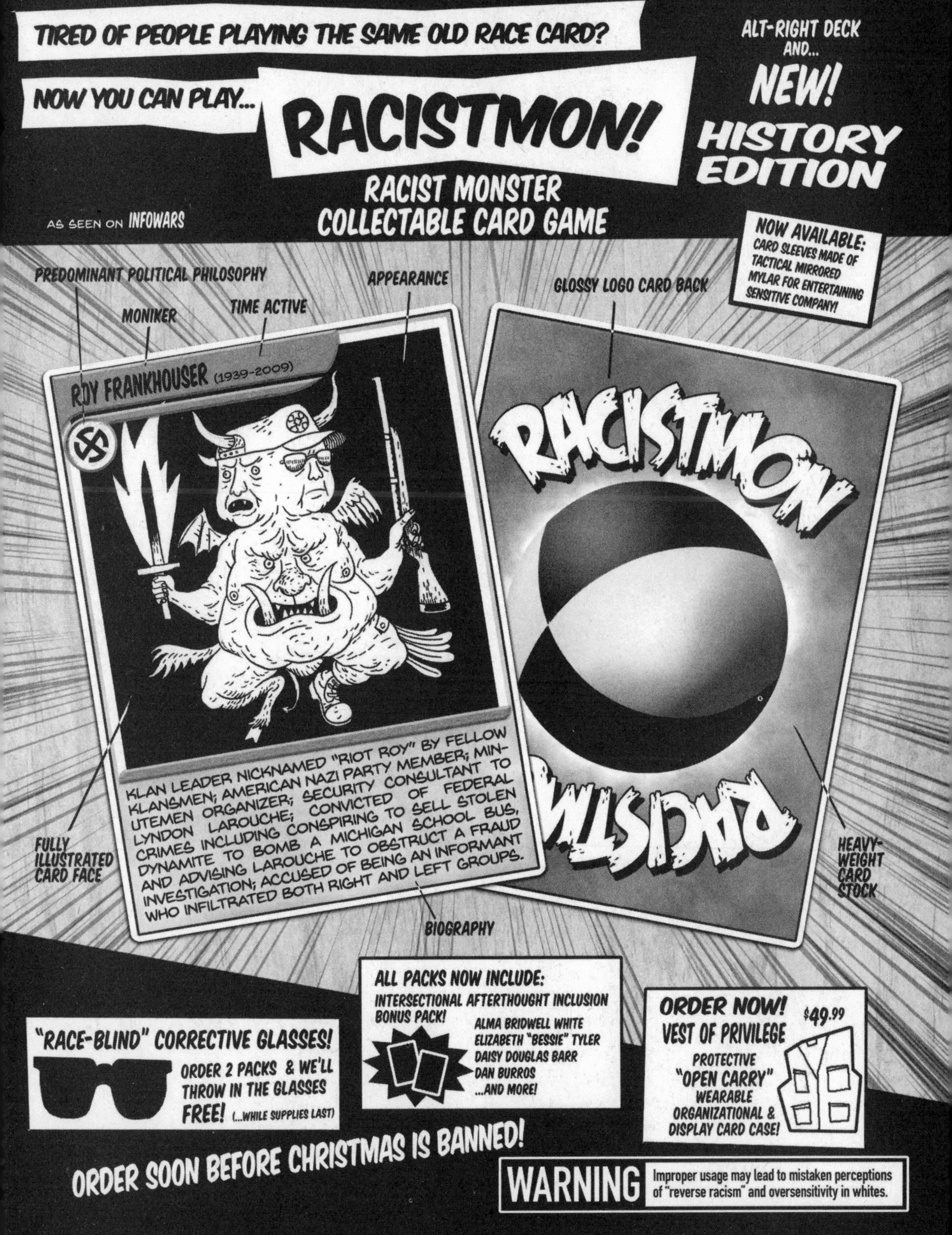

TIRED OF PEOPLE PLAYING THE SAME OLD RACE CARD?
NOW YOU CAN PLAY...
RACISTMON!
RACIST MONSTER
COLLECTABLE CARD GAME
AS SEEN ON INFOWARS
ALT-RIGHT DECK
AND...
NEW!
HISTORY EDITION
NOW AVAILABLE:
CARD SLEEVES MADE OF TACTICAL MIRRORED MYLAR FOR ENTERTAINING SENSITIVE COMPANY!
PREDOMINANT POLITICAL PHILOSOPHY
MONIKER
TIME ACTIVE
APPEARANCE
GLOSSY LOGO CARD BACK
ROY FRANKHOUSER (1939-2009)
KLAN LEADER NICKNAMED "RIOT ROY" BY FELLOW KLANSMEN; AMERICAN NAZI PARTY MEMBER; MINUTEMEN ORGANIZER; SECURITY CONSULTANT TO LYNDON LAROUCHE; CONVICTED OF FEDERAL CRIMES INCLUDING CONSPIRING TO SELL STOLEN DYNAMITE TO BOMB A MICHIGAN SCHOOL BUS, AND ADVISING LAROUCHE TO OBSTRUCT A FRAUD INVESTIGATION; ACCUSED OF BEING AN INFORMANT WHO INFILTRATED BOTH RIGHT AND LEFT GROUPS.
RACISTMON
RACISTMON
FULLY ILLUSTRATED CARD FACE
BIOGRAPHY
HEAVY-WEIGHT CARD STOCK
ALL PACKS NOW INCLUDE:
INTERSECTIONAL AFTERTHOUGHT INCLUSION BONUS PACK!
ALMA BRIDWELL WHITE
ELIZABETH "BESSIE" TYLER
DAISY DOUGLAS BARR
DAN BURROS
...AND MORE!
"RACE-BLIND" CORRECTIVE GLASSES!
ORDER 2 PACKS & WE'LL THROW IN THE GLASSES FREE! (...WHILE SUPPLIES LAST)
ORDER NOW!
$49.99
VEST OF PRIVILEGE
PROTECTIVE "OPEN CARRY" WEARABLE ORGANIZATIONAL & DISPLAY CARD CASE!
ORDER SOON BEFORE CHRISTMAS IS BANNED!
WARNING
Improper usage may lead to mistaken perceptions of "reverse racism" and oversensitivity in whites.

HENRY LAMONT "MIKE" BEACH (1903-1989)

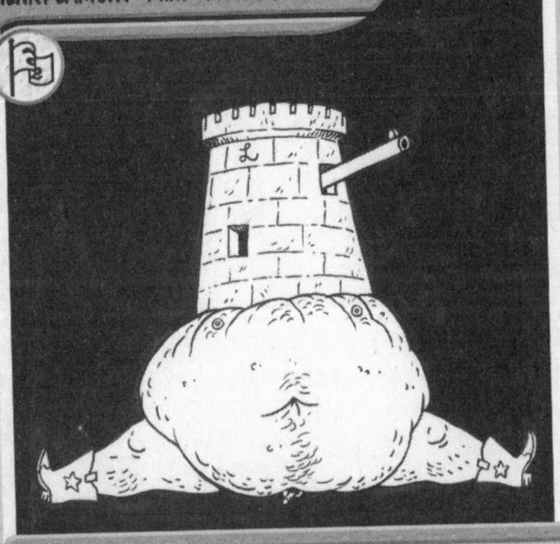
L

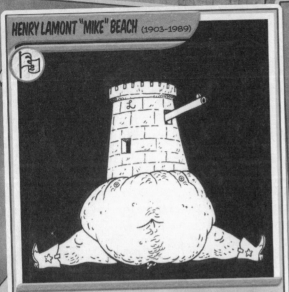

A RETIRED DRY CLEANER, ONE-TIME MEMBER OF THE SILVER SHIRTS AND FOUNDER OF POSSE COMITATUS, INSPIRED BY WILLIAM POTTER GALE'S UNITED CHRISTIAN POSSE ASSOCIATION; BEACH BELIEVED THAT THERE IS NO LEGITIMATE FORM OF GOVERNMENT ABOVE THAT OF THE COUNTY LEVEL AND NO HIGHER LAW AUTHORITY THAN THE COUNTY SHERIFF.

DON BLACK (1953-)

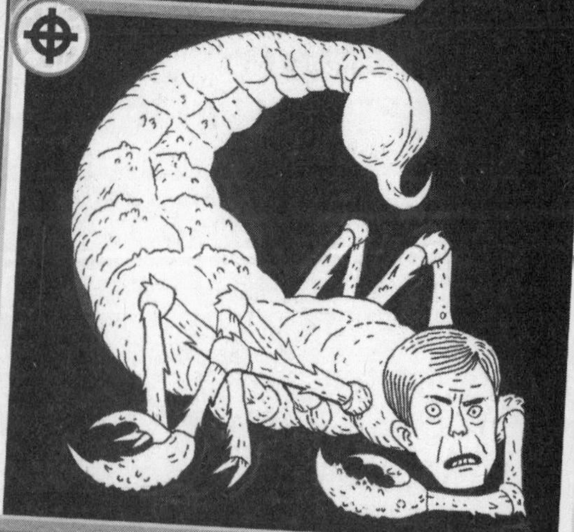

OWNER AND FOUNDER OF STORMFRONT, THE FIRST WHITE NATIONALIST INTERNET FORUM; MEMBER OF NATIONAL SOCIALIST WHITE PEOPLE'S PARTY AND KNIGHTS OF THE KU KLUX KLAN; SERVED TIME IN JAIL AFTER HE AND NINE OTHER WHITE SUPREMACISTS WERE ARRESTED TRYING TO INVADE THE CARIBBEAN ISLAND OF DOMINICA AND OVERTHROW ITS GOVERNMENT.

SAMUEL BOWERS (1924-2006)

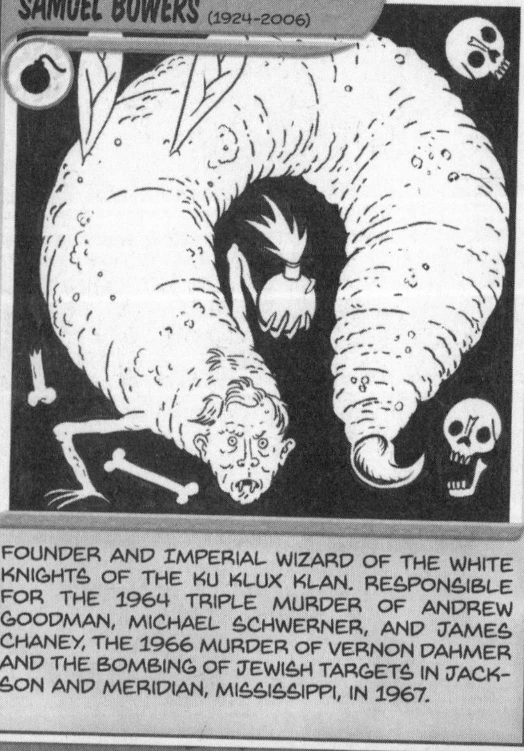

FOUNDER AND IMPERIAL WIZARD OF THE WHITE KNIGHTS OF THE KU KLUX KLAN. RESPONSIBLE FOR THE 1964 TRIPLE MURDER OF ANDREW GOODMAN, MICHAEL SCHWERNER, AND JAMES CHANEY, THE 1966 MURDER OF VERNON DAHMER AND THE BOMBING OF JEWISH TARGETS IN JACKSON AND MERIDIAN, MISSISSIPPI, IN 1967.

PRESCOTT BUSH (1895-1972)

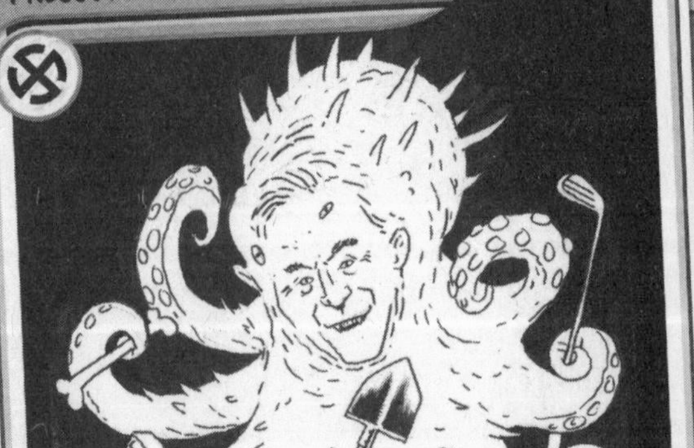

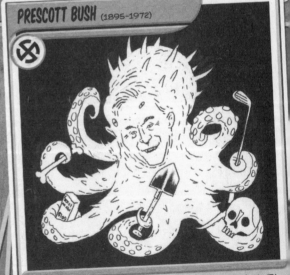

AMERICAN BANKER AND SENATOR; WAS A DIRECTOR AND SHAREHOLDER OF COMPANIES THAT PROFITED FROM INVOLVEMENT WITH THE FINANCIAL BACKERS OF NAZI GERMANY AND PRESSURED THE U.S. GOVERNMENT UNDER ROOSEVELT NOT TO INTERVENE AND ATTEMPT TO RESCUE EUROPEAN JEWS BY BOMBING RAILWAY LINES AND BRIDGES FROM HUNGARY TO AUSCHWITZ.

RICHARD GIRNT BUTLER (1918-2004)

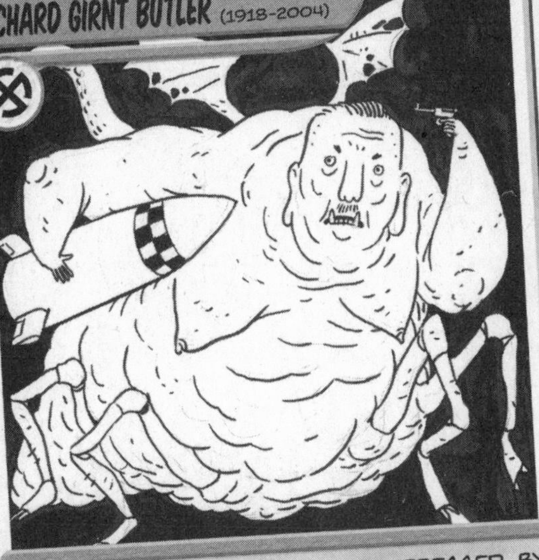

AEROSPACE ENGINEER; DEEPLY IMPRESSED BY INDIA'S CASTE SYSTEM, FOUNDED ARYAN NATIONS, BASED ON HIS 20-ACRE COMPOUND IN IDAHO, SEEKING A WHITE NATION IN THE U.S. NORTHWEST. INSPIRED MANY FAR-RIGHT PARAMILITARIES -- AND THE CREATION BY IDAHOANS OF ORGANIZATIONS, MONUMENTS AND RESOLUTIONS OPPOSING RACISM AND PROMOTING HUMAN RIGHTS.

JOHN C. CALHOUN (1782-1850)

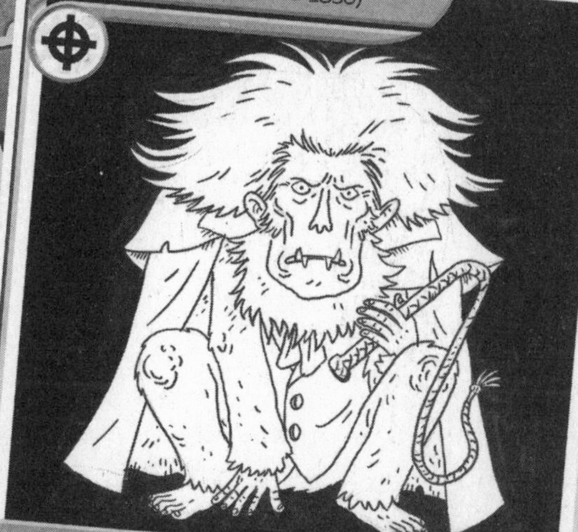

SEVENTH U.S. VICE PRESIDENT AND SOUTH CAROLINA SENATOR; WHITE SUPREMACIST AND OUTSPOKEN PROPONENT OF THE INSTITUTION OF SLAVERY, WHICH HE FAMOUSLY DEFENDED AS A "POSITIVE GOOD" RATHER THAN AS A "NECESSARY EVIL"; BELIEVED THAT ALL SOCIETIES ARE RULED BY AN ELITE GROUP THAT ENJOYS THE FRUITS OF THE LABOR OF A LESS-EXCEPTIONAL GROUP.

WILLIAM J. CAMERON (1878-1955)

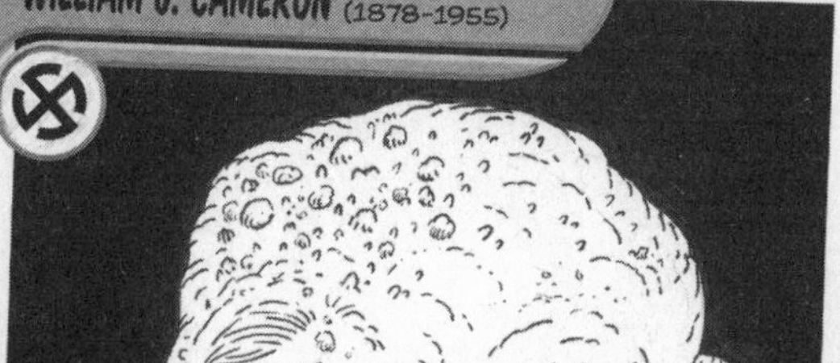
THE INTERNATIONAL
JEW:
THE WORLD'S
PROBLEM

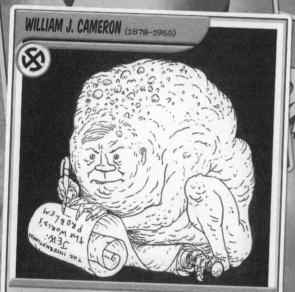

JOURNALIST AND PUBLIC RELATIONS REPRESENTATIVE FOR HENRY FORD, HE EDITED THE DEARBORN INDEPENDENT. CAMERON WROTE A SERIES OF ARTICLES FOR THE PAPER, WHICH WERE LATER PUBLISHED IN THE BOOK "THE INTERNATIONAL JEW: THE WORLD'S FOREMOST PROBLEM." HE IS THE CREATOR OF "THE PROTOCOLS OF THE ELDERS OF ZION."

THOMAS DIXON JR. (1864-1946)

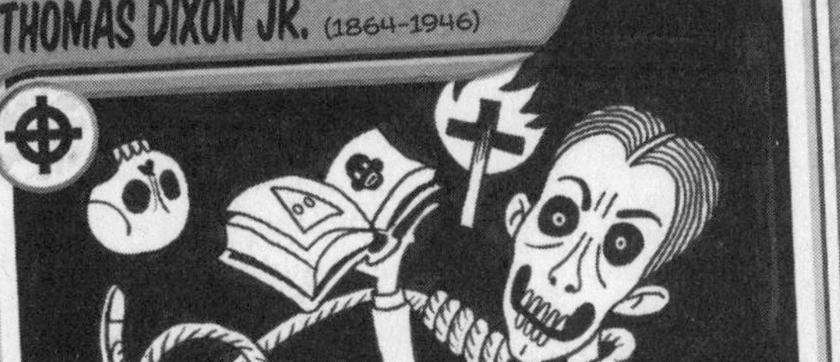

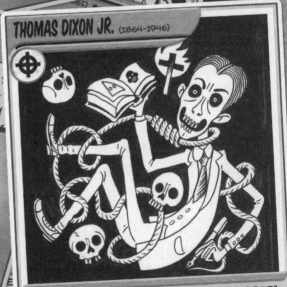

NOVELIST WHO WROTE "THE LEOPARD'S SPOTS: A ROMANCE OF THE WHITE MAN'S BURDEN, 1865-1900" AND "THE CLANSMAN," WHICH IN 1915 WAS MADE INTO "THE BIRTH OF A NATION," DIRECTED BY D.W. GRIFFITH, THE FIRST MOVIE TO BE SCREENED IN THE WHITE HOUSE. THE FILM LED TO THE FOUNDING OF THE 2ND KU KLUX KLAN.

DAVID DUKE (1950-)

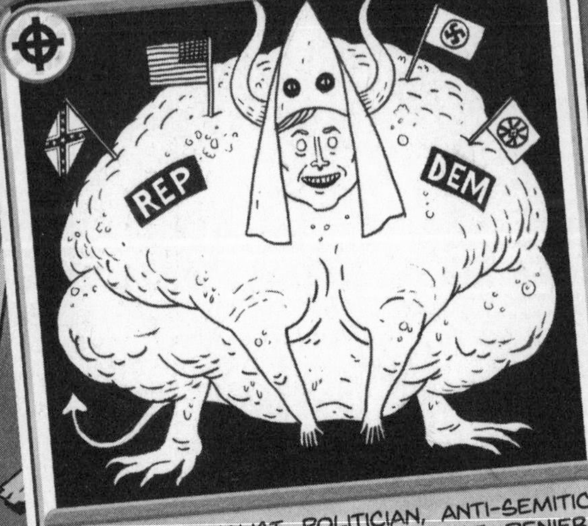
REP
DEM

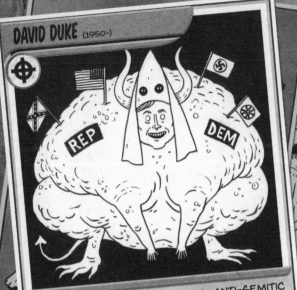

WHITE NATIONALIST, POLITICIAN, ANTI-SEMITIC CONSPIRACY THEORIST, HOLOCAUST DENIER, AND FORMER IMPERIAL WIZARD OF THE KU KLUX KLAN; FOUNDER OF THE NATIONAL ASSOCIATION FOR THE ADVANCEMENT OF WHITE PEOPLE (NAAWP); IN 1992 LED AN UNSUCCESSFUL PRESIDENTIAL RUN WITH THE CAMPAIGN SLOGAN "AMERICA FIRST."

HENRY FORD (1863-1947)

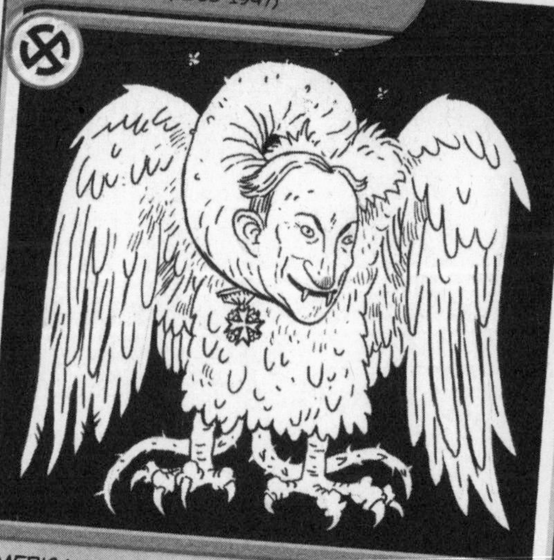

AMERICAN INDUSTRIALIST, FOUNDER OF THE FORD MOTOR COMPANY, SPONSORED THE DEVELOPMENT OF THE ASSEMBLY LINE FOR MASS PRODUCTION. IN THE EARLY 1920S, PUBLISHED A WEEKLY NEWSPAPER THAT PUBLISHED STRONGLY ANTI SEMITIC VIEWS; BLAMED WWII ON JEWISH "FINANCIERS" AND DID BUSINESS WITH NAZI GERMANY, EVEN MANUFACTURING WAR MATERIALS; A GERMAN FORD SUBSIDIARY COMPANY USED SLAVE LABOR.

COL. WILLIAM POTTER GALE (1917-1988)

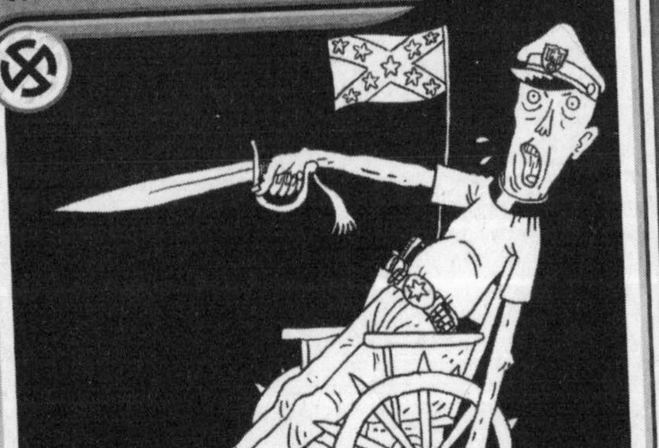

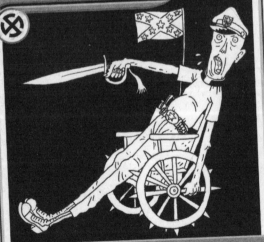

SELF-DESCRIBED REVEREND IN THE CHRISTIAN IDENTITY MOVEMENT PREVIOUSLY AN AIDE TO GENERAL MACARTHUR, COORDINATED GUERRILLA RESISTANCE IN THE PHILIPPINES DURING WWII. BECAME A LEADING FIGURE IN THE ANTI-TAX AND PARAMILITARY MOVEMENTS OF THE 1970S AND 1980S, INCLUDING HIS GROUP UNITED CHRISTIAN POSSE ASSOCIATION, THE CALIFORNIA RANGERS AND POSSE COMITATUS. HELPED FOUND THE MILITIA MOVEMENT.

ERICH GLIEBE (1963-) INACTIVE

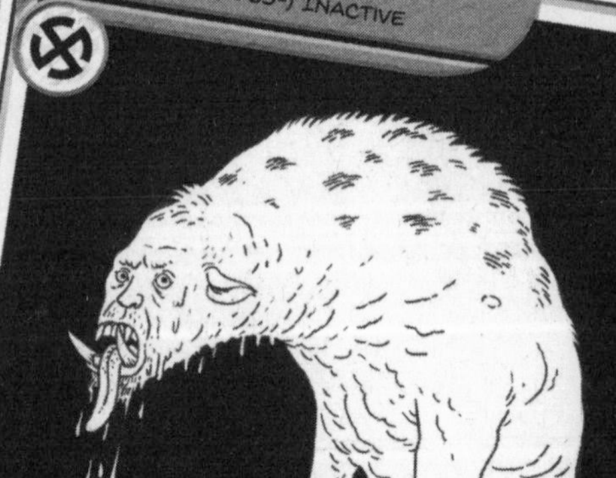

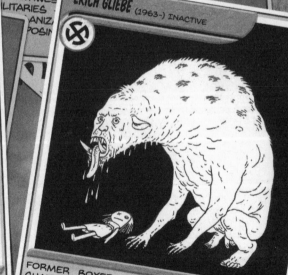

FORMER BOXER "THE ARYAN BARBARIAN" AND CHAIRMAN OF THE NATIONAL ALLIANCE, A GENOCIDAL NEO-NAZI GROUP THAT CALLS FOR THE ERADICATION OF THE JEWS AND OTHER RACES AND THE CREATION OF AN ALL-WHITE HOMELAND; MANAGED WHITE-POWER MUSIC LABELS LIFE RUNE RECORDS AND RESISTANCE RECORDS. RESIGNED AS NATIONAL ALLIANCE CHAIRMAN AMIDST ALLEGATIONS OF PEDOPHILIA.

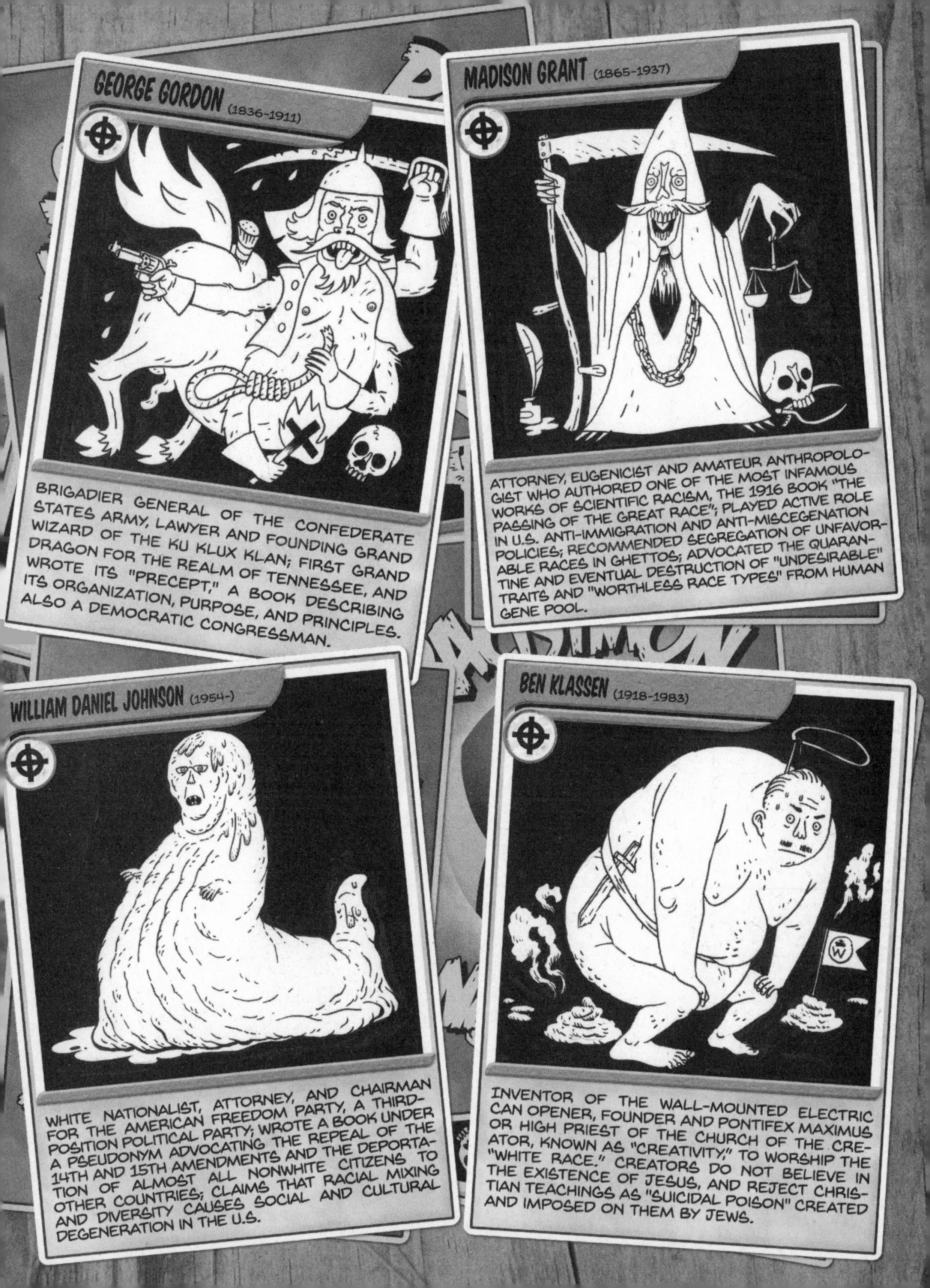
GEORGE GORDON (1836-1911)
BRIGADIER GENERAL OF THE CONFEDERATE STATES ARMY, LAWYER AND FOUNDING GRAND WIZARD OF THE KU KLUX KLAN; FIRST GRAND DRAGON FOR THE REALM OF TENNESSEE, AND WROTE ITS "PRECEPT," A BOOK DESCRIBING ITS ORGANIZATION, PURPOSE, AND PRINCIPLES. ALSO A DEMOCRATIC CONGRESSMAN.
MADISON GRANT (1865-1937)
ATTORNEY, EUGENICIST AND AMATEUR ANTHROPOLOGIST WHO AUTHORED ONE OF THE MOST INFAMOUS WORKS OF SCIENTIFIC RACISM, THE 1916 BOOK "THE PASSING OF THE GREAT RACE"; PLAYED ACTIVE ROLE IN U.S. ANTI-IMMIGRATION AND ANTI-MISCEGENATION POLICIES; RECOMMENDED SEGREGATION OF UNFAVORABLE RACES IN GHETTOS; ADVOCATED THE QUARANTINE AND EVENTUAL DESTRUCTION OF "UNDESIRABLE" TRAITS AND "WORTHLESS RACE TYPES" FROM HUMAN GENE POOL.
WILLIAM DANIEL JOHNSON (1954-)
WHITE NATIONALIST, ATTORNEY, AND CHAIRMAN FOR THE AMERICAN FREEDOM PARTY, A THIRD-POSITION POLITICAL PARTY; WROTE A BOOK UNDER A PSEUDONYM ADVOCATING THE REPEAL OF THE 14TH AND 15TH AMENDMENTS AND THE DEPORTATION OF ALMOST ALL NONWHITE CITIZENS TO OTHER COUNTRIES; CLAIMS THAT RACIAL MIXING AND DIVERSITY CAUSES SOCIAL AND CULTURAL DEGENERATION IN THE U.S.
BEN KLASSEN (1918-1983)
INVENTOR OF THE WALL-MOUNTED ELECTRIC CAN OPENER, FOUNDER AND PONTIFEX MAXIMUS OR HIGH PRIEST OF THE CHURCH OF THE CREATOR, KNOWN AS "CREATIVITY," TO WORSHIP THE "WHITE RACE." CREATORS DO NOT BELIEVE IN THE EXISTENCE OF JESUS, AND REJECT CHRISTIAN TEACHINGS AS "SUICIDAL POISON" CREATED AND IMPOSED ON THEM BY JEWS.

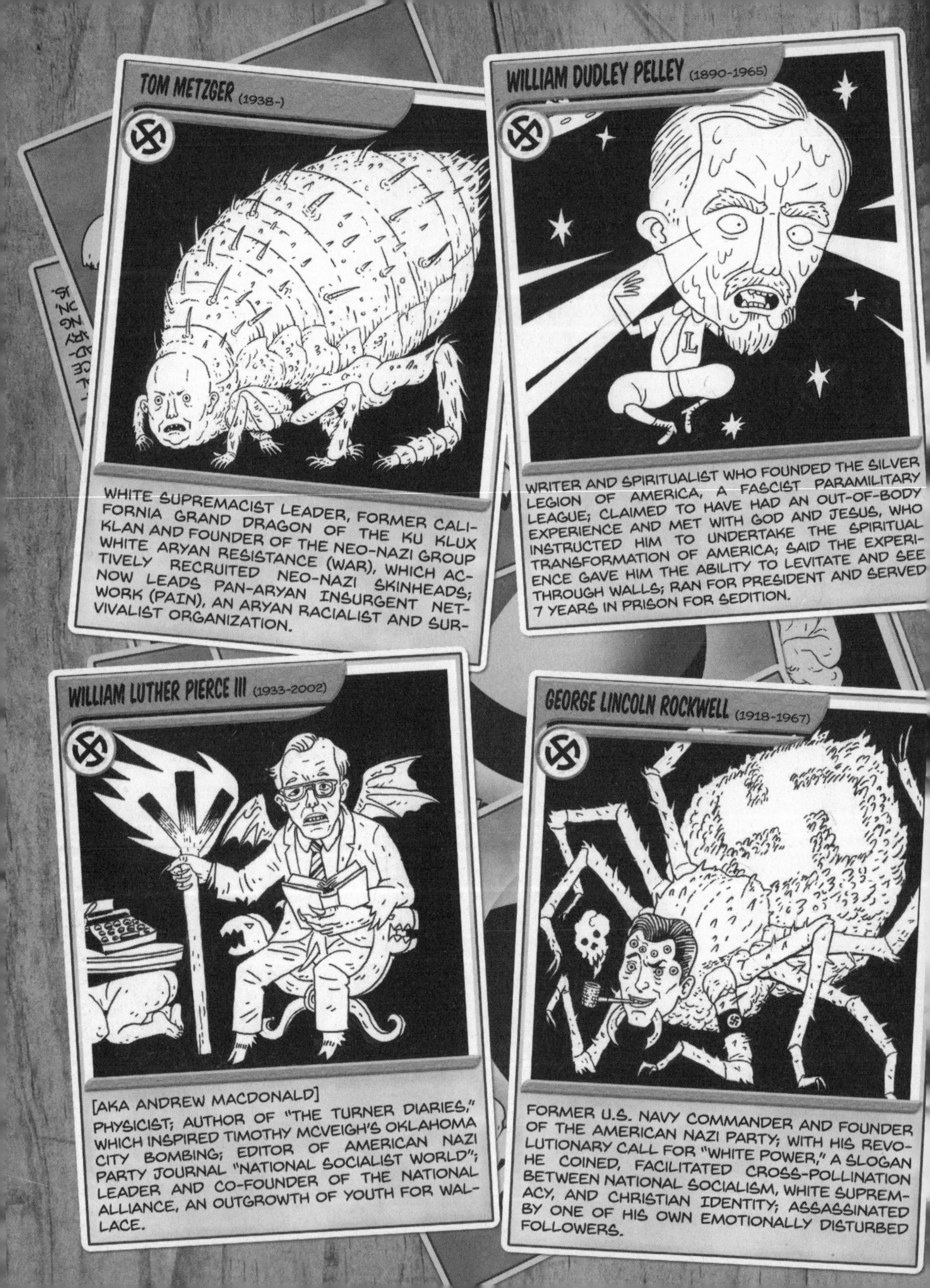
TOM METZGER (1938-)
WHITE SUPREMACIST LEADER, FORMER CALIFORNIA GRAND DRAGON OF THE KU KLUX KLAN AND FOUNDER OF THE NEO-NAZI GROUP WHITE ARYAN RESISTANCE (WAR), WHICH ACTIVELY RECRUITED NEO-NAZI SKINHEADS; NOW LEADS PAN-ARYAN INSURGENT NETWORK (PAIN), AN ARYAN RACIALIST AND SURVIVALIST ORGANIZATION.
WILLIAM DUDLEY PELLEY (1890-1965)
L
WRITER AND SPIRITUALIST WHO FOUNDED THE SILVER LEGION OF AMERICA, A FASCIST PARAMILITARY LEAGUE; CLAIMED TO HAVE HAD AN OUT-OF-BODY EXPERIENCE AND MET WITH GOD AND JESUS, WHO INSTRUCTED HIM TO UNDERTAKE THE SPIRITUAL TRANSFORMATION OF AMERICA; SAID THE EXPERIENCE GAVE HIM THE ABILITY TO LEVITATE AND SEE THROUGH WALLS; RAN FOR PRESIDENT AND SERVED 7 YEARS IN PRISON FOR SEDITION.
WILLIAM LUTHER PIERCE III (1933-2002)
[AKA ANDREW MACDONALD]
PHYSICIST; AUTHOR OF "THE TURNER DIARIES," WHICH INSPIRED TIMOTHY MCVEIGH'S OKLAHOMA CITY BOMBING; EDITOR OF AMERICAN NAZI PARTY JOURNAL "NATIONAL SOCIALIST WORLD"; LEADER AND CO-FOUNDER OF THE NATIONAL ALLIANCE, AN OUTGROWTH OF YOUTH FOR WALLACE.
GEORGE LINCOLN ROCKWELL (1918-1967)
FORMER U.S. NAVY COMMANDER AND FOUNDER OF THE AMERICAN NAZI PARTY; WITH HIS REVOLUTIONARY CALL FOR "WHITE POWER," A SLOGAN HE COINED, FACILITATED CROSS-POLLINATION BETWEEN NATIONAL SOCIALISM, WHITE SUPREMACY, AND CHRISTIAN IDENTITY; ASSASSINATED BY ONE OF HIS OWN EMOTIONALLY DISTURBED FOLLOWERS.

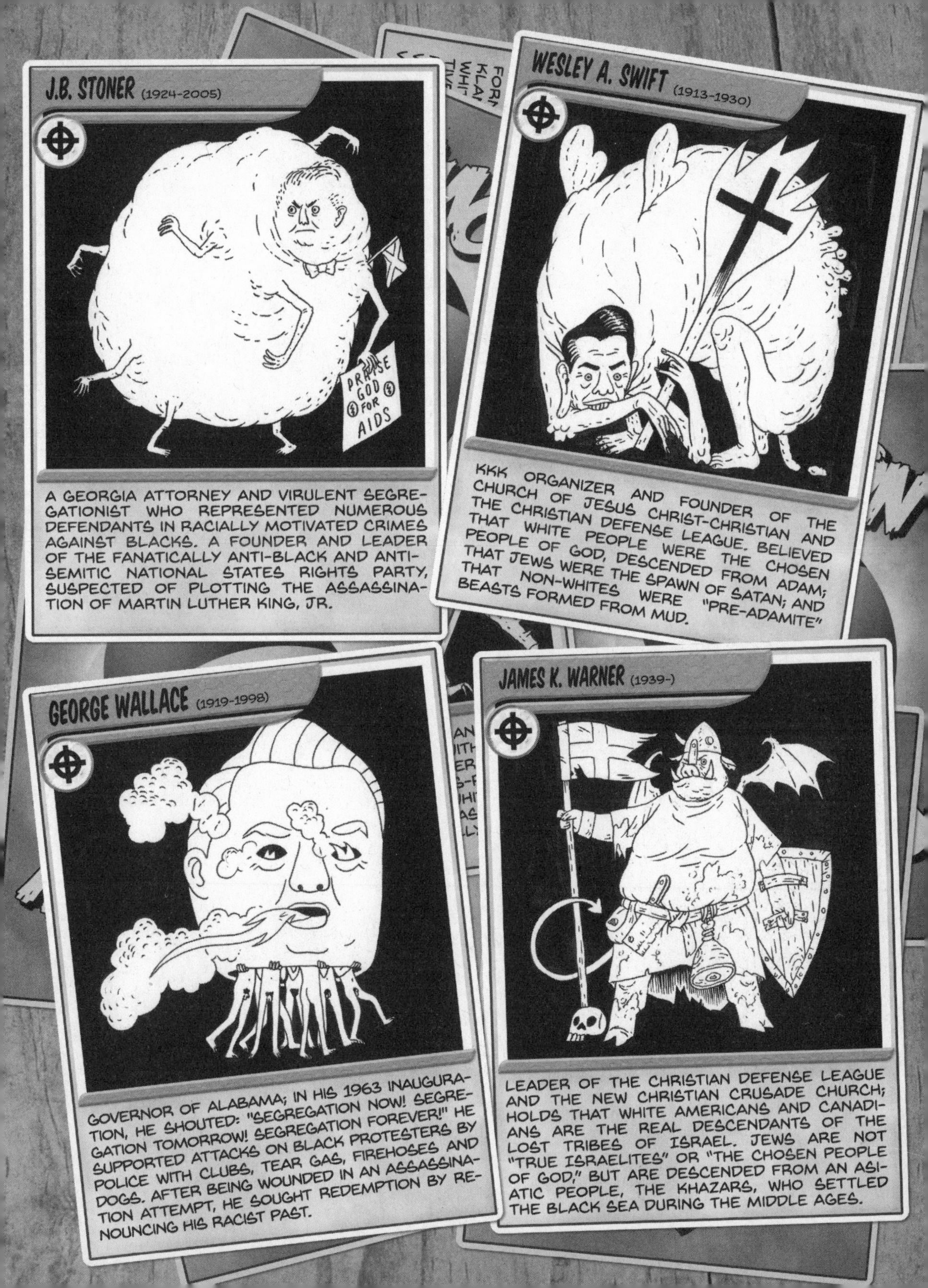
J.B. STONER (1924-2005)
PRAISE GOD FOR AIDS
A GEORGIA ATTORNEY AND VIRULENT SEGREGATIONIST WHO REPRESENTED NUMEROUS DEFENDANTS IN RACIALLY MOTIVATED CRIMES AGAINST BLACKS. A FOUNDER AND LEADER OF THE FANATICALLY ANTI-BLACK AND ANTI-SEMITIC NATIONAL STATES RIGHTS PARTY, SUSPECTED OF PLOTTING THE ASSASSINATION OF MARTIN LUTHER KING, JR.
WESLEY A. SWIFT (1913-1930)
KKK ORGANIZER AND FOUNDER OF THE
CHURCH OF JESUS CHRIST-CHRISTIAN AND
THE CHRISTIAN DEFENSE LEAGUE. BELIEVED
THAT WHITE PEOPLE WERE THE CHOSEN
PEOPLE OF GOD, DESCENDED FROM ADAM;
THAT JEWS WERE THE SPAWN OF SATAN; AND
THAT NON-WHITES WERE "PRE-ADAMITE"
BEASTS FORMED FROM MUD.
GEORGE WALLACE (1919-1998)
GOVERNOR OF ALABAMA; IN HIS 1963 INAUGURATION, HE SHOUTED: "SEGREGATION NOW! SEGREGATION TOMORROW! SEGREGATION FOREVER!" HE SUPPORTED ATTACKS ON BLACK PROTESTERS BY POLICE WITH CLUBS, TEAR GAS, FIREHOSES AND DOGS. AFTER BEING WOUNDED IN AN ASSASSINATION ATTEMPT, HE SOUGHT REDEMPTION BY RENOUNCING HIS RACIST PAST.
JAMES K. WARNER (1939-)
LEADER OF THE CHRISTIAN DEFENSE LEAGUE AND THE NEW CHRISTIAN CRUSADE CHURCH; HOLDS THAT WHITE AMERICANS AND CANADIANS ARE THE REAL DESCENDANTS OF THE LOST TRIBES OF ISRAEL. JEWS ARE NOT "TRUE ISRAELITES" OR "THE CHOSEN PEOPLE OF GOD," BUT ARE DESCENDED FROM AN ASIATIC PEOPLE, THE KHAZARS, WHO SETTLED THE BLACK SEA DURING THE MIDDLE AGES.

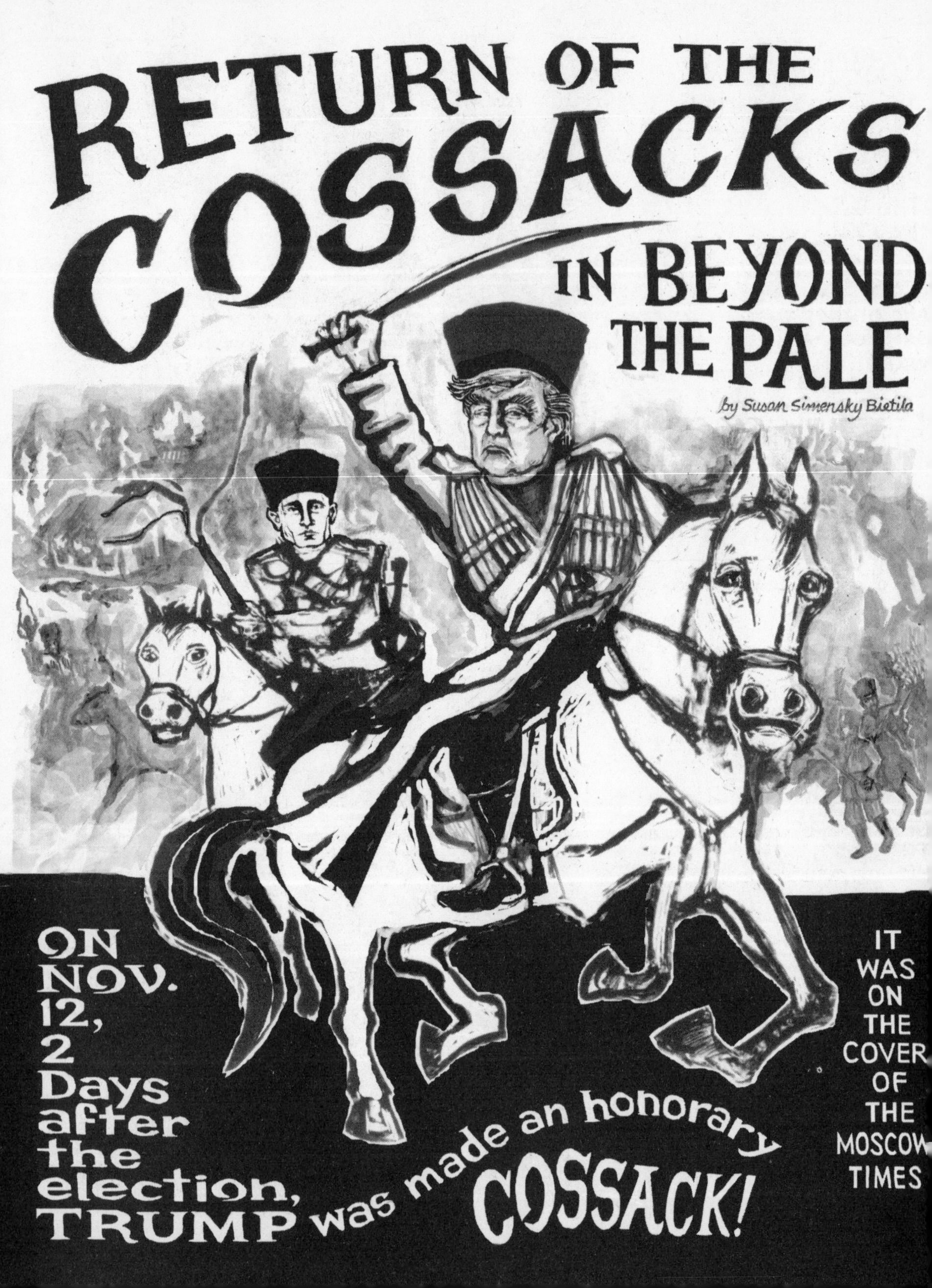

RETURN OF THE COSSACKS

IN BEYOND THE PALE

by Susan Simensky Bietila

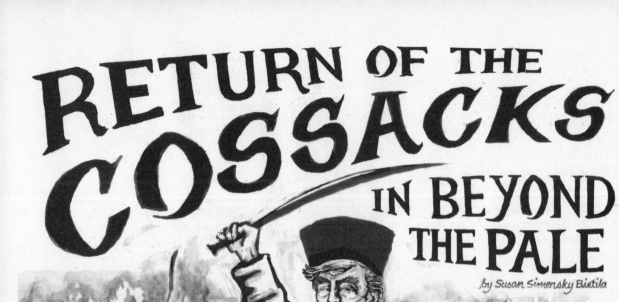

ON NOV. 12, 2 Days after the election, TRUMP was made an honorary COSSACK!

IT WAS ON THE COVER OF THE MOSCOW TIMES

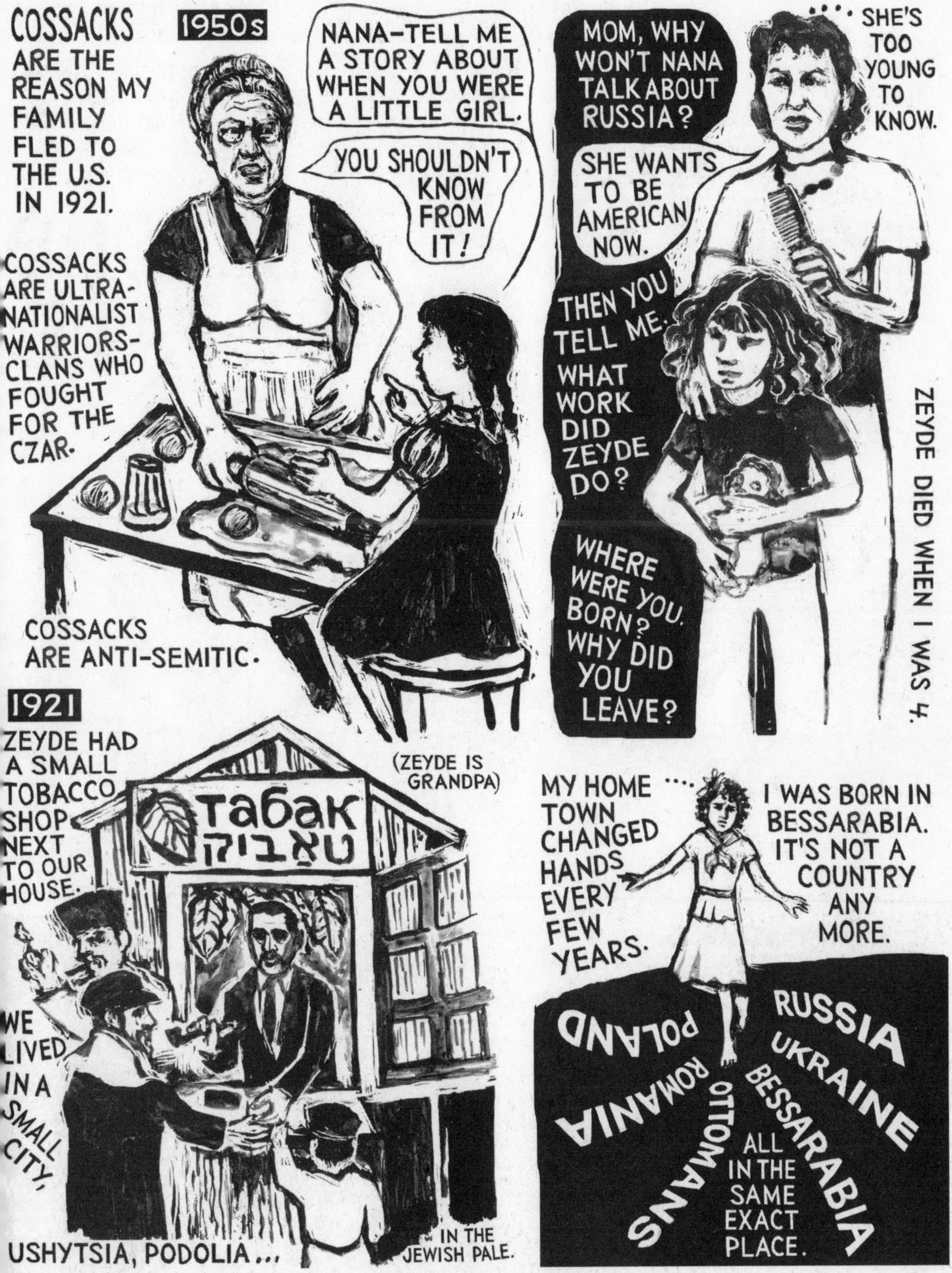
COSSACKS ARE THE REASON MY FAMILY FLED TO THE U.S. IN 1921.
1950s
NANA–TELL ME A STORY ABOUT WHEN YOU WERE A LITTLE GIRL.
YOU SHOULDN'T KNOW FROM IT!
COSSACKS ARE ULTRA-NATIONALIST WARRIORS-CLANS WHO FOUGHT FOR THE CZAR.
COSSACKS ARE ANTI-SEMITIC.
MOM, WHY WON'T NANA TALK ABOUT RUSSIA?
...SHE'S TOO YOUNG TO KNOW.
SHE WANTS TO BE AMERICAN NOW.
THEN YOU TELL ME.
WHAT WORK DID ZEYDE DO?
WHERE WERE YOU BORN? WHY DID YOU LEAVE?
ZEYDE DIED WHEN I WAS 4.
1921
ZEYDE HAD A SMALL TOBACCO SHOP NEXT TO OUR HOUSE.
(ZEYDE IS GRANDPA)
табак
טאַביק
WE LIVED IN A SMALL CITY,
USHYTSIA, PODOLIA...
IN THE JEWISH PALE.
MY HOME TOWN CHANGED HANDS EVERY FEW YEARS....
I WAS BORN IN BESSARABIA. IT'S NOT A COUNTRY ANY MORE.
RUSSIA
UKRAINE
POLAND
ROMANIA
OTTOMANS
BESSARABIA
ALL IN THE SAME EXACT PLACE.

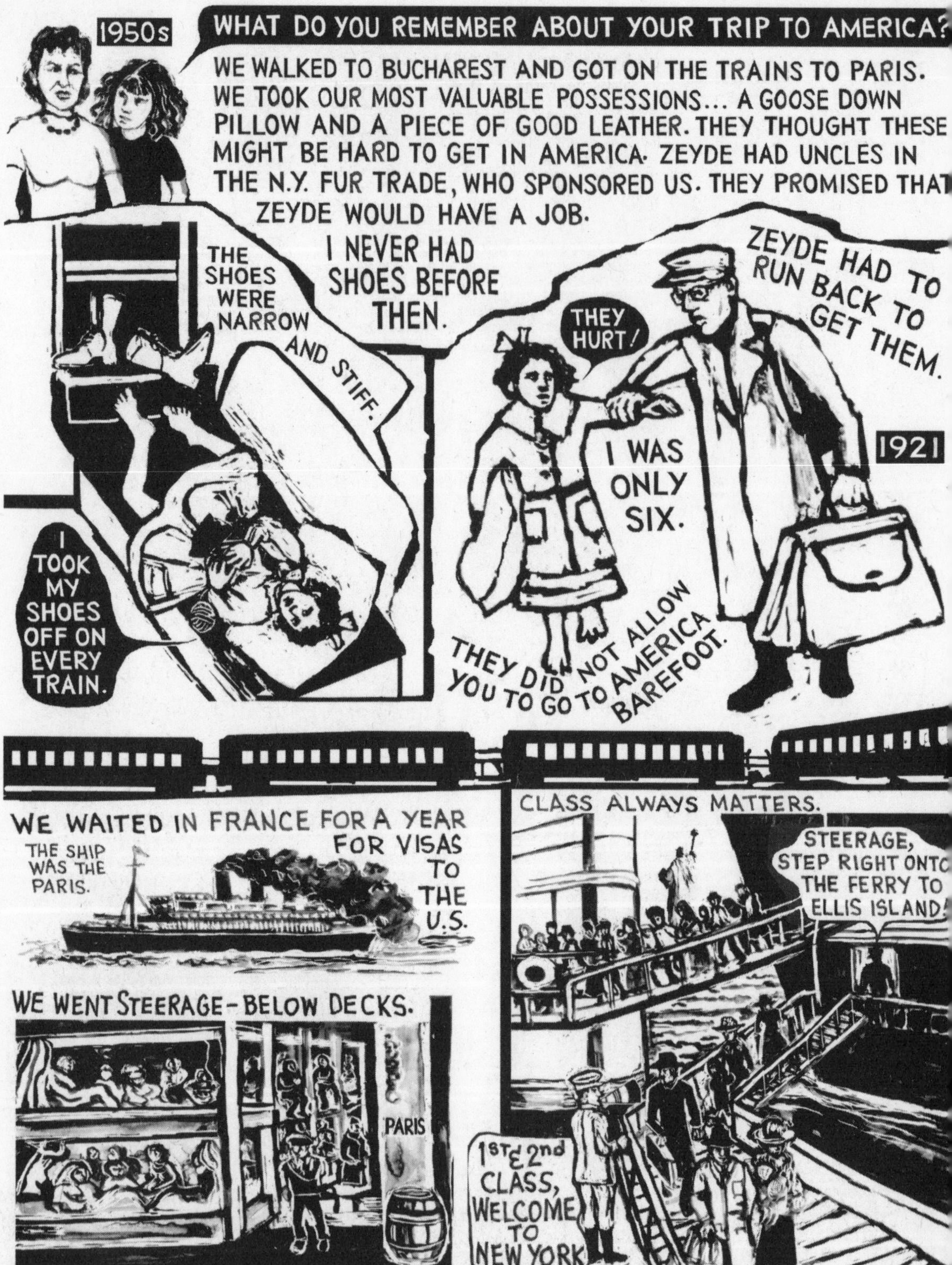
1950s
WHAT DO YOU REMEMBER ABOUT YOUR TRIP TO AMERICA?
WE WALKED TO BUCHAREST AND GOT ON THE TRAINS TO PARIS. WE TOOK OUR MOST VALUABLE POSSESSIONS... A GOOSE DOWN PILLOW AND A PIECE OF GOOD LEATHER. THEY THOUGHT THESE MIGHT BE HARD TO GET IN AMERICA. ZEYDE HAD UNCLES IN THE N.Y. FUR TRADE, WHO SPONSORED US. THEY PROMISED THAT ZEYDE WOULD HAVE A JOB.
THE SHOES WERE NARROW AND STIFF.
I NEVER HAD SHOES BEFORE THEN.
I TOOK MY SHOES OFF ON EVERY TRAIN.
ZEYDE HAD TO RUN BACK TO GET THEM.
THEY HURT!
1921
I WAS ONLY SIX.
THEY DID NOT ALLOW YOU TO GO TO AMERICA BAREFOOT.
WE WAITED IN FRANCE FOR A YEAR FOR VISAS TO THE U.S.
THE SHIP WAS THE PARIS.
WE WENT STEERAGE - BELOW DECKS.
PARIS
CLASS ALWAYS MATTERS.
STEERAGE, STEP RIGHT ONTO THE FERRY TO ELLIS ISLAND!
1ST & 2nd CLASS, WELCOME TO NEW YORK

THE 1920s WAS NOT A GOOD TIME TO ARRIVE.

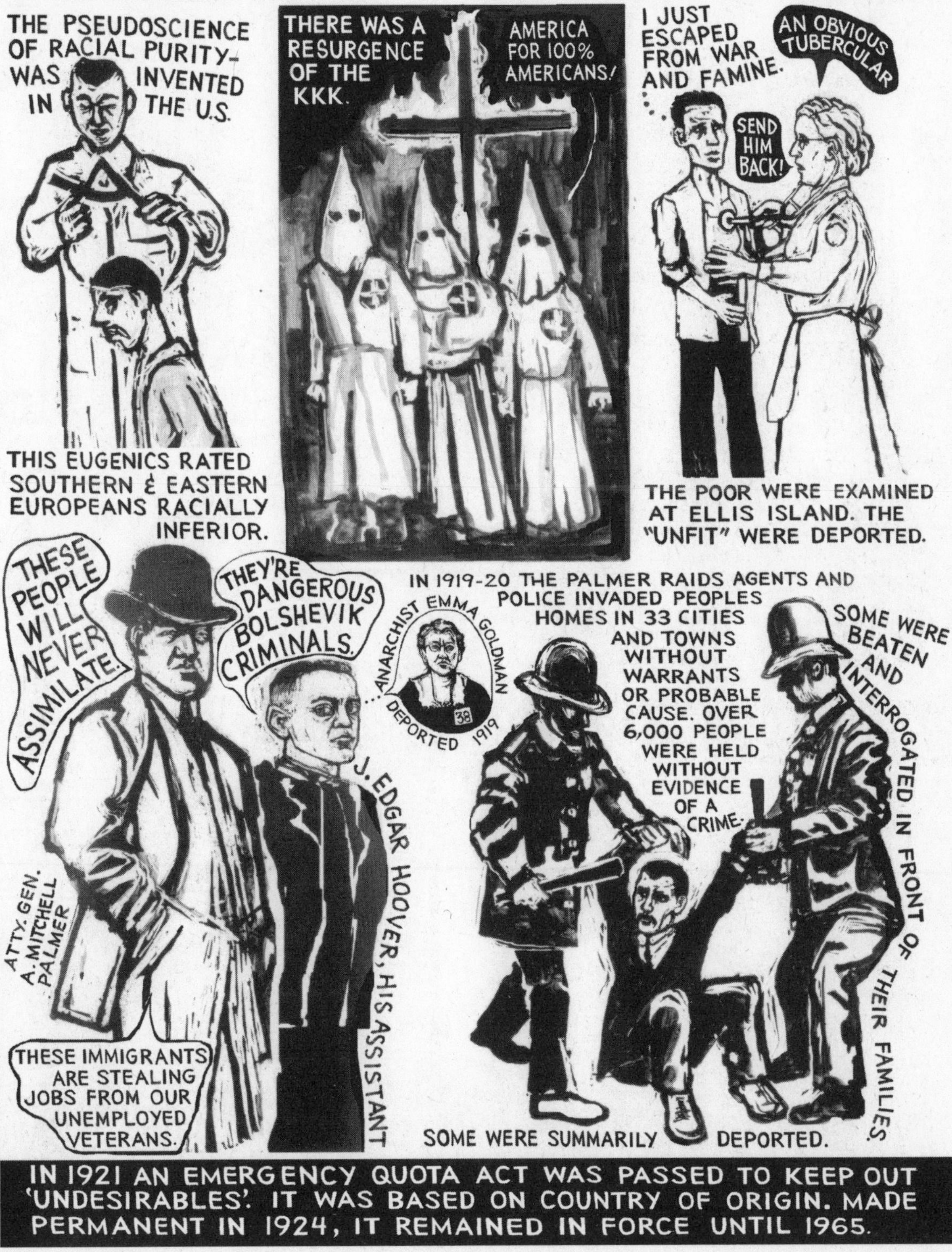
THE PSEUDOSCIENCE OF RACIAL PURITY- WAS INVENTED IN THE U.S.
THIS EUGENICS RATED SOUTHERN & EASTERN EUROPEANS RACIALLY INFERIOR.
THERE WAS A RESURGENCE OF THE KKK.
AMERICA FOR 100% AMERICANS!
I JUST ESCAPED FROM WAR AND FAMINE.
AN OBVIOUS TUBERCULAR
SEND HIM BACK!
THE POOR WERE EXAMINED AT ELLIS ISLAND. THE "UNFIT" WERE DEPORTED.
THESE PEOPLE WILL NEVER ASSIMILATE.
THEY'RE DANGEROUS BOLSHEVIK CRIMINALS.
ATTY. GEN. A. MITCHELL PALMER
THESE IMMIGRANTS ARE STEALING JOBS FROM OUR UNEMPLOYED VETERANS.
J. EDGAR HOOVER, HIS ASSISTANT
ANARCHIST EMMA GOLDMAN DEPORTED 1919
38
IN 1919-20 THE PALMER RAIDS AGENTS AND POLICE INVADED PEOPLES HOMES IN 33 CITIES AND TOWNS WITHOUT WARRANTS OR PROBABLE CAUSE. OVER 6,000 PEOPLE WERE HELD WITHOUT EVIDENCE OF A CRIME.
SOME WERE BEATEN AND INTERROGATED IN FRONT OF THEIR FAMILIES.
SOME WERE SUMMARILY DEPORTED.

IN 1921 AN EMERGENCY QUOTA ACT WAS PASSED TO KEEP OUT 'UNDESIRABLES'. IT WAS BASED ON COUNTRY OF ORIGIN. MADE PERMANENT IN 1924, IT REMAINED IN FORCE UNTIL 1965.

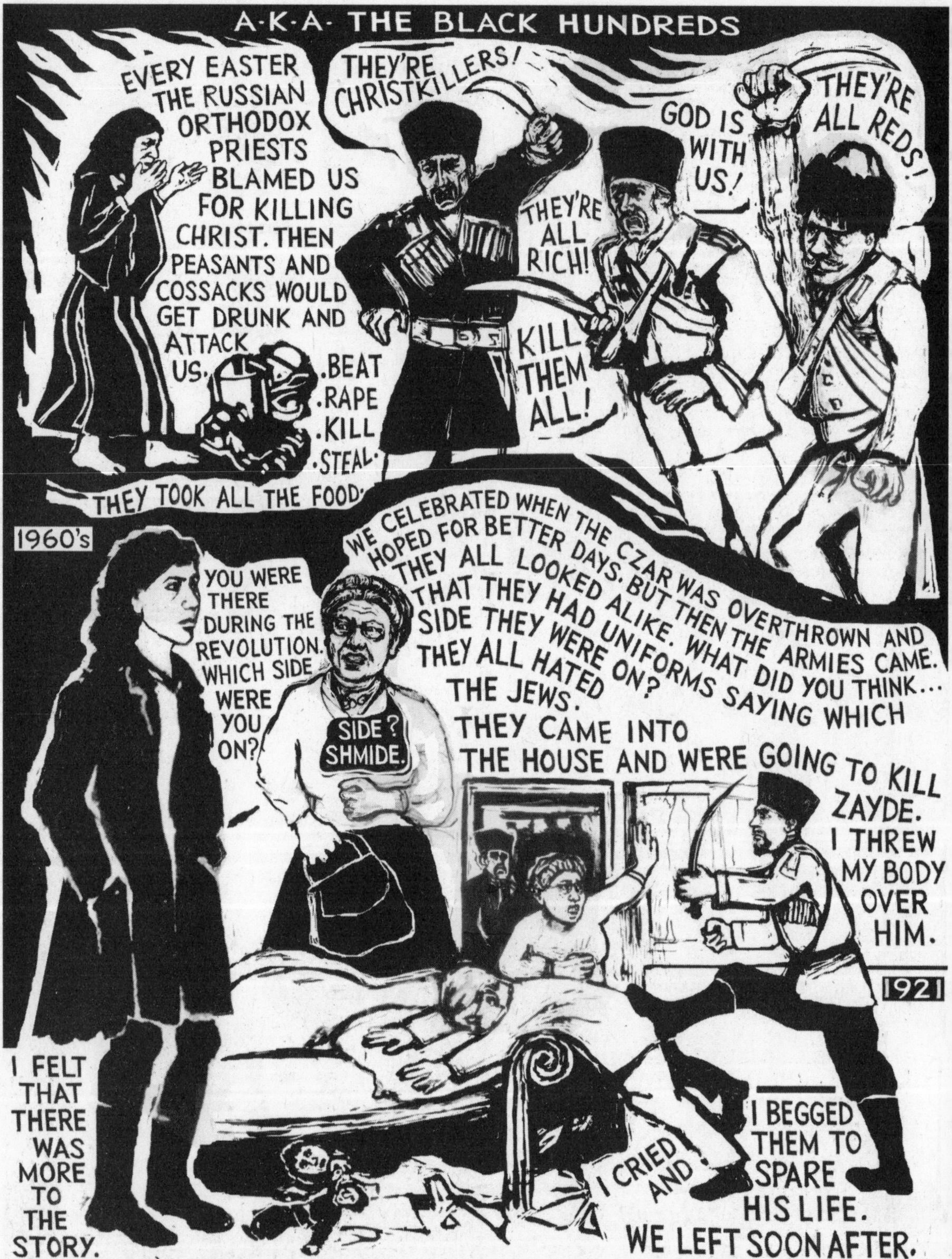
A·K·A· THE BLACK HUNDREDS
EVERY EASTER THE RUSSIAN ORTHODOX PRIESTS BLAMED US FOR KILLING CHRIST. THEN PEASANTS AND COSSACKS WOULD GET DRUNK AND ATTACK US.
.BEAT
.RAPE
.KILL
.STEAL.
THEY TOOK ALL THE FOOD.
THEY'RE CHRISTKILLERS!
THEY'RE ALL RICH!
KILL THEM ALL!
GOD IS WITH US!
THEY'RE ALL REDS!
1960's
YOU WERE THERE DURING THE REVOLUTION. WHICH SIDE WERE YOU ON?
SIDE? SHMIDE.
WE CELEBRATED WHEN THE CZAR WAS OVERTHROWN AND HOPED FOR BETTER DAYS. BUT THEN THE ARMIES CAME. THEY ALL LOOKED ALIKE. WHAT DID YOU THINK... THAT THEY HAD UNIFORMS SAYING WHICH SIDE THEY WERE ON?
THEY ALL HATED THE JEWS.
THEY CAME INTO THE HOUSE AND WERE GOING TO KILL ZAYDE.
I THREW MY BODY OVER HIM.
1921
I FELT THAT THERE WAS MORE TO THE STORY.
I CRIED AND
I BEGGED THEM TO SPARE HIS LIFE.
WE LEFT SOON AFTER.

It's still dark far to the East.
Ancestors with secrets
Even their graves buried under water
Along with their town.

There is no place to stand where they once stood
To cry for their all but forgotten murders
No one to tell their story
Nothing solid to connect with them
Only words on paper
History chapters about the worst Pogroms
during the Russian Civil War.

Silent memories of famine
They fattened me with huge steaks
And heaps of buttery mashed potatoes
I was not allowed
To leave the table
Until I ate it all.
Then they scolded me for getting fat
But they never spoke of their starvation
When the White Armies had stolen all their food.

The lucky ones fled, carrying only their fear
Then lived their lives, screaming and vomiting up
The horrors they had seen without relief.
They burdened my generation
With grandiose expectations.
How could we not thrive here in America?

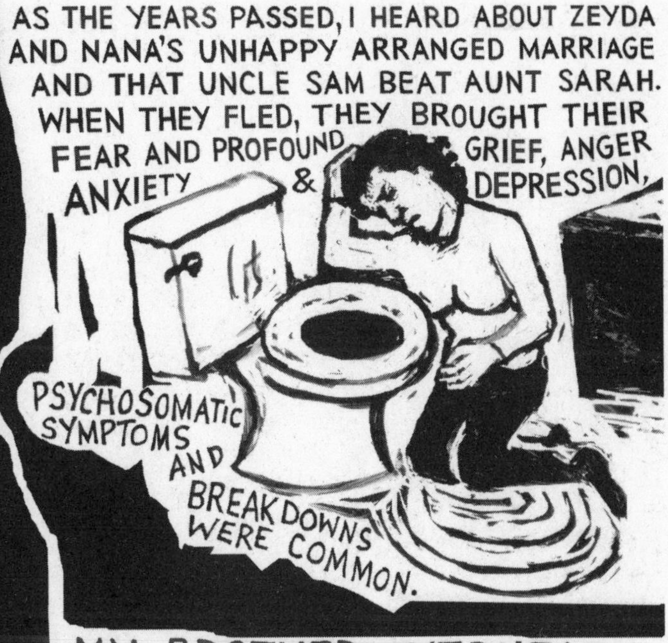
AS THE YEARS PASSED, I HEARD ABOUT ZEYDA AND NANA'S UNHAPPY ARRANGED MARRIAGE AND THAT UNCLE SAM BEAT AUNT SARAH. WHEN THEY FLED, THEY BROUGHT THEIR FEAR AND PROFOUND GRIEF, ANGER
ANXIETY & DEPRESSION,
PSYCHOSOMATIC SYMPTOMS AND BREAKDOWNS WERE COMMON.

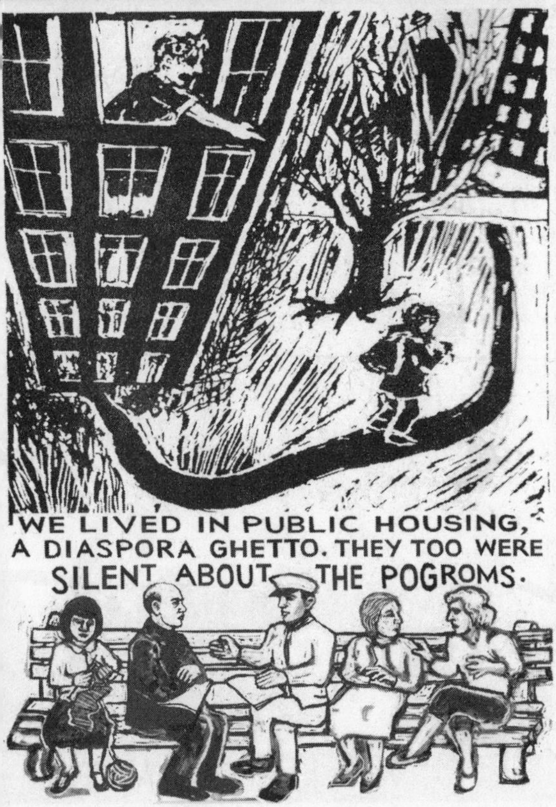
WE LIVED IN PUBLIC HOUSING, A DIASPORA GHETTO. THEY TOO WERE SILENT ABOUT THE POGROMS.

MY BROTHER OVERHEARD MORE OF THE STORY....

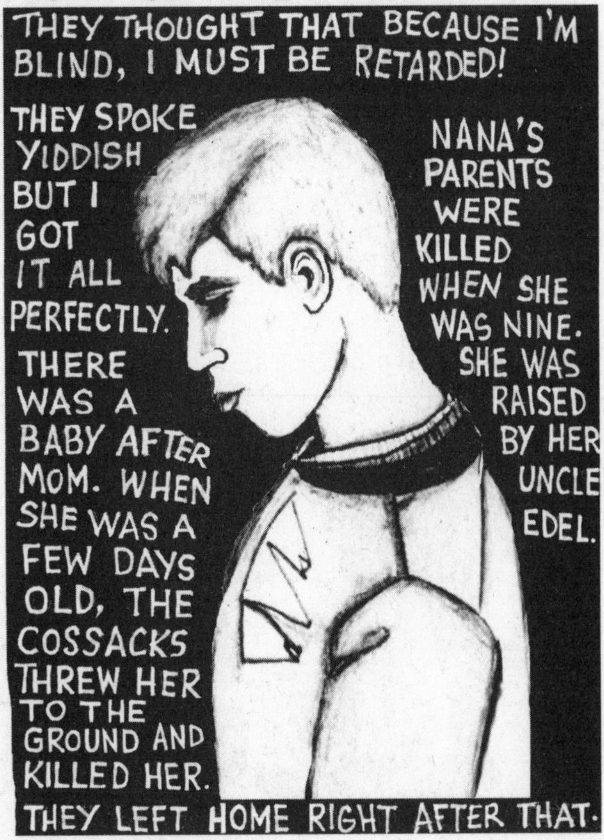
THEY THOUGHT THAT BECAUSE I'M BLIND, I MUST BE RETARDED!
THEY SPOKE YIDDISH BUT I GOT IT ALL PERFECTLY.
THERE WAS A BABY AFTER MOM. WHEN SHE WAS A FEW DAYS OLD, THE COSSACKS THREW HER TO THE GROUND AND KILLED HER.
NANA'S PARENTS WERE KILLED WHEN SHE WAS NINE. SHE WAS RAISED BY HER UNCLE EDEL.
THEY LEFT HOME RIGHT AFTER THAT.

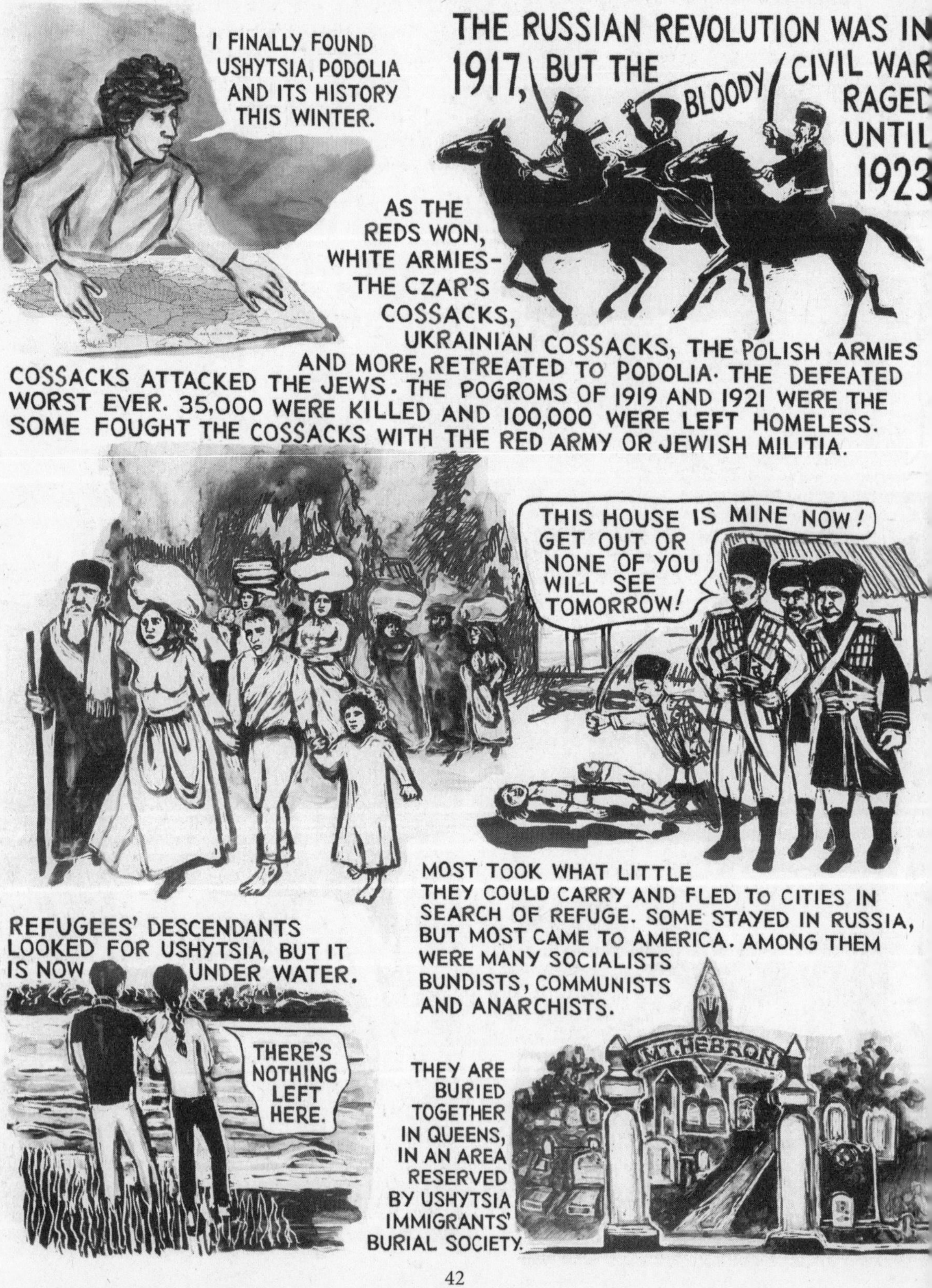
I FINALLY FOUND USHYTSIA, PODOLIA AND ITS HISTORY THIS WINTER.
THE RUSSIAN REVOLUTION WAS IN 1917, BUT THE BLOODY CIVIL WAR RAGED UNTIL 1923
AS THE REDS WON, WHITE ARMIES- THE CZAR'S COSSACKS, UKRAINIAN COSSACKS, THE POLISH ARMIES AND MORE, RETREATED TO PODOLIA. THE DEFEATED COSSACKS ATTACKED THE JEWS. THE POGROMS OF 1919 AND 1921 WERE THE WORST EVER. 35,000 WERE KILLED AND 100,000 WERE LEFT HOMELESS. SOME FOUGHT THE COSSACKS WITH THE RED ARMY OR JEWISH MILITIA.
THIS HOUSE IS MINE NOW! GET OUT OR NONE OF YOU WILL SEE TOMORROW!
MOST TOOK WHAT LITTLE THEY COULD CARRY AND FLED TO CITIES IN SEARCH OF REFUGE. SOME STAYED IN RUSSIA, BUT MOST CAME TO AMERICA. AMONG THEM WERE MANY SOCIALISTS BUNDISTS, COMMUNISTS AND ANARCHISTS.
REFUGEES' DESCENDANTS LOOKED FOR USHYTSIA, BUT IT IS NOW UNDER WATER.
THERE'S NOTHING LEFT HERE.
THEY ARE BURIED TOGETHER IN QUEENS, IN AN AREA RESERVED BY USHYTSIA IMMIGRANTS' BURIAL SOCIETY.
MT. HEBRON

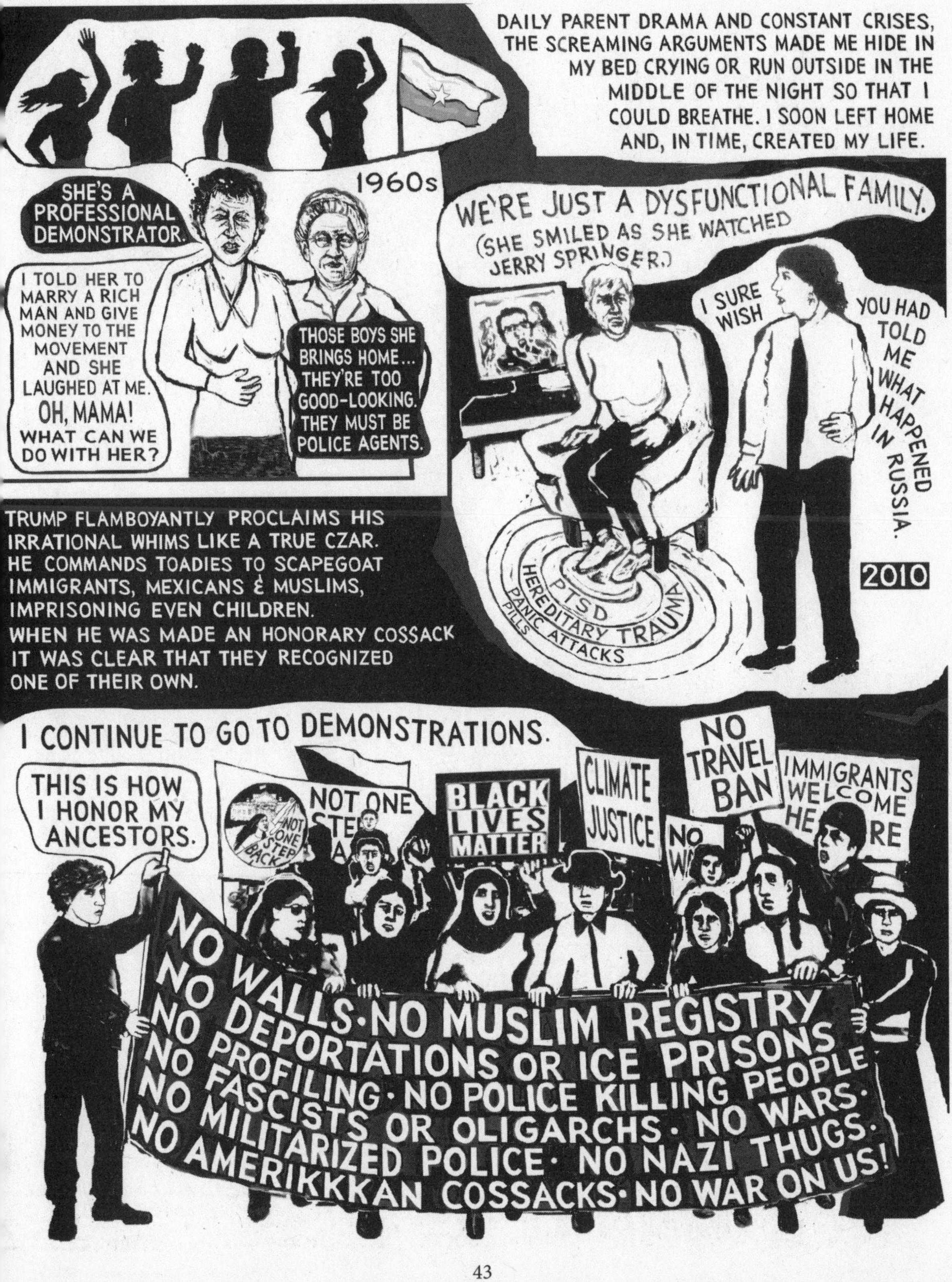
DAILY PARENT DRAMA AND CONSTANT CRISES, THE SCREAMING ARGUMENTS MADE ME HIDE IN MY BED CRYING OR RUN OUTSIDE IN THE MIDDLE OF THE NIGHT SO THAT I COULD BREATHE. I SOON LEFT HOME AND, IN TIME, CREATED MY LIFE.
1960s
SHE'S A PROFESSIONAL DEMONSTRATOR.
I TOLD HER TO MARRY A RICH MAN AND GIVE MONEY TO THE MOVEMENT AND SHE LAUGHED AT ME. OH, MAMA! WHAT CAN WE DO WITH HER?
THOSE BOYS SHE BRINGS HOME... THEY'RE TOO GOOD-LOOKING. THEY MUST BE POLICE AGENTS.
WE'RE JUST A DYSFUNCTIONAL FAMILY. (SHE SMILED AS SHE WATCHED JERRY SPRINGER.)
I SURE WISH YOU HAD TOLD ME WHAT HAPPENED IN RUSSIA.
PTSD
HEREDITARY TRAUMA
PANIC ATTACKS
PILLS
2010
TRUMP FLAMBOYANTLY PROCLAIMS HIS IRRATIONAL WHIMS LIKE A TRUE CZAR. HE COMMANDS TOADIES TO SCAPEGOAT IMMIGRANTS, MEXICANS & MUSLIMS, IMPRISONING EVEN CHILDREN. WHEN HE WAS MADE AN HONORARY COSSACK IT WAS CLEAR THAT THEY RECOGNIZED ONE OF THEIR OWN.
I CONTINUE TO GO TO DEMONSTRATIONS.
THIS IS HOW I HONOR MY ANCESTORS.
NOT ONE STEP BACK
NOT ONE
BLACK LIVES MATTER
CLIMATE JUSTICE
NO TRAVEL BAN
IMMIGRANTS WELCOME HERE
NO WALLS · NO MUSLIM REGISTRY
NO DEPORTATIONS OR ICE PRISONS
NO PROFILING · NO POLICE KILLING PEOPLE
NO FASCISTS OR OLIGARCHS · NO WARS ·
NO MILITARIZED POLICE · NO NAZI THUGS ·
NO AMERIKKKAN COSSACKS · NO WAR ON US!

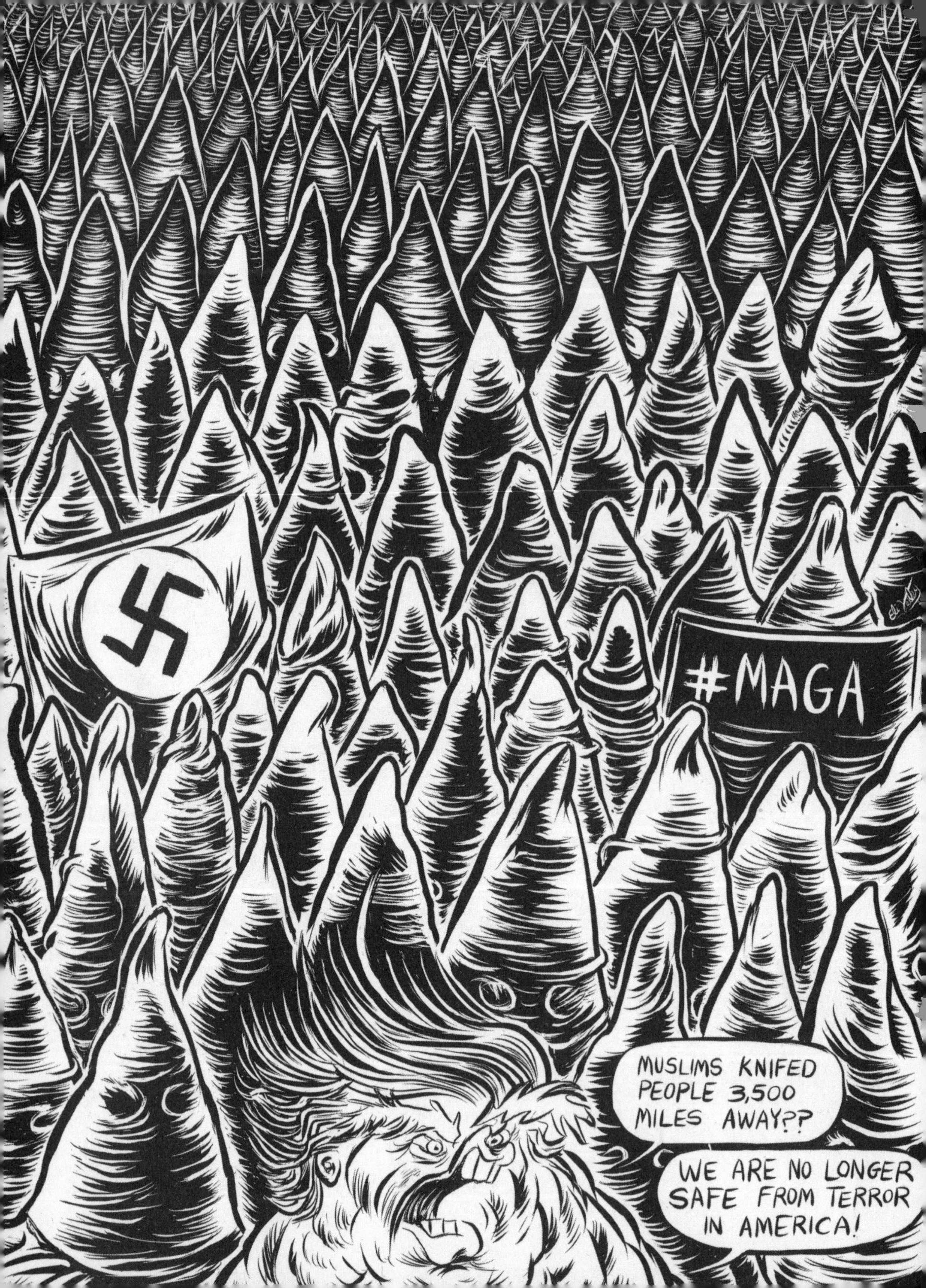
#MAGA
MUSLIMS KNIFED PEOPLE 3,500 MILES AWAY??
WE ARE NO LONGER SAFE FROM TERROR IN AMERICA!

A Sheltered White Girls Decent into Lesbianism & the Far-Left

by Taylor Hollingsworth

if you had told me when I was 14 that in 6 years I would be a Communist Dyke who was a proponent for beating the shit out of facist,

I would have told you:

I don't know what any of those words mean..

and I'm a Pacifist.

hmph...

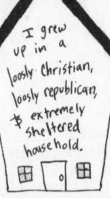

I grew up in a loosly Christian, loosly republican, & extremely sheltered household.

I didnt know what

Gay!!

meant until I was 12 years old.

It's when men like to have sex with other men.

my mom after I got in trouble for calling another kid 'gay' at school.

I also didnt hear the word gay used to mean something other than an insult or sex until I was in eighth grade, when Maine was voting to legalize gay marriage for the first time.

I've always leaned a little to the left.

Impeach Bush!!

→ me, age 9

My mom says it's 'cause I'm an empath

momma's little liberal!

pbbt

YES on 1

MARRIAGE MATTERS TO ALL FAMILIES

www.Mainesunited.org

But I think it's because I've experienced life through the lens of a closeted, gender non-conforming Lesbian in a largely conservative area.

ha! gay.

stfu F*g.

I'm terrified & I don't know why...

my empathy isnt some god-given super power.

its rooted in my understanding of confusion, fear & isolation.

fucking f*#g!!

what are you? a Dyke?

ha ha Queer!

gay ppl are just gross!

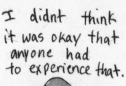

I didnt think it was okay that anyone had to experience that.

This is so fucked up!

When I realized I was gay at 17, I wasnt in a place where I was comfortable being out to anyone...

So I found community online.

Alone in my Room

watched hundreds of Youtube videos,

coming out, being trans

Read up on LGBT feminist theory,

compulsory heterosexuality & the lesbian experience

Gender trouble

and about LGBT history...

Stonewall: the riots that sparked

Body Counts: a memoir of

Why marriage matters

which led me to journals about racism, xenophobia, white supremacy in the USA.

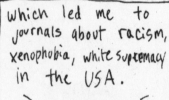

Even though I was living my life as a straight cis person pretending to be unfazed by everyday bigotry

I became obsessed with learning about homophobia, transphobia, racism, classism, ect...

and how those things are intertwined with racism, capitalism & the american government

I know a lot of people see that as insane, like I'm trying to demonize the US while playing the victim.

But they dont understand I was born into this fight & coming to that conclusion wasnt an option.

It was an inevitability.

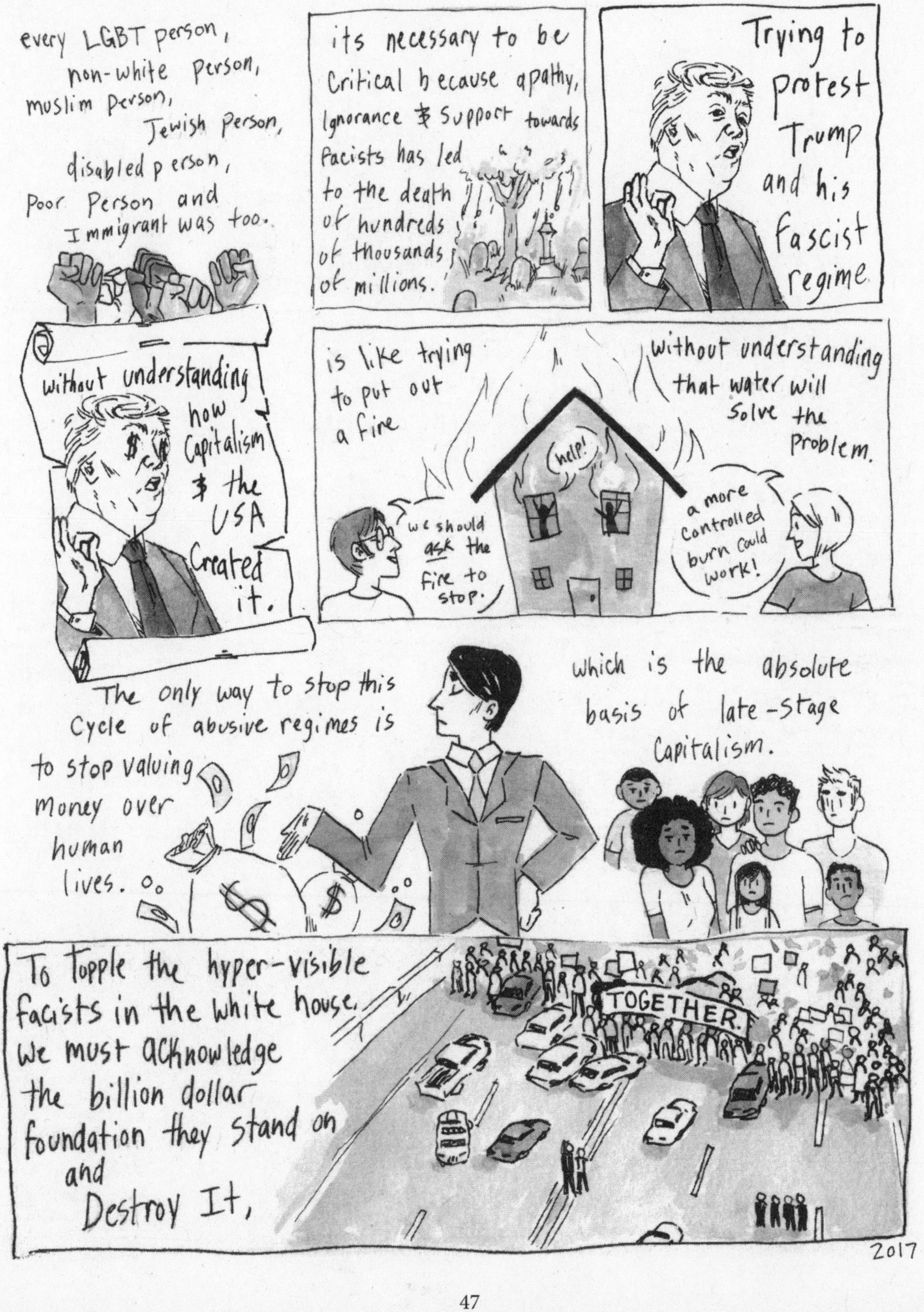
every LGBT person,
non-white person,
muslim person,
Jewish person,
disabled person,
Poor Person and
Immigrant was too.
its necessary to be Critical because apathy, Ignorance & Support towards facists has led to the death of hundreds of thousands of millions.
Trying to protest Trump and his fascist regime
without understanding how Capitalism & the USA Created it.
is like trying to put out a fire
without understanding that water will solve the problem.
help!
we should ask the fire to stop.
a more controlled burn could work!
The only way to stop this Cycle of abusive regimes is to stop valuing money over human lives.
which is the absolute basis of late-stage Capitalism.
To topple the hyper-visible facists in the white house, we must acknowledge the billion dollar foundation they stand on and Destroy It,
TOGETHER.
2017

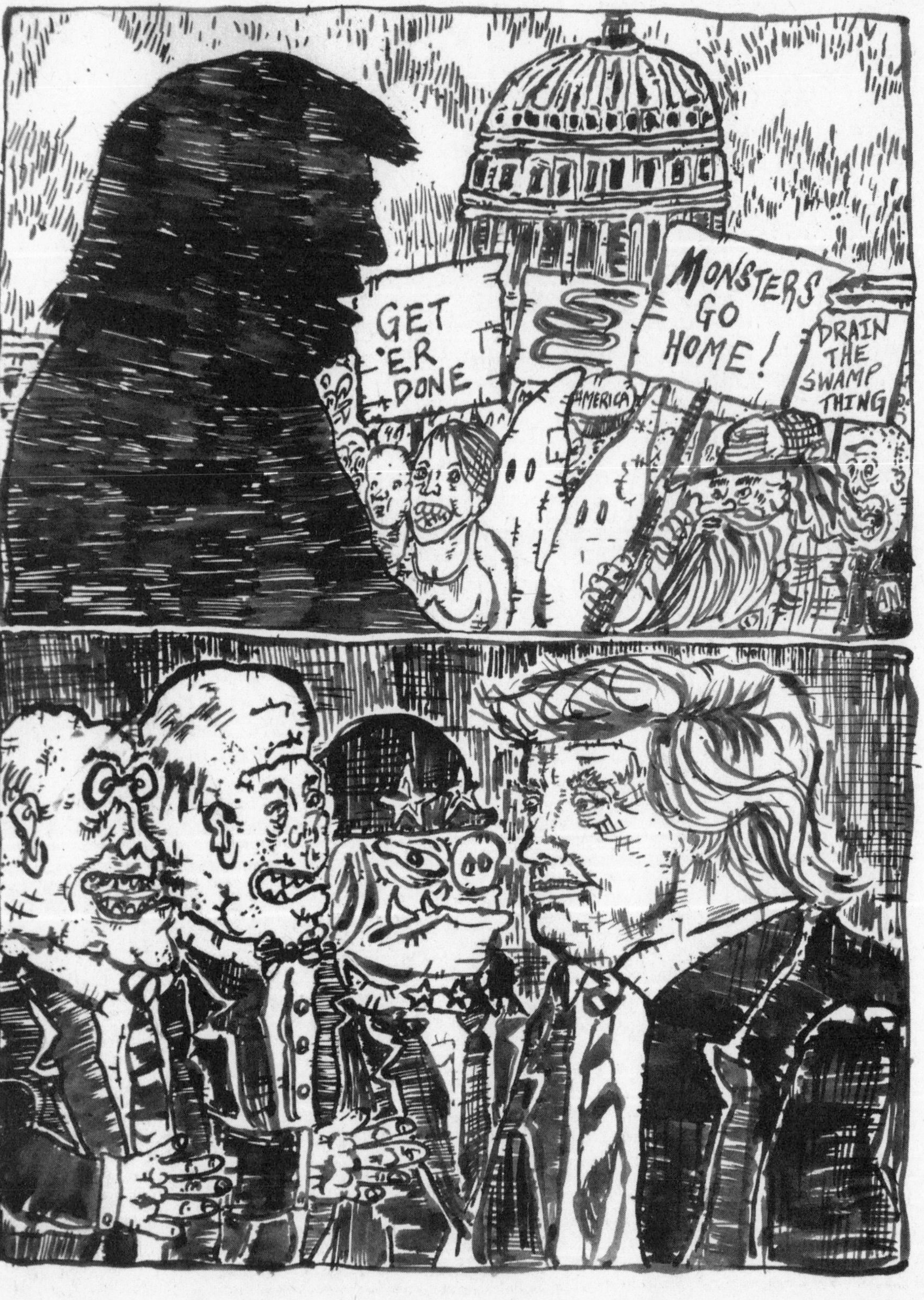
GET 'ER DONE
MONSTERS GO HOME!
DRAIN THE SWAMP THING
AMERICA

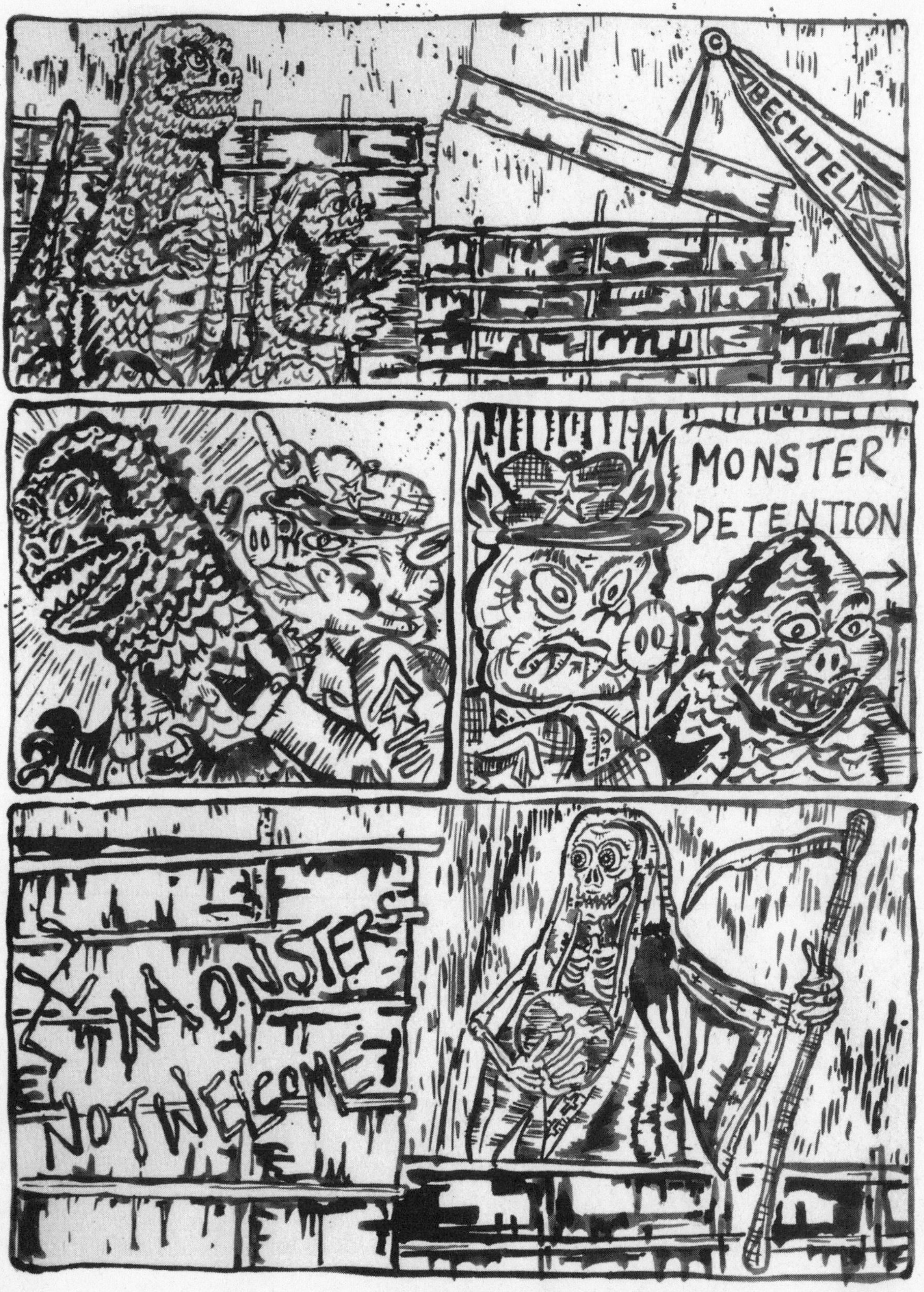
BECHTEL
MONSTER
DETENTION
MONSTERS
NOT WELCOME

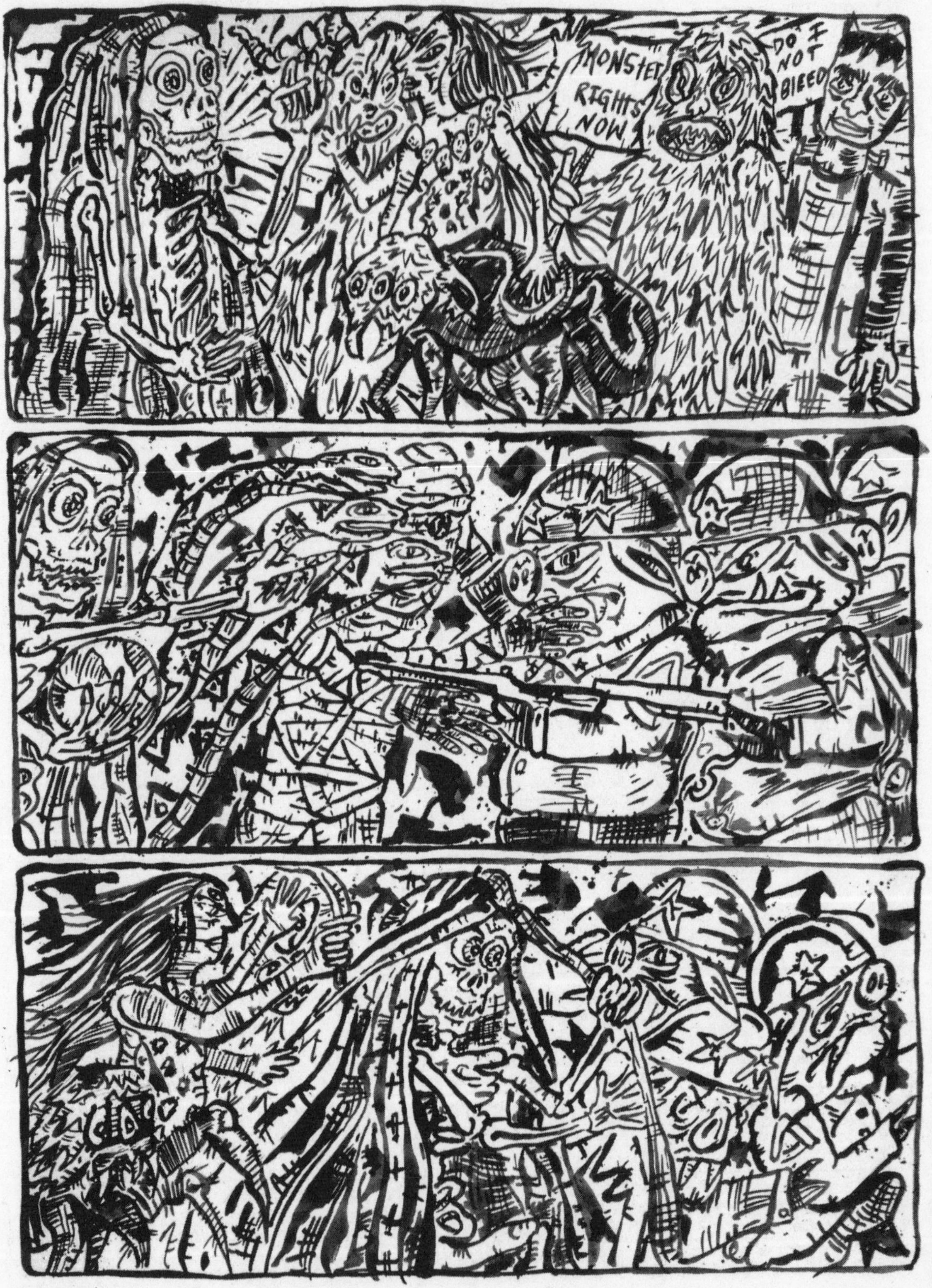
MONSTER RIGHTS NOW
DO I NOT BLEED

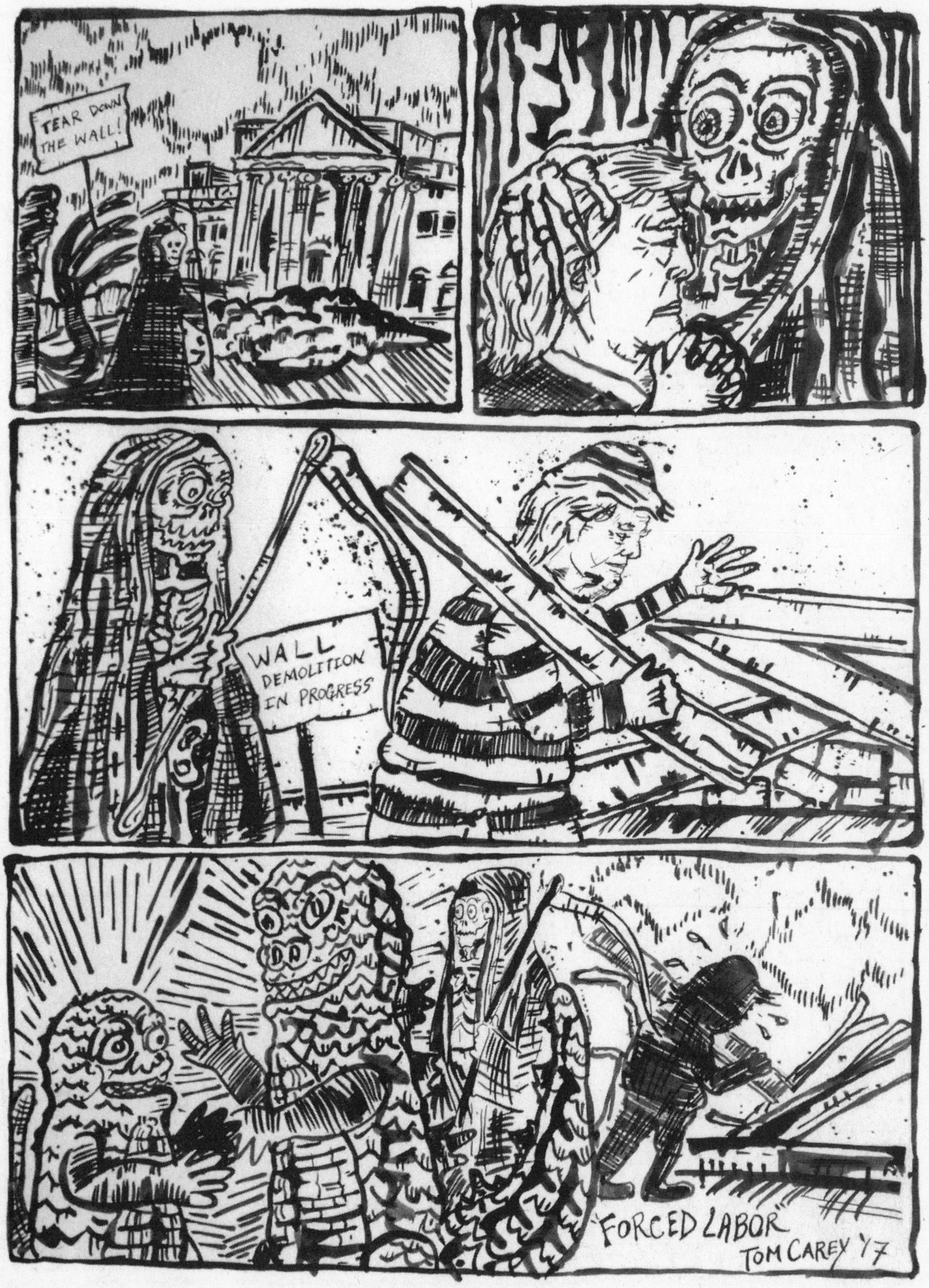
TEAR DOWN THE WALL!
WALL DEMOLITION IN PROGRESS
FORCED LABOR
TOM CAREY '17

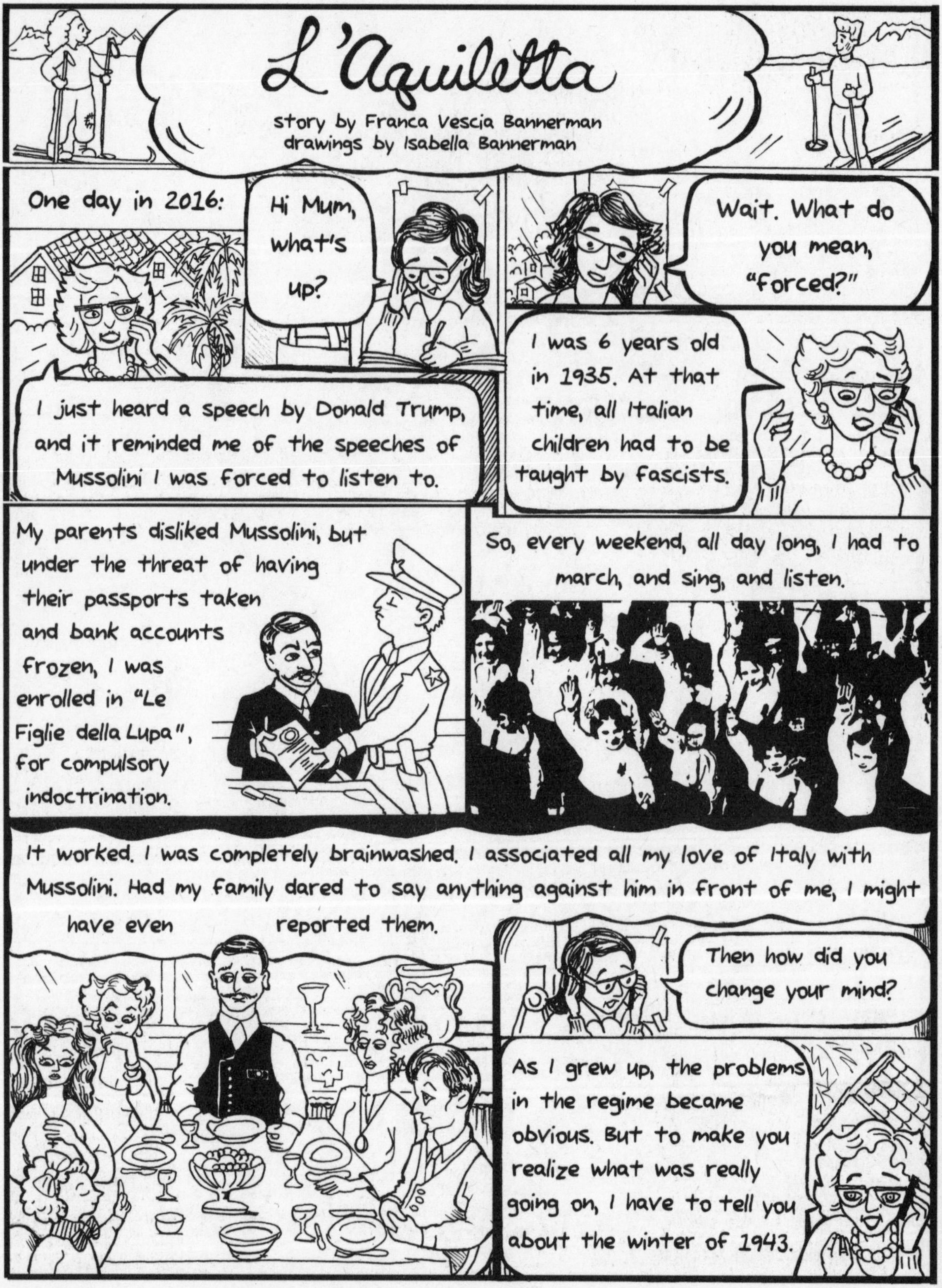
L'Aquiletta
story by Franca Vescia Bannerman
drawings by Isabella Bannerman
One day in 2016:
Hi Mum, what's up?
I just heard a speech by Donald Trump, and it reminded me of the speeches of Mussolini I was forced to listen to.
Wait. What do you mean, "forced?"
I was 6 years old in 1935. At that time, all Italian children had to be taught by fascists.
My parents disliked Mussolini, but under the threat of having their passports taken and bank accounts frozen, I was enrolled in "Le Figlie della Lupa", for compulsory indoctrination.
So, every weekend, all day long, I had to march, and sing, and listen.
It worked. I was completely brainwashed. I associated all my love of Italy with Mussolini. Had my family dared to say anything against him in front of me, I might have even reported them.
Then how did you change your mind?
As I grew up, the problems in the regime became obvious. But to make you realize what was really going on, I have to tell you about the winter of 1943.

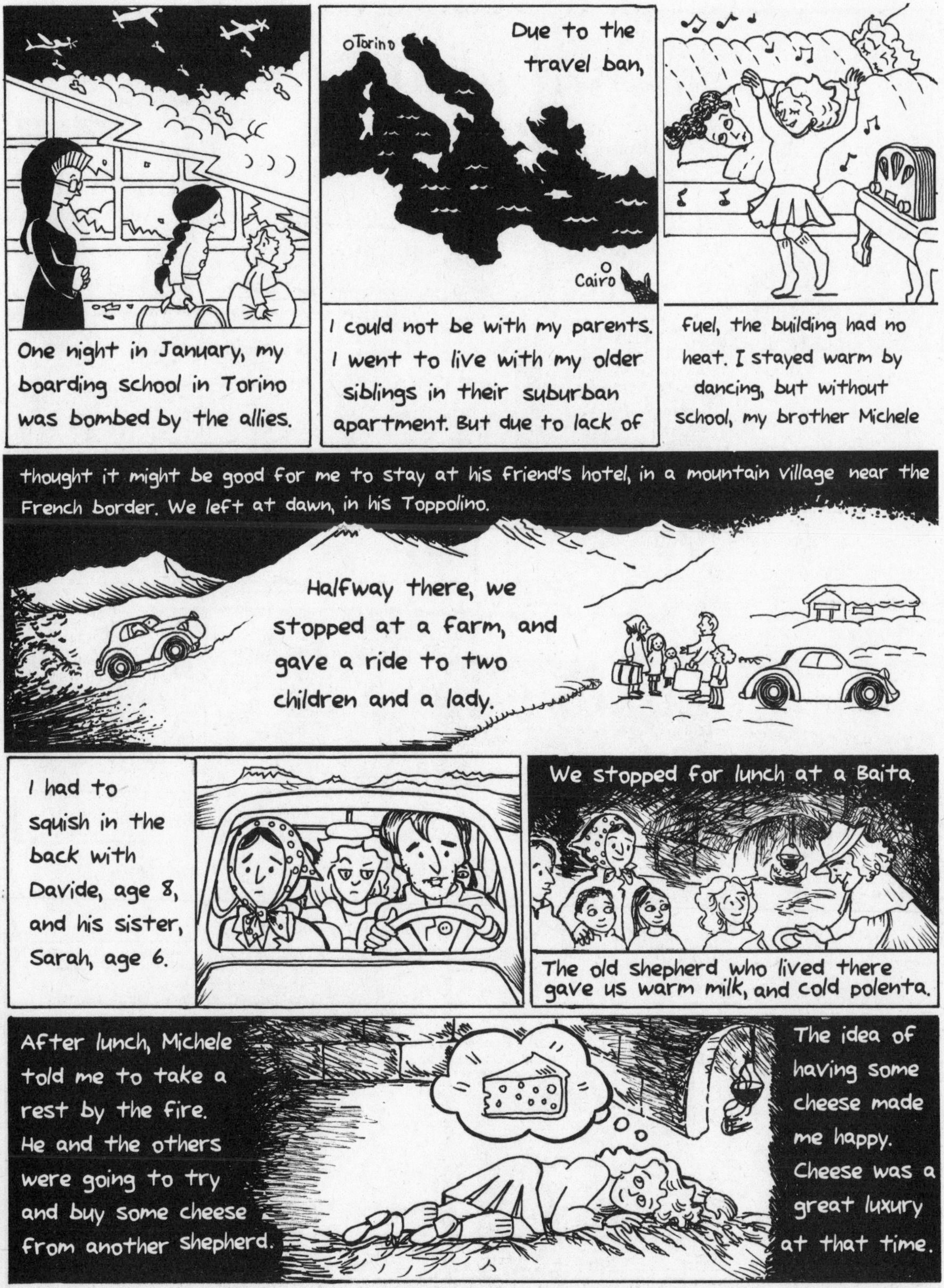

One night in January, my boarding school in Torino was bombed by the allies.
Torino
Cairo
Due to the travel ban,
I could not be with my parents. I went to live with my older siblings in their suburban apartment. But due to lack of
fuel, the building had no heat. I stayed warm by dancing, but without school, my brother Michele
thought it might be good for me to stay at his friend's hotel, in a mountain village near the French border. We left at dawn, in his Toppolino.
Halfway there, we stopped at a farm, and gave a ride to two children and a lady.
I had to squish in the back with Davide, age 8, and his sister, Sarah, age 6.
We stopped for lunch at a Baita.
The old shepherd who lived there gave us warm milk, and cold polenta.
After lunch, Michele told me to take a rest by the fire. He and the others were going to try and buy some cheese from another shepherd.
The idea of having some cheese made me happy. Cheese was a great luxury at that time.

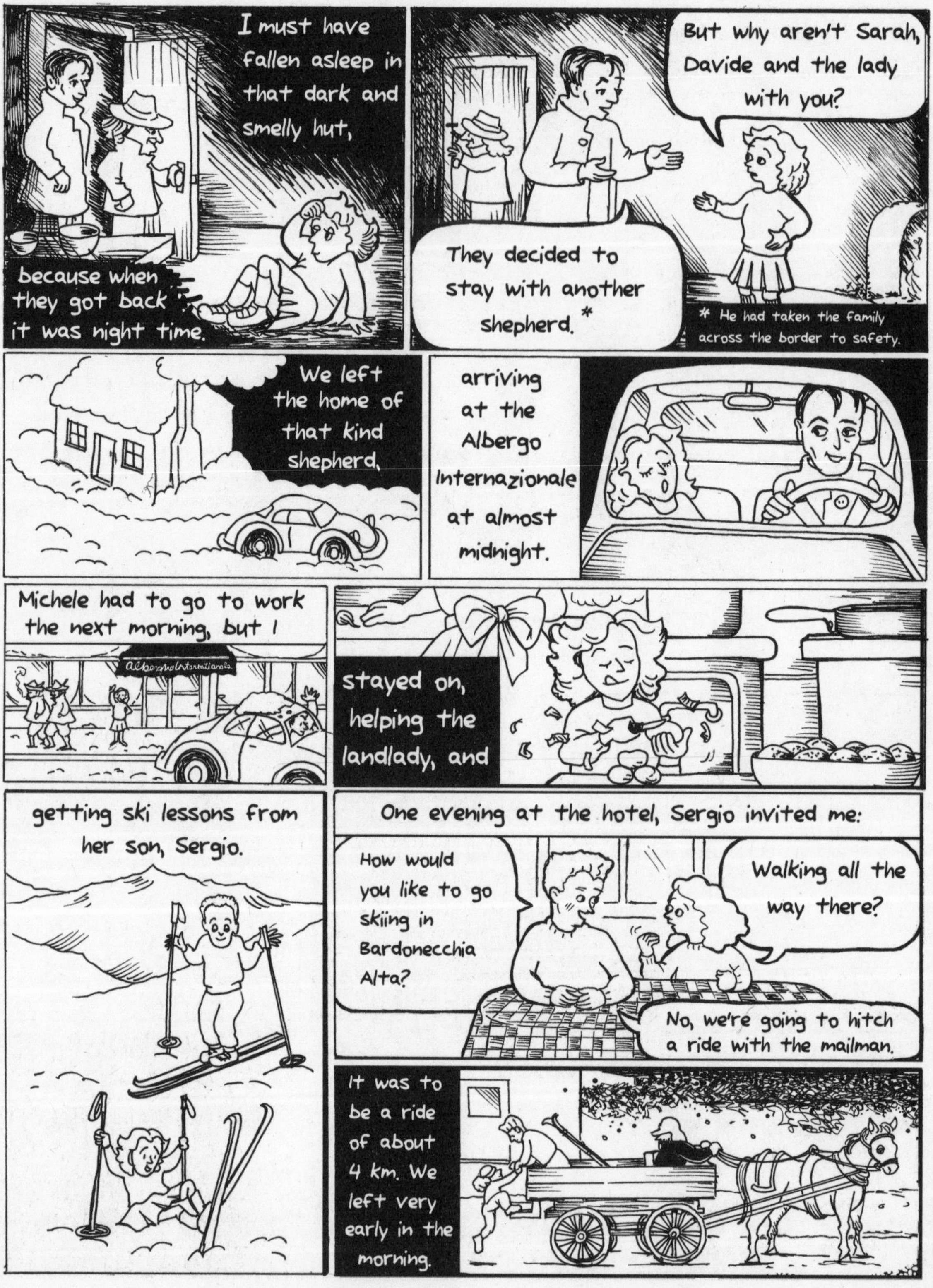
I must have fallen asleep in that dark and smelly hut,
because when they got back it was night time.
But why aren't Sarah, Davide and the lady with you?
They decided to stay with another shepherd.*
* He had taken the family across the border to safety.
We left the home of that kind shepherd,
arriving at the Albergo Internazionale at almost midnight.
Michele had to go to work the next morning, but I
stayed on, helping the landlady, and
getting ski lessons from her son, Sergio.
One evening at the hotel, Sergio invited me:
How would you like to go skiing in Bardonecchia Alta?
Walking all the way there?
No, we're going to hitch a ride with the mailman.
It was to be a ride of about 4 km. We left very early in the morning.

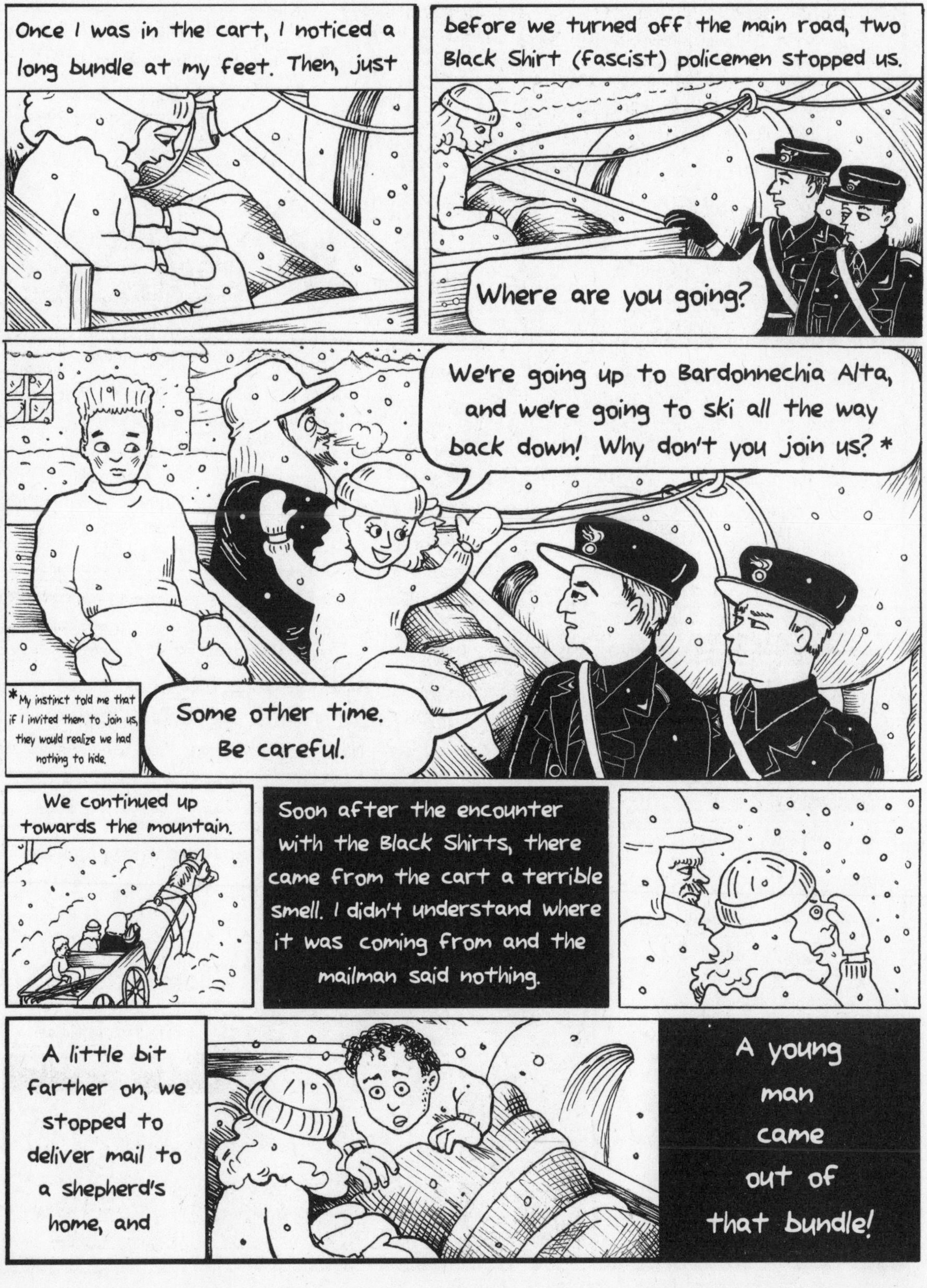
Once I was in the cart, I noticed a long bundle at my feet. Then, just
before we turned off the main road, two Black Shirt (fascist) policemen stopped us.
Where are you going?
We're going up to Bardonnechia Alta, and we're going to ski all the way back down! Why don't you join us? *
Some other time. Be careful.
*My instinct told me that if I invited them to join us, they would realize we had nothing to hide.
We continued up towards the mountain.
Soon after the encounter with the Black Shirts, there came from the cart a terrible smell. I didn't understand where it was coming from and the mailman said nothing.
A little bit farther on, we stopped to deliver mail to a shepherd's home, and
A young man came out of that bundle!

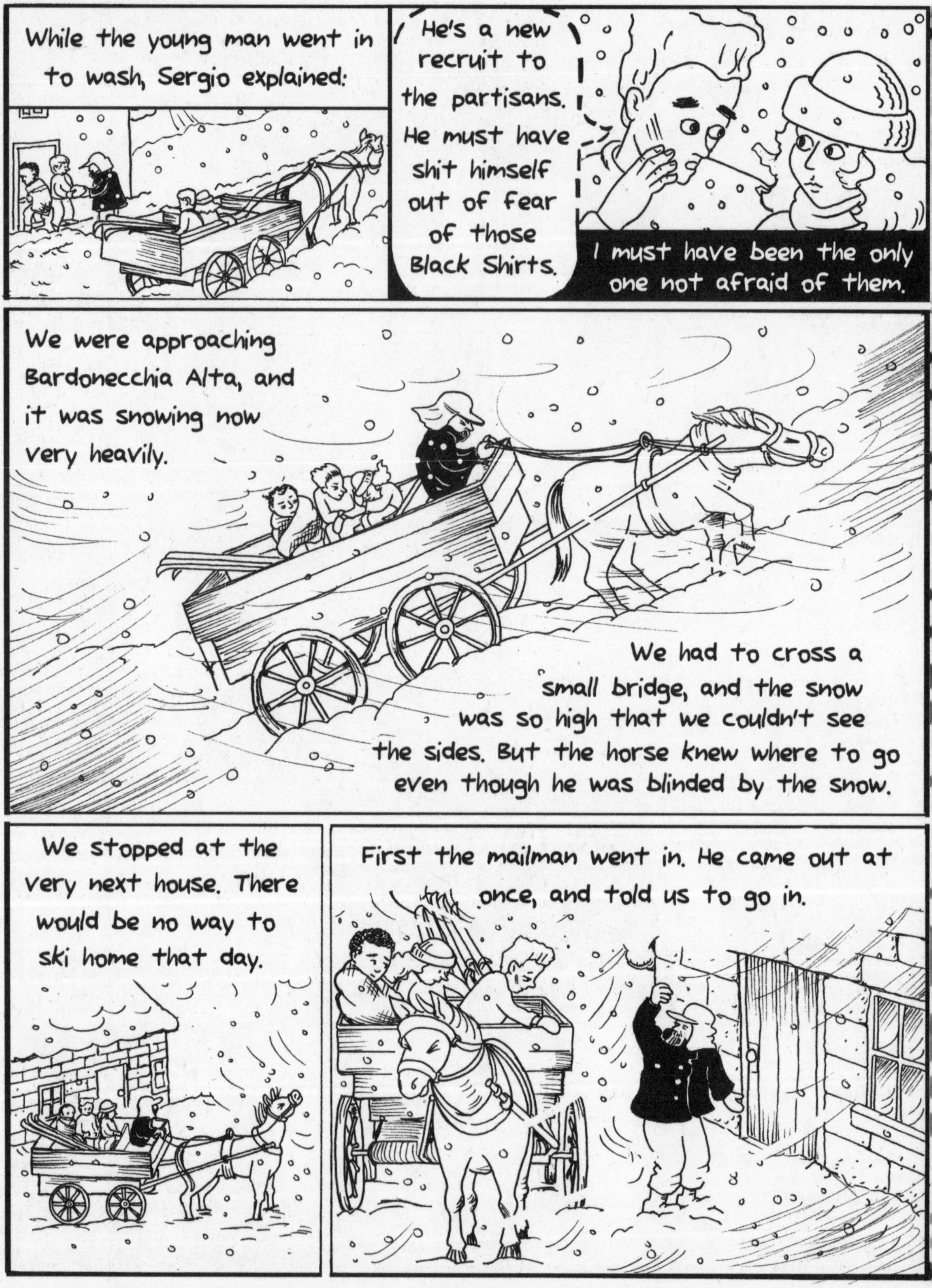
While the young man went in to wash, Sergio explained:
He's a new recruit to the partisans. He must have shit himself out of fear of those Black Shirts.
I must have been the only one not afraid of them.
We were approaching Bardonecchia Alta, and it was snowing now very heavily.
We had to cross a small bridge, and the snow was so high that we couldn't see the sides. But the horse knew where to go even though he was blinded by the snow.
We stopped at the very next house. There would be no way to ski home that day.
First the mailman went in. He came out at once, and told us to go in.

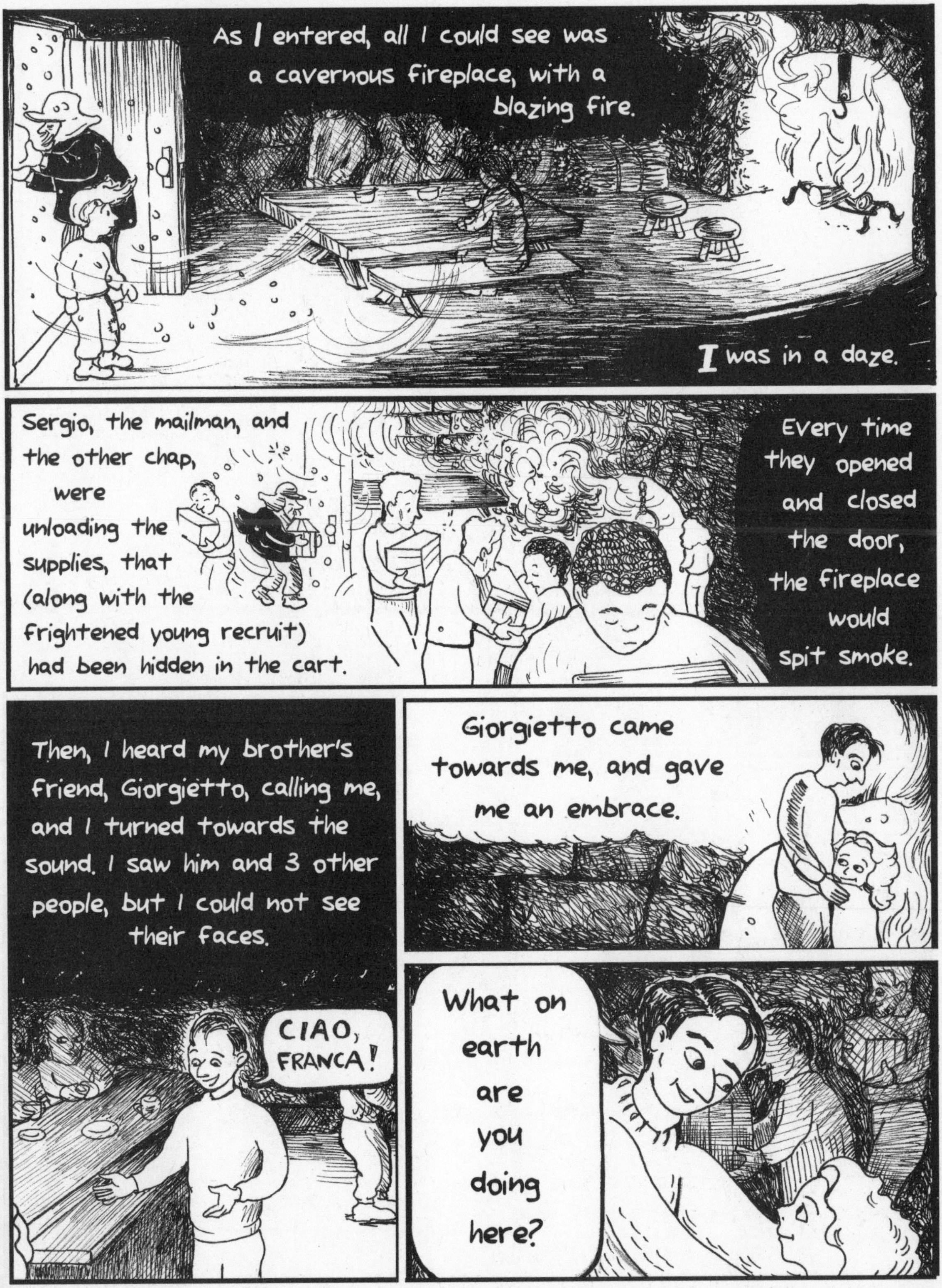
As I entered, all I could see was a cavernous fireplace, with a blazing fire.
I was in a daze.
Sergio, the mailman, and the other chap, were unloading the supplies, that (along with the frightened young recruit) had been hidden in the cart.
Every time they opened and closed the door, the fireplace would spit smoke.
Then, I heard my brother's friend, Giorgietto, calling me, and I turned towards the sound. I saw him and 3 other people, but I could not see their faces.
CIAO, FRANCA!
Giorgietto came towards me, and gave me an embrace.
What on earth are you doing here?

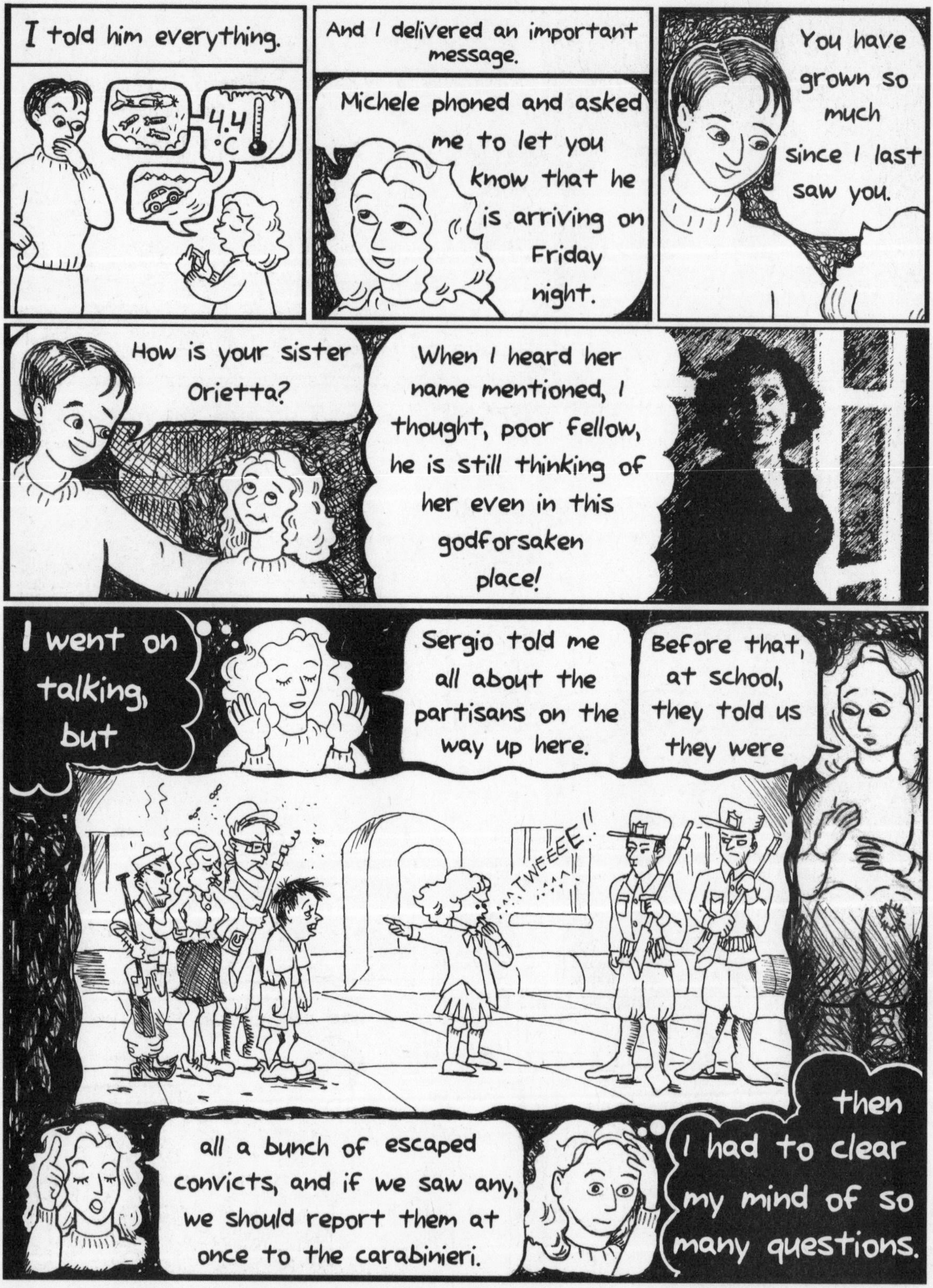
I told him everything.
4.4 °C
And I delivered an important message.
Michele phoned and asked me to let you know that he is arriving on Friday night.
You have grown so much since I last saw you.
How is your sister Orietta?
When I heard her name mentioned, I thought, poor fellow, he is still thinking of her even in this godforsaken place!
I went on talking, but
Sergio told me all about the partisans on the way up here.
Before that, at school, they told us they were
TWEEEEE!!
all a bunch of escaped convicts, and if we saw any, we should report them at once to the carabinieri.
then I had to clear my mind of so many questions.

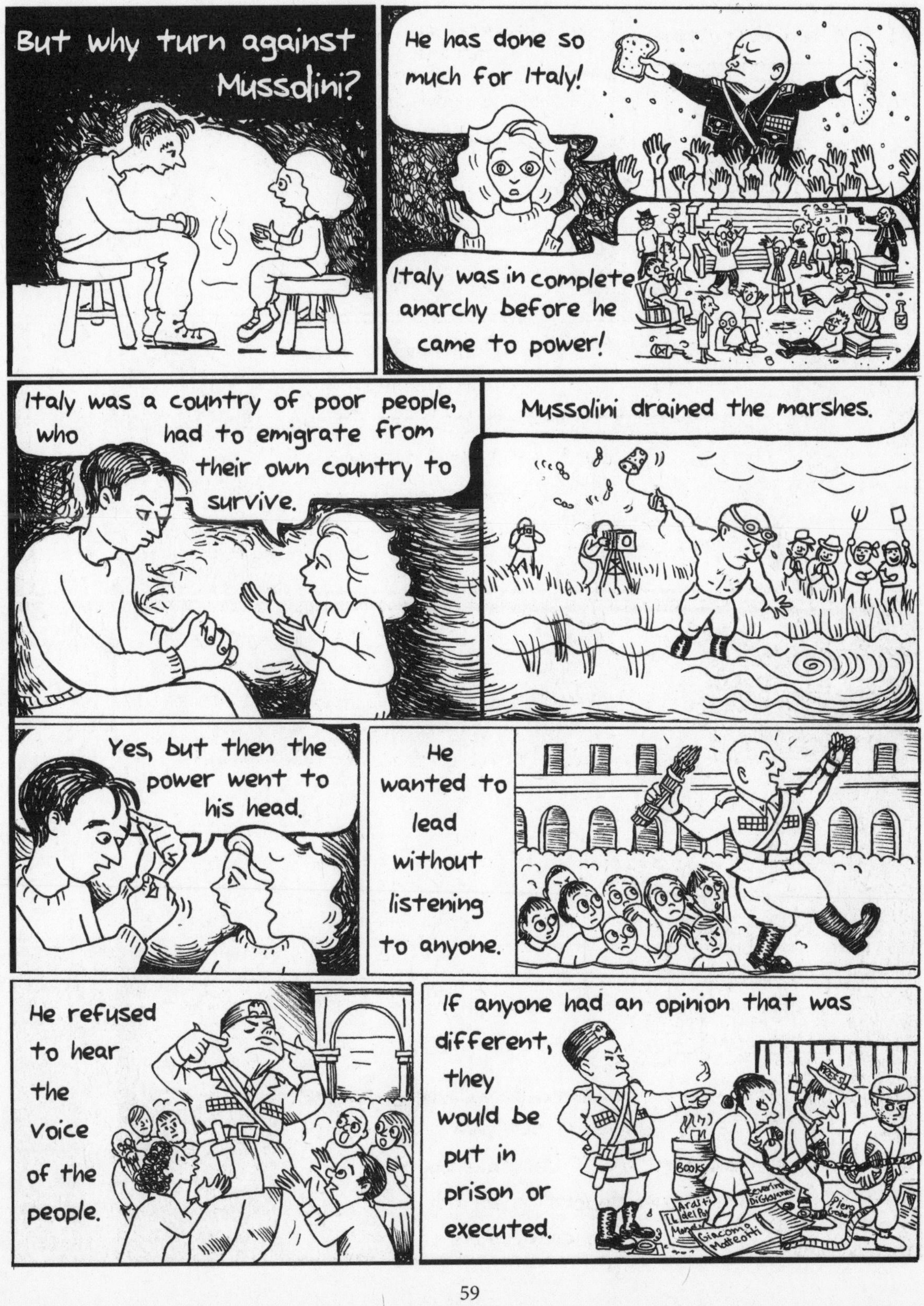
But why turn against Mussolini?
He has done so much for Italy!
Italy was in complete anarchy before he came to power!
Italy was a country of poor people, who had to emigrate from their own country to survive.
Mussolini drained the marshes.
Yes, but then the power went to his head.
He wanted to lead without listening to anyone.
He refused to hear the voice of the people.
If anyone had an opinion that was different, they would be put in prison or executed.
Books
Giacomo Matteotti

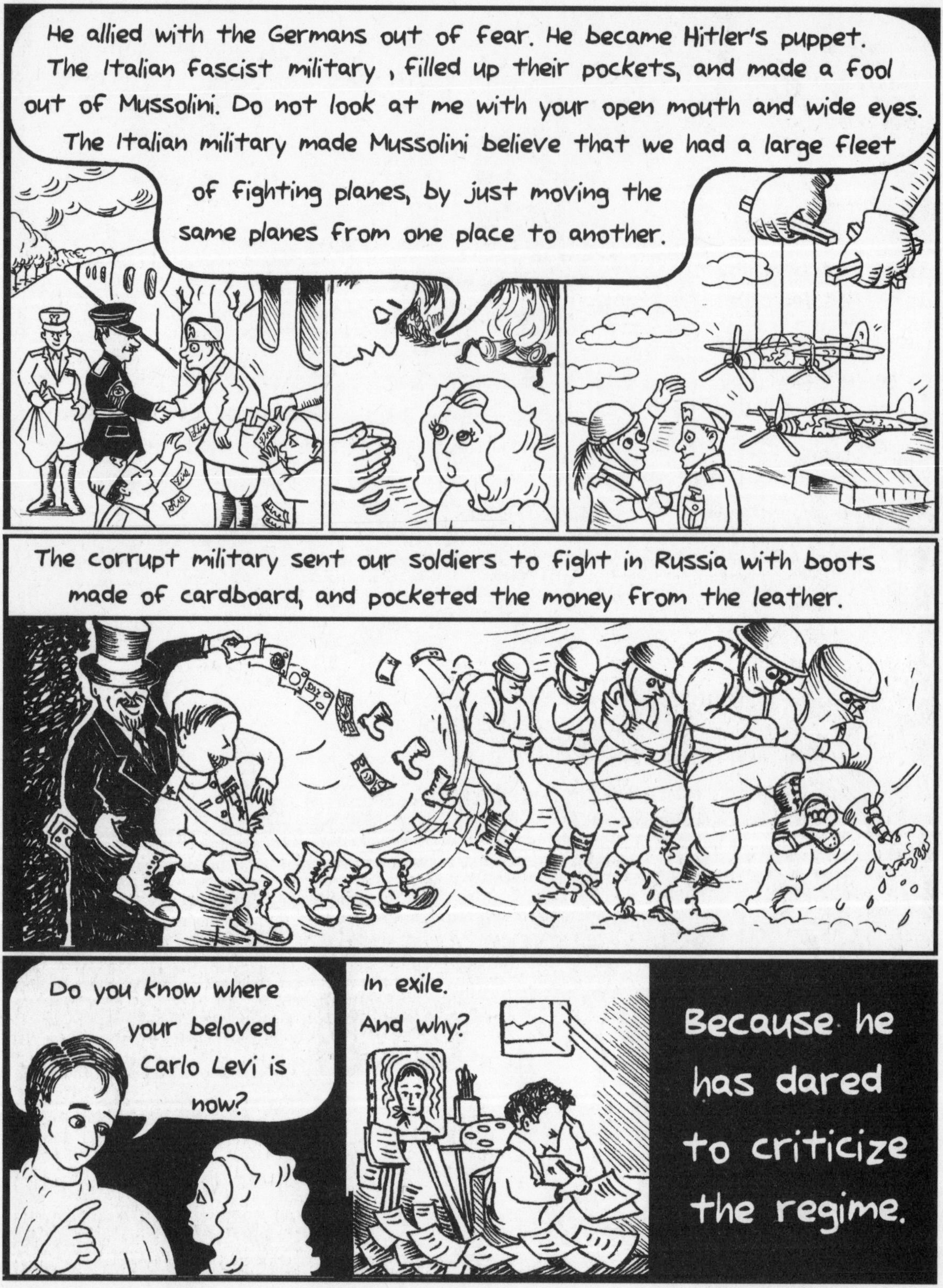
He allied with the Germans out of fear. He became Hitler's puppet. The Italian fascist military , filled up their pockets, and made a fool out of Mussolini. Do not look at me with your open mouth and wide eyes. The Italian military made Mussolini believe that we had a large fleet of fighting planes, by just moving the same planes from one place to another.
The corrupt military sent our soldiers to fight in Russia with boots made of cardboard, and pocketed the money from the leather.
Do you know where your beloved Carlo Levi is now?
In exile.
And why?
Because he has dared to criticize the regime.

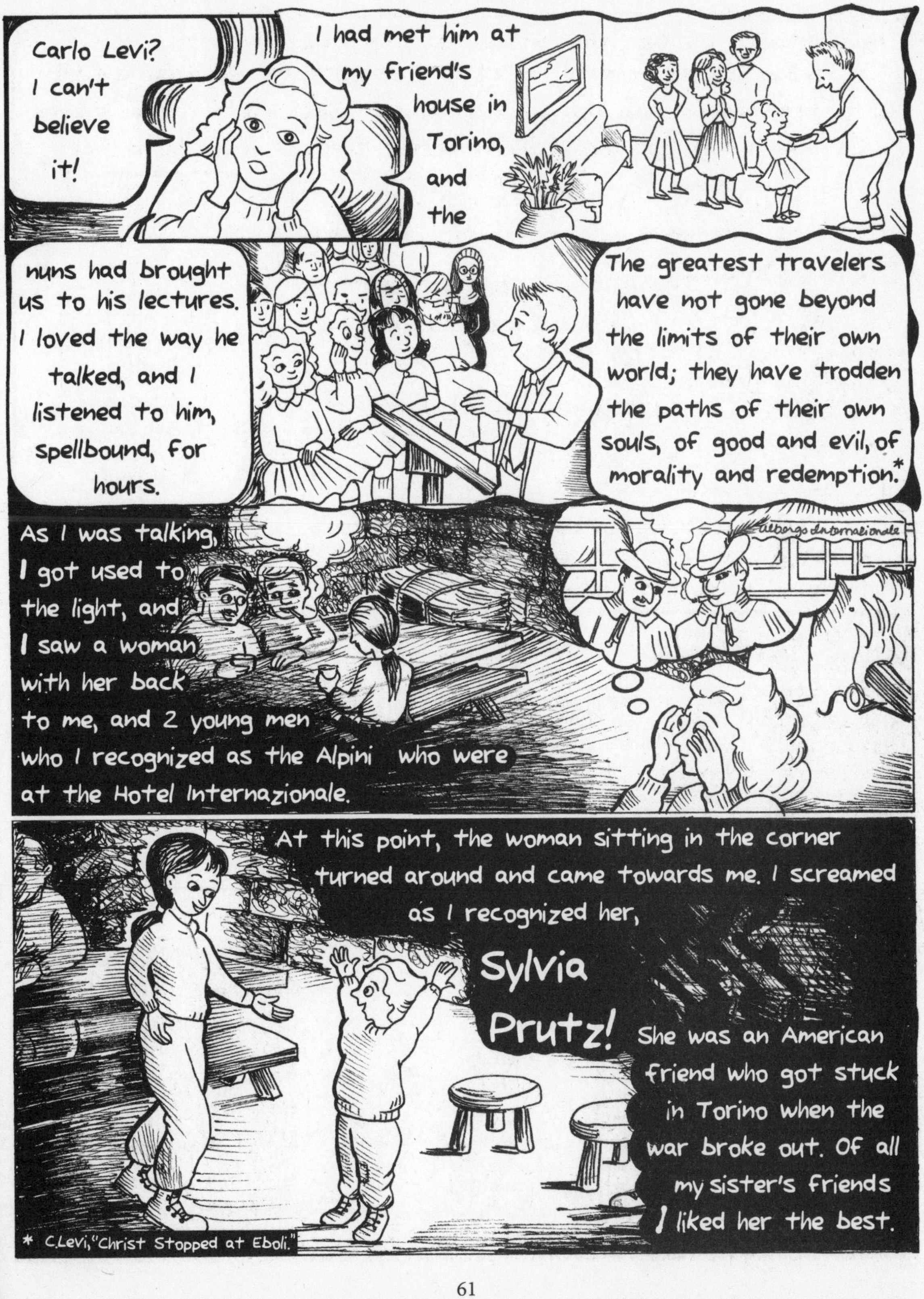
Carlo Levi? I can't believe it!
I had met him at my friend's house in Torino, and the
nuns had brought us to his lectures. I loved the way he talked, and I listened to him, spellbound, for hours.
The greatest travelers have not gone beyond the limits of their own world; they have trodden the paths of their own souls, of good and evil, of morality and redemption.*
As I was talking, I got used to the light, and I saw a woman with her back to me, and 2 young men who I recognized as the Alpini who were at the Hotel Internazionale.
Albergo Internazionale
At this point, the woman sitting in the corner turned around and came towards me. I screamed as I recognized her,
Sylvia Prutz!
She was an American friend who got stuck in Torino when the war broke out. Of all my sister's friends I liked her the best.
* C.Levi, "Christ Stopped at Eboli."

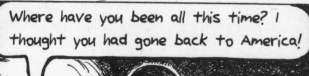

Where have you been all this time? I thought you had gone back to America!

Once the United States entered the war, I did go to Switzerland, but then I came back,

to help your brother and his friends.

When I had spoken to Giorgietto, I did not feel altogether persuaded. After all, many years of propaganda do not get erased in 10 minutes. But the fact that Sylvia was with them was another matter. I turned

and said to them all,

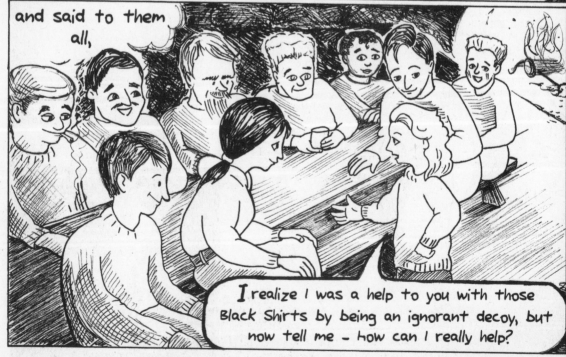

I realize I was a help to you with those Black Shirts by being an ignorant decoy, but now tell me - how can I really help?

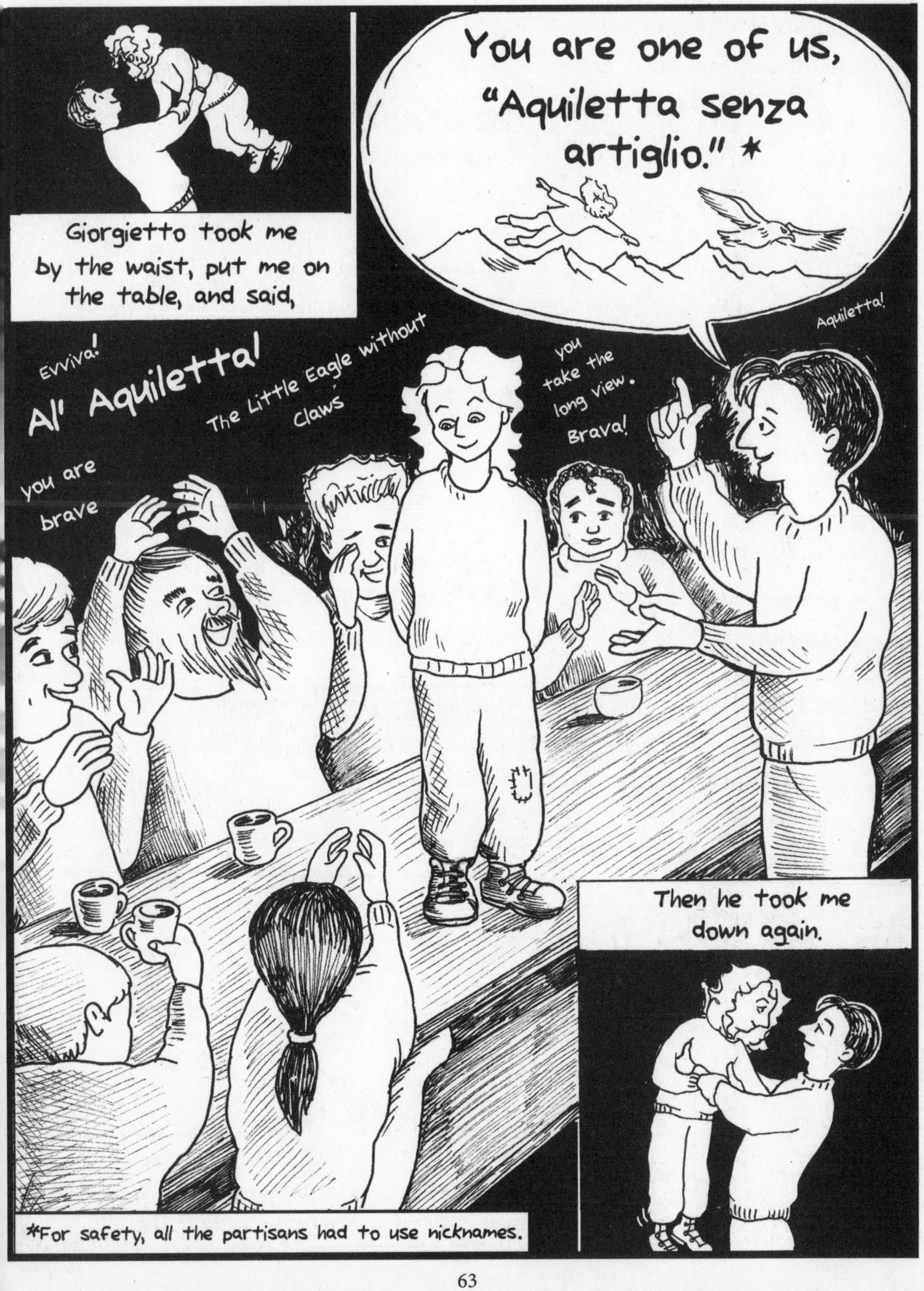
Giorgietto took me by the waist, put me on the table, and said,
You are one of us, "Aquiletta senza artiglio." *
Evviva!
Al' Aquiletta!
The Little Eagle without Claws
you take the long view. Brava!
Aquiletta!
you are brave
Then he took me down again.
*For safety, all the partisans had to use nicknames.

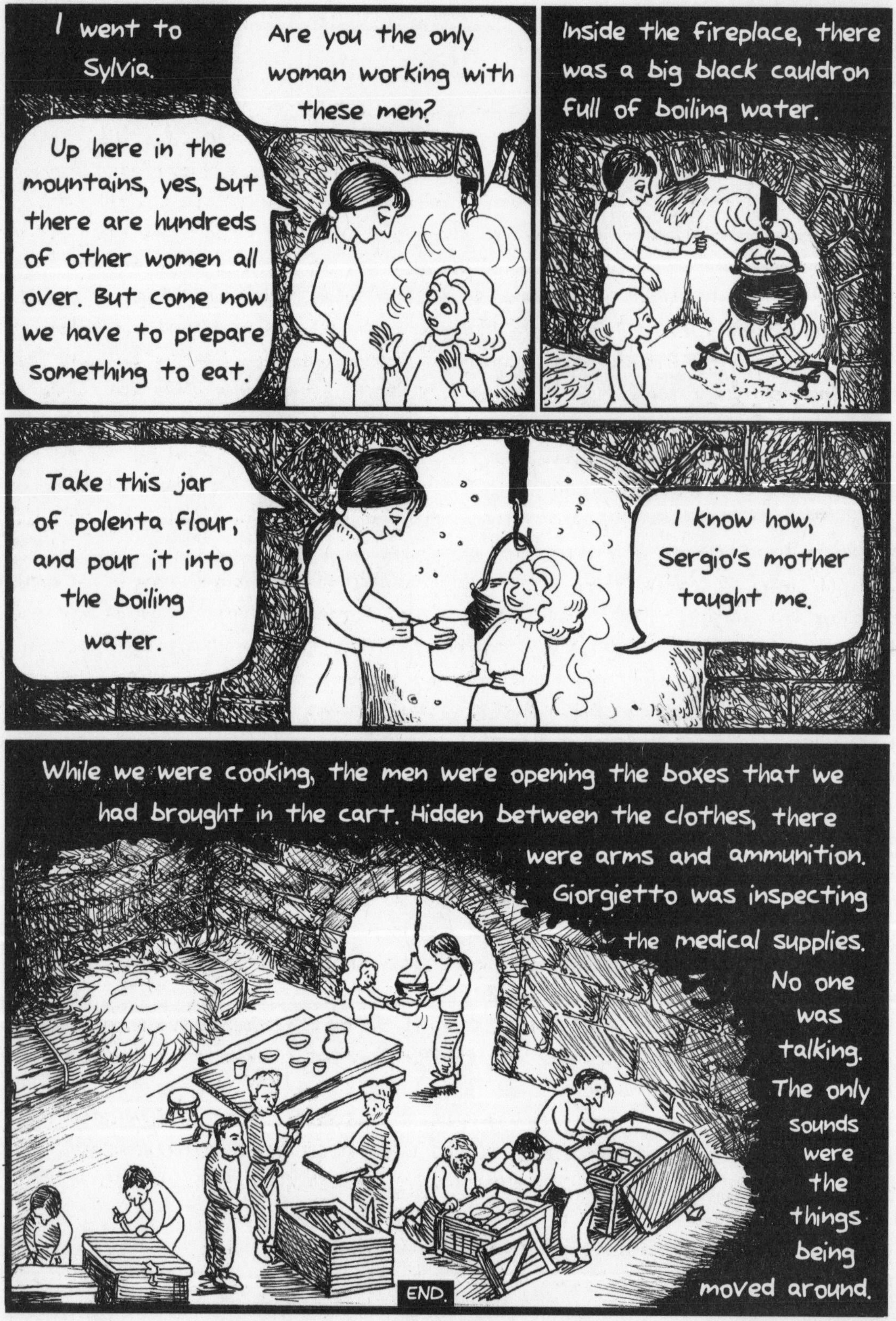
I went to Sylvia.
Are you the only woman working with these men?
Up here in the mountains, yes, but there are hundreds of other women all over. But come now we have to prepare something to eat.
Inside the fireplace, there was a big black cauldron full of boiling water.
Take this jar of polenta flour, and pour it into the boiling water.
I know how, Sergio's mother taught me.
While we were cooking, the men were opening the boxes that we had brought in the cart. Hidden between the clothes, there were arms and ammunition. Giorgietto was inspecting the medical supplies. No one was talking. The only sounds were the things being moved around.
END.

(74 years later, my mother, now an American citizen, wrote this letter to her daughters.)

January 2017

I watched Donald Trump's inauguration speech, then read it on the web. It was incredible how the theme of his speech was the same that Benito Mussolini used.

Mussolini believed that he was going to bring us Italians to the glories of the Roman Empire. That we had to get rid of all foreign influences. We had to build a strong Italy. Our genius, our hard work, must not be for the profit of other nations. We must stand united, and show the world that Italy would be again like our ancestors the Romans.

He made us Italians believe in him. I was 6 years old when I first heard Mussolini speak. All of us schoolchildren had to follow him. I remember my school friends and I, in uniform, marching 3 by 3 on the street, then listening to fascist indoctrination for an hour. Then, we each had to take a tablespoon of cod liver oil (I still remember the horrible taste) to strengthen our bodies. Then, we were given lunch, and let out to play freely in the courtyard, followed by an hour of exercise, then we were allowed to go home.

To me, Mussolini represented ITALY. By the time I was 10 years old, I believed that not to follow "Il Duce" was not only betraying him, but Italy. I would have died for that belief. But all that changed for me, when he allied with Hitler.

I looked today at Donald Trump - the way he talked, what he said. Echoing in my head was what I saw and heard in 1939, 78 years ago. I cannot forget it. Donald Trump is not evil. The only thing is that we must learn from the past. But remember that now it is the future. Circumstances are not the same. Even if the power and glory of 1960's America could return, it would not suit this generation of Americans. Our children and grandchildren do not understand or approve of our past. They ask, "How could you have lived with a telephone where every call had to go through an operator? How was it possible not to have a computer? Credit cards?" Scientific progress has made each generation different, but social life is also different.

On my first visit to the USA, in 1956, I visited South Carolina. I was horrified to see notices that forbade "blacks" to drink from the same water fountains I did.

Two generations later, we had an African American President.

Is it possible that a man of Donald Trump's upbringing can become so blinded by his ego, that he believes what he is preaching?

Darwin proved the evolution of animals. Could it be that our human evolution goes unseen because it is inside our brains? But that once it has changed, it can never return?

My message to Donald Trump:

IN A HUMBLE WAY, AND AS AN OLD WOMAN WHO HAS BEEN GIFTED WITH A GOOD MEMORY, I WOULD LIKE TO ASK YOU NOT TO LET YOUR POSITION GO TO YOUR HEAD. ALREADY, AFTER YOUR SPEECH, IT SEEMED THAT YOU AND YOUR FAMILY WALKED AS IF YOU WERE CROWNED KING OF THE USA?

(I wonder how many others were struck by that view.)

PLEASE! FOR AMERICA'S SAKE! FOR THE WORLD AND HUMANITY - GET OFF THAT IMAGINARY THRONE.

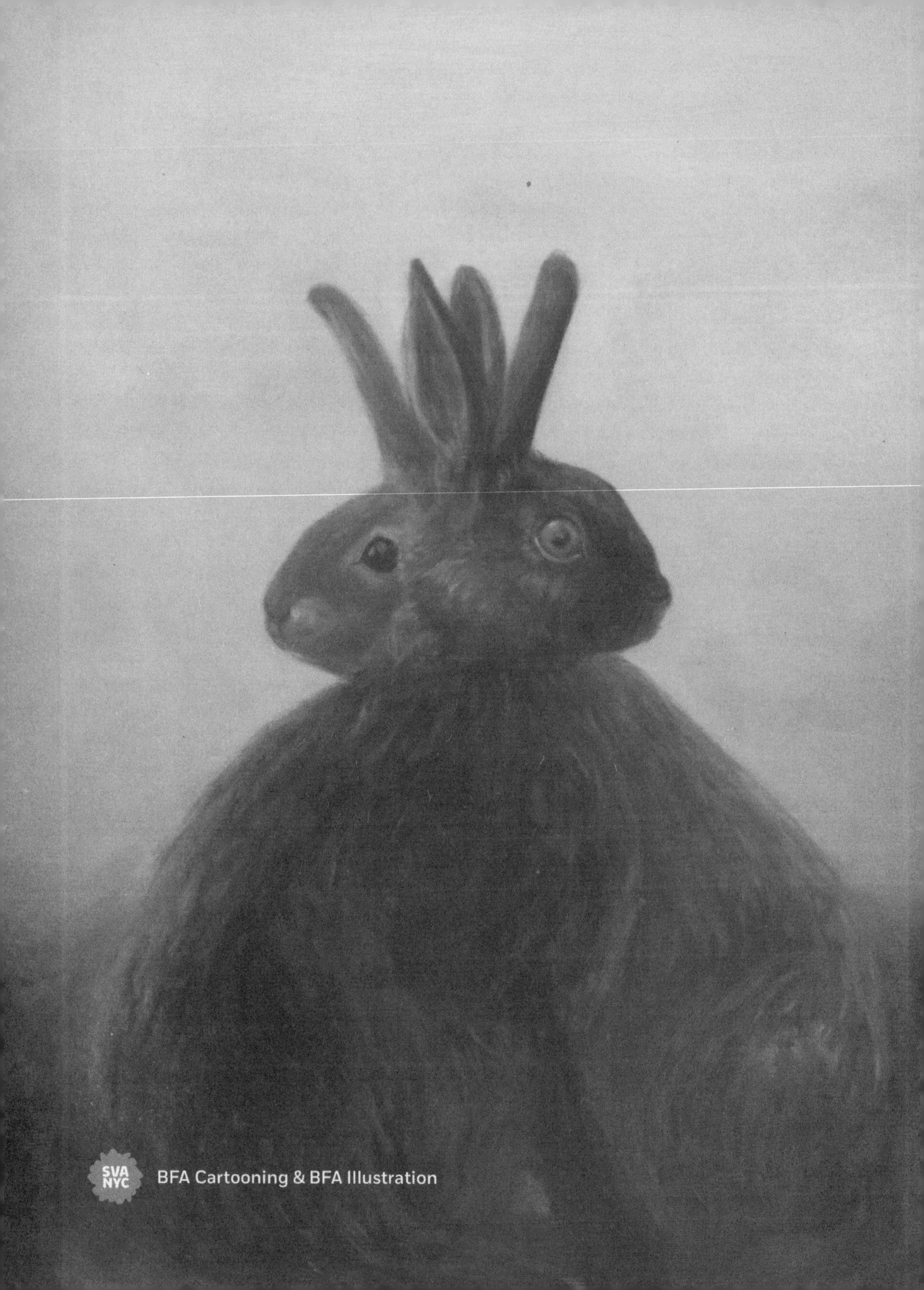
SVA NYC
BFA Cartooning & BFA Illustration

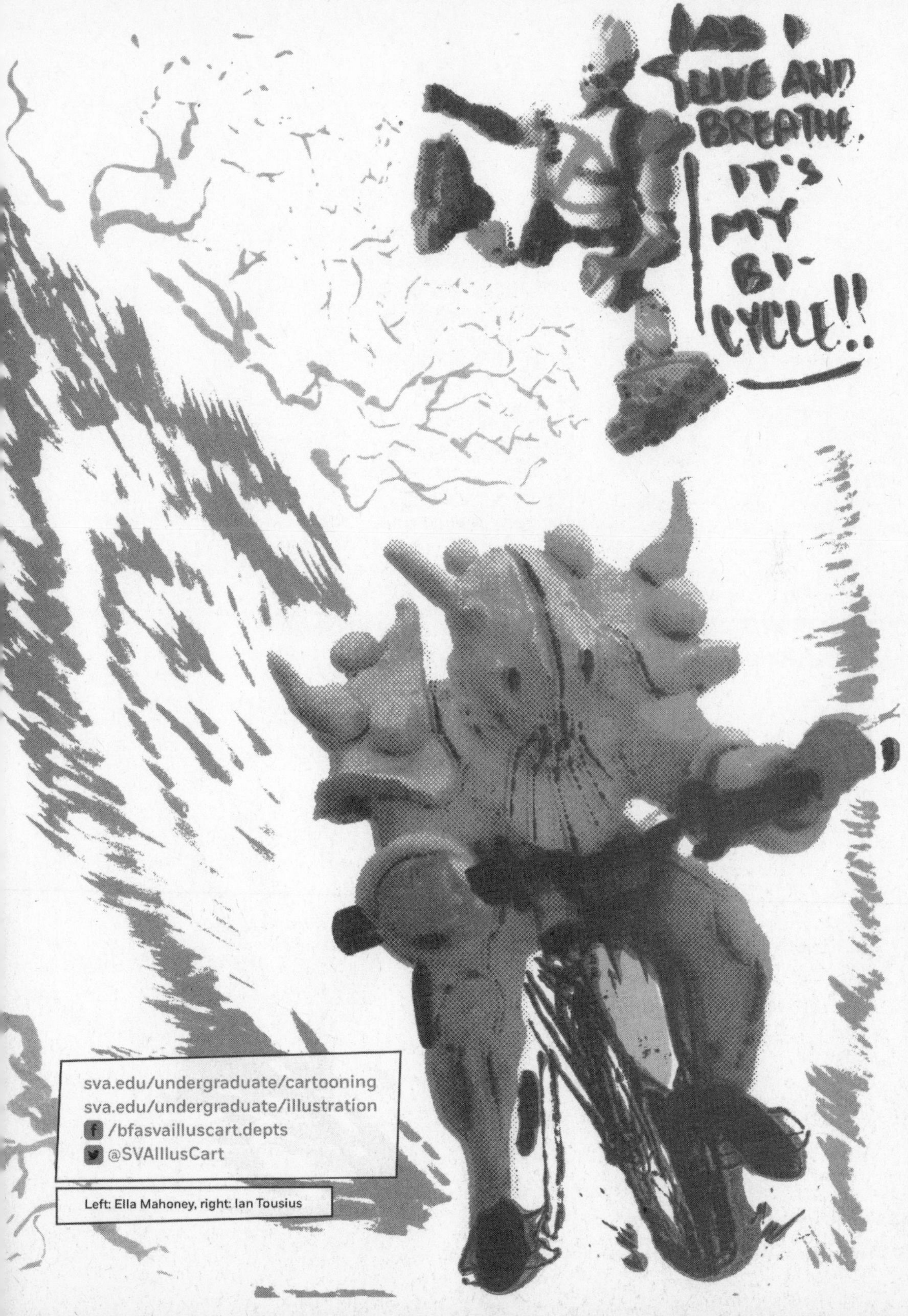
AS I
LIVE AND
BREATHE
IT'S
MY
BI-
CYCLE!!

Left: Ella Mahoney, right: Ian Tousius

COMICS AS A POLITICAL WEAPON

YOU DON'T HAVE TO FUCK PEOPLE OVER

TO SURVIVE

This year I will be teaching a class in what I have done for most of my life, writing and drawing political comics. If that interests you, contact the School Of Visual Arts Dept. of Continuing Education: 212.592.2050, sva.edu/ce

Thanks,
Seth Tobocman

http://www.sva.edu/continuing-education/cartooning/comics-as-a-political-weapon-17-cs-cic-2237-a

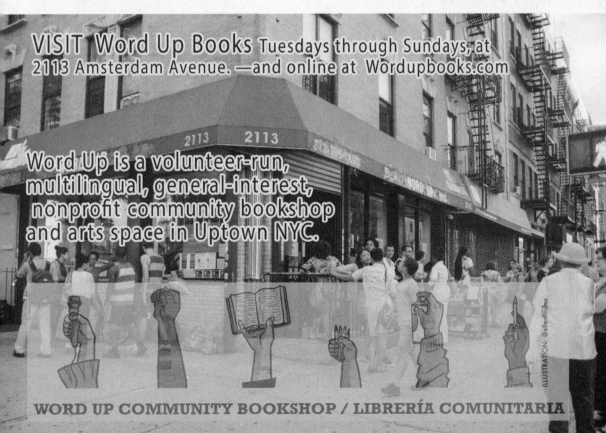

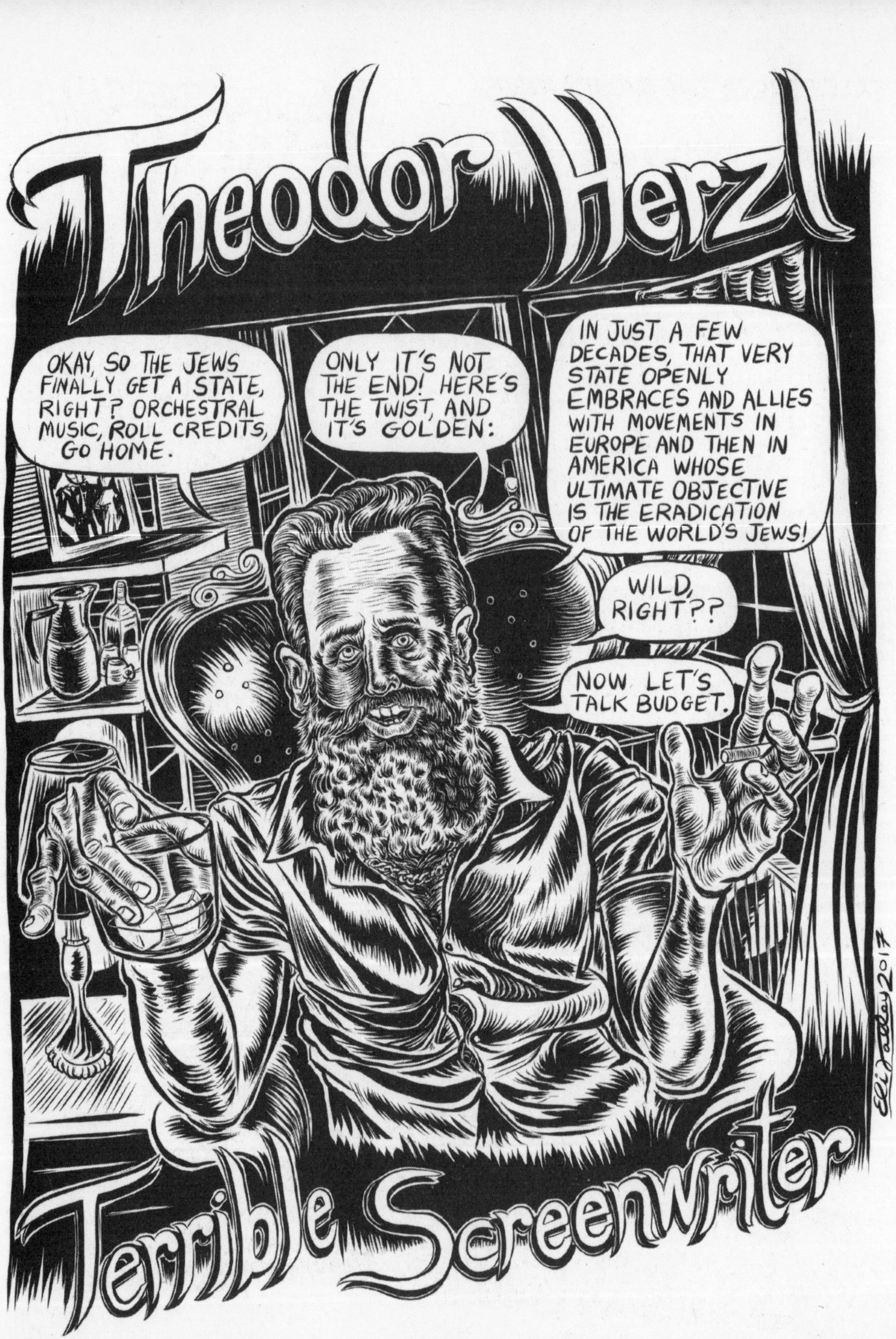
Theodor Herzl
OKAY, SO THE JEWS FINALLY GET A STATE, RIGHT? ORCHESTRAL MUSIC, ROLL CREDITS, GO HOME.
ONLY IT'S NOT THE END! HERE'S THE TWIST, AND IT'S GOLDEN:
IN JUST A FEW DECADES, THAT VERY STATE OPENLY EMBRACES AND ALLIES WITH MOVEMENTS IN EUROPE AND THEN IN AMERICA WHOSE ULTIMATE OBJECTIVE IS THE ERADICATION OF THE WORLD'S JEWS!
WILD, RIGHT??
NOW LET'S TALK BUDGET.
Terrible Screenwriter

TALES FROM THE CAMPAIGN!

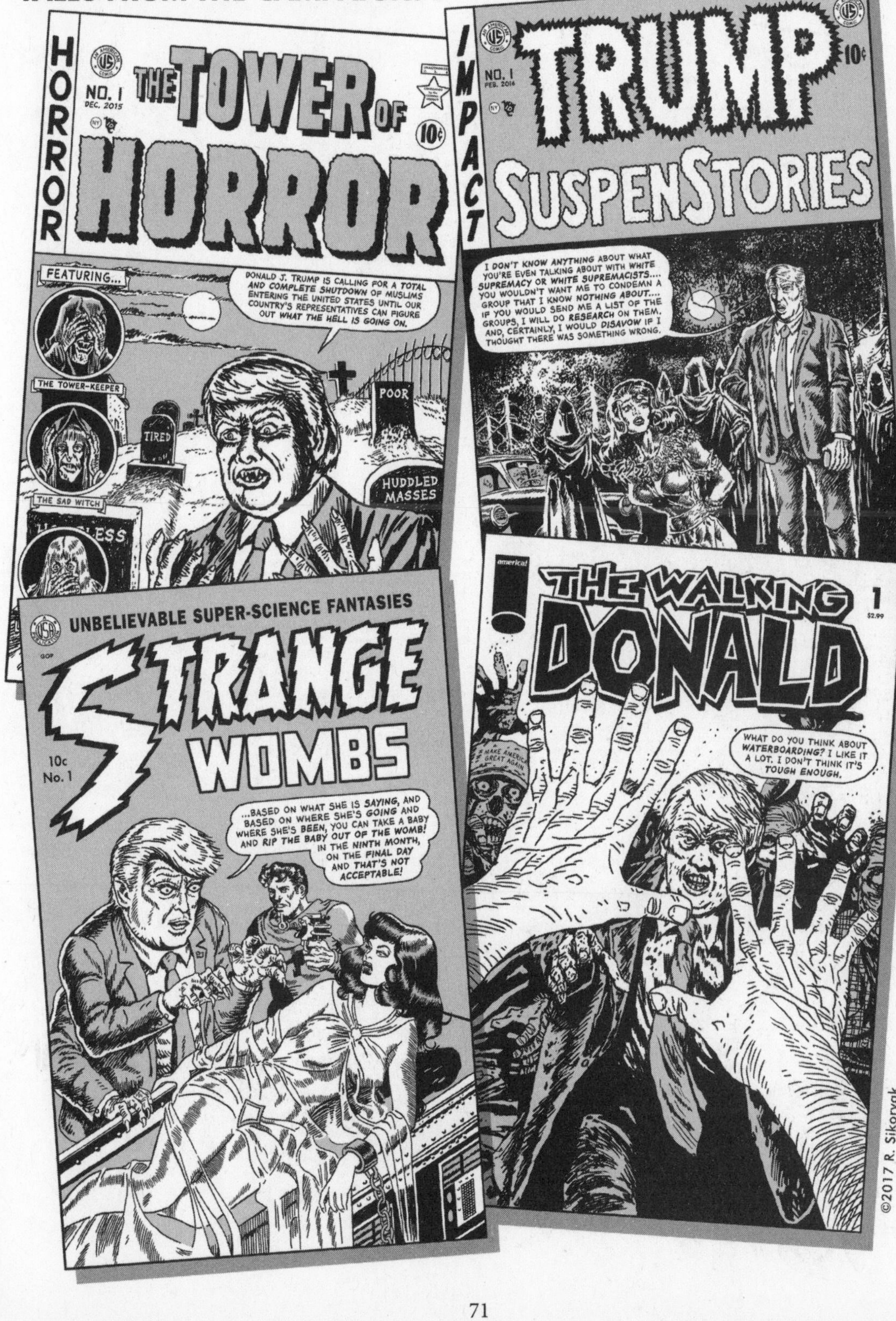

HORROR
NO. 1
DEC. 2015
THE TOWER OF HORROR
10¢
FEATURING...
THE TOWER-KEEPER
THE SAD WITCH
DONALD J. TRUMP IS CALLING FOR A TOTAL AND COMPLETE SHUTDOWN OF MUSLIMS ENTERING THE UNITED STATES UNTIL OUR COUNTRY'S REPRESENTATIVES CAN FIGURE OUT WHAT THE HELL IS GOING ON.
TIRED
POOR
HUDDLED MASSES
IMPACT
NO. 1
FEB. 2016
TRUMP
10¢
SUSPENSTORIES
I DON'T KNOW ANYTHING ABOUT WHAT YOU'RE EVEN TALKING ABOUT WITH WHITE SUPREMACY OR WHITE SUPREMACISTS.... YOU WOULDN'T WANT ME TO CONDEMN A GROUP THAT I KNOW NOTHING ABOUT.... IF YOU WOULD SEND ME A LIST OF THE GROUPS, I WILL DO RESEARCH ON THEM. AND, CERTAINLY, I WOULD DISAVOW IF I THOUGHT THERE WAS SOMETHING WRONG.
UNBELIEVABLE SUPER-SCIENCE FANTASIES
GOP
STRANGE WOMBS
10c
No. 1
...BASED ON WHAT SHE IS SAYING, AND BASED ON WHERE SHE'S GOING AND WHERE SHE'S BEEN, YOU CAN TAKE A BABY AND RIP THE BABY OUT OF THE WOMB! IN THE NINTH MONTH, ON THE FINAL DAY AND THAT'S NOT ACCEPTABLE!
america!
THE WALKING DONALD
1
$2.99
WHAT DO YOU THINK ABOUT WATERBOARDING? I LIKE IT A LOT. I DON'T THINK IT'S TOUGH ENOUGH.

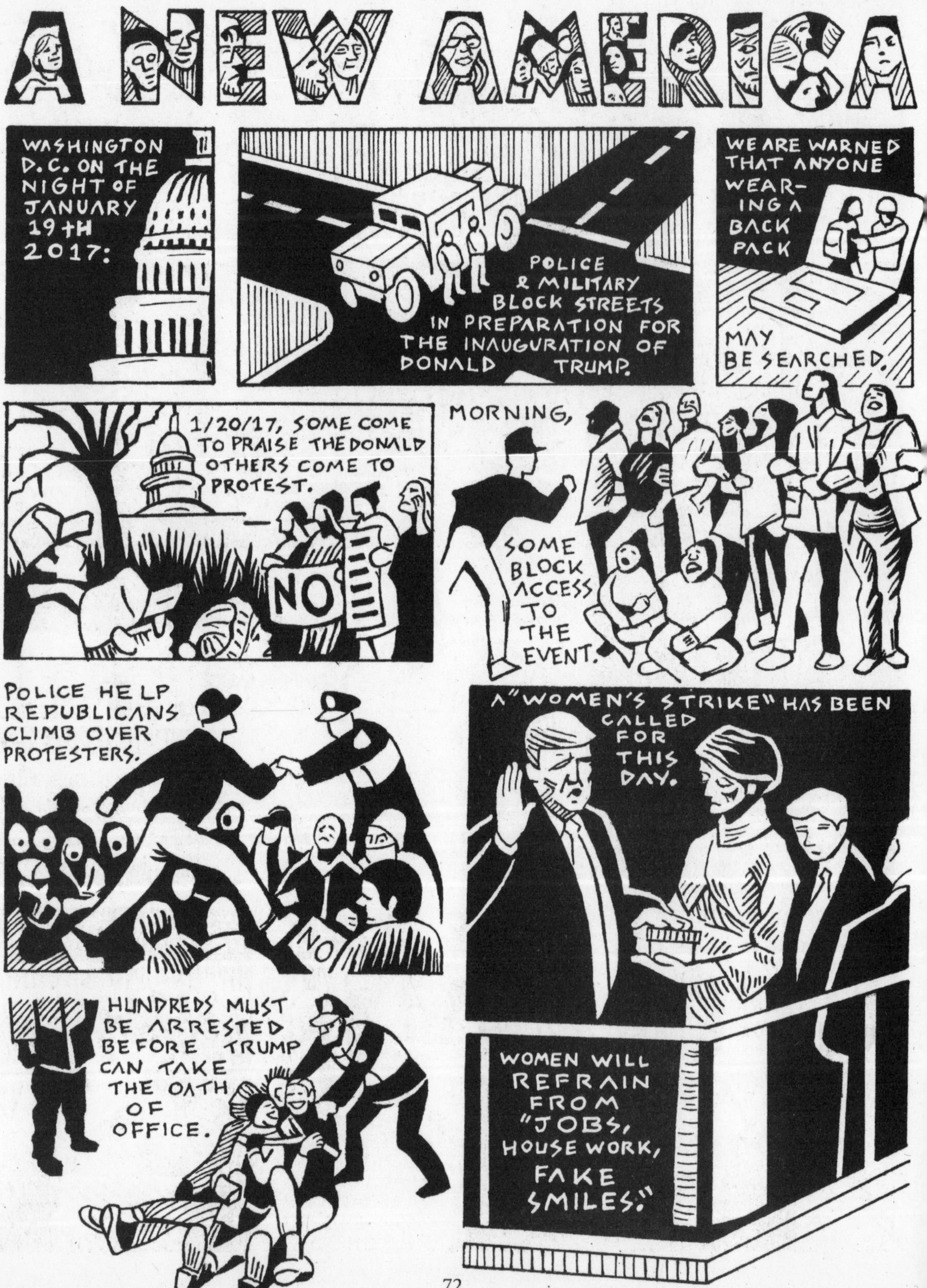
A NEW AMERICA
WASHINGTON D.C. ON THE NIGHT OF JANUARY 19TH 2017:
POLICE & MILITARY BLOCK STREETS IN PREPARATION FOR THE INAUGURATION OF DONALD TRUMP.
WE ARE WARNED THAT ANYONE WEAR-ING A BACK PACK
MAY BE SEARCHED.
1/20/17, SOME COME TO PRAISE THE DONALD OTHERS COME TO PROTEST.
NO
MORNING,
SOME BLOCK ACCESS TO THE EVENT.
POLICE HELP REPUBLICANS CLIMB OVER PROTESTERS.
NO
A "WOMEN'S STRIKE" HAS BEEN CALLED FOR THIS DAY.
HUNDREDS MUST BE ARRESTED BEFORE TRUMP CAN TAKE THE OATH OF OFFICE.
WOMEN WILL REFRAIN FROM "JOBS, HOUSE WORK, FAKE SMILES."

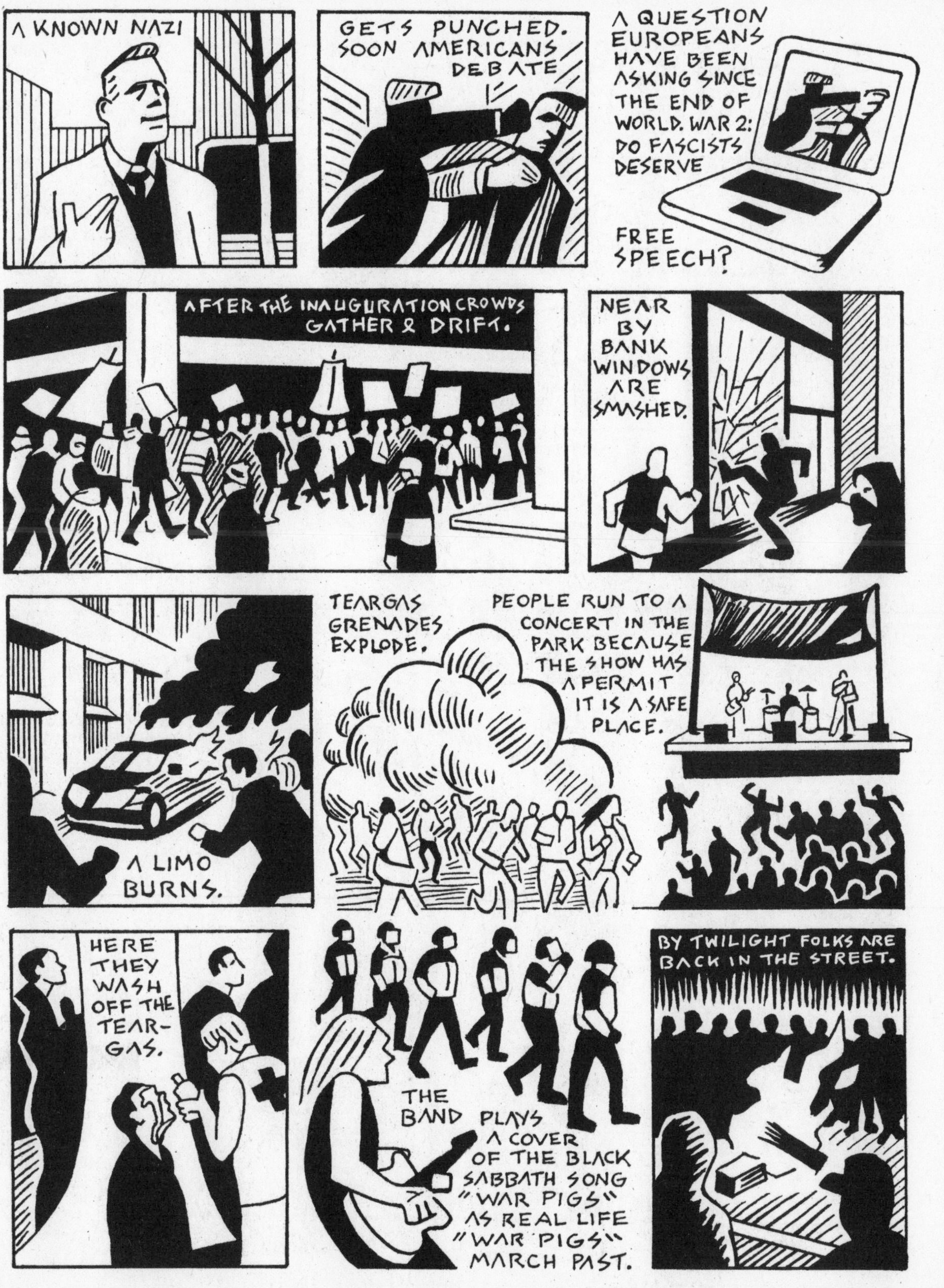
A KNOWN NAZI
GETS PUNCHED. SOON AMERICANS DEBATE
A QUESTION EUROPEANS HAVE BEEN ASKING SINCE THE END OF WORLD WAR 2: DO FASCISTS DESERVE
FREE SPEECH?
AFTER THE INAUGURATION CROWDS GATHER & DRIFT.
NEAR BY BANK WINDOWS ARE SMASHED.
A LIMO BURNS.
TEARGAS GRENADES EXPLODE.
PEOPLE RUN TO A CONCERT IN THE PARK BECAUSE THE SHOW HAS A PERMIT IT IS A SAFE PLACE.
HERE THEY WASH OFF THE TEAR-GAS.
THE BAND PLAYS A COVER OF THE BLACK SABBATH SONG "WAR PIGS" AS REAL LIFE "WAR PIGS" MARCH PAST.
BY TWILIGHT FOLKS ARE BACK IN THE STREET.

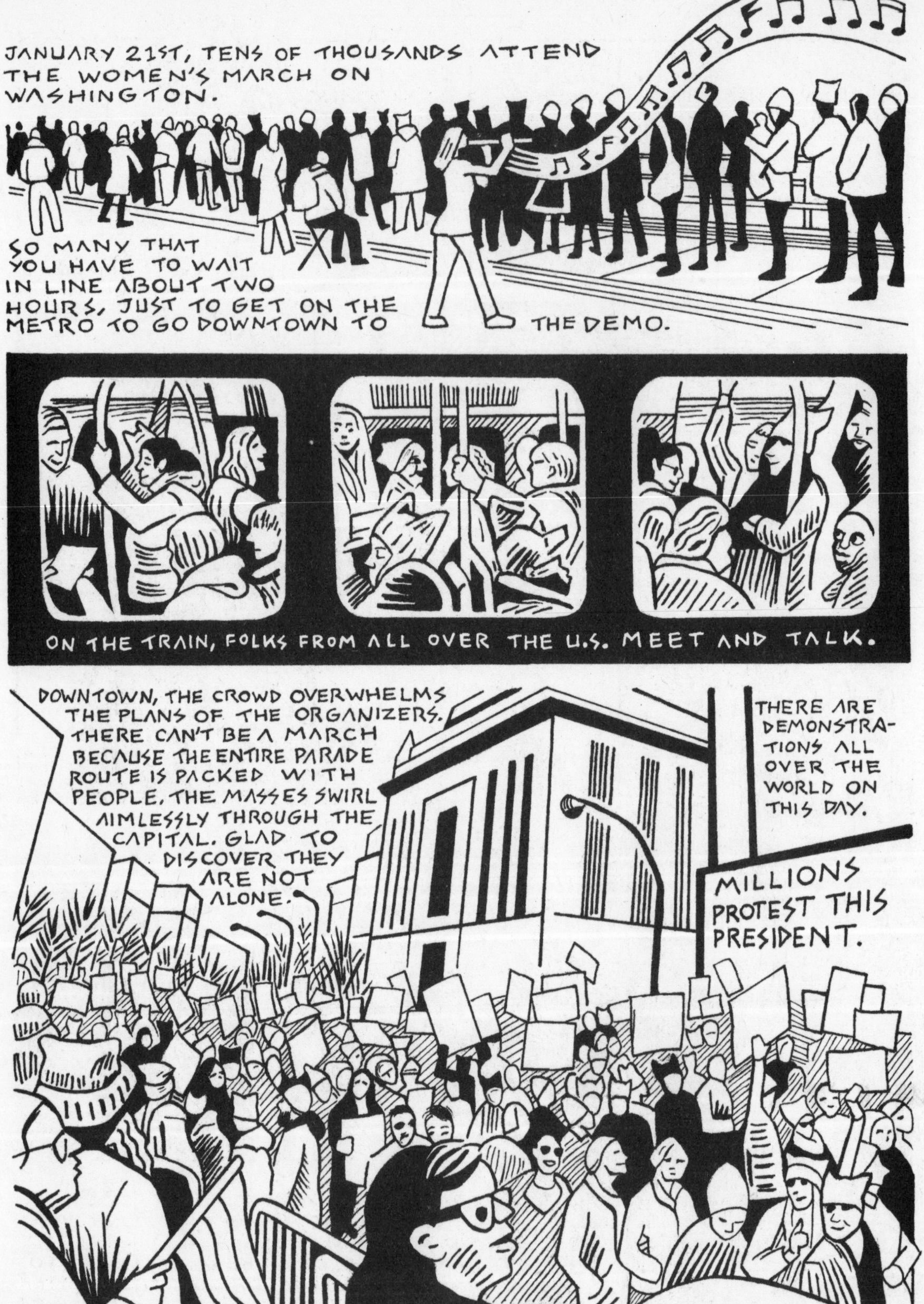
JANUARY 21ST, TENS OF THOUSANDS ATTEND THE WOMEN'S MARCH ON WASHINGTON.
SO MANY THAT YOU HAVE TO WAIT IN LINE ABOUT TWO HOURS, JUST TO GET ON THE METRO TO GO DOWNTOWN TO
THE DEMO.
ON THE TRAIN, FOLKS FROM ALL OVER THE U.S. MEET AND TALK.
DOWNTOWN, THE CROWD OVERWHELMS THE PLANS OF THE ORGANIZERS. THERE CAN'T BE A MARCH BECAUSE THE ENTIRE PARADE ROUTE IS PACKED WITH PEOPLE. THE MASSES SWIRL AIMLESSLY THROUGH THE CAPITAL. GLAD TO DISCOVER THEY ARE NOT ALONE.
THERE ARE DEMONSTRATIONS ALL OVER THE WORLD ON THIS DAY.
MILLIONS PROTEST THIS PRESIDENT.

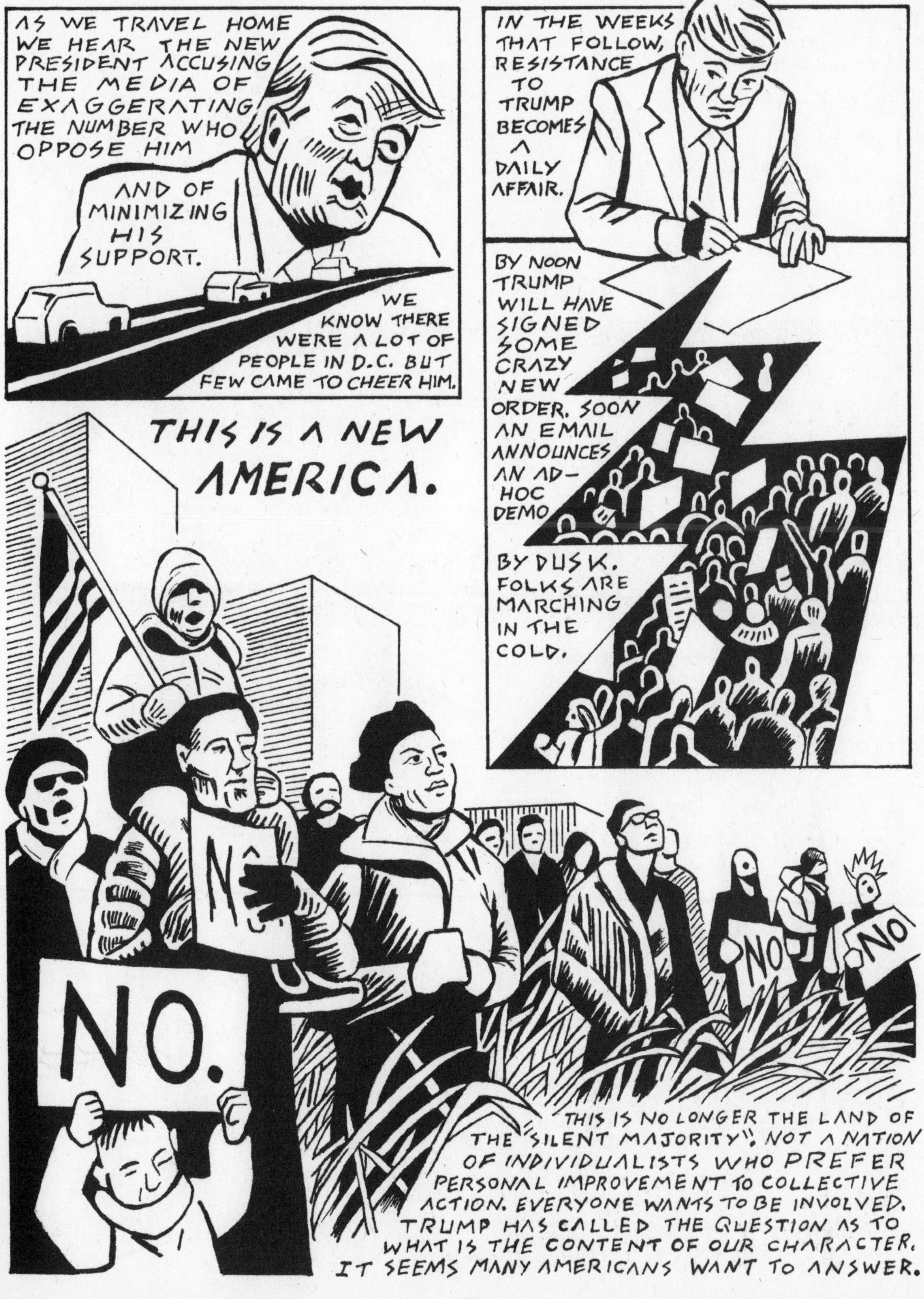
AS WE TRAVEL HOME WE HEAR THE NEW PRESIDENT ACCUSING THE MEDIA OF EXAGGERATING THE NUMBER WHO OPPOSE HIM
AND OF MINIMIZING HIS SUPPORT.
WE KNOW THERE WERE A LOT OF PEOPLE IN D.C. BUT FEW CAME TO CHEER HIM.
IN THE WEEKS THAT FOLLOW, RESISTANCE TO TRUMP BECOMES A DAILY AFFAIR.
BY NOON TRUMP WILL HAVE SIGNED SOME CRAZY NEW ORDER. SOON AN EMAIL ANNOUNCES AN AD-HOC DEMO
BY DUSK. FOLKS ARE MARCHING IN THE COLD.
THIS IS A NEW AMERICA.
NO
NO.
NO
NO
THIS IS NO LONGER THE LAND OF THE "SILENT MAJORITY". NOT A NATION OF INDIVIDUALISTS WHO PREFER PERSONAL IMPROVEMENT TO COLLECTIVE ACTION. EVERYONE WANTS TO BE INVOLVED. TRUMP HAS CALLED THE QUESTION AS TO WHAT IS THE CONTENT OF OUR CHARACTER. IT SEEMS MANY AMERICANS WANT TO ANSWER.

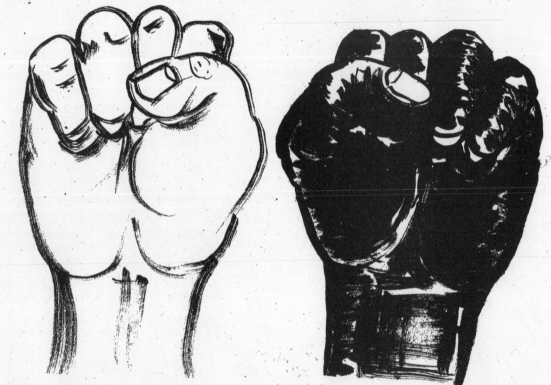

NORMALIZE THIS

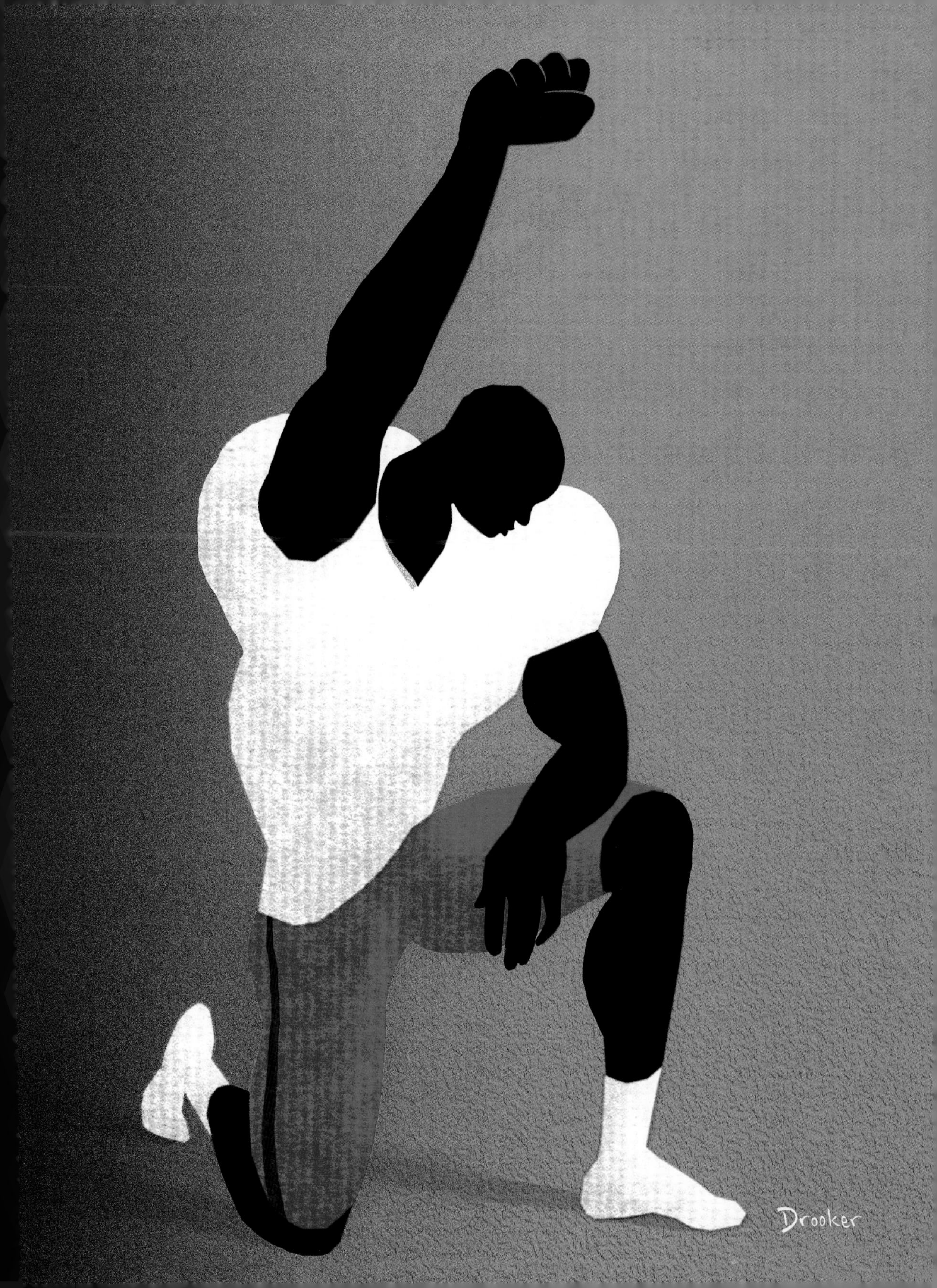
Drooker

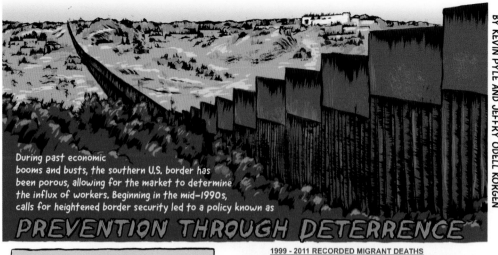

BY KEVIN PYLE AND JEFFRY ODELL KORGEN

During past economic booms and busts, the southern U.S. border has been porous, allowing for the market to determine the influx of workers. Beginning in the mid-1990s, calls for heightened border security led to a policy known as

PREVENTION THROUGH DETERRENCE

The militarization of the border—the wall and more agents and surveillance technology at urban border crossings led to fewer successful crossings in places like San Diego and El Paso. The policy intensified after 9-11.

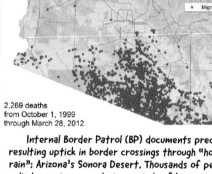

1999 - 2011 RECORDED MIGRANT DEATHS

* Migrant Deaths

2,269 deaths from October 1, 1999 through March 28, 2012.

Internal Border Patrol (BP) documents predicted the resulting uptick in border crossings through "hostile terrain": Arizona's Sonora Desert. Thousands of people have died crossing, even during periods of low migration. The desert itself has become a weapon of enforcement.

240 bodies were found in 2015 but the figure reached twice that in the mid-2000's. These figures don't include those never found.

In addition to the dangerous conditions, migrants are vulnerable to kidnapping or forced smuggling at the hand of the drug cartels.

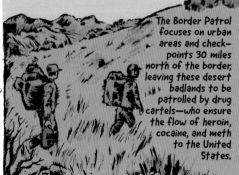

The Border Patrol focuses on urban areas and checkpoints 30 miles north of the border, leaving these desert badlands to be patrolled by drug cartels—who ensure the flow of heroin, cocaine, and meth to the United States.

After the desert crossing, migrants then pass through American ranches on their way to pick up points. Ranchers like Jim and Sue respect the migrants, but want the drug traffickers gone!

You want to know who's guarding the border—it's him!

Statistics give us part of the story—but who are these migrants who cross at their own peril?

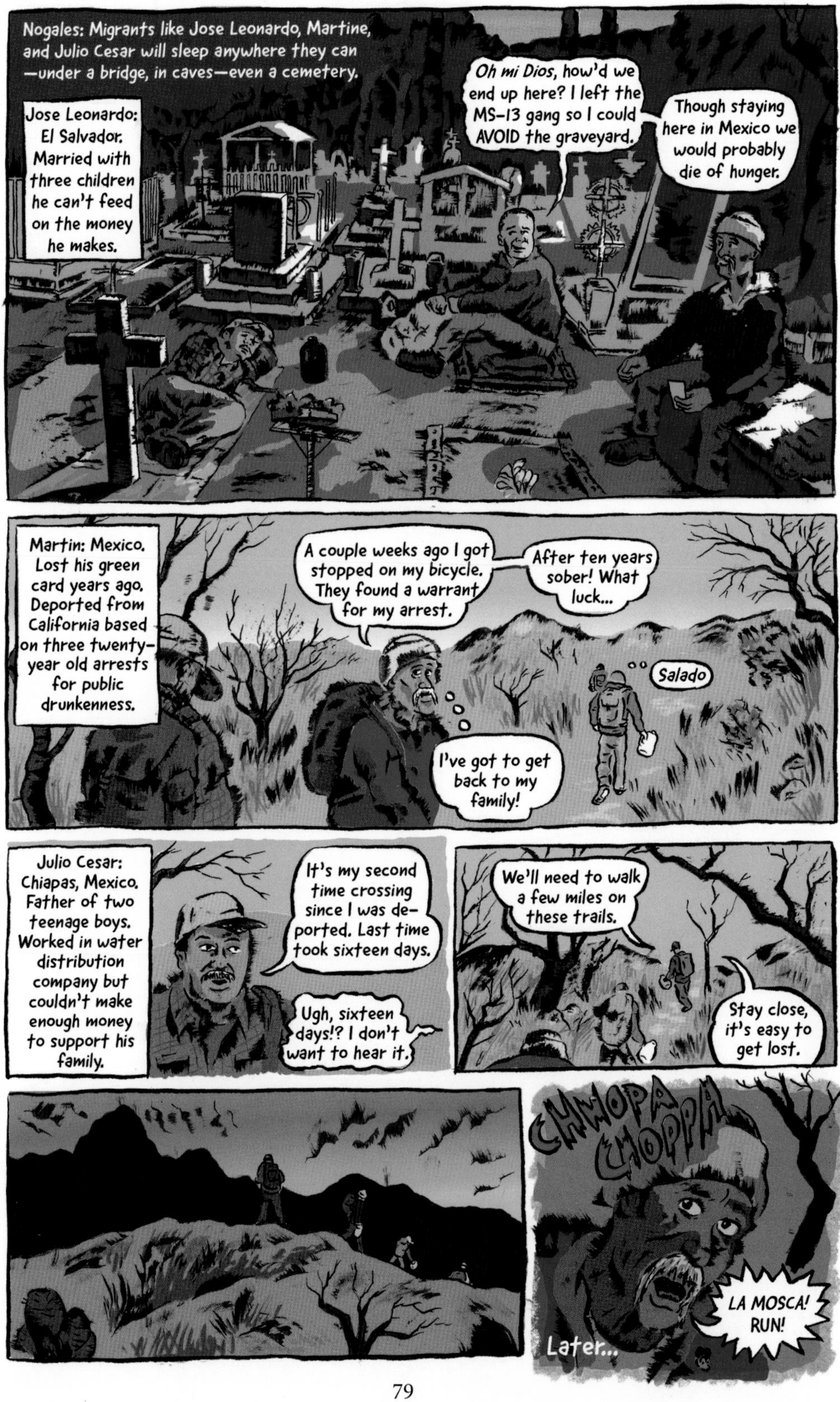

Nogales: Migrants like Jose Leonardo, Martine, and Julio Cesar will sleep anywhere they can —under a bridge, in caves—even a cemetery.
Jose Leonardo: El Salvador. Married with three children he can't feed on the money he makes.
Oh mi Dios, how'd we end up here? I left the MS-13 gang so I could AVOID the graveyard.
Though staying here in Mexico we would probably die of hunger.
Martin: Mexico. Lost his green card years ago. Deported from California based on three twenty-year old arrests for public drunkenness.
A couple weeks ago I got stopped on my bicycle. They found a warrant for my arrest.
After ten years sober! What luck...
Salado
I've got to get back to my family!
Julio Cesar: Chiapas, Mexico. Father of two teenage boys. Worked in water distribution company but couldn't make enough money to support his family.
It's my second time crossing since I was deported. Last time took sixteen days.
Ugh, sixteen days!? I don't want to hear it.
We'll need to walk a few miles on these trails.
Stay close, it's easy to get lost.
CHWOPA CHOPPA
LA MOSCA! RUN!
Later...

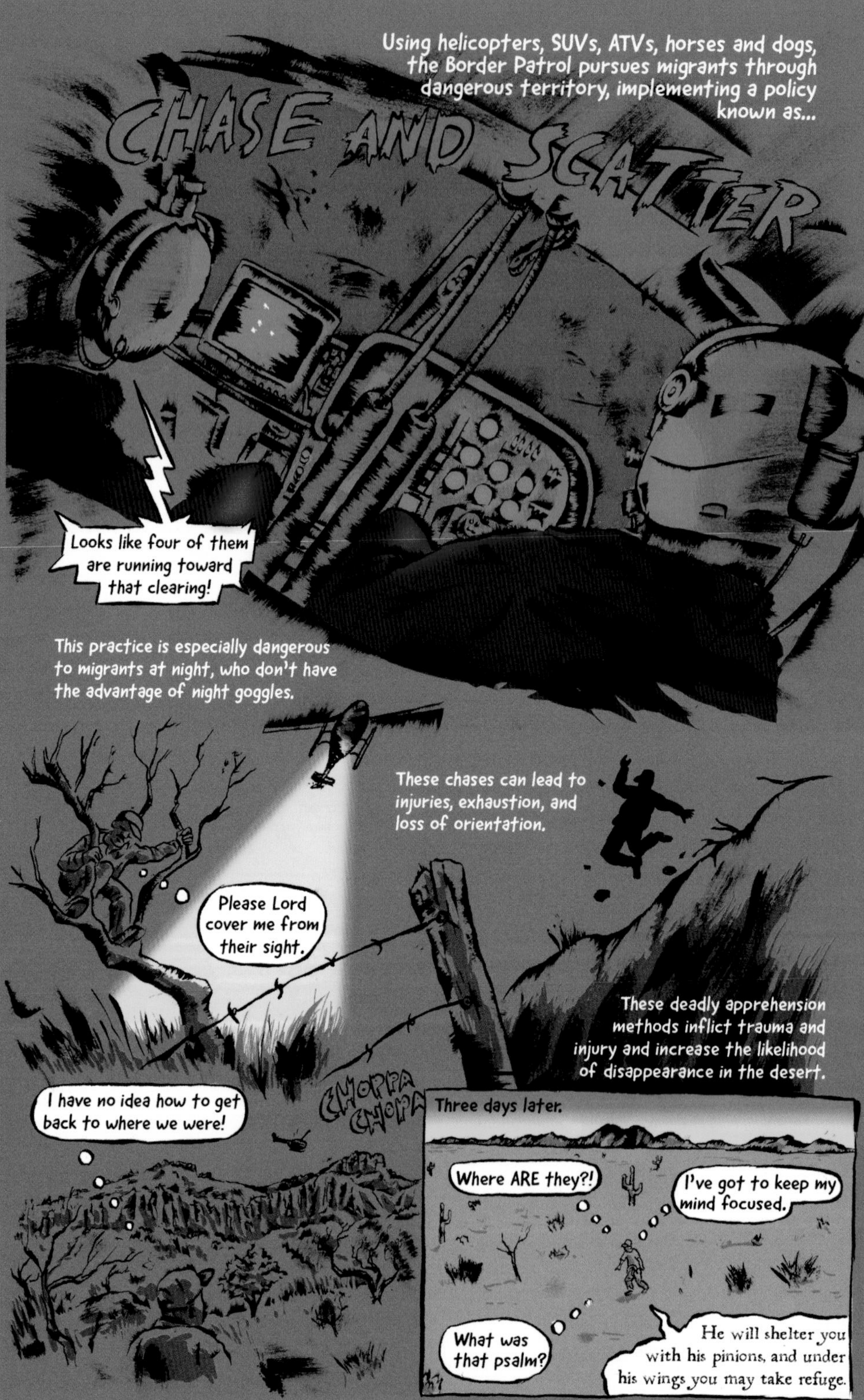
Using helicopters, SUVs, ATVs, horses and dogs, the Border Patrol pursues migrants through dangerous territory, implementing a policy known as...
CHASE AND SCATTER
Looks like four of them are running toward that clearing!
This practice is especially dangerous to migrants at night, who don't have the advantage of night goggles.
These chases can lead to injuries, exhaustion, and loss of orientation.
Please Lord cover me from their sight.
These deadly apprehension methods inflict trauma and injury and increase the likelihood of disappearance in the desert.
I have no idea how to get back to where we were!
CHOPPA
Three days later.
Where ARE they?!
I've got to keep my mind focused.
What was that psalm?
He will shelter you with his pinions, and under his wings you may take refuge.

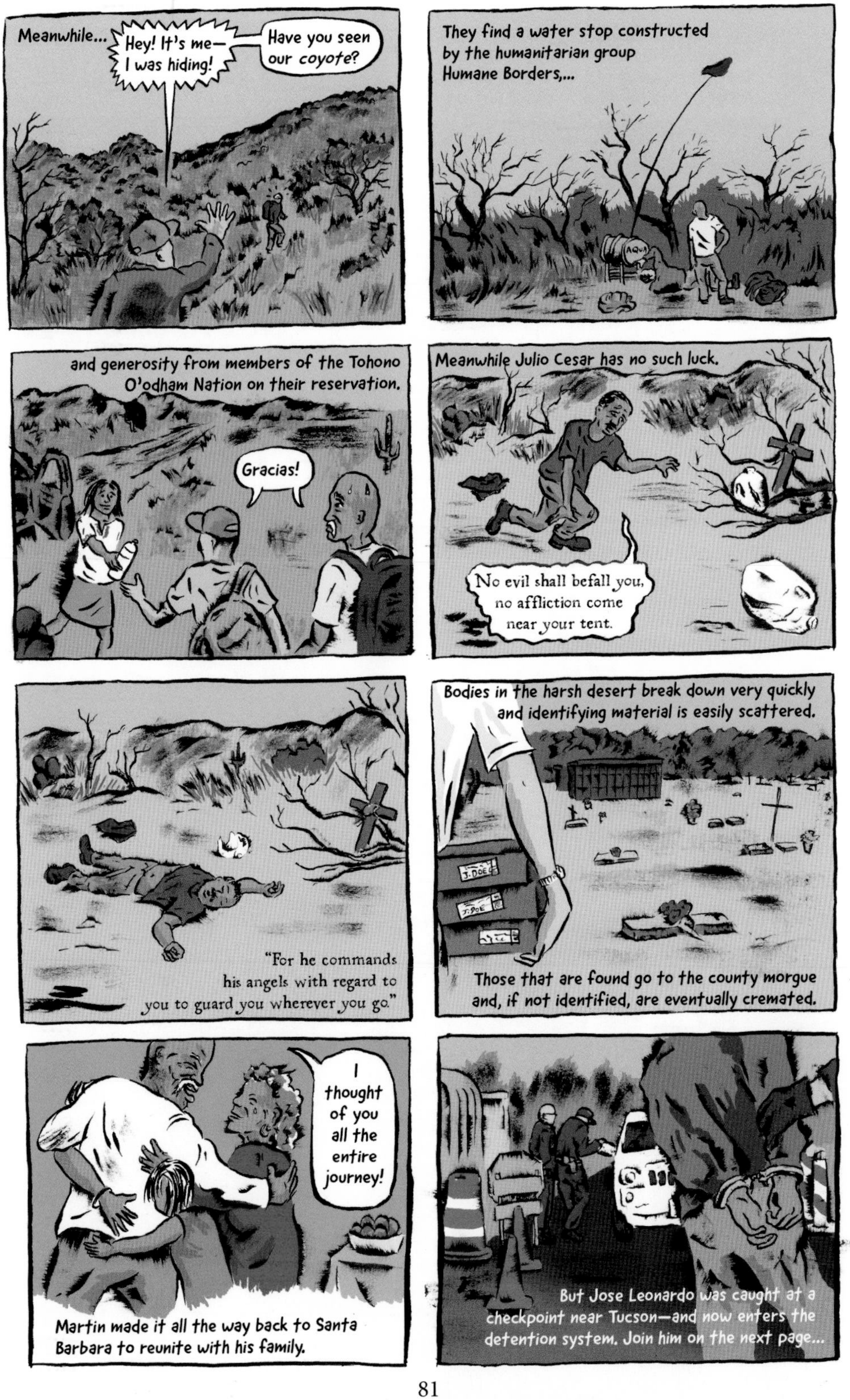
Meanwhile...
Hey! It's me— I was hiding!
Have you seen our coyote?
They find a water stop constructed by the humanitarian group Humane Borders,...
AQUA
and generosity from members of the Tohono O'odham Nation on their reservation.
Gracias!
Meanwhile Julio Cesar has no such luck.
No evil shall befall you, no affliction come near your tent.
"For he commands his angels with regard to you to guard you wherever you go."
Bodies in the harsh desert break down very quickly and identifying material is easily scattered.
J. DOE
J. DOE
Those that are found go to the county morgue and, if not identified, are eventually cremated.
I thought of you all the entire journey!
Martin made it all the way back to Santa Barbara to reunite with his family.
But Jose Leonardo was caught at a checkpoint near Tucson—and now enters the detention system. Join him on the next page...

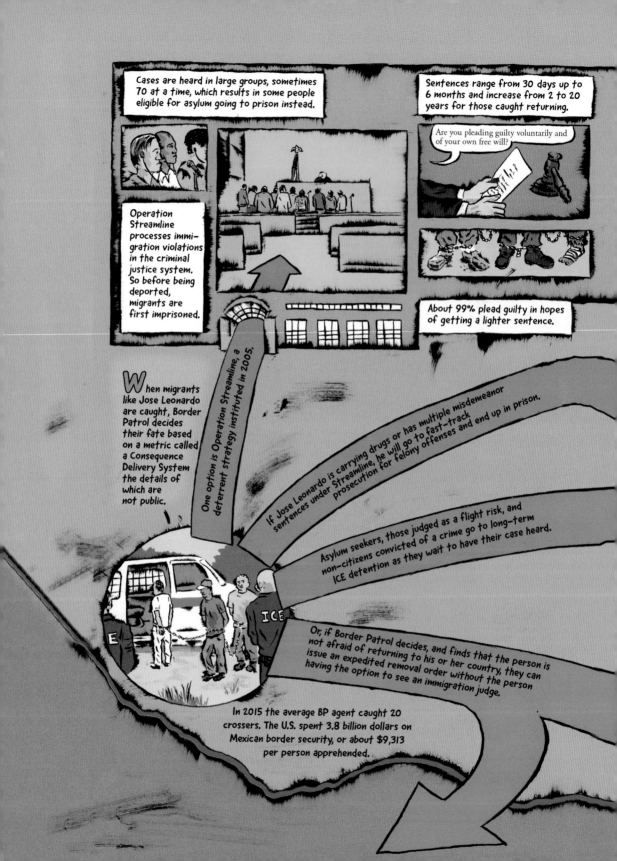

Cases are heard in large groups, sometimes 70 at a time, which results in some people eligible for asylum going to prison instead.

Sentences range from 30 days up to 6 months and increase from 2 to 20 years for those caught returning.

Are you pleading guilty voluntarily and of your own free will?

Operation Streamline processes immigration violations in the criminal justice system. So before being deported, migrants are first imprisoned.

About 99% plead guilty in hopes of getting a lighter sentence.

When migrants like Jose Leonardo are caught, Border Patrol decides their fate based on a metric called a Consequence Delivery System the details of which are not public.

One option is Operation Streamline, a deterrent strategy instituted in 2005.

If Jose Leonardo is carrying drugs or has multiple misdemeanor sentences under Streamline, he will go to fast-track prosecution for felony offenses and end up in prison.

Asylum seekers, those judged as a flight risk, and non-citizens convicted of a crime go to long-term ICE detention as they wait to have their case heard.

Or, if Border Patrol decides, and finds that the person is not afraid of returning to his or her country, they can issue an expedited removal order without the person having the option to see an immigration judge.

In 2015 the average BP agent caught 20 crossers. The U.S. spent 3.8 billion dollars on Mexican border security, or about $9,313 per person apprehended.

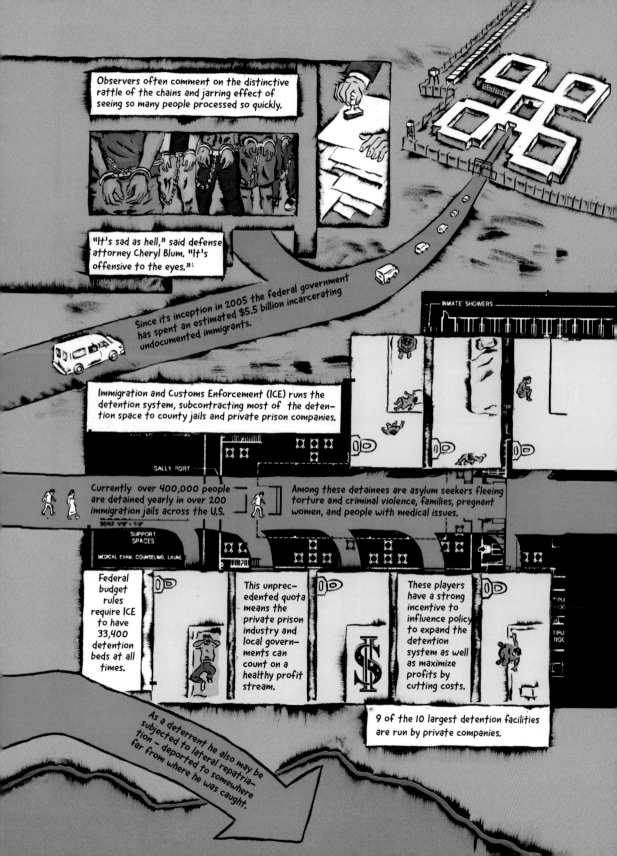

Observers often comment on the distinctive rattle of the chains and jarring effect of seeing so many people processed so quickly.

"It's sad as hell," said defense attorney Cheryl Blum. "It's offensive to the eyes."[1]

Since its inception in 2005 the federal government has spent an estimated $5.5 billion incarcerating undocumented immigrants.

Immigration and Customs Enforcement (ICE) runs the detention system, subcontracting most of the detention space to county jails and private prison companies.

INMATE SHOWERS

SALLY PORT

Currently over 400,000 people are detained yearly in over 200 immigration jails across the U.S.

SCALE 1/16" = 1'-0"

Among these detainees are asylum seekers fleeing torture and criminal violence, families, pregnant women, and people with medical issues.

SUPPORT SPACES

MEDICAL EXAM, COUNSELING, LAUND

Federal budget rules require ICE to have 33,400 detention beds at all times.

This unprecedented quota means the private prison industry and local governments can count on a healthy profit stream.

These players have a strong incentive to influence policy to expand the detention system as well as maximize profits by cutting costs.

As a deterrent he also may be subjected to lateral repatriation – deported to somewhere far from where he was caught.

9 of the 10 largest detention facilities are run by private companies.

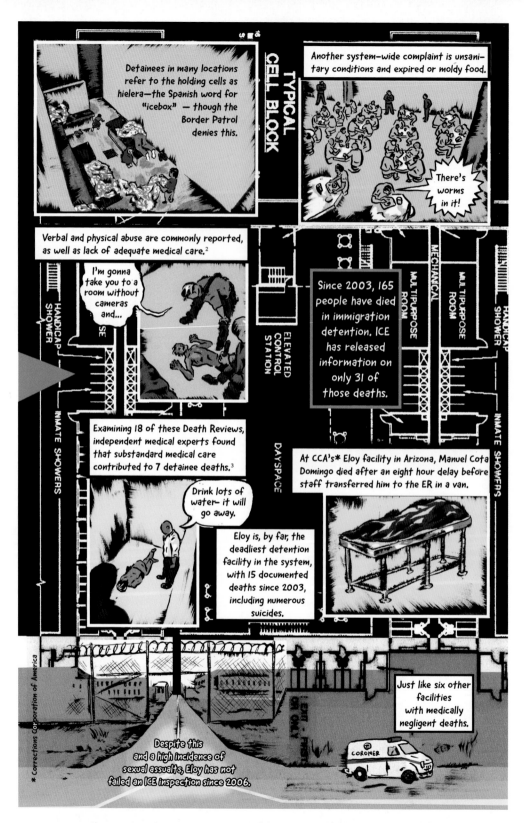

TYPICAL CELL BLOCK

Detainees in many locations refer to the holding cells as hielera—the Spanish word for "icebox" — though the Border Patrol denies this.

Another system-wide complaint is unsanitary conditions and expired or moldy food.

There's worms in it!

Verbal and physical abuse are commonly reported, as well as lack of adequate medical care.[2]

I'm gonna take you to a room without cameras and...

Since 2003, 165 people have died in immigration detention. ICE has released information on only 31 of those deaths.

Examining 18 of these Death Reviews, independent medical experts found that substandard medical care contributed to 7 detainee deaths.[3]

Drink lots of water— it will go away.

At CCA's* Eloy facility in Arizona, Manuel Cota Domingo died after an eight hour delay before staff transferred him to the ER in a van.

Eloy is, by far, the deadliest detention facility in the system, with 15 documented deaths since 2003, including numerous suicides.

Just like six other facilities with medically negligent deaths.

Despite this and a high incidence of sexual assaults, Eloy has not failed an ICE inspection since 2006.

* Corrections Corporation of America

CORONER

HANDICAP SHOWER

INMATE SHOWERS

ELEVATED CONTROL STATION

DAYSPACE

MECHANICAL

MULTIPURPOSE ROOM

MULTIPURPOSE ROOM

HANDICAP SHOWER

INMATE SHOWERS

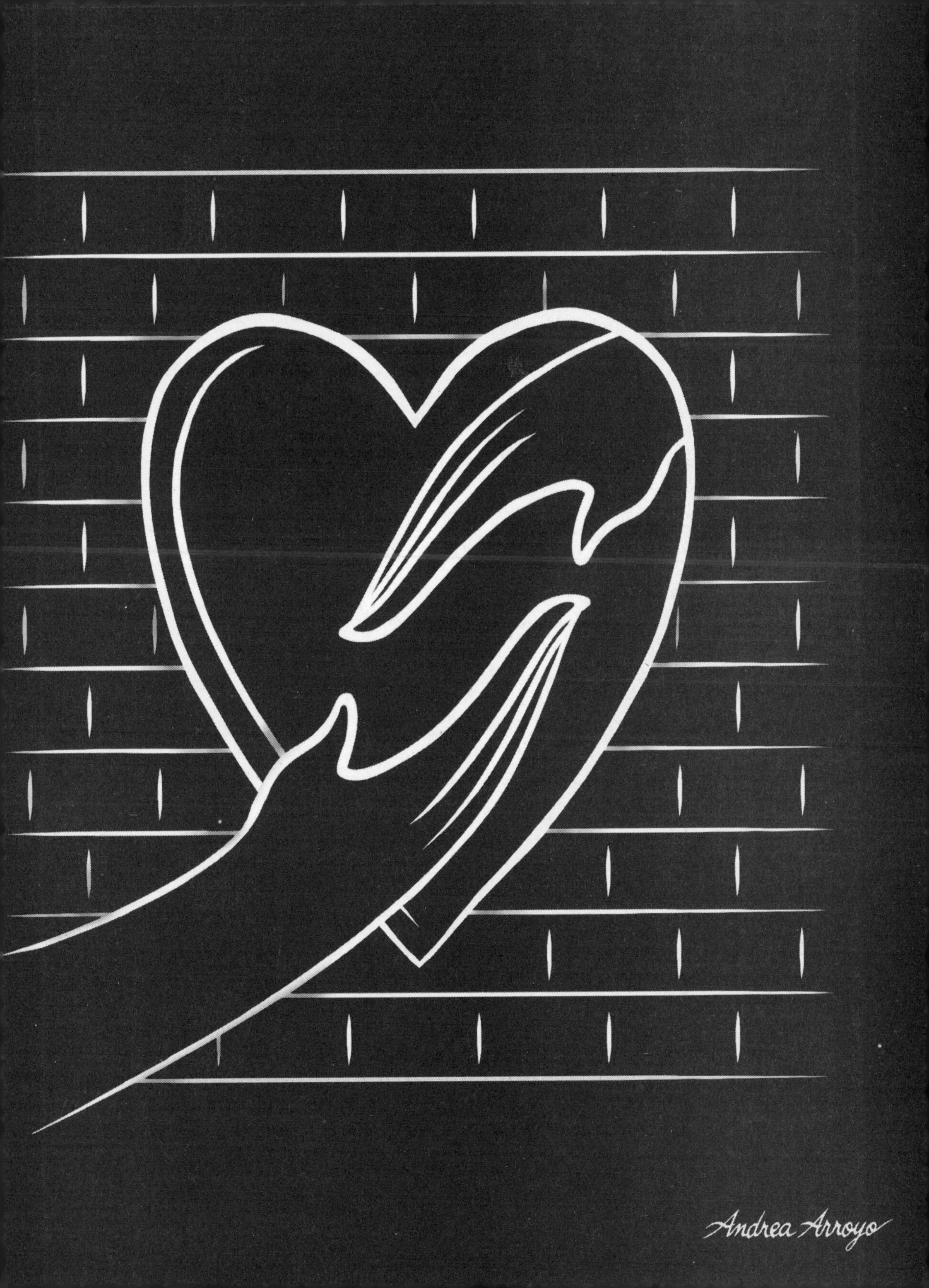
Andrea Arroyo

NOS CUBRIMOS LAS ESPALDAS

COMMUNITY SELF-DEFENSE

Ethan Heitner 7/17

Thanks to those who shared info with me, and every-one doing the work

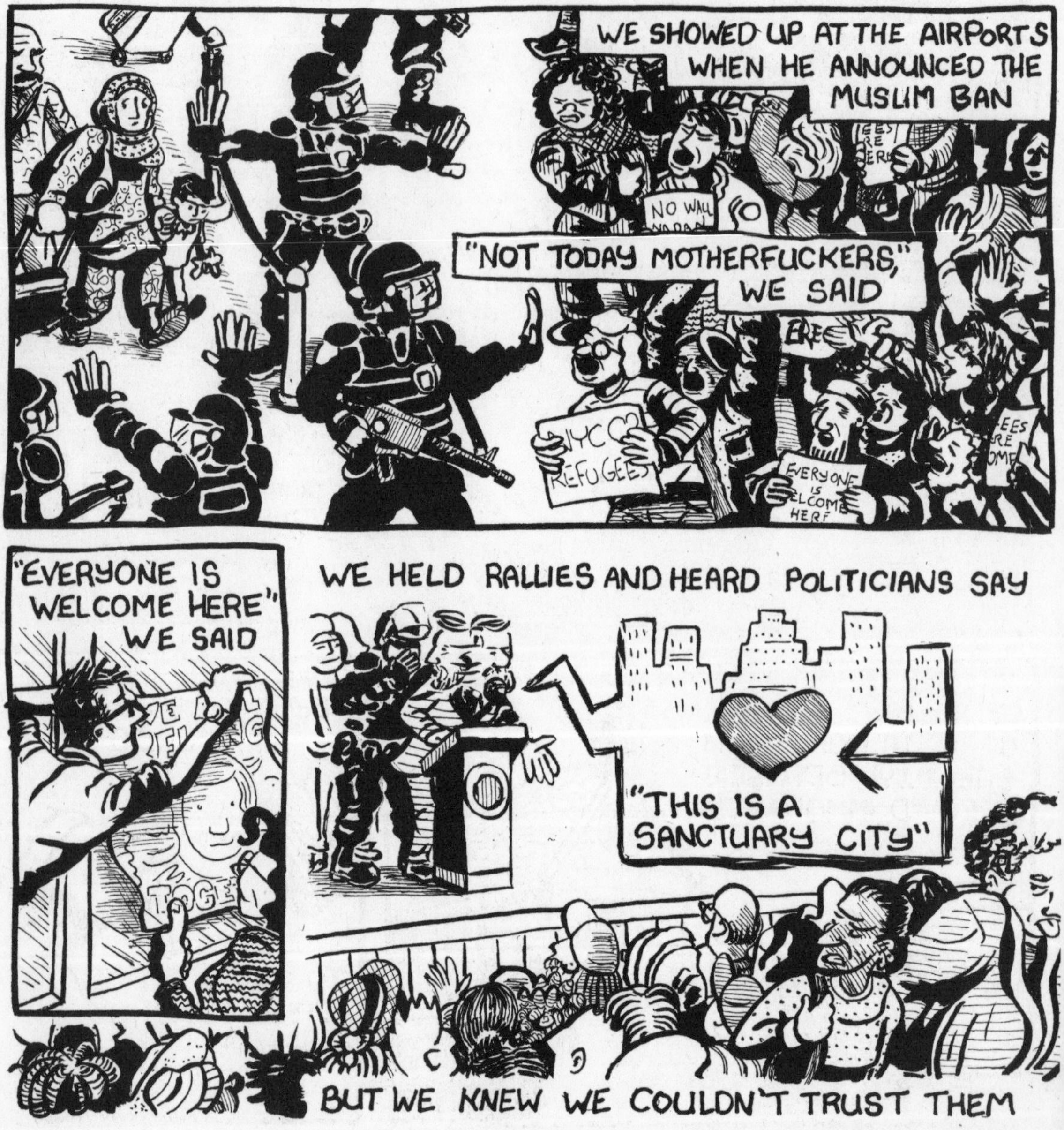
WE SHOWED UP AT THE AIRPORTS WHEN HE ANNOUNCED THE MUSLIM BAN
"NOT TODAY MOTHERFUCKERS," WE SAID
NO WALL
NYC ♡ REFUGEES
"EVERYONE IS WELCOME HERE" WE SAID
WE HELD RALLIES AND HEARD POLITICIANS SAY
"THIS IS A SANCTUARY CITY"
BUT WE KNEW WE COULDN'T TRUST THEM

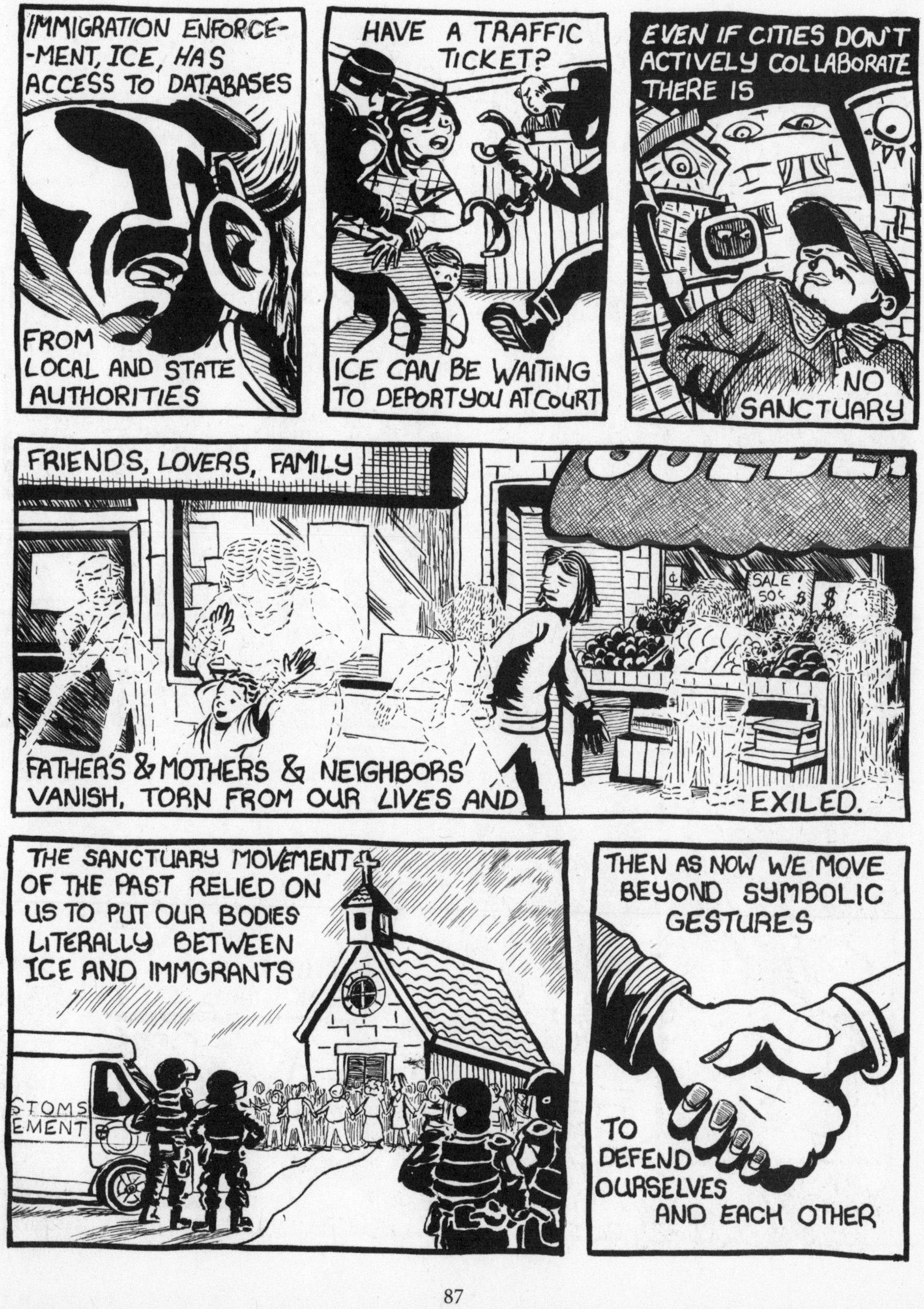
IMMIGRATION ENFORCE-
-MENT, ICE, HAS
ACCESS TO DATABASES
FROM
LOCAL AND STATE
AUTHORITIES
HAVE A TRAFFIC
TICKET?
ICE CAN BE WAITING
TO DEPORT YOU AT COURT
EVEN IF CITIES DON'T
ACTIVELY COLLABORATE
THERE IS
NO
SANCTUARY
FRIENDS, LOVERS, FAMILY
SALE!
50¢
FATHER'S & MOTHERS & NEIGHBORS
VANISH, TORN FROM OUR LIVES AND
EXILED.
THE SANCTUARY MOVEMENT
OF THE PAST RELIED ON
US TO PUT OUR BODIES
LITERALLY BETWEEN
ICE AND IMMGRANTS
STOMS
EMENT
THEN AS NOW WE MOVE
BEYOND SYMBOLIC
GESTURES
TO
DEFEND
OURSELVES
AND EACH OTHER

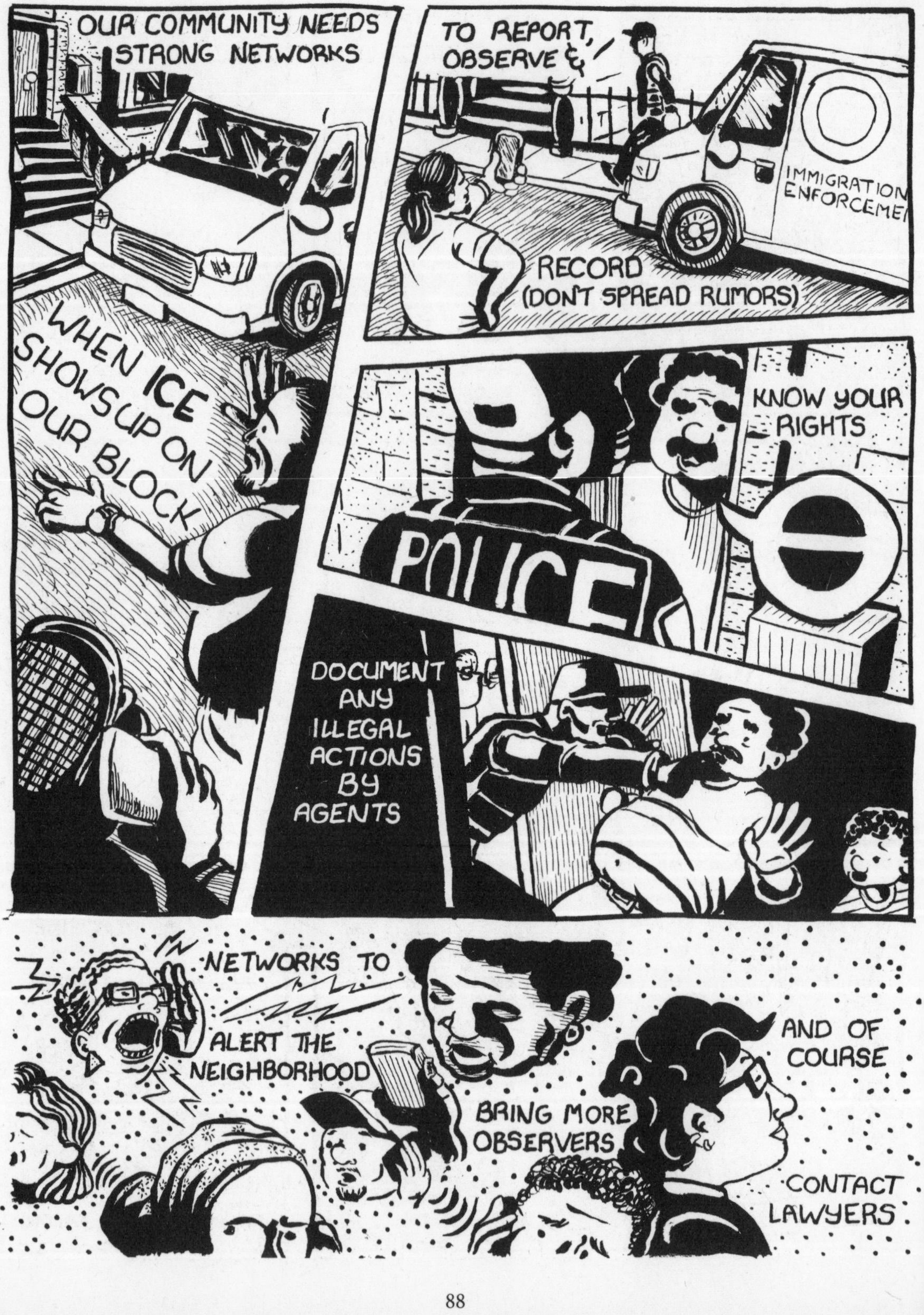
OUR COMMUNITY NEEDS STRONG NETWORKS
TO REPORT, OBSERVE &
IMMIGRATION ENFORCEME
RECORD (DON'T SPREAD RUMORS)
WHEN ICE SHOWS UP ON OUR BLOCK
KNOW YOUR RIGHTS
POLICE
DOCUMENT ANY ILLEGAL ACTIONS BY AGENTS
NETWORKS TO
ALERT THE NEIGHBORHOOD
BRING MORE OBSERVERS
AND OF COURSE
CONTACT LAWYERS

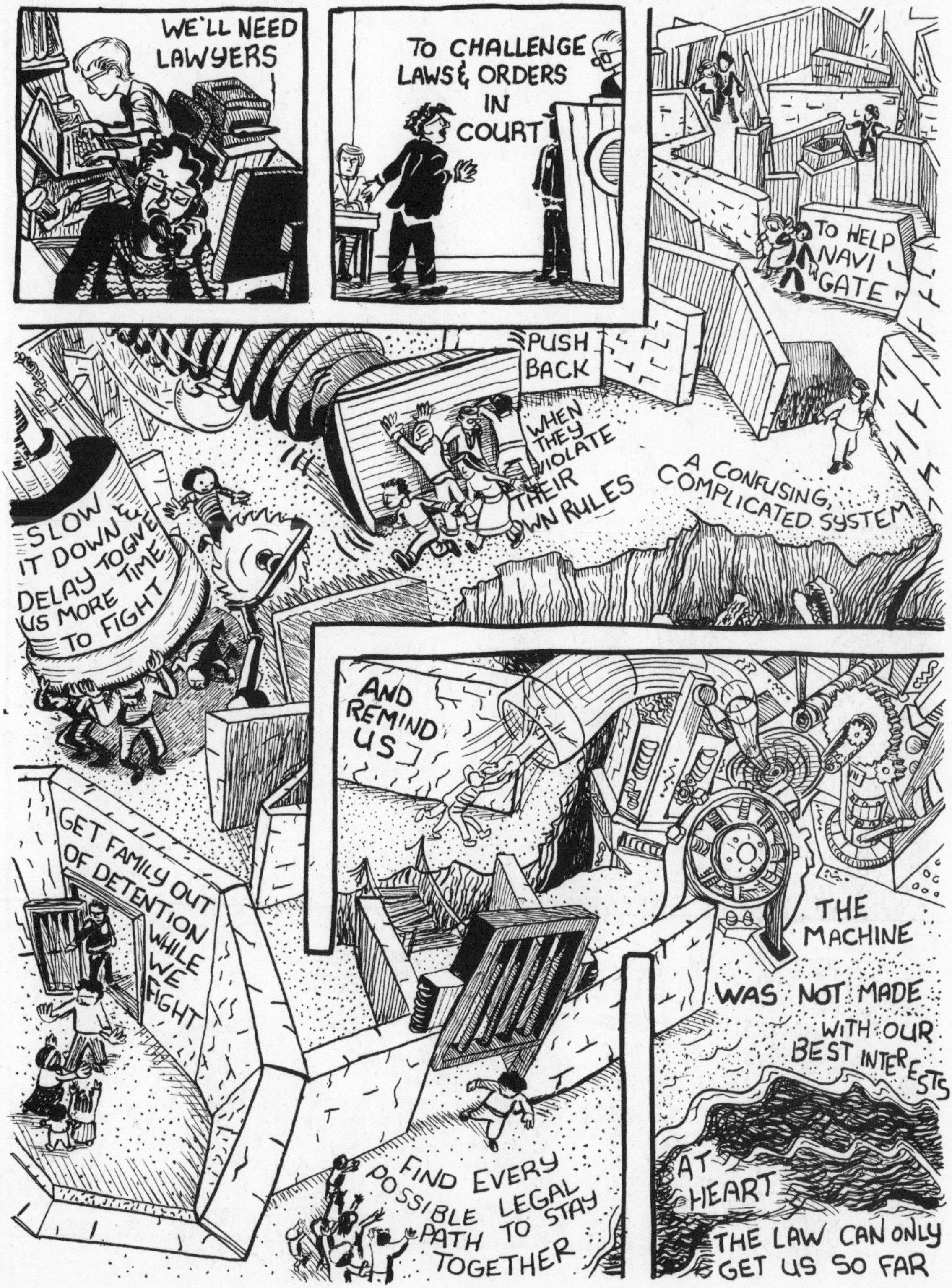
WE'LL NEED LAWYERS
TO CHALLENGE LAWS & ORDERS IN COURT
TO HELP NAVIGATE
A CONFUSING, COMPLICATED SYSTEM
PUSH BACK
WHEN THEY VIOLATE THEIR OWN RULES
SLOW IT DOWN
DELAY TO GIVE US MORE TIME TO FIGHT
AND REMIND US
GET FAMILY OUT OF DETENTION WHILE WE FIGHT
FIND EVERY POSSIBLE LEGAL PATH TO STAY TOGETHER
THE MACHINE
WAS NOT MADE
WITH OUR BEST INTERESTS
AT HEART
THE LAW CAN ONLY GET US SO FAR

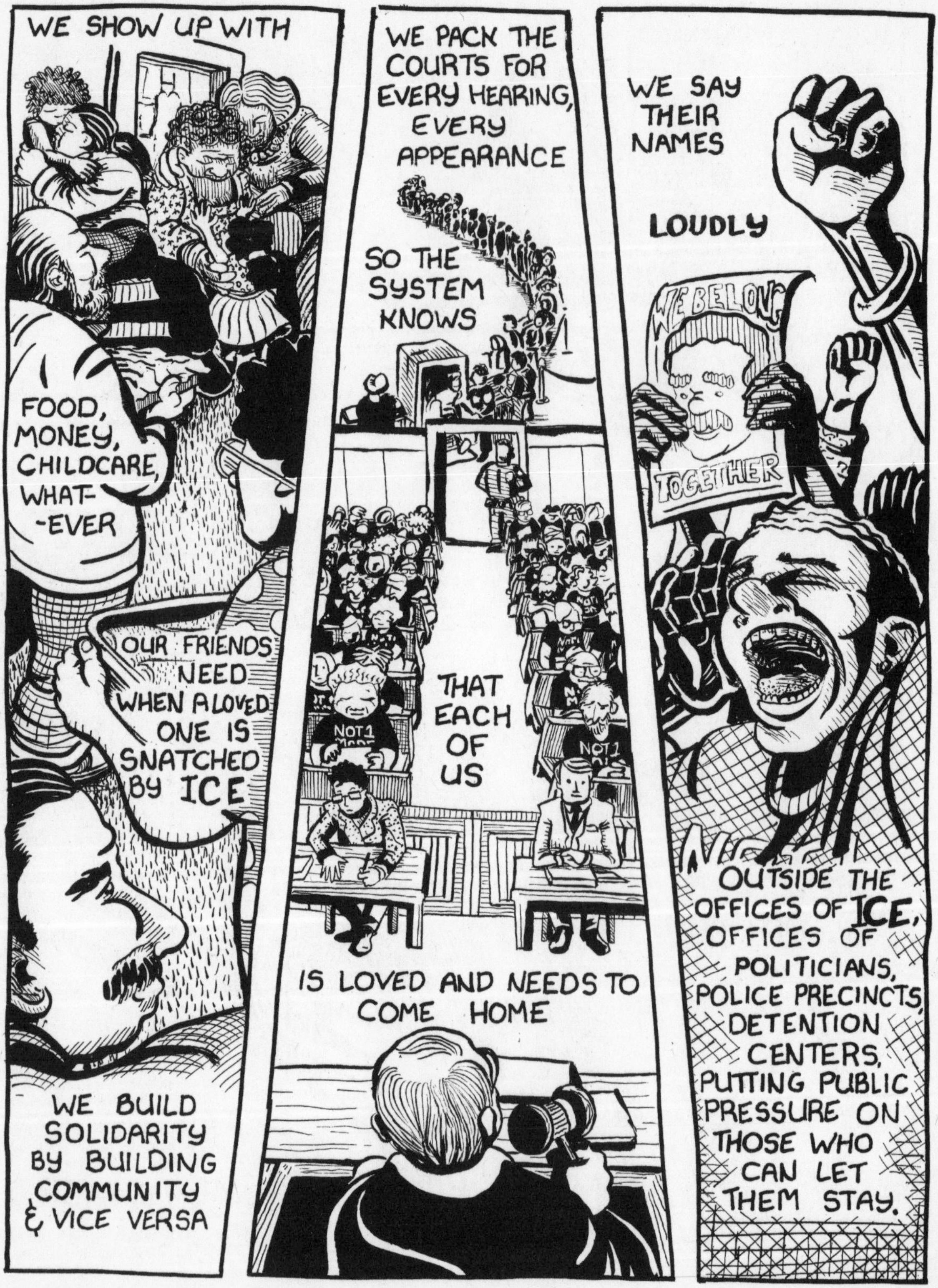
WE SHOW UP WITH
FOOD, MONEY, CHILDCARE, WHAT-EVER
OUR FRIENDS NEED WHEN A LOVED ONE IS SNATCHED BY ICE
WE BUILD SOLIDARITY BY BUILDING COMMUNITY & VICE VERSA
WE PACK THE COURTS FOR EVERY HEARING, EVERY APPEARANCE
SO THE SYSTEM KNOWS
THAT EACH OF US
IS LOVED AND NEEDS TO COME HOME
NOT1
NOT1
WE SAY THEIR NAMES
LOUDLY
WE BELONG
TOGETHER
OUTSIDE THE OFFICES OF ICE, OFFICES OF POLITICIANS, POLICE PRECINCTS, DETENTION CENTERS, PUTTING PUBLIC PRESSURE ON THOSE WHO CAN LET THEM STAY.

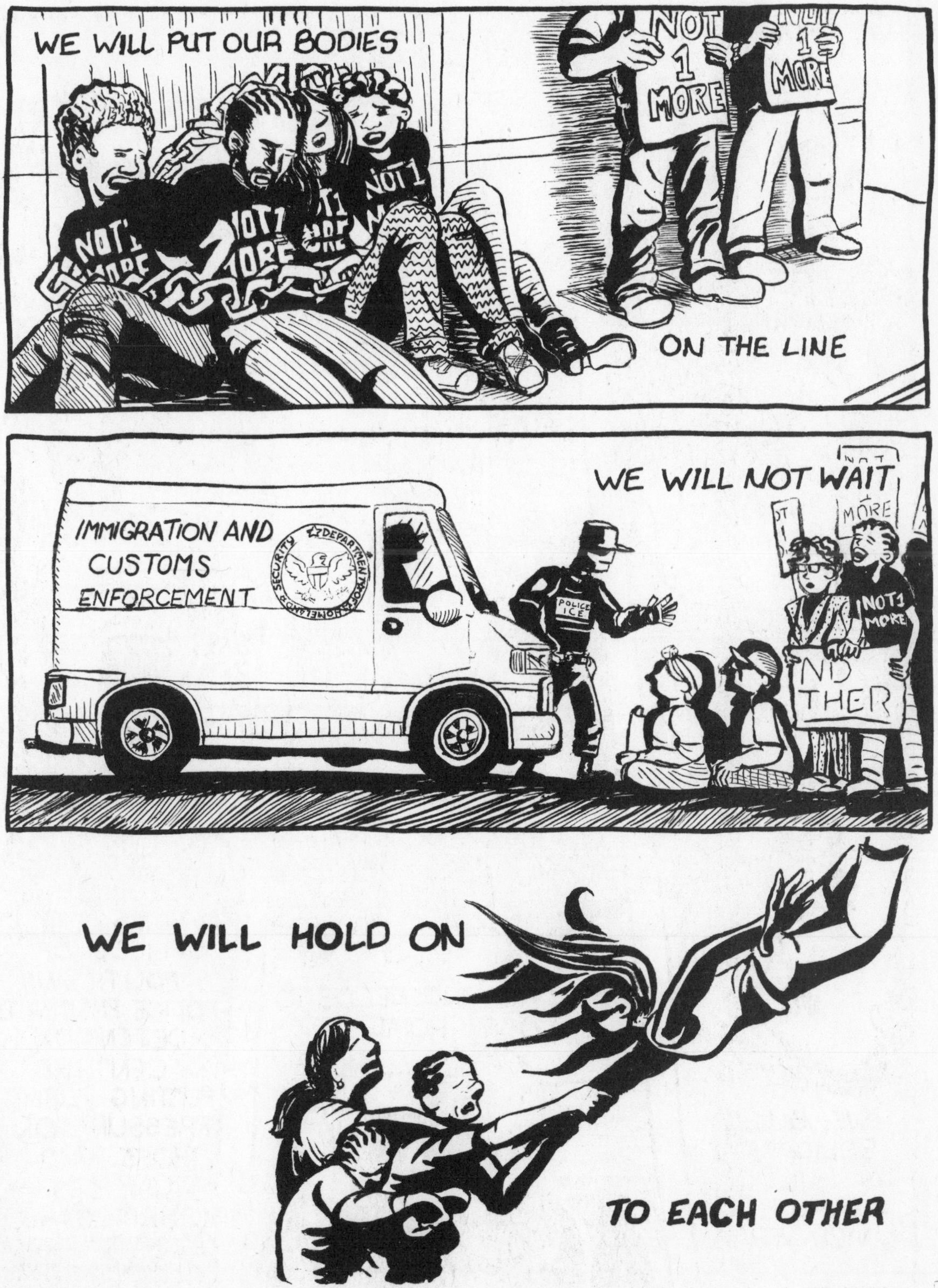
WE WILL PUT OUR BODIES
NOT 1 MORE
NOT 1 MORE
ON THE LINE
WE WILL NOT WAIT
IMMIGRATION AND CUSTOMS ENFORCEMENT
DEPARTMENT OF HOMELAND SECURITY
POLICE ICE
NOT1 MORE
WE WILL HOLD ON
TO EACH OTHER

FIGHTING NAZIS in Charlottesville

a photo essay by John Penley

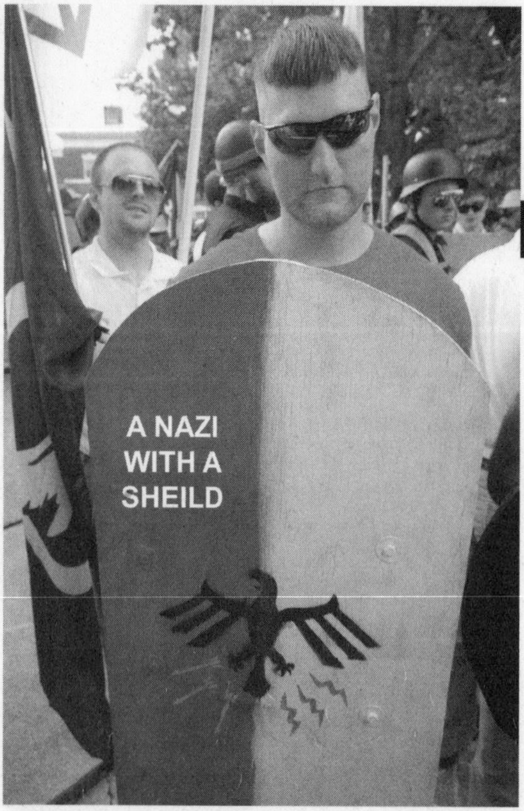

A NAZI WITH A SHEILD

John Penley is a courageous and talented photo journalist and an activist with a long history of organizing and documenting anti-Klan, anti-nuclear and anti-capitalist protest. He has a unique eye for the odd moments that occur at such events. This year he was involved with actions in Charlottesville where American Neo-Nazis and the so-called "Alt-Right" held their "Unite-the-Right" protest and anti-fascists showed up to oppose them.. He says " I feel like I just got back from a war." Judge for yourself.

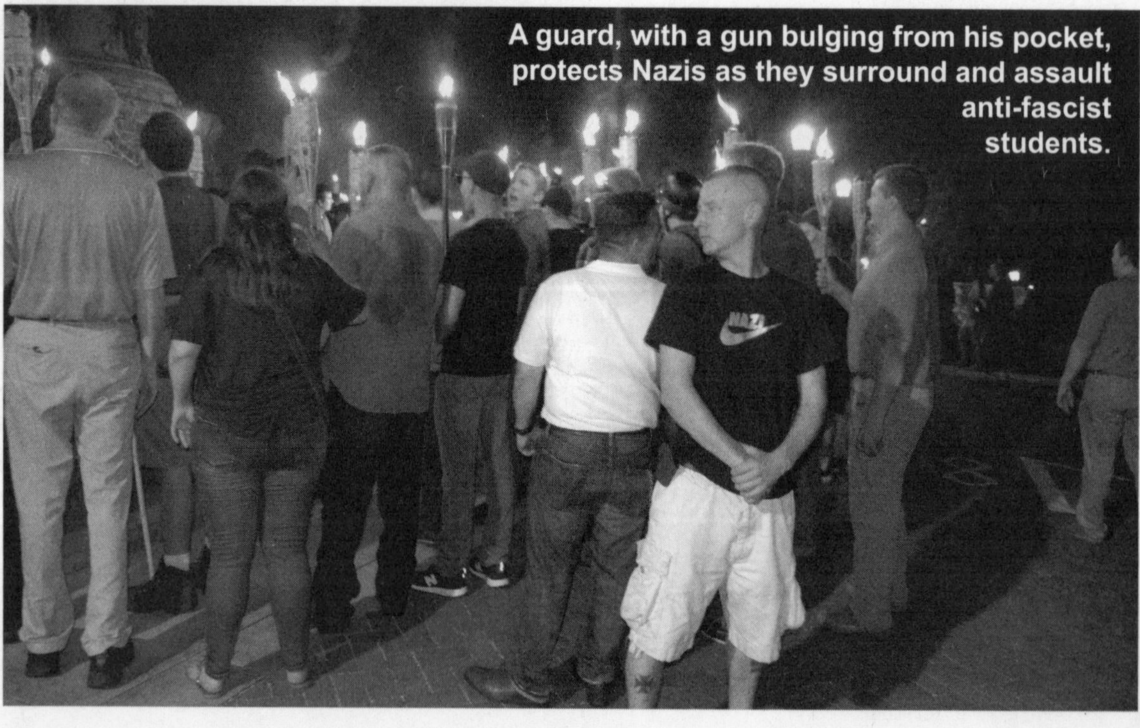

A guard, with a gun bulging from his pocket, protects Nazis as they surround and assault anti-fascist students.

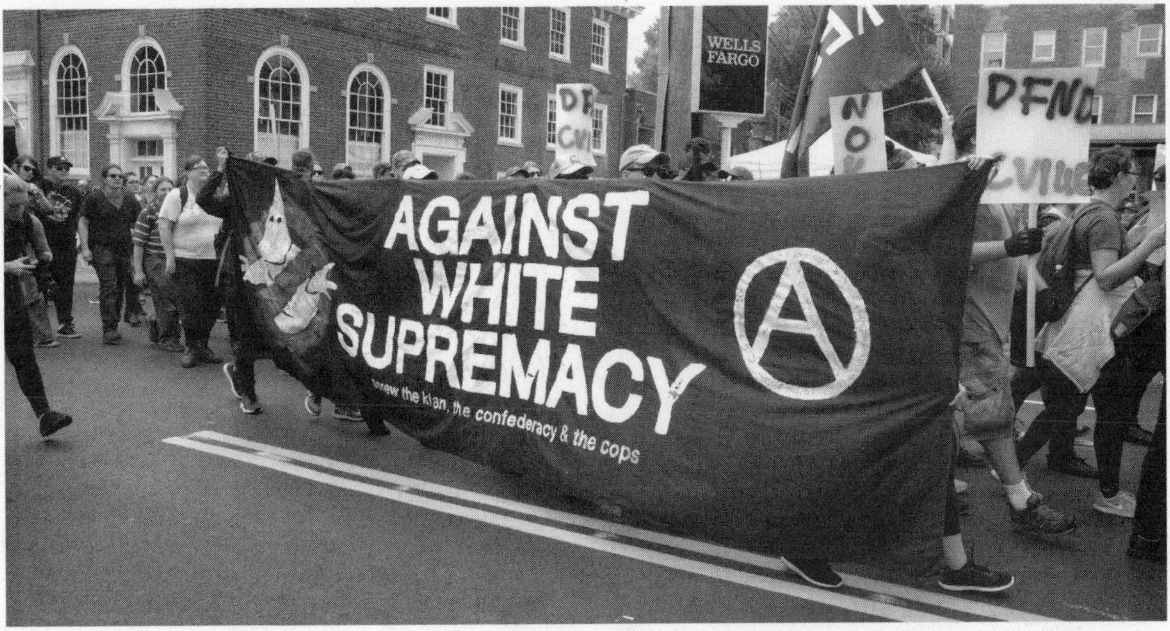
WELLS FARGO
AGAINST WHITE SUPREMACY
the klan, the confederacy & the cops

BELOW: A face-off between a militia member, and an anti-fascist counterprotester.

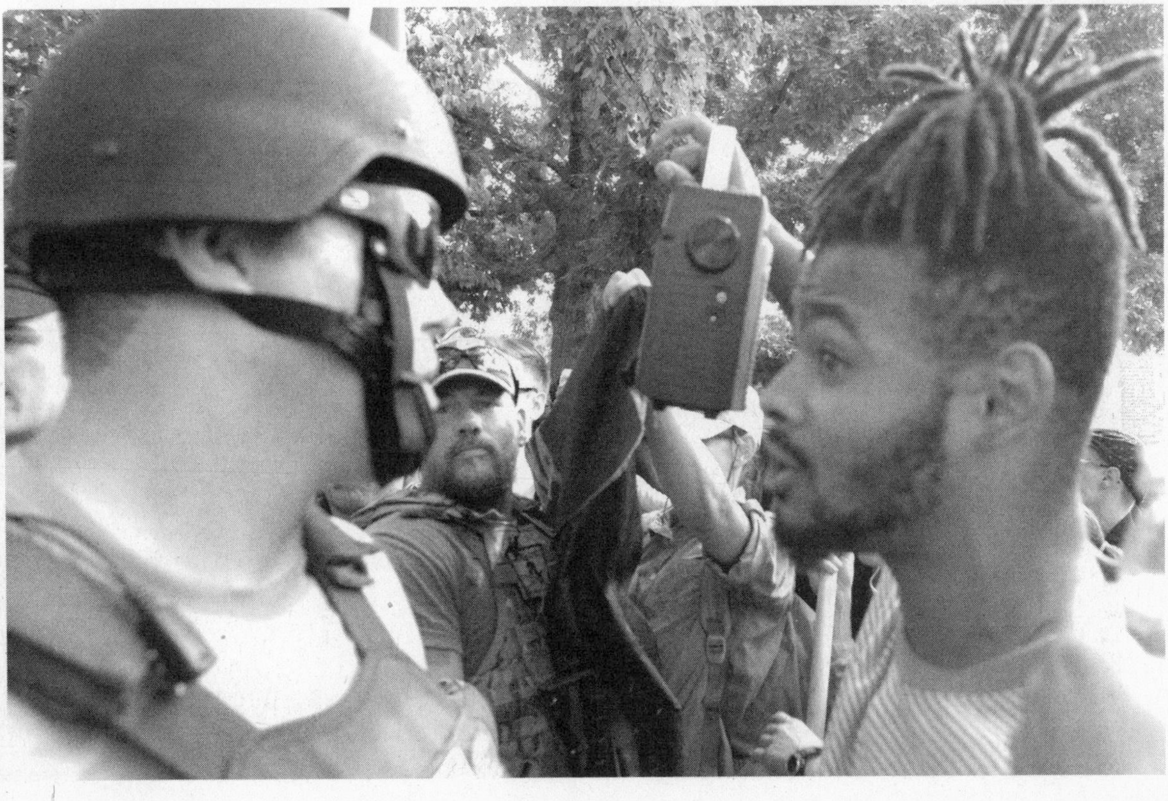

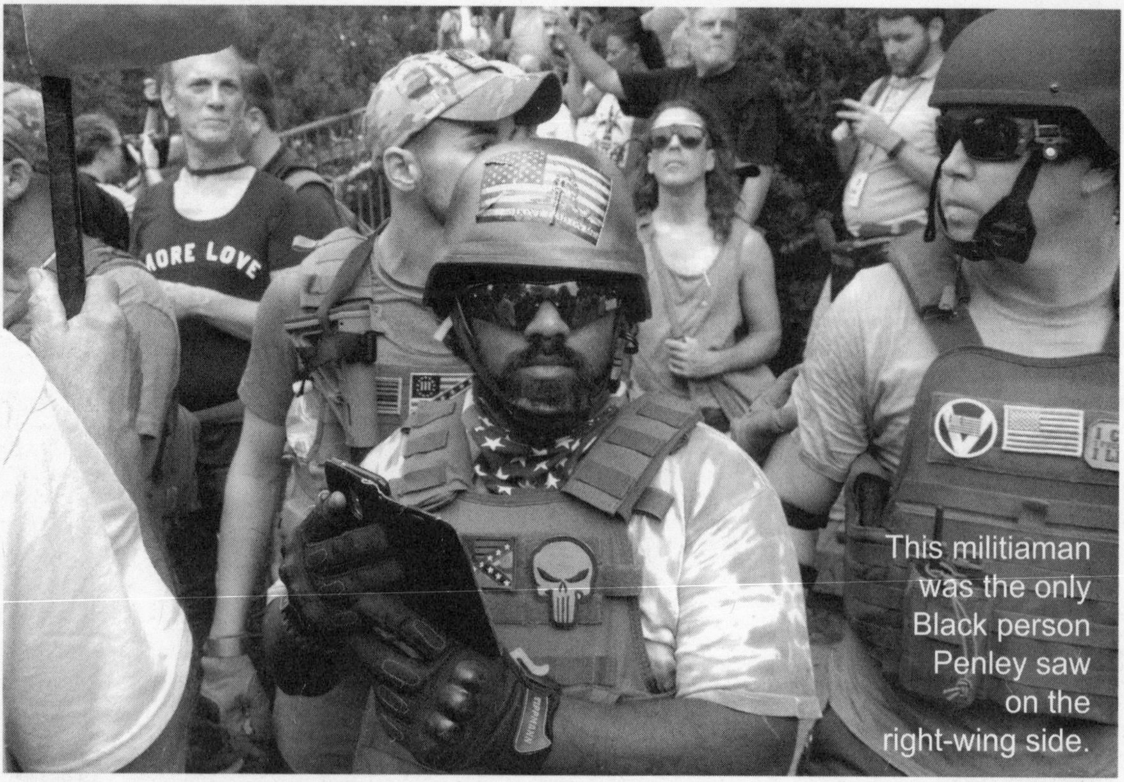

This militiaman was the only Black person Penley saw on the right-wing side.

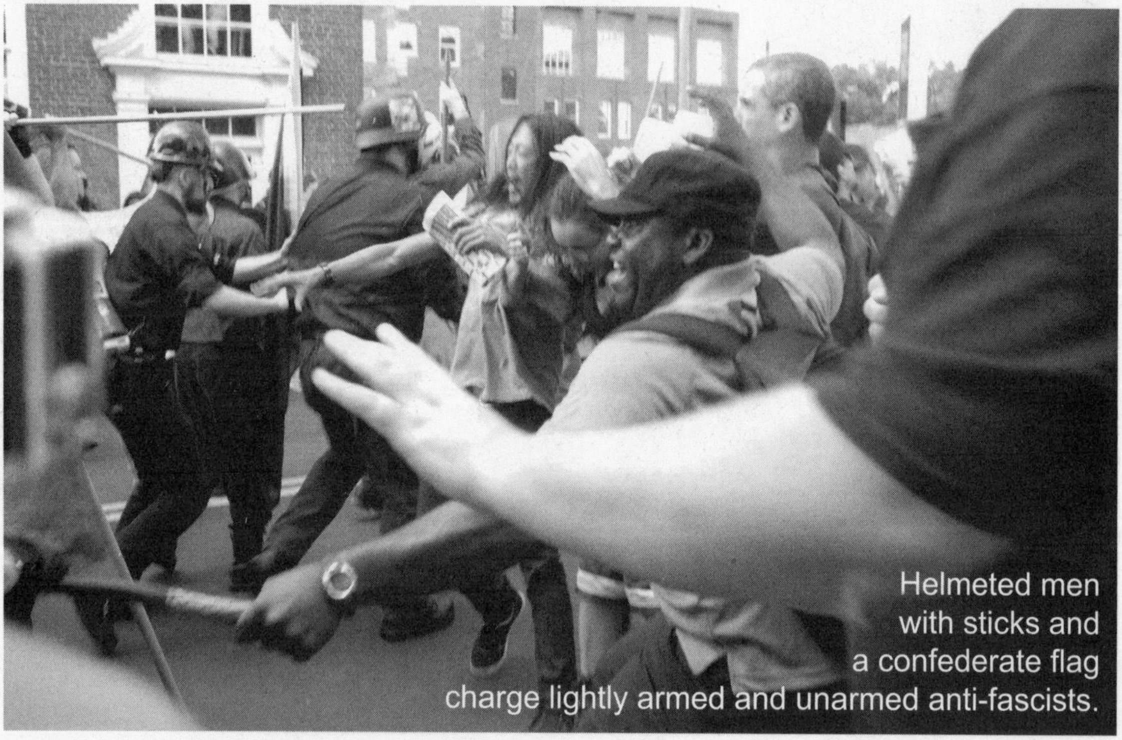

Helmeted men with sticks and a confederate flag charge lightly armed and unarmed anti-fascists.

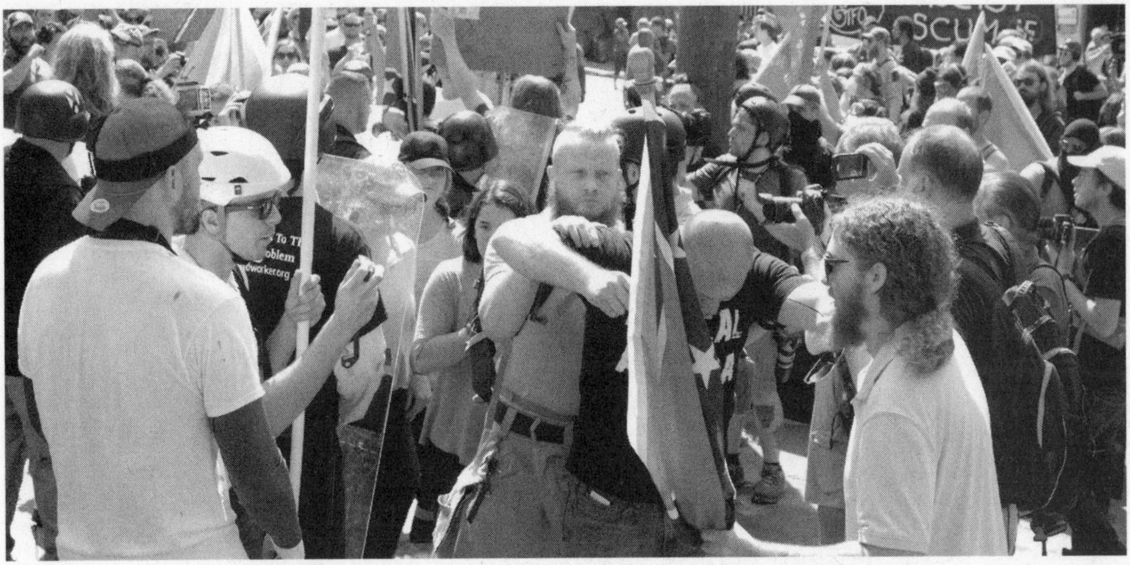

At "Unite-the-Right" marches anti-Semitic chants were common.
At one point the congregants of a synagogue were afraid to walk out because their temple was surrounded by an armed mob. Christopher Cantwell became an instant celebrity for making anti Jewish statements while showing off his gun collection on VICE news. Above we see Cantwell being carried off the street after getting his ass kicked by anti-fascists.

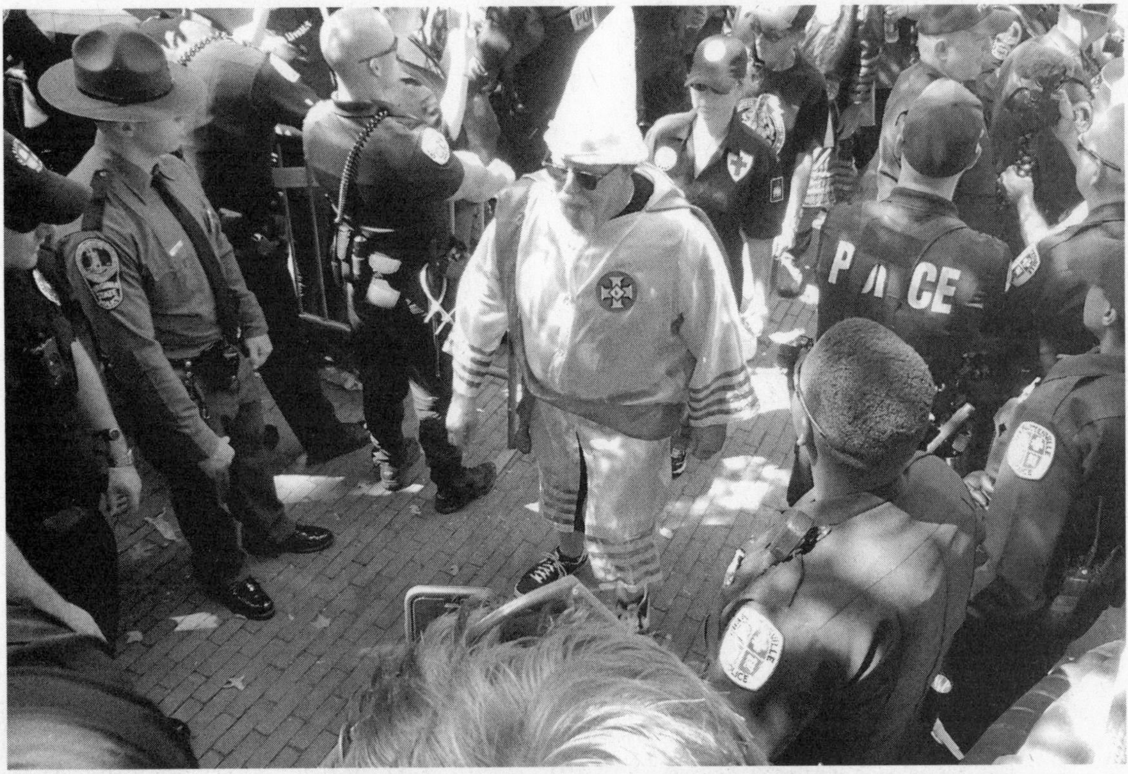

POLICE PROTECT KLANSMEN.

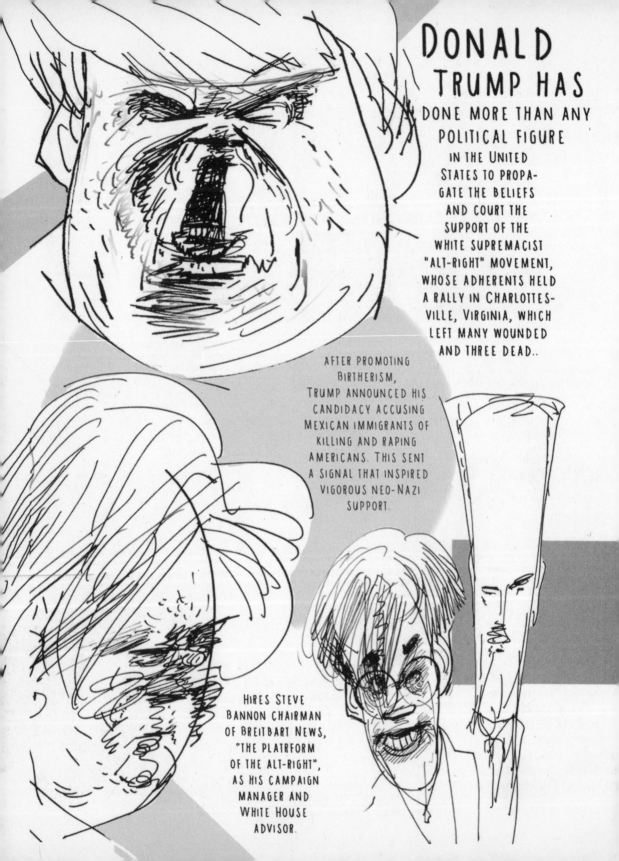

DONALD TRUMP HAS

DONE MORE THAN ANY POLITICAL FIGURE IN THE UNITED STATES TO PROPAGATE THE BELIEFS AND COURT THE SUPPORT OF THE WHITE SUPREMACIST "ALT-RIGHT" MOVEMENT, WHOSE ADHERENTS HELD A RALLY IN CHARLOTTESVILLE, VIRGINIA, WHICH LEFT MANY WOUNDED AND THREE DEAD..

AFTER PROMOTING BIRTHERISM, TRUMP ANNOUNCED HIS CANDIDACY ACCUSING MEXICAN IMMIGRANTS OF KILLING AND RAPING AMERICANS. THIS SENT A SIGNAL THAT INSPIRED VIGOROUS NEO-NAZI SUPPORT.

HIRES STEVE BANNON CHAIRMAN OF BREITBART NEWS, "THE PLATRFORM OF THE ALT-RIGHT", AS HIS CAMPAIGN MANAGER AND WHITE HOUSE ADVISOR.

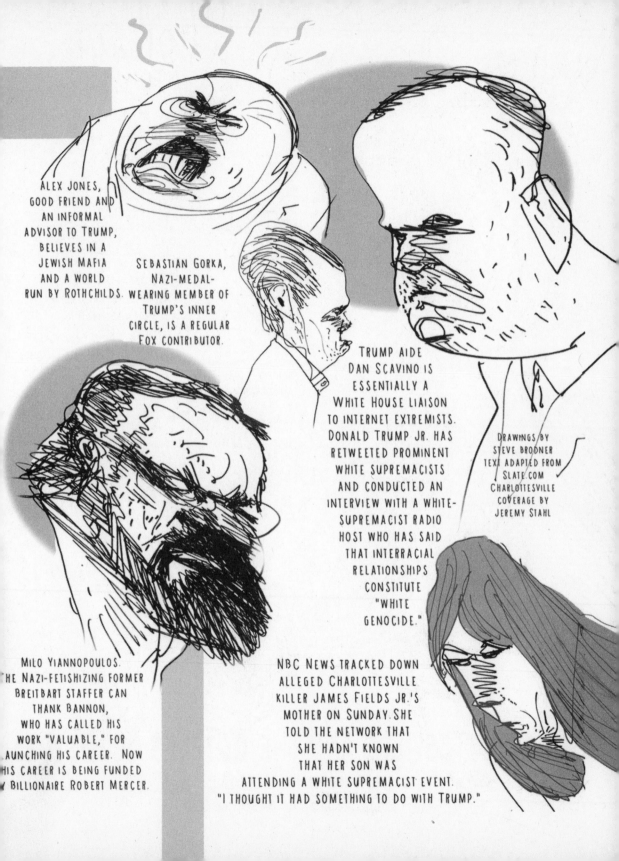

ALEX JONES, GOOD FRIEND AND AN INFORMAL ADVISOR TO TRUMP, BELIEVES IN A JEWISH MAFIA AND A WORLD RUN BY ROTHCHILDS.

SEBASTIAN GORKA, NAZI-MEDAL-WEARING MEMBER OF TRUMP'S INNER CIRCLE, IS A REGULAR FOX CONTRIBUTOR.

TRUMP AIDE DAN SCAVINO IS ESSENTIALLY A WHITE HOUSE LIAISON TO INTERNET EXTREMISTS. DONALD TRUMP JR. HAS RETWEETED PROMINENT WHITE SUPREMACISTS AND CONDUCTED AN INTERVIEW WITH A WHITE-SUPREMACIST RADIO HOST WHO HAS SAID THAT INTERRACIAL RELATIONSHIPS CONSTITUTE "WHITE GENOCIDE."

DRAWINGS BY STEVE BRODNER TEXT ADAPTED FROM SLATE.COM CHARLOTTESVILLE COVERAGE BY JEREMY STAHL

MILO YIANNOPOULOS. THE NAZI-FETISHIZING FORMER BREITBART STAFFER CAN THANK BANNON, WHO HAS CALLED HIS WORK "VALUABLE," FOR LAUNCHING HIS CAREER. NOW HIS CAREER IS BEING FUNDED BY BILLIONAIRE ROBERT MERCER.

NBC NEWS TRACKED DOWN ALLEGED CHARLOTTESVILLE KILLER JAMES FIELDS JR.'S MOTHER ON SUNDAY. SHE TOLD THE NETWORK THAT SHE HADN'T KNOWN THAT HER SON WAS ATTENDING A WHITE SUPREMACIST EVENT. "I THOUGHT IT HAD SOMETHING TO DO WITH TRUMP."

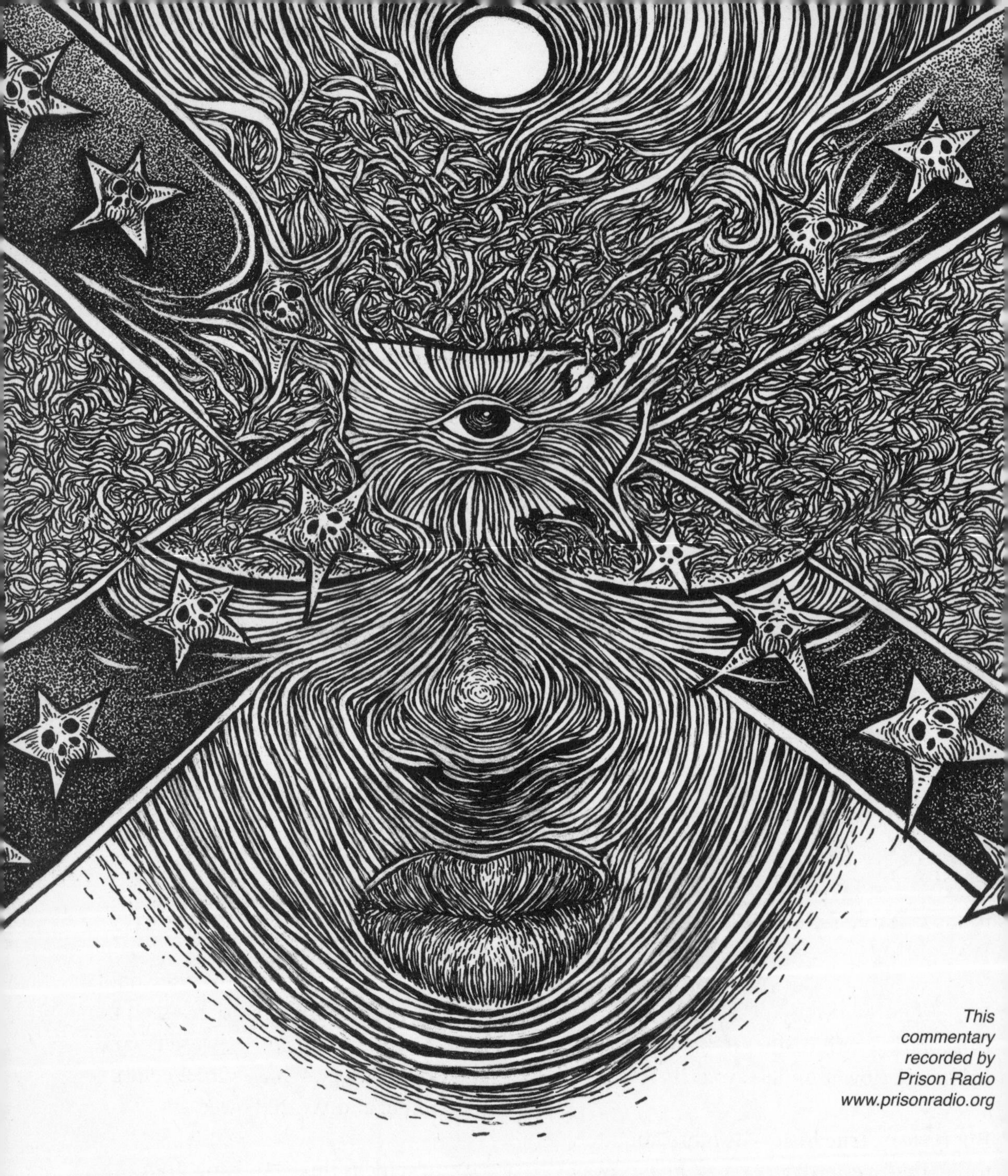

This
commentary
recorded by
Prison Radio
www.prisonradio.org

CHARLOTTESVILLE AND THE BATTLES OF HISTORY

written by Mumia-Abu-Jamal
illustrated by Mac McGill

The events surrounding Charlottesville, Virginia have a resonance far beyond the borders of Old Dominion. Even though they began as a strictly local affair, they quickly assumed a national character, because this strictly local event stems from the nation's history—a history that remains not only contested but bitterly unresolved.

That history, of course is the toxic poison of White Supremacy, and the trigger thereof—African Slavery—the intentional, centuries-long economic, social, communal and psychic exploitation of Africans for the financial and psychological benefits of the White Nation. This toxin has tainted the bloodstream of the Nation, and infected all segments of society, and was integral to the very development of Whiteness as a core identity for millions of people who call themselves "Americans."

As we look at protests rolling throughout the country, the first thing we must recognize is that this isn't about monuments. Nor is it about the Civil War.

It is about the Present. It is about how this country will define itself, how it sees itself, and how it understands its future.

But history, true history is more about today than yesterday, for it is the pathway to tomorrow, and it lives or dies in the minds of the young who learn, or unlearn, how this country came to be, and what role they play in the days to come.

The great Black freedom fighter, Malcolm X repeatedly said, "Of all our studies, history best rewards our research." He knew this not only because he was taught this by his Teacher (Honorable Elijah Muhammed) but because he learned this in the very expression of his life. For, as a state prisoner, a man so hated that he was called "Satan," his learning of a deeper history of Black people literally made him a new man. It gave him confidence, it turned his loathing into loving, it gave him purpose—and perhaps more importantly, perspective.

Perspective. How to look at the world. How to interpret it. How to understand why things are the way they are. That's the real value of History.

It teaches Perspective of Now—not Then.

And that's the reason why monuments, turned green by oxidation and pigeon poop, are seemingly at the center of these controversies.

The Trump presidency signaled a Great Leap – Backwards. It was the expression of a deep, profound fear of the Future, of Change, of Transformation. So, they hold on to Yesterday, invoking Tradition—as if the central Tradition of America wasn't—and isn't—Black Slavery, which launched it into an Economic and World Power.

Charlottesville is thus a turning point—a pivot point upon which the Nation turns back, or moves forward, creating a New History.

This only the people of America will decide.

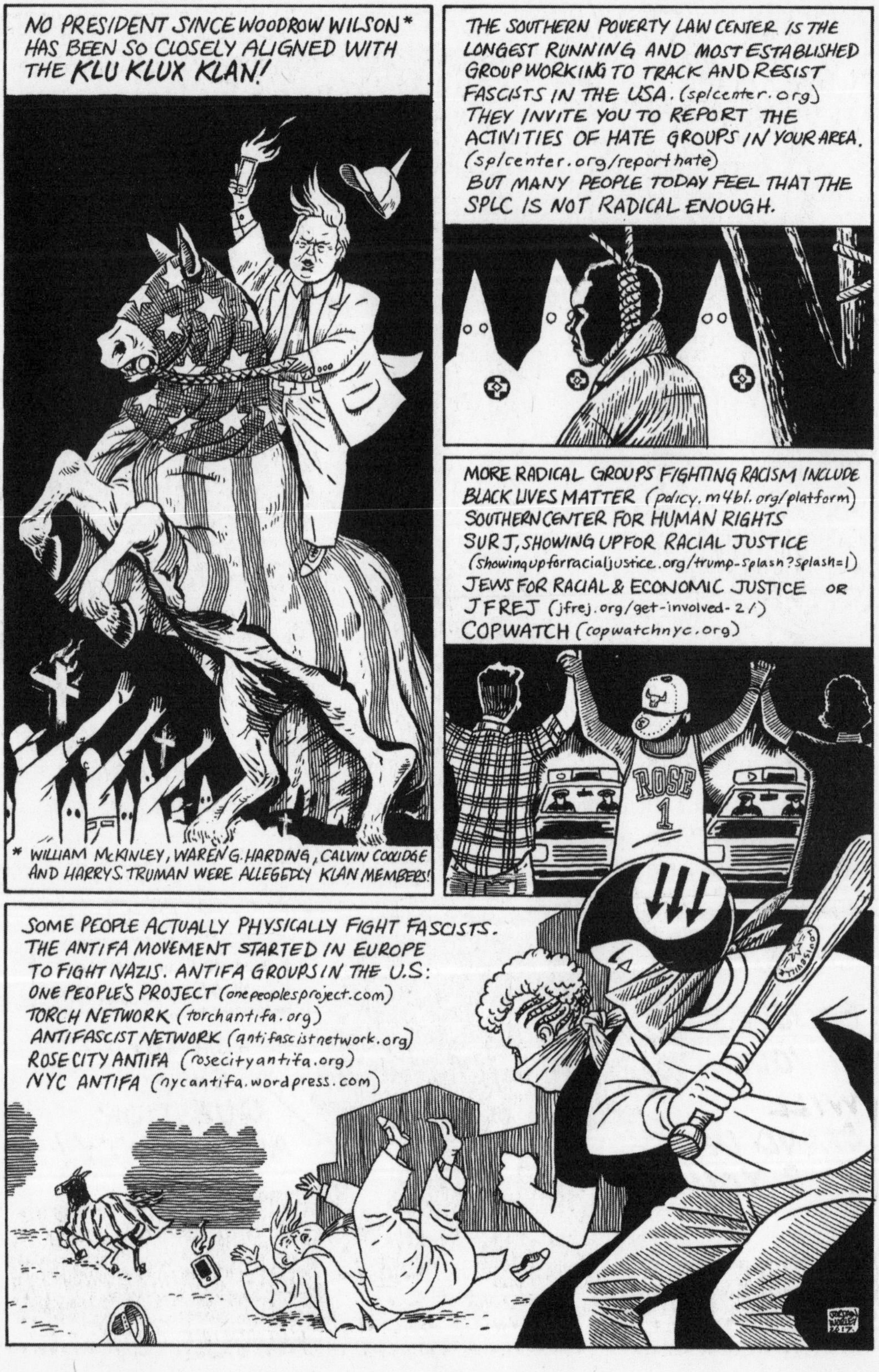
NO PRESIDENT SINCE WOODROW WILSON* HAS BEEN SO CLOSELY ALIGNED WITH THE KLU KLUX KLAN!
* WILLIAM McKINLEY, WAREN G. HARDING, CALVIN COOLIDGE AND HARRY S. TRUMAN WERE ALLEGEDLY KLAN MEMBERS!
THE SOUTHERN POVERTY LAW CENTER IS THE LONGEST RUNNING AND MOST ESTABLISHED GROUP WORKING TO TRACK AND RESIST FASCISTS IN THE USA. (splcenter.org)
THEY INVITE YOU TO REPORT THE ACTIVITIES OF HATE GROUPS IN YOUR AREA. (splcenter.org/reporthate)
BUT MANY PEOPLE TODAY FEEL THAT THE SPLC IS NOT RADICAL ENOUGH.
MORE RADICAL GROUPS FIGHTING RACISM INCLUDE
BLACK LIVES MATTER (policy.m4bl.org/platform)
SOUTHERN CENTER FOR HUMAN RIGHTS
SURJ, SHOWING UP FOR RACIAL JUSTICE (showingupforracialjustice.org/trump-splash?splash=1)
JEWS FOR RACIAL & ECONOMIC JUSTICE OR JFREJ (jfrej.org/get-involved-2/)
COPWATCH (copwatchnyc.org)
ROSE
1
SOME PEOPLE ACTUALLY PHYSICALLY FIGHT FASCISTS.
THE ANTIFA MOVEMENT STARTED IN EUROPE TO FIGHT NAZIS. ANTIFA GROUPS IN THE U.S:
ONE PEOPLE'S PROJECT (onepeoplesproject.com)
TORCH NETWORK (torchantifa.org)
ANTIFASCIST NETWORK (antifascistnetwork.org)
ROSE CITY ANTIFA (rosecityantifa.org)
NYC ANTIFA (nycantifa.wordpress.com)

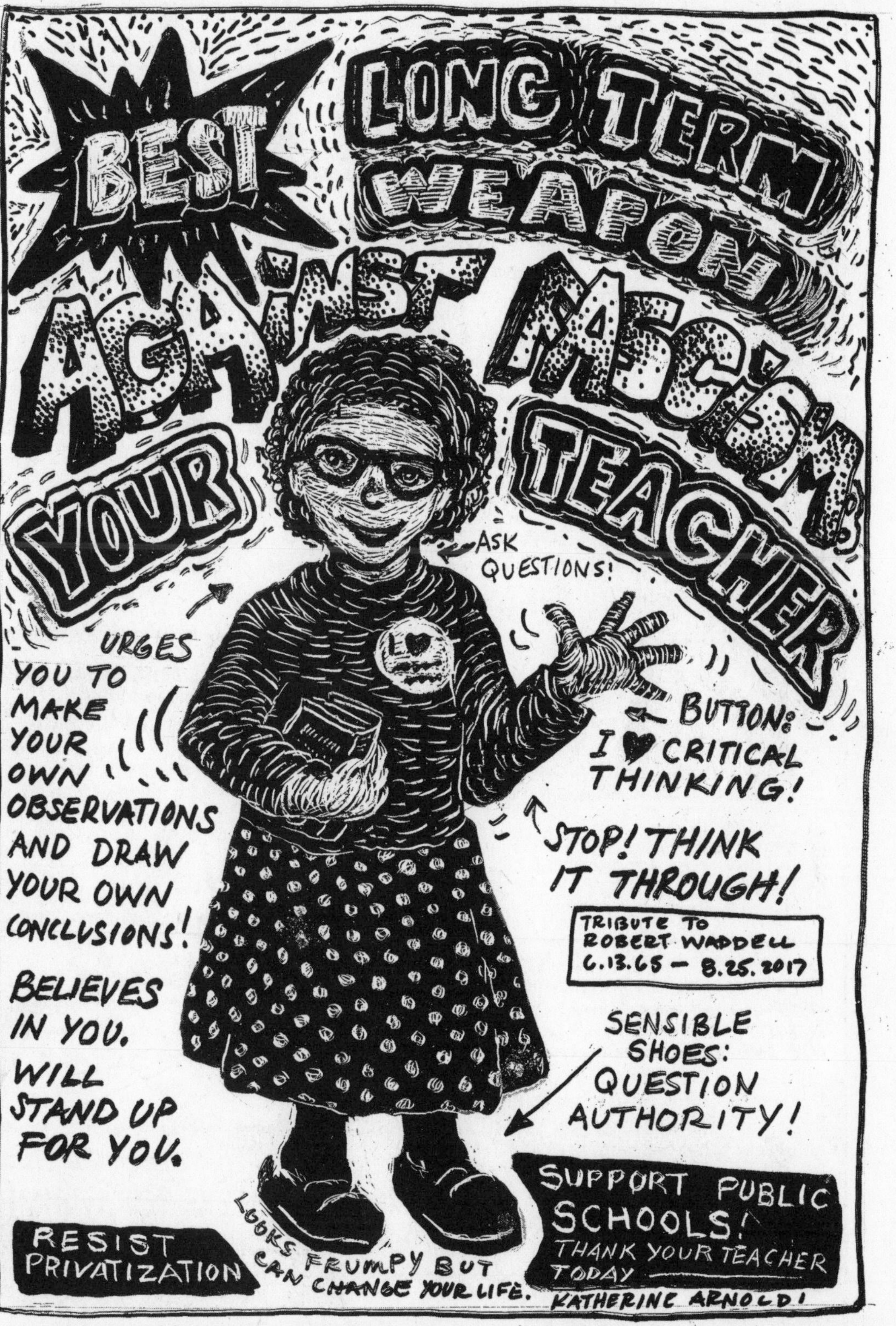
BEST LONG TERM WEAPON AGAINST FASCISM: YOUR TEACHER
ASK QUESTIONS!
URGES YOU TO MAKE YOUR OWN OBSERVATIONS AND DRAW YOUR OWN CONCLUSIONS!
BELIEVES IN YOU.
WILL STAND UP FOR YOU.
BUTTON: I ♥ CRITICAL THINKING!
STOP! THINK IT THROUGH!
TRIBUTE TO ROBERT WADDELL 6.13.65 – 8.25.2017
SENSIBLE SHOES: QUESTION AUTHORITY!
RESIST PRIVATIZATION
LOOKS FRUMPY BUT CAN CHANGE YOUR LIFE.
SUPPORT PUBLIC SCHOOLS!
THANK YOUR TEACHER TODAY
KATHERINE ARNOLD!

THE INTERNATIONAL ANTI-FASCIST DEFENCE FUND

Defending & Supporting Antifa Since 2015

SOLIDARITY IS OUR WEAPON!

Donate today!

The International Anti-Fascist Defence Fund provides direct, immediate support to anti-fascists and anti-racists anywhere in the world, whenever they find themselves in a difficult situation as a result of their stand against hate.

Whether it's replacing damaged or stolen property, paying medical bills, helping them find a safe place to stay, funding legal defence, helping their families, or doing antifa prisoner support, the Fund seeks to alleviate harm that results from doing the right thing.

In its first year alone, the International Anti-Fascist Defence Fund donated thousands of dollars to more than three dozen anti-fascists and anti-racists in ten countries.

Anyone can make a proposal to support an anti-fascist/anti-racist by emailing us at:

antifaintl@gmail.com

We depend on donations to do our work and can accept monthly recurring donations or one-time donations via Patreon, PayPal or credit card. Any group or individual that donates more than $20US/€20/£15 will be invited to help make decisions on proposals the Fund receives.

To donate:

https://intlantifadefence.wordpress.com/donate/

The International Anti-Fascist Defence Fund is a way to show real solidarity with anti-fascists and anti-racists worldwide when they need our support the most!

Find out more:

intlantifadefence.wordpress.com

FIGHTING HATE IS NOT A CRIME!
ANTI-FASCISM = SELF-DEFENCE!

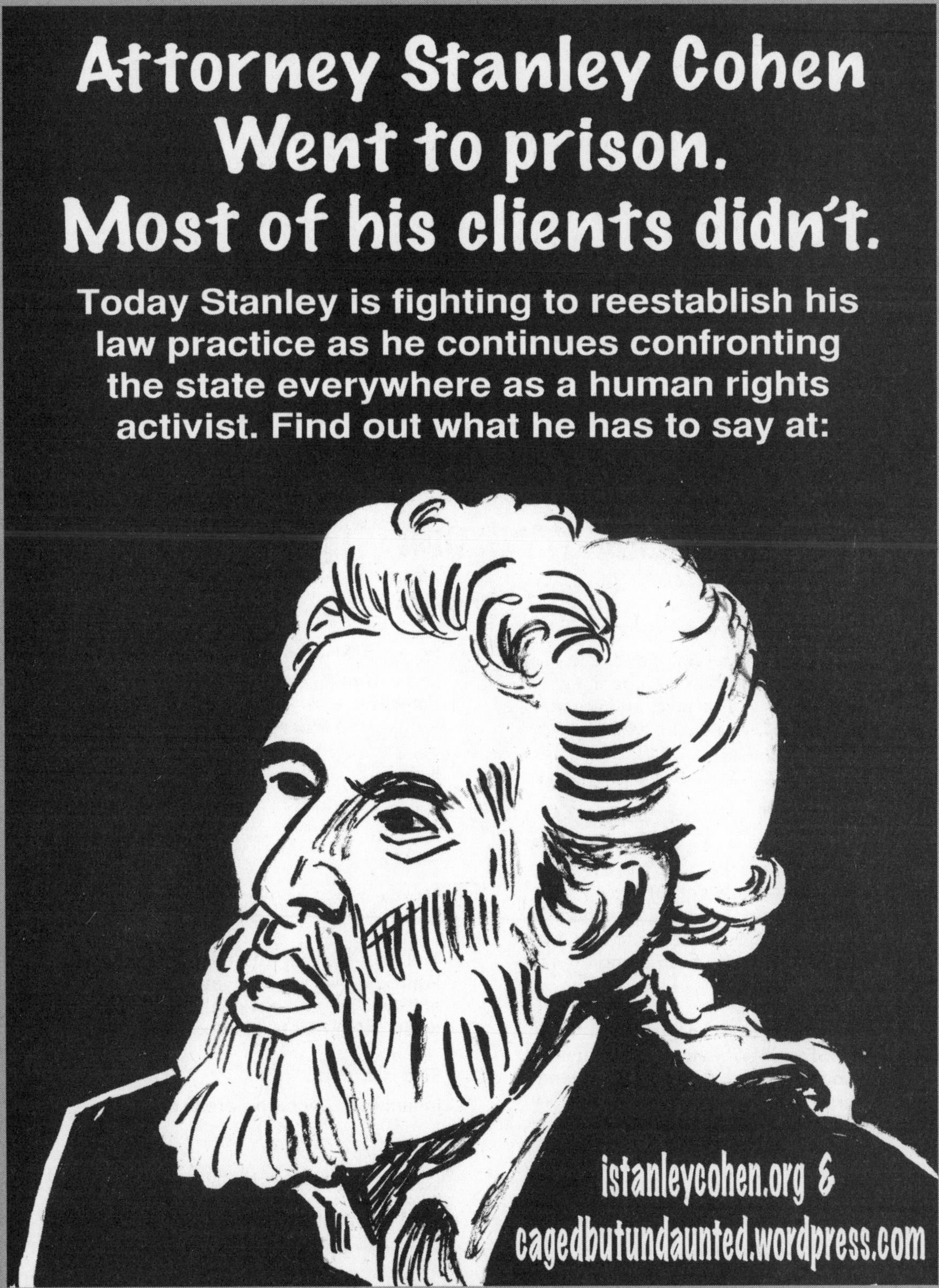
Attorney Stanley Cohen
Went to prison.
Most of his clients didn't.
Today Stanley is fighting to reestablish his law practice as he continues confronting the state everywhere as a human rights activist. Find out what he has to say at:
istanleycohen.org &
cagedbutundaunted.wordpress.com

HEY KIDS, POLITICS!

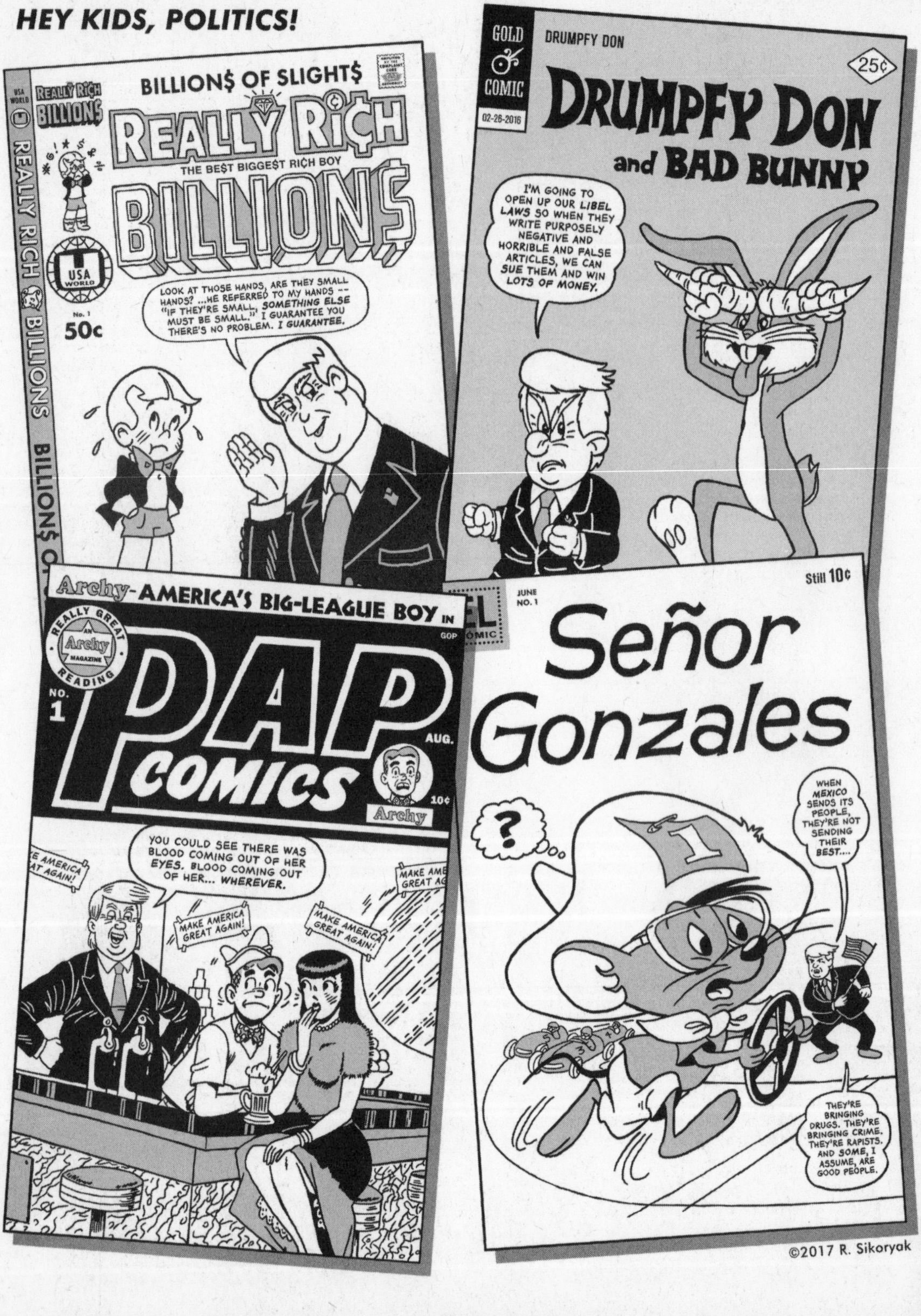

BILLION$ OF SLIGHT$
REALLY RICH BILLION$
REALLY RICH
THE BE$T BIGGE$T RICH BOY
BILLION$
USA WORLD
No. 1
50c
LOOK AT THOSE HANDS, ARE THEY SMALL HANDS? ...HE REFERRED TO MY HANDS -- "IF THEY'RE SMALL, SOMETHING ELSE MUST BE SMALL." I GUARANTEE YOU THERE'S NO PROBLEM. I GUARANTEE.
REALLY RICH BILLIONS BILLION$
GOLD COMIC
02-26-2016
DRUMPFY DON
25¢
DRUMPFY DON
and BAD BUNNY
I'M GOING TO OPEN UP OUR LIBEL LAWS SO WHEN THEY WRITE PURPOSELY NEGATIVE AND HORRIBLE AND FALSE ARTICLES, WE CAN SUE THEM AND WIN LOTS OF MONEY.
Archy-AMERICA'S BIG-LEAGUE BOY IN
REALLY GREAT Archy MAGAZINE READING
GOP
NO. 1
PAP
AUG.
COMICS
10¢
Archy
YOU COULD SEE THERE WAS BLOOD COMING OUT OF HER EYES. BLOOD COMING OUT OF HER... WHEREVER.
MAKE AMERICA GREAT AGAIN!
MAKE AMERICA GREAT AGAIN!
JUNE NO. 1
Still 10¢
Señor Gonzales
?
WHEN MEXICO SENDS ITS PEOPLE, THEY'RE NOT SENDING THEIR BEST....
THEY'RE BRINGING DRUGS. THEY'RE BRINGING CRIME. THEY'RE RAPISTS. AND SOME, I ASSUME, ARE GOOD PEOPLE.

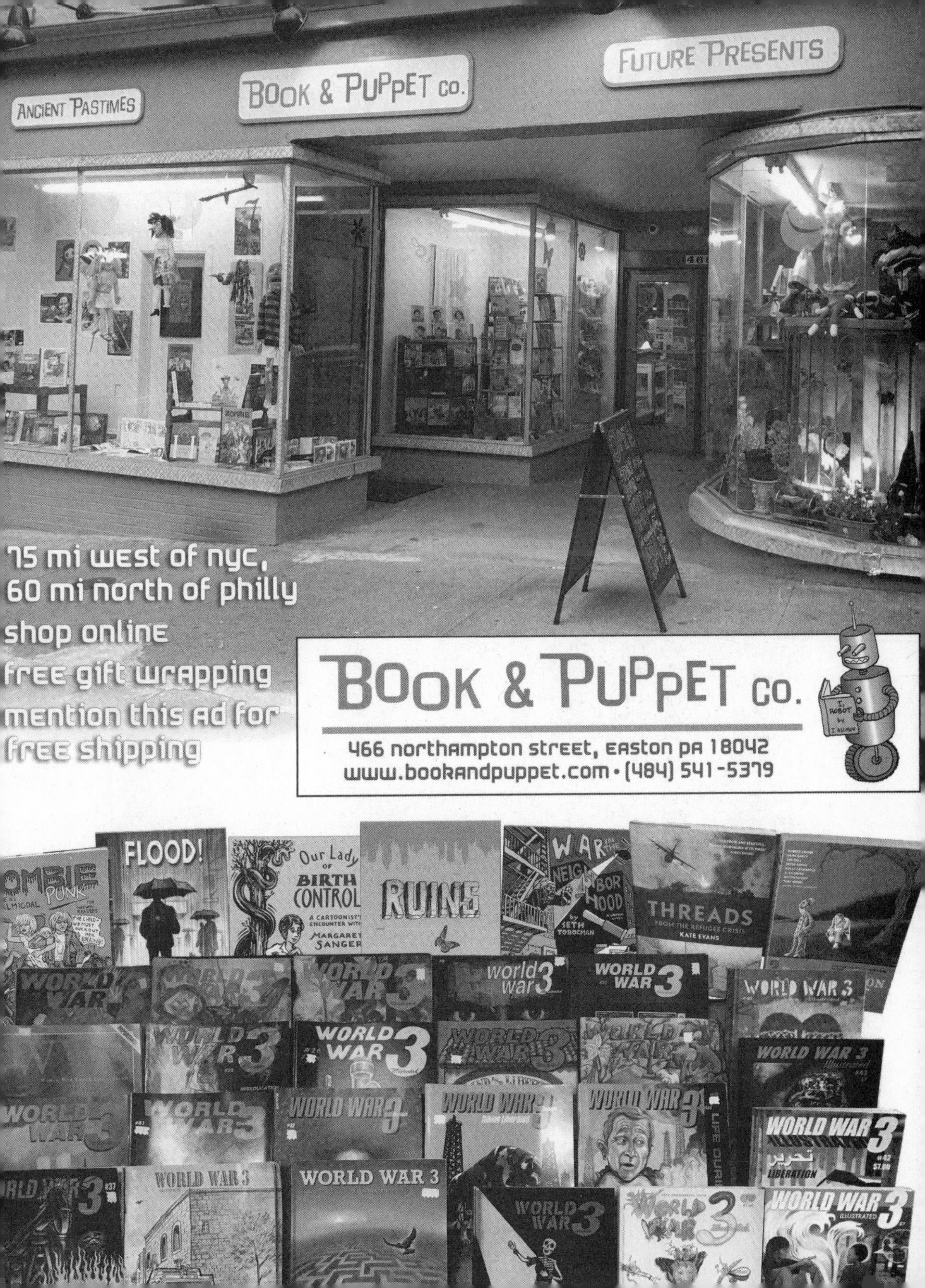
ANCIENT PASTIMES
BOOK & PUPPET CO.
FUTURE PRESENTS
75 mi west of nyc,
60 mi north of philly
shop online
free gift wrapping
mention this ad for
free shipping
BOOK & PUPPET CO.
466 northampton street, easton pa 18042
www.bookandpuppet.com • (484) 541-5379
I, ROBOT by I. ASIMOV

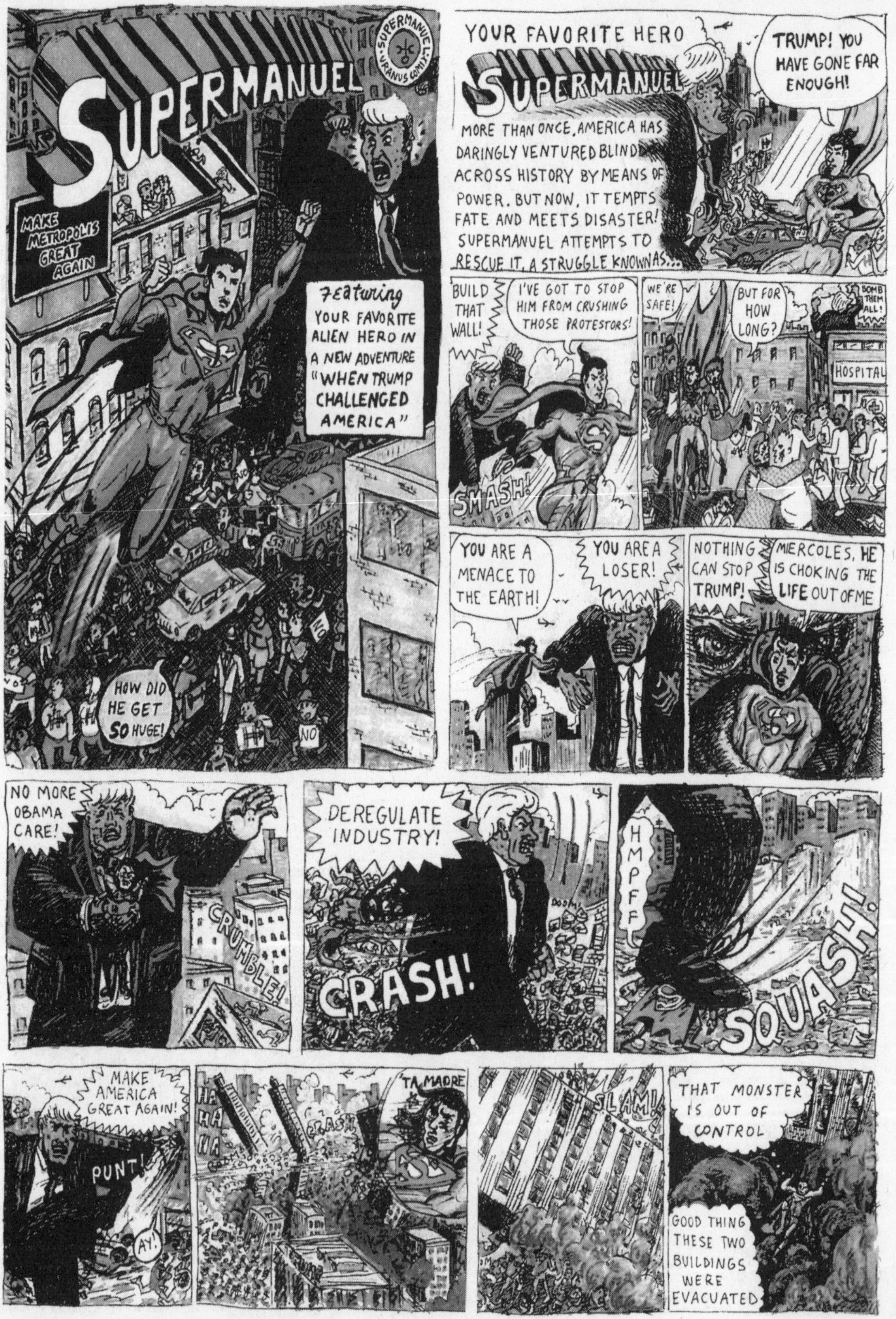
SUPERMANUEL
SUPERMANUEL URANUS COMIX
MAKE METROPOLIS GREAT AGAIN
Featuring YOUR FAVORITE ALIEN HERO IN A NEW ADVENTURE "WHEN TRUMP CHALLENGED AMERICA"
HOW DID HE GET SO HUGE!
NO
YOUR FAVORITE HERO
SUPERMANUEL
MORE THAN ONCE, AMERICA HAS DARINGLY VENTURED BLIND ACROSS HISTORY BY MEANS OF POWER. BUT NOW, IT TEMPTS FATE AND MEETS DISASTER! SUPERMANUEL ATTEMPTS TO RESCUE IT, A STRUGGLE KNOWN AS...
TRUMP! YOU HAVE GONE FAR ENOUGH!
BUILD THAT WALL!
I'VE GOT TO STOP HIM FROM CRUSHING THOSE PROTESTORS!
SMASH!
WE'RE SAFE!
BUT FOR HOW LONG?
BOMB THEM ALL!
HOSPITAL
YOU ARE A MENACE TO THE EARTH!
YOU ARE A LOSER!
NOTHING CAN STOP TRUMP!
MIERCOLES, HE IS CHOKING THE LIFE OUT OF ME
NO MORE OBAMA CARE!
CRUMBLE!
DEREGULATE INDUSTRY!
CRASH!
HMPFF
SQUASH!
MAKE AMERICA GREAT AGAIN!
PUNT!
AY!
HA HA HA
TA MADRE
SLAM!
THAT MONSTER IS OUT OF CONTROL
GOOD THING THESE TWO BUILDINGS WERE EVACUATED

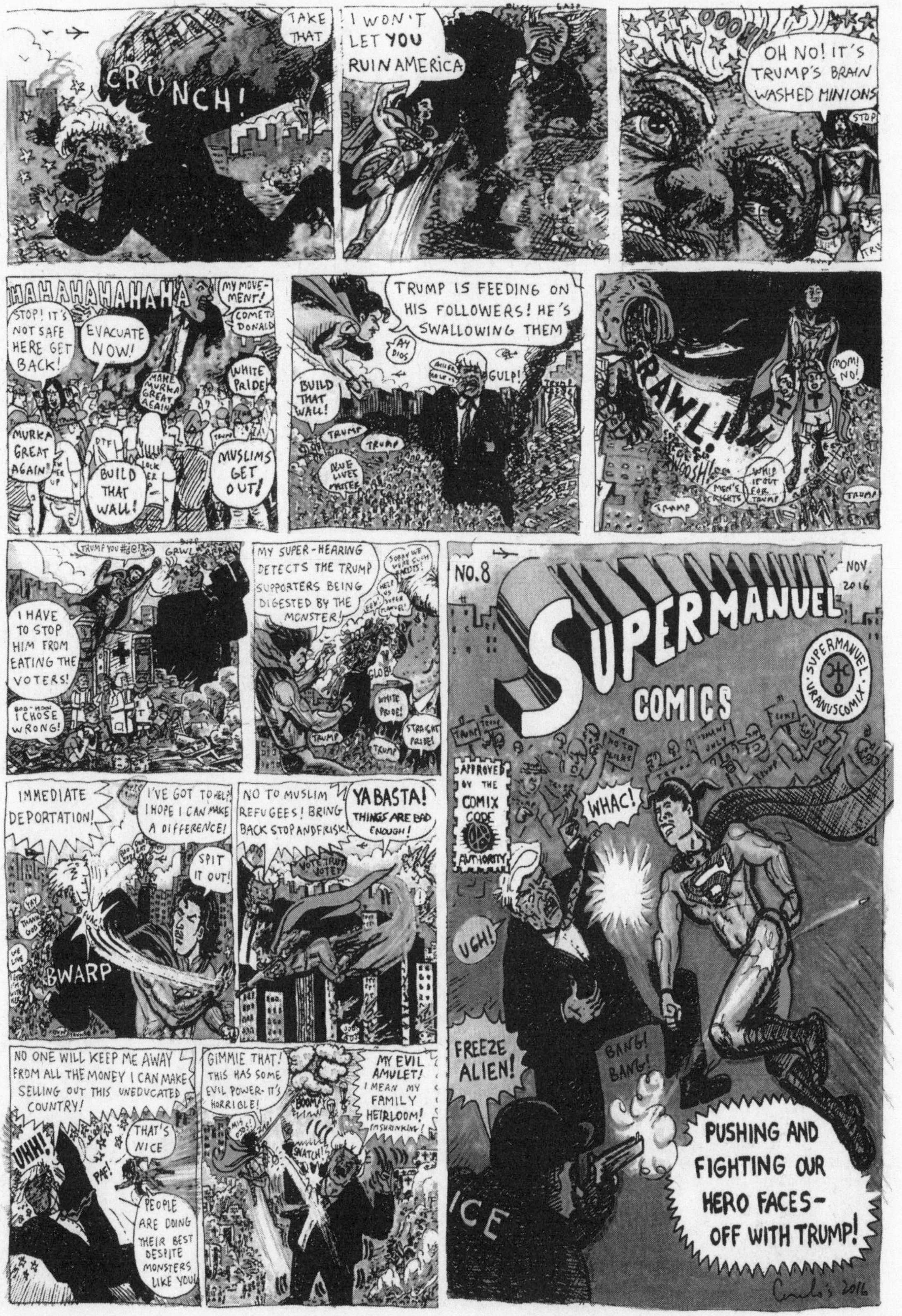
CRUNCH!
TAKE THAT
I WON'T LET YOU RUIN AMERICA
OOOH!
OH NO! IT'S TRUMP'S BRAIN WASHED MINIONS
STOP!
HAHAHAHAHAHA
MY MOVEMENT!
COMET: DONALD
STOP! IT'S NOT SAFE HERE GET BACK!
EVACUATE NOW!
MAKE MURKA GREAT AGAIN
WHITE PRIDE!
MURKA GREAT AGAIN
BUILD THAT WALL!
MUSLIMS GET OUT!
TRUMP IS FEEDING ON HIS FOLLOWERS! HE'S SWALLOWING THEM
AY DIOS
BUILD THAT WALL!
GULP!
TRUMP
TRUMP
BLUE LIVES MATTER
RAWL!!!
MOM! NO!
WHOOSH!
MEN'S RIGHTS
WHIP IT OUT FOR TRUMP
TRUMP
GRWL
I HAVE TO STOP HIM FROM EATING THE VOTERS!
BOO-HOO! I CHOSE WRONG!
MY SUPER-HEARING DETECTS THE TRUMP SUPPORTERS BEING DIGESTED BY THE MONSTER!
GLOB!
WHITE PRIDE!
STRAIGHT PRIDE!
TRUMP
IMMEDIATE DEPORTATION!
I'VE GOT TO HELP! I HOPE I CAN MAKE A DIFFERENCE!
SPIT IT OUT!
BWARP
NO TO MUSLIM REFUGEES! BRING BACK STOP AND FRISK!
YA BASTA! THINGS ARE BAD ENOUGH!
NO ONE WILL KEEP ME AWAY FROM ALL THE MONEY I CAN MAKE SELLING OUT THIS UNEDUCATED COUNTRY!
UHH!
THAT'S NICE
PAF!
PEOPLE ARE DOING THEIR BEST DESPITE MONSTERS LIKE YOU!
GIMMIE THAT! THIS HAS SOME EVIL POWER- IT'S HORRIBLE!
BOOM!
MY EVIL AMULET! I MEAN MY FAMILY HEIRLOOM!
SNATCH!
NO.8
SUPERMANUEL
NOV. 2016
COMICS
SUPERMANUEL URANUSCOMIX
APPROVED BY THE COMIX CODE AUTHORITY
WHAC!
UGH!
FREEZE ALIEN!
BANG! BANG!
ICE
PUSHING AND FIGHTING OUR HERO FACES-OFF WITH TRUMP!
Carlos 2016

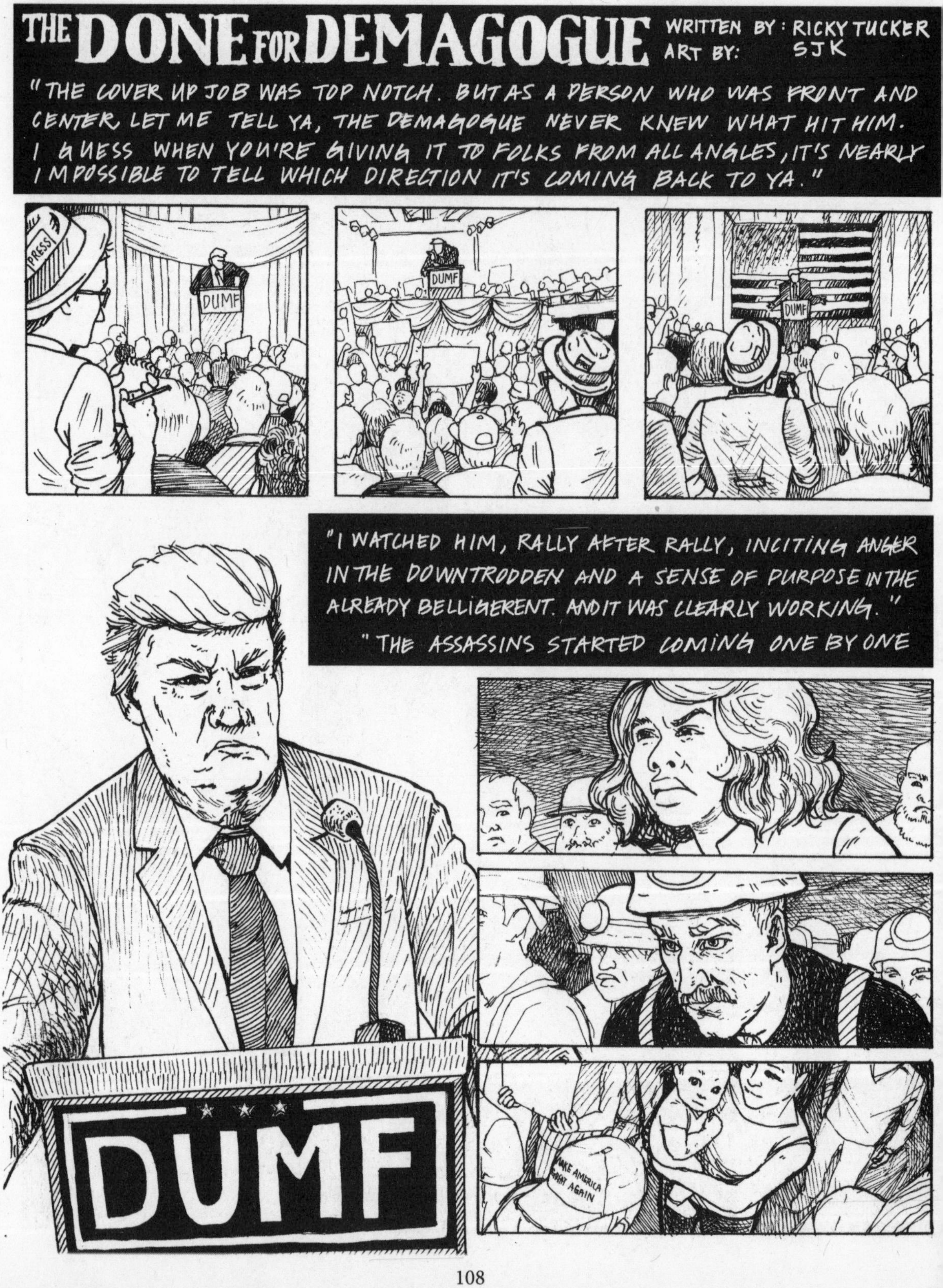
THE DONE FOR DEMAGOGUE
WRITTEN BY: RICKY TUCKER
ART BY: SJK
"THE COVER UP JOB WAS TOP NOTCH. BUT AS A PERSON WHO WAS FRONT AND CENTER, LET ME TELL YA, THE DEMAGOGUE NEVER KNEW WHAT HIT HIM. I GUESS WHEN YOU'RE GIVING IT TO FOLKS FROM ALL ANGLES, IT'S NEARLY IMPOSSIBLE TO TELL WHICH DIRECTION IT'S COMING BACK TO YA."
PRESS
DUMF
DUMF
DUMF
"I WATCHED HIM, RALLY AFTER RALLY, INCITING ANGER IN THE DOWNTRODDEN AND A SENSE OF PURPOSE IN THE ALREADY BELLIGERENT. AND IT WAS CLEARLY WORKING."
"THE ASSASSINS STARTED COMING ONE BY ONE
DUMF
MAKE AMERICA GREAT AGAIN

"THE CALIFORNIA CONGRESSWOMAN WAS BRASSY AND RESPECTED. SHE'D BEEN MAKING THE ROUNDS, REFERRING TO THE DEMAGOGUE AS A FRAUD ON SUNDAY'S BROADCAST ROUND UPS, AND STORMING IMMEDIATELY OUT OF INTERVIEWS WHERE HIS NONSENSE WAS EVEN SLIGHTLY ENTERTAINED. I WATCHED AS SHE MADE A BEELINE UP THE AISLE OF THE CONVENTION CENTER IN TULSA THAT DAY. KNIFE IN PURSE IN TOW."

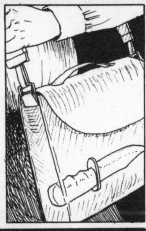

"HER STRIDE WAS QUICK, BOLD AND BRASH — BUT UNFORTUNATELY SHE WAS ALSO BLACK."

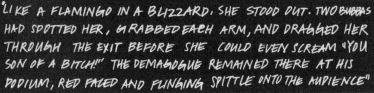

"LIKE A FLAMINGO IN A BLIZZARD. SHE STOOD OUT. TWO BUBBAS HAD SPOTTED HER, GRABBED EACH ARM, AND DRAGGED HER THROUGH THE EXIT BEFORE SHE COULD EVEN SCREAM "YOU SON OF A BITCH!" THE DEMAGOGUE REMAINED THERE AT HIS PODIUM, RED FACED AND FLINGING SPITTLE ONTO THE AUDIENCE"

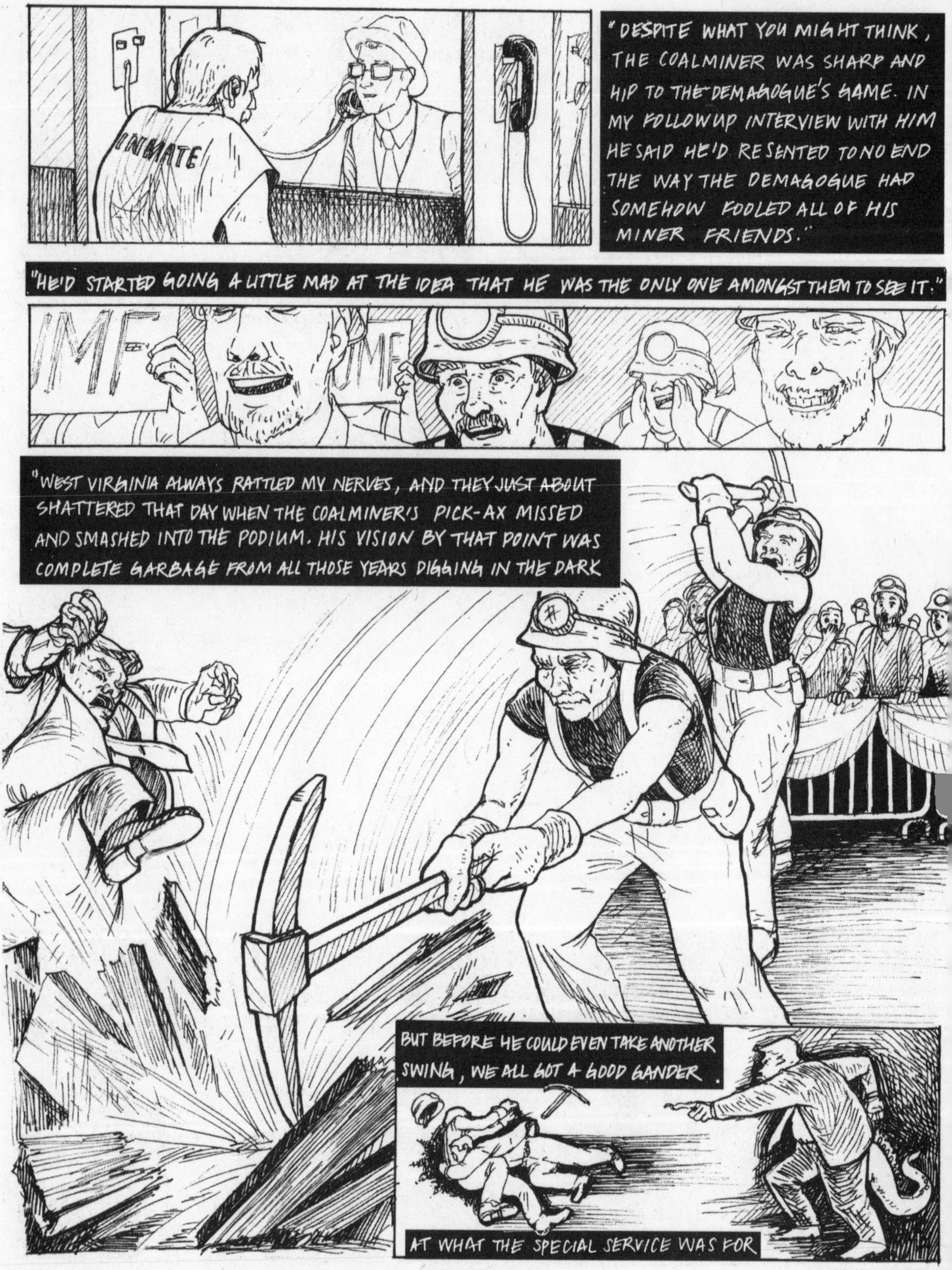
INMATE
"DESPITE WHAT YOU MIGHT THINK, THE COALMINER WAS SHARP AND HIP TO THE DEMAGOGUE'S GAME. IN MY FOLLOWUP INTERVIEW WITH HIM HE SAID HE'D RESENTED TO NO END THE WAY THE DEMAGOGUE HAD SOMEHOW FOOLED ALL OF HIS MINER FRIENDS."
"HE'D STARTED GOING A LITTLE MAD AT THE IDEA THAT HE WAS THE ONLY ONE AMONGST THEM TO SEE IT."
"WEST VIRGINIA ALWAYS RATTLED MY NERVES, AND THEY JUST ABOUT SHATTERED THAT DAY WHEN THE COALMINER'S PICK-AX MISSED AND SMASHED INTO THE PODIUM. HIS VISION BY THAT POINT WAS COMPLETE GARBAGE FROM ALL THOSE YEARS DIGGING IN THE DARK
BUT BEFORE HE COULD EVEN TAKE ANOTHER SWING, WE ALL GOT A GOOD GANDER
AT WHAT THE SPECIAL SERVICE WAS FOR

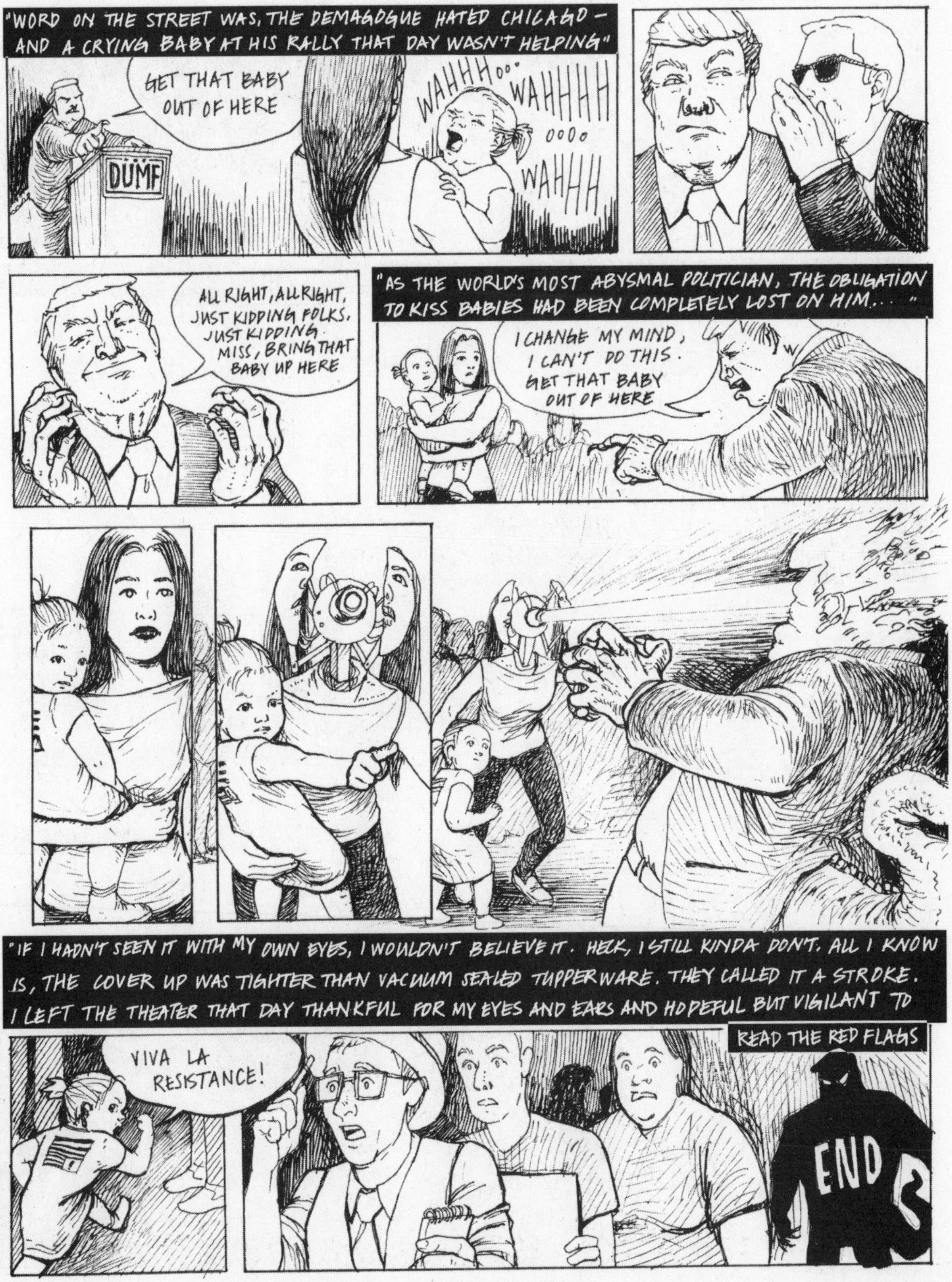

"WORD ON THE STREET WAS, THE DEMAGOGUE HATED CHICAGO — AND A CRYING BABY AT HIS RALLY THAT DAY WASN'T HELPING"
GET THAT BABY OUT OF HERE
DÜMF
WAHHHooo WAHHHHH oooo WAHHHH
ALL RIGHT, ALL RIGHT, JUST KIDDING FOLKS. JUST KIDDING. MISS, BRING THAT BABY UP HERE
"AS THE WORLD'S MOST ABYSMAL POLITICIAN, THE OBLIGATION TO KISS BABIES HAD BEEN COMPLETELY LOST ON HIM..."
I CHANGE MY MIND, I CAN'T DO THIS. GET THAT BABY OUT OF HERE
"IF I HADN'T SEEN IT WITH MY OWN EYES, I WOULDN'T BELIEVE IT. HECK, I STILL KINDA DON'T. ALL I KNOW IS, THE COVER UP WAS TIGHTER THAN VACUUM SEALED TUPPERWARE. THEY CALLED IT A STROKE. I LEFT THE THEATER THAT DAY THANKFUL FOR MY EYES AND EARS AND HOPEFUL BUT VIGILANT TO READ THE RED FLAGS
VIVA LA RESISTANCE!
END

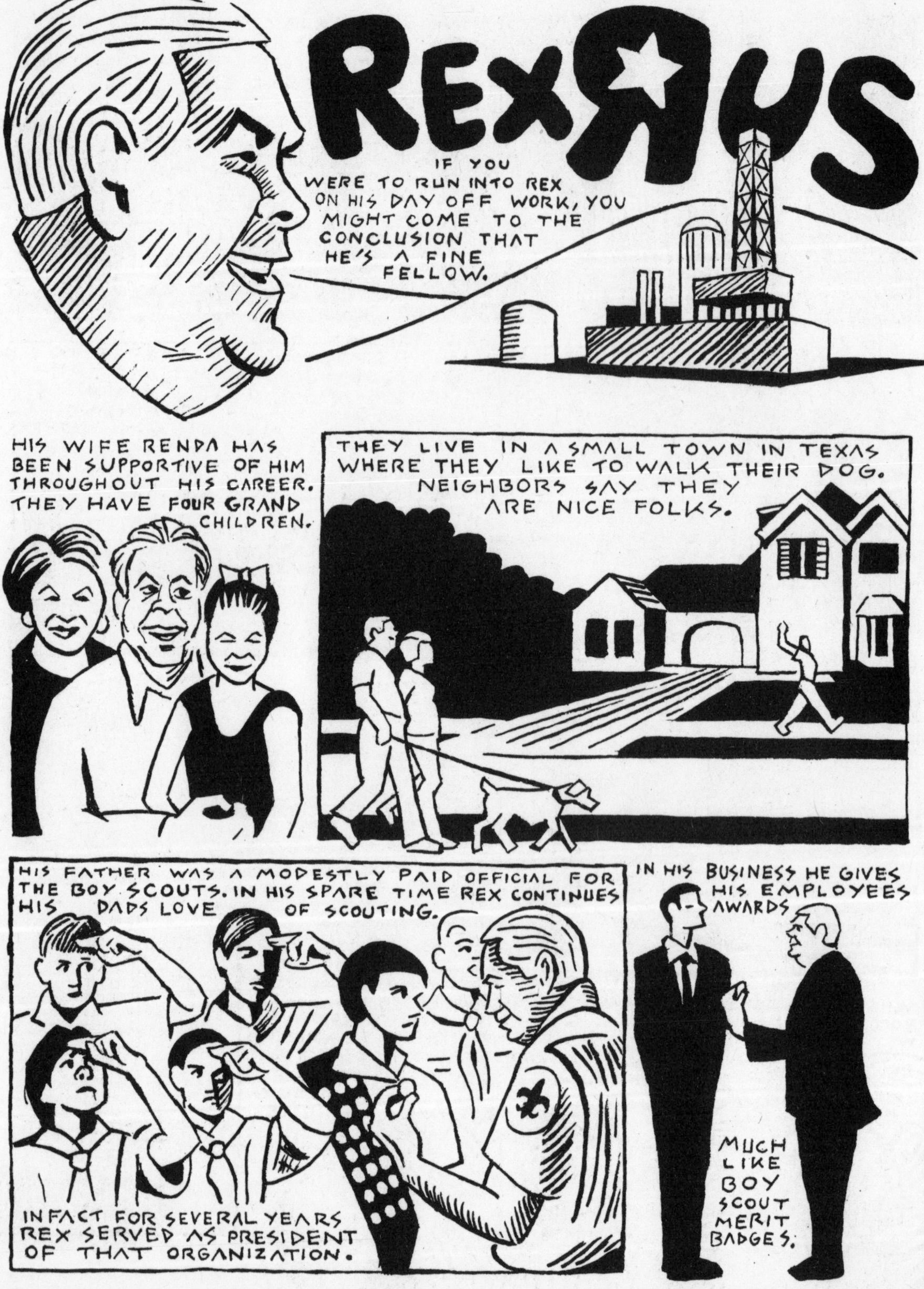

REX R US
IF YOU WERE TO RUN INTO REX ON HIS DAY OFF WORK, YOU MIGHT COME TO THE CONCLUSION THAT HE'S A FINE FELLOW.
HIS WIFE RENDA HAS BEEN SUPPORTIVE OF HIM THROUGHOUT HIS CAREER. THEY HAVE FOUR GRAND CHILDREN.
THEY LIVE IN A SMALL TOWN IN TEXAS WHERE THEY LIKE TO WALK THEIR DOG. NEIGHBORS SAY THEY ARE NICE FOLKS.
HIS FATHER WAS A MODESTLY PAID OFFICIAL FOR THE BOY SCOUTS. IN HIS SPARE TIME REX CONTINUES HIS DADS LOVE OF SCOUTING.
INFACT FOR SEVERAL YEARS REX SERVED AS PRESIDENT OF THAT ORGANIZATION.
IN HIS BUSINESS HE GIVES HIS EMPLOYEES AWARDS
MUCH LIKE BOY SCOUT MERIT BADGES.

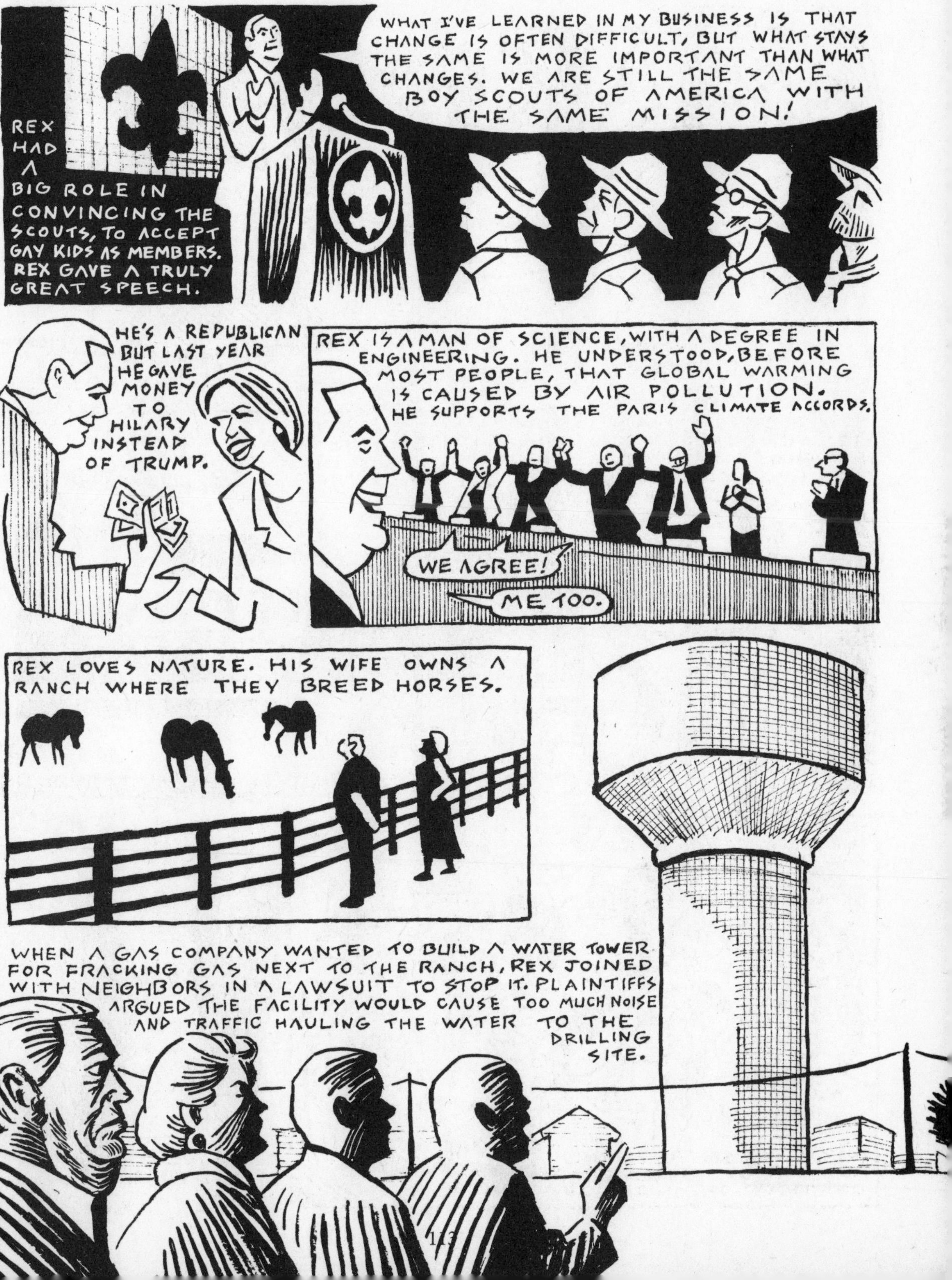

REX HAD A BIG ROLE IN CONVINCING THE SCOUTS, TO ACCEPT GAY KIDS AS MEMBERS. REX GAVE A TRULY GREAT SPEECH.
WHAT I'VE LEARNED IN MY BUSINESS IS THAT CHANGE IS OFTEN DIFFICULT, BUT WHAT STAYS THE SAME IS MORE IMPORTANT THAN WHAT CHANGES. WE ARE STILL THE SAME BOY SCOUTS OF AMERICA WITH THE SAME MISSION!
HE'S A REPUBLICAN BUT LAST YEAR HE GAVE MONEY TO HILARY INSTEAD OF TRUMP.
REX IS A MAN OF SCIENCE, WITH A DEGREE IN ENGINEERING. HE UNDERSTOOD, BEFORE MOST PEOPLE, THAT GLOBAL WARMING IS CAUSED BY AIR POLLUTION. HE SUPPORTS THE PARIS CLIMATE ACCORDS.
WE AGREE!
ME TOO.
REX LOVES NATURE. HIS WIFE OWNS A RANCH WHERE THEY BREED HORSES.
WHEN A GAS COMPANY WANTED TO BUILD A WATER TOWER FOR FRACKING GAS NEXT TO THE RANCH, REX JOINED WITH NEIGHBORS IN A LAWSUIT TO STOP IT. PLAINTIFFS ARGUED THE FACILITY WOULD CAUSE TOO MUCH NOISE AND TRAFFIC HAULING THE WATER TO THE DRILLING SITE.

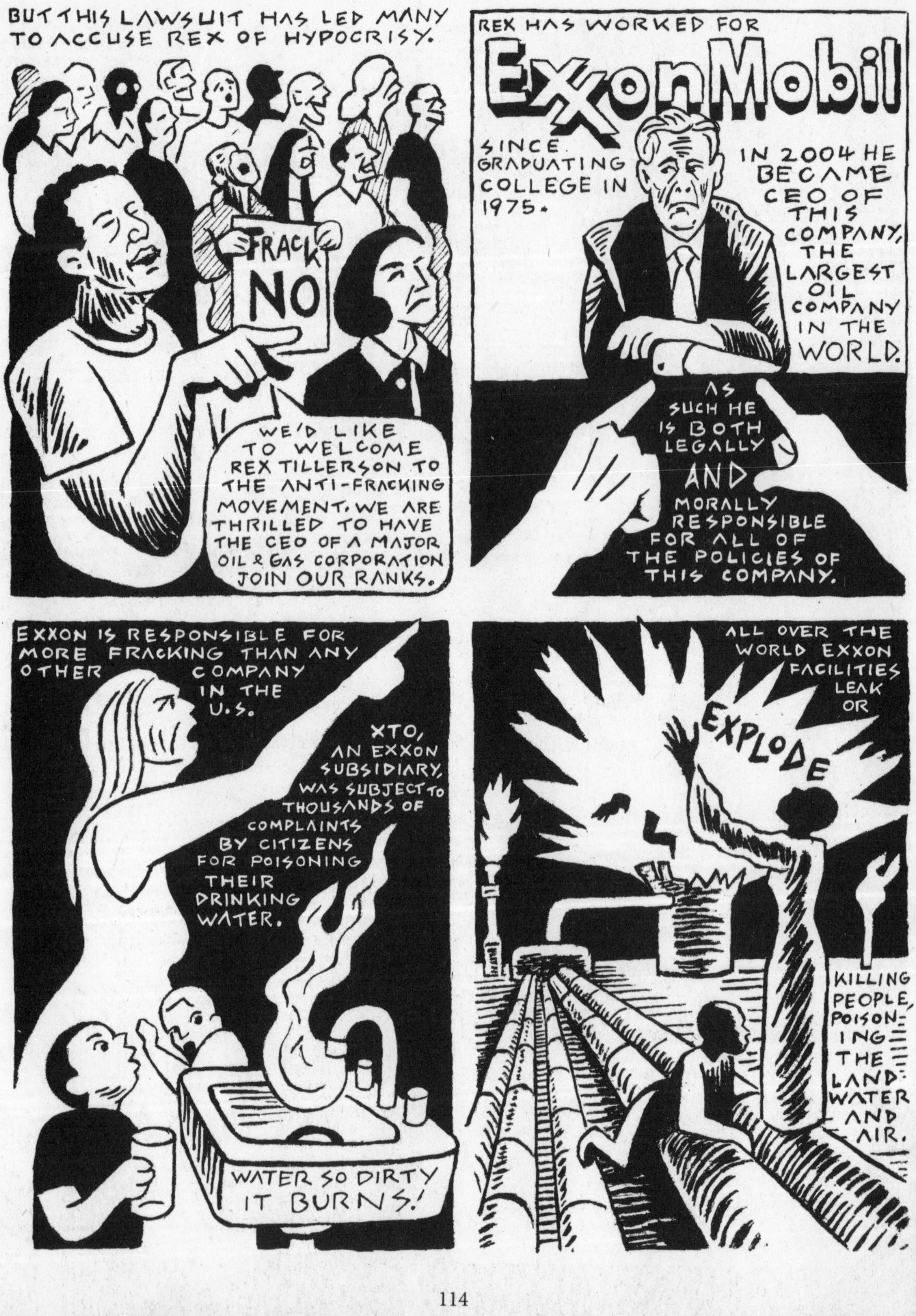
BUT THIS LAWSUIT HAS LED MANY TO ACCUSE REX OF HYPOCRISY.
FRACK NO
WE'D LIKE TO WELCOME REX TILLERSON TO THE ANTI-FRACKING MOVEMENT. WE ARE THRILLED TO HAVE THE CEO OF A MAJOR OIL & GAS CORPORATION JOIN OUR RANKS.
REX HAS WORKED FOR
ExxonMobil
SINCE GRADUATING COLLEGE IN 1975.
IN 2004 HE BECAME CEO OF THIS COMPANY, THE LARGEST OIL COMPANY IN THE WORLD.
AS SUCH HE IS BOTH LEGALLY AND MORALLY RESPONSIBLE FOR ALL OF THE POLICIES OF THIS COMPANY.
EXXON IS RESPONSIBLE FOR MORE FRACKING THAN ANY OTHER COMPANY IN THE U.S.
XTO, AN EXXON SUBSIDIARY, WAS SUBJECT TO THOUSANDS OF COMPLAINTS BY CITIZENS FOR POISONING THEIR DRINKING WATER.
WATER SO DIRTY IT BURNS!
ALL OVER THE WORLD EXXON FACILITIES LEAK OR
EXPLODE
KILLING PEOPLE, POISONING THE LAND WATER AND AIR.

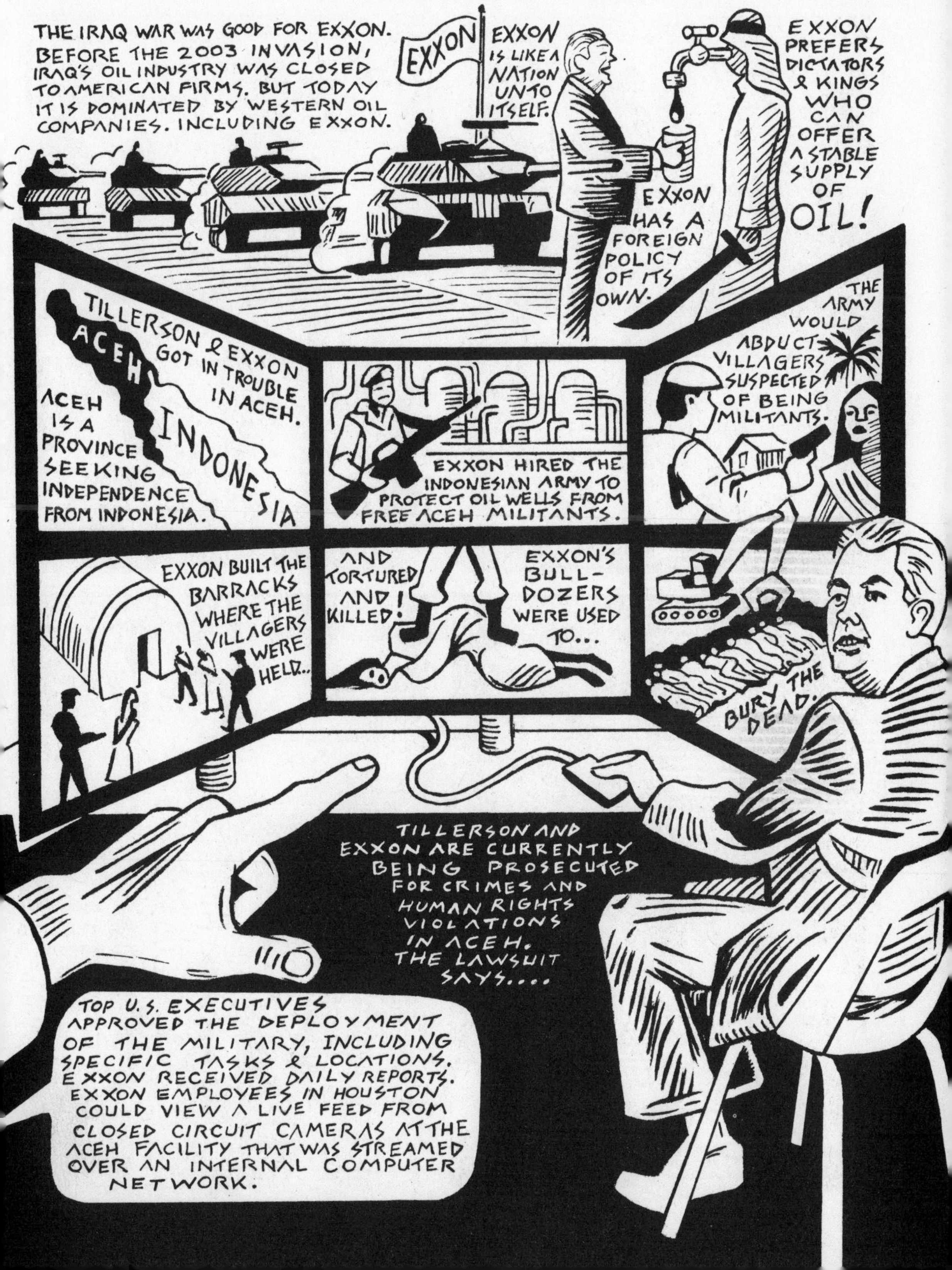
THE IRAQ WAR WAS GOOD FOR EXXON. BEFORE THE 2003 INVASION, IRAQ'S OIL INDUSTRY WAS CLOSED TO AMERICAN FIRMS. BUT TODAY IT IS DOMINATED BY WESTERN OIL COMPANIES. INCLUDING EXXON.
EXXON
EXXON IS LIKE A NATION UNTO ITSELF.
EXXON PREFERS DICTATORS & KINGS WHO CAN OFFER A STABLE SUPPLY OF OIL!
EXXON HAS A FOREIGN POLICY OF ITS OWN.
TILLERSON & EXXON GOT IN TROUBLE IN ACEH.
ACEH
INDONESIA
ACEH IS A PROVINCE SEEKING INDEPENDENCE FROM INDONESIA.
EXXON HIRED THE INDONESIAN ARMY TO PROTECT OIL WELLS FROM FREE ACEH MILITANTS.
THE ARMY WOULD ABDUCT VILLAGERS SUSPECTED OF BEING MILITANTS.
EXXON BUILT THE BARRACKS WHERE THE VILLAGERS WERE HELD...
AND TORTURED AND KILLED!
EXXON'S BULL-DOZERS WERE USED TO...
BURY THE DEAD.
TILLERSON AND EXXON ARE CURRENTLY BEING PROSECUTED FOR CRIMES AND HUMAN RIGHTS VIOLATIONS IN ACEH. THE LAWSUIT SAYS....
TOP U.S. EXECUTIVES APPROVED THE DEPLOYMENT OF THE MILITARY, INCLUDING SPECIFIC TASKS & LOCATIONS. EXXON RECEIVED DAILY REPORTS. EXXON EMPLOYEES IN HOUSTON COULD VIEW A LIVE FEED FROM CLOSED CIRCUIT CAMERAS AT THE ACEH FACILITY THAT WAS STREAMED OVER AN INTERNAL COMPUTER NETWORK.

LIKE AN ICEBERG, MUCH OF EXXON IS HIDDEN.

EXXON LIED ABOUT CLIMATE CHANGE. IN THE 1970s EXXON'S SCIENTISTS INFORMED THEM THAT BURNING FOSSIL FUELS WOULD LEAD TO CATASTROPHIC GLOBAL WARMING. BUT EXXON DIDN'T SHARE THIS WITH THE PUBLIC. INSTEAD THEY COVERED IT UP. EXXON AND TILLERSON ARE BEING SUED FOR THIS TOO.

TILLERSON WAS ALSO PRESIDENT OF EXXON-NEFTGAS, THE SUBSIDIARY RESPONSIBLE FOR DEALING WITH RUSSIA. HE MADE EXTENSIVE DEALS THERE. AS A RESULT, EXXON NOW HAS ACCESS TO MORE OIL IN RUSSIA THAN THEY DO IN THE UNITED STATES.

REX HAS A GOOD RELATIONSHIP WITH MR. PUTIN.

BECAUSE OF RUSSIA'S ATTEMPT TO DOMINATE UKRAINE...

THE OBAMA ADMINISTRATION PLACED SANCTIONS ON RUSSIA.

THESE SANCTIONS PREVENT EXXON FROM SELLING THEIR RUSSIAN OIL.

UKRAINE

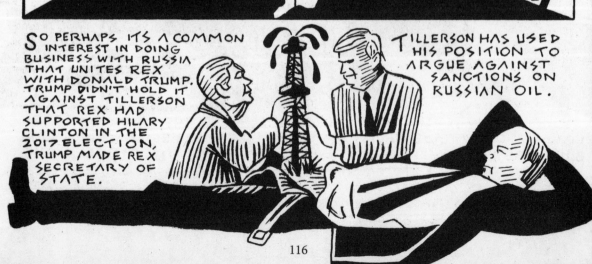

SO PERHAPS ITS A COMMON INTEREST IN DOING BUSINESS WITH RUSSIA THAT UNITES REX WITH DONALD TRUMP. TRUMP DIDN'T HOLD IT AGAINST TILLERSON THAT REX HAD SUPPORTED HILARY CLINTON IN THE 2017 ELECTION. TRUMP MADE REX SECRETARY OF STATE.

TILLERSON HAS USED HIS POSITION TO ARGUE AGAINST SANCTIONS ON RUSSIAN OIL.

TRUMPS CABINET WAS SPLIT.

REX OPPOSSED TRUMPS DECISION TO PULL OUT OF THE PARIS CLIMATE ACCORD. BUT IN THE END...

WELL, IT WAS A POLICY DECISION, & I THINK IT'S IMPORTANT EVERYONE RECOGNIZE THE U.S. HAS A TERRIFIC RECORD OF CUTTING CARBON EMISSIONS. THAT WONT CHANGE....

REX TRIED TO CALM FEARS ABOUT TRUMP POLICIES.

SO REX APPEARS TO BE THE "GROWN-UP IN THE ROOM". IN THIS CAR-LOAD OF CLIMATE DENIALISTS HE LOOKS LIKE THE DESIGNATED DRIVER. BUT THERE'S ANOTHER WAY OF LOOKING AT IT. IF TILLERSON IS ONE OF THE ONLY CABINET MEMBERS WHO BELIEVES IN CLIMATE CHANGE, THEN ANY REGULATIONS ON POLLUTION THAT COME OUT OF THIS ADMINISTRATION WILL BE THOSE PROPOSED BY REX AND ACCEPTABLE TO EXXON. MR. EXXON IS IN THE DRIVER'S SEAT.

SO WHO IS REX TILLERSON? THE NICE NEIGHBOR? THE BOY SCOUT LEADER?

OR T-REX? OR MAYBE HE'S BOTH?

WE'VE ALL GOT CONTRADICTIONS.

UNDER PRESSURE FROM A WELL ORGANIZED PUBLIC GOVERNOR CUOMO HAS BANNED FRACKING IN NEW YORK STATE.

BUT CUOMO HAS APPROVED PIPELINES THAT CARRY FRACKED GAS FROM OTHER STATES.

NONE OF US WANTS OIL AND GAS INFRASTRUCTURE ON OUR BLOCK.

IF IT DOESN'T EXPLODE IT WILL GIVE YOU CANCER.

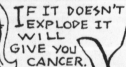

WE ALL USE THE ENERGY PRODUCED THROUGH BURNING FOSSIL FUELS.

SO FOSSIL FUEL FACILITIES WIND UP BEING BUILT IN SOME ONE ELSE'S BACK YARD. USUALLY SOMEONE POOR.

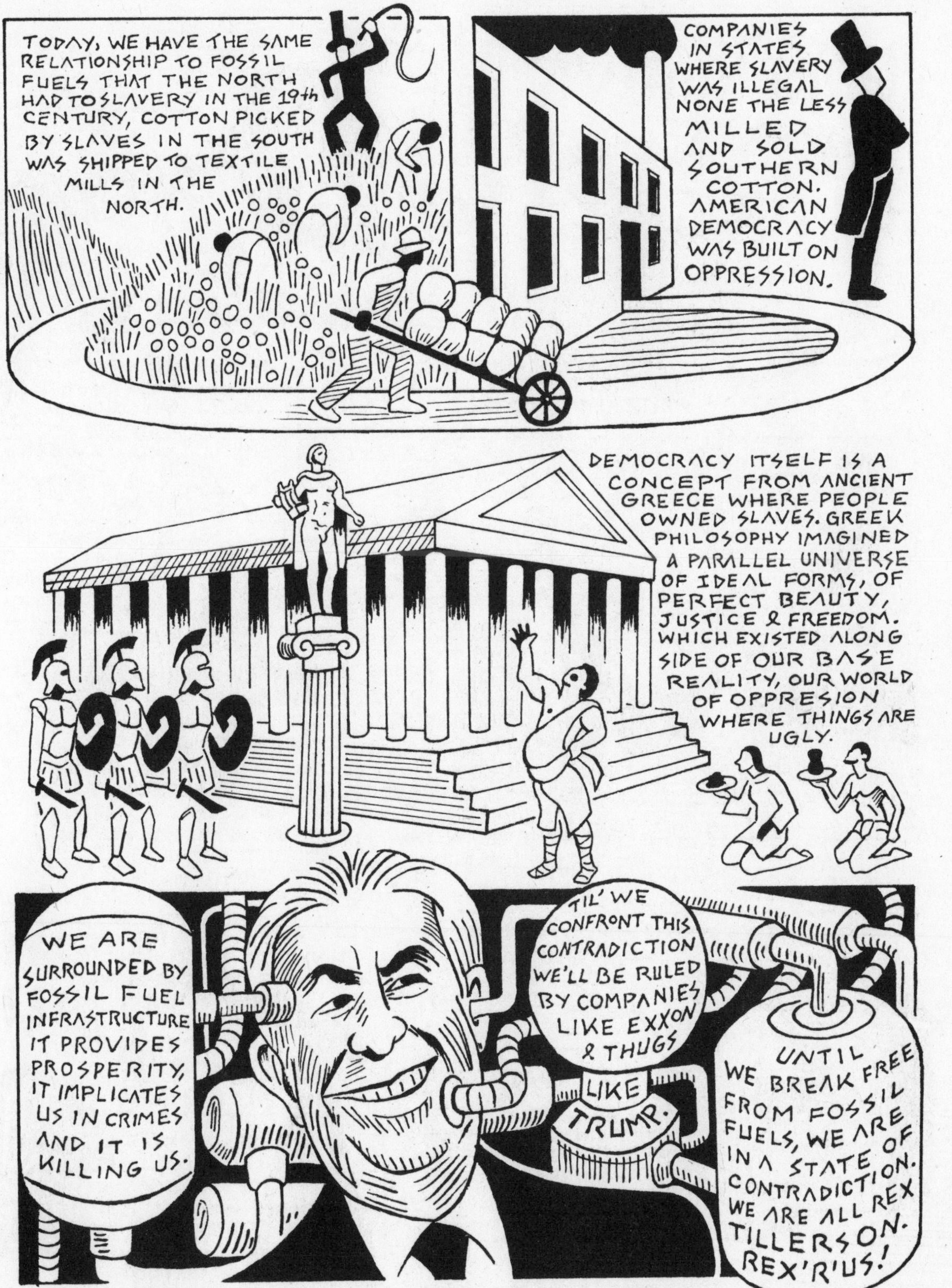
TODAY, WE HAVE THE SAME RELATIONSHIP TO FOSSIL FUELS THAT THE NORTH HAD TO SLAVERY IN THE 19th CENTURY, COTTON PICKED BY SLAVES IN THE SOUTH WAS SHIPPED TO TEXTILE MILLS IN THE NORTH.
COMPANIES IN STATES WHERE SLAVERY WAS ILLEGAL NONE THE LESS MILLED AND SOLD SOUTHERN COTTON. AMERICAN DEMOCRACY WAS BUILT ON OPPRESSION.
DEMOCRACY ITSELF IS A CONCEPT FROM ANCIENT GREECE WHERE PEOPLE OWNED SLAVES. GREEK PHILOSOPHY IMAGINED A PARALLEL UNIVERSE OF IDEAL FORMS, OF PERFECT BEAUTY, JUSTICE & FREEDOM. WHICH EXISTED ALONG SIDE OF OUR BASE REALITY, OUR WORLD OF OPPRESION WHERE THINGS ARE UGLY.
WE ARE SURROUNDED BY FOSSIL FUEL INFRASTRUCTURE IT PROVIDES PROSPERITY, IT IMPLICATES US IN CRIMES AND IT IS KILLING US.
TIL' WE CONFRONT THIS CONTRADICTION WE'LL BE RULED BY COMPANIES LIKE EXXON & THUGS
LIKE
TRUMP.
UNTIL WE BREAK FREE FROM FOSSIL FUELS, WE ARE IN A STATE OF CONTRADICTION. WE ARE ALL REX TILLERSON. REX'R'US!

HOW YOU'VE BEEN HOLDING UP

a conversation about healthcare w. Erin Schick by Avy Lora

ERIN:
· POET
· SOCIAL WORKER
· ACTIVIST

ERIN AND I TALK A LOT ABOUT WHAT IT MEANS TO LIVE WITH A DISABILITY.

ERIN'S CHAIR

I GUESS IT COMES WITH THE TERRITORY.

THESE DAYS IT COMES UP MORE + MORE.

NOT JUST BETWEEN US, BUT BETWEEN THE WORLD AND OUR PRE-EXISTING CONDITIONS.

BUT FOR A LOT OF US, THAT DIALOGUE DIRECTLY IMPACTS OUR ABILITY TO SURVIVE.

I MEAN-- WE'RE ALL REALLY VULNERABLE RIGHT NOW.

I'M LUCKY TO HAVE GOOD INSURANCE, BUT THAT'S ONLY AVAILABLE TO ME BECAUSE OF THE ACA-- AND RACE + CLASS PRIVILEGE-- ANY CHANGES TO THAT COULD MAKE ME UNINSURABLE IN THE NEXT FEW YEARS.

AND MEDICAID IS UP IN THE AIR, WHICH ALLOWS DISABLED PEOPLE TO STAY ALIVE AND IN THEIR HOMES-- INSTEAD OF IN NURSING HOMES-- IF MEDICAID IS CUT, I HAVE FRIENDS WHO WON'T HAVE AIDES TO HOOK UP THEIR MACHINES, OR GET THEM OUT OF BED IN THE MORNING.

I'M TRYING TO QUALIFY FOR MEDICAID + SSI RIGHT NOW--

I DON'T KNOW WHAT I'LL DO IF IT'S NOT AVAILABLE.

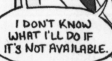

ERIN'S REGULAR TREATMENTS ADD UP TO TENS OF THOUSANDS OF DOLLARS YEARLY.

WITHOUT COVERAGE, THEY CAN'T PAY AND WITHOUT TREATMENT, THEY WOULD DIE.

I TRY NOT TO IMAGINE WHAT WOULD HAPPEN TO THE PEOPLE IN MY LIFE IF THE PROPOSED CUTS GO THROUGH.

YEAH, MY PARTNER'S ON MEDICAID...

NOT ONLY ARE HIS CONDITIONS DISQUALIFYING, BUT HIS MOTHER'S AS WELL, WHO'S HAVING A BABY SOON.

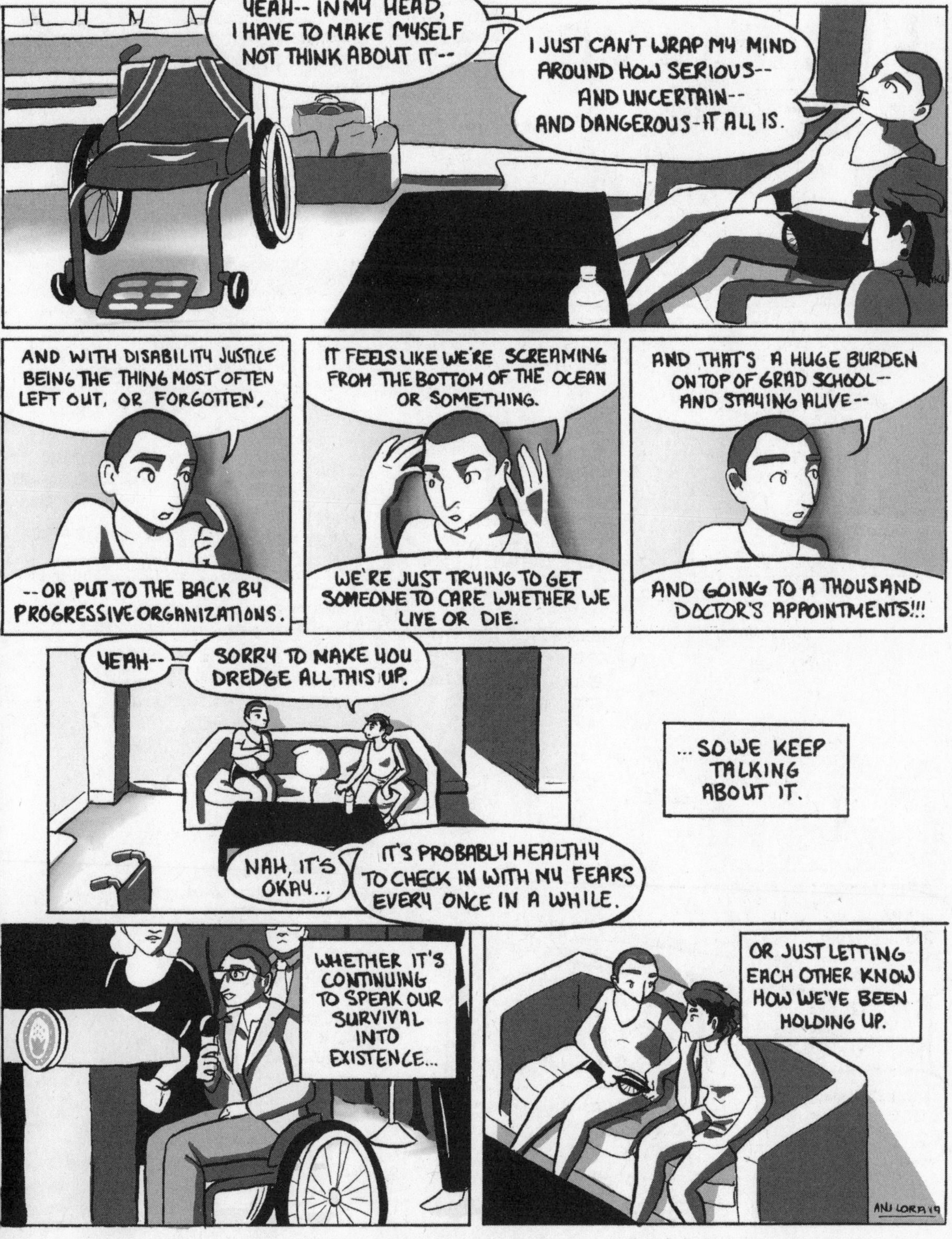
YEAH-- IN MY HEAD, I HAVE TO MAKE MYSELF NOT THINK ABOUT IT--
I JUST CAN'T WRAP MY MIND AROUND HOW SERIOUS-- AND UNCERTAIN-- AND DANGEROUS- IT ALL IS.
AND WITH DISABILITY JUSTICE BEING THE THING MOST OFTEN LEFT OUT, OR FORGOTTEN,
--OR PUT TO THE BACK BY PROGRESSIVE ORGANIZATIONS.
IT FEELS LIKE WE'RE SCREAMING FROM THE BOTTOM OF THE OCEAN OR SOMETHING.
WE'RE JUST TRYING TO GET SOMEONE TO CARE WHETHER WE LIVE OR DIE.
AND THAT'S A HUGE BURDEN ON TOP OF GRAD SCHOOL-- AND STAYING ALIVE--
AND GOING TO A THOUSAND DOCTOR'S APPOINTMENTS!!!
YEAH--
SORRY TO MAKE YOU DREDGE ALL THIS UP.
NAH, IT'S OKAY...
IT'S PROBABLY HEALTHY TO CHECK IN WITH MY FEARS EVERY ONCE IN A WHILE.
...SO WE KEEP TALKING ABOUT IT.
WHETHER IT'S CONTINUING TO SPEAK OUR SURVIVAL INTO EXISTENCE...
OR JUST LETTING EACH OTHER KNOW HOW WE'VE BEEN HOLDING UP.

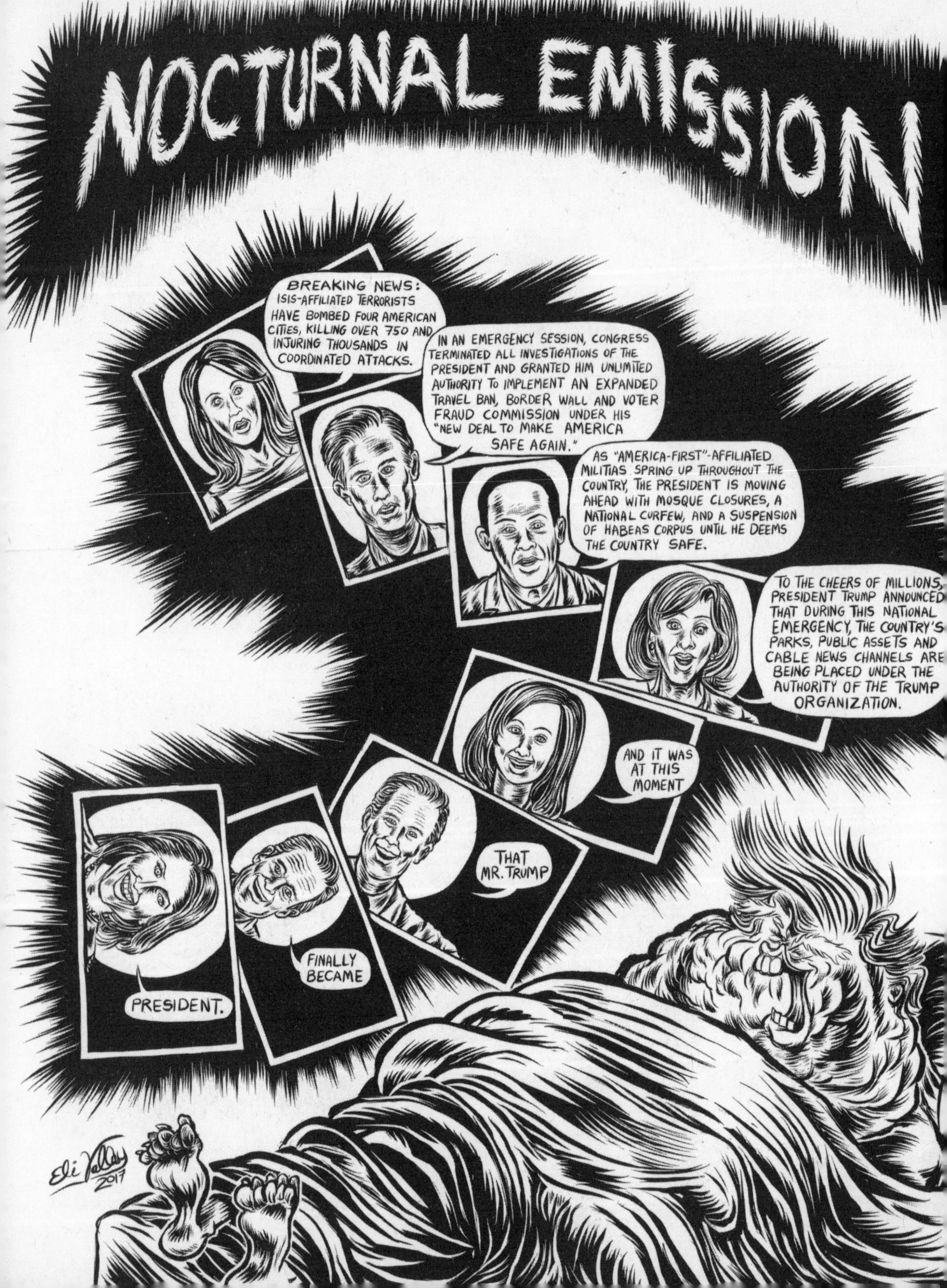
NOCTURNAL EMISSION
BREAKING NEWS: ISIS-AFFILIATED TERRORISTS HAVE BOMBED FOUR AMERICAN CITIES, KILLING OVER 750 AND INJURING THOUSANDS IN COORDINATED ATTACKS.
IN AN EMERGENCY SESSION, CONGRESS TERMINATED ALL INVESTIGATIONS OF THE PRESIDENT AND GRANTED HIM UNLIMITED AUTHORITY TO IMPLEMENT AN EXPANDED TRAVEL BAN, BORDER WALL AND VOTER FRAUD COMMISSION UNDER HIS "NEW DEAL TO MAKE AMERICA SAFE AGAIN."
AS "AMERICA-FIRST"-AFFILIATED MILITIAS SPRING UP THROUGHOUT THE COUNTRY, THE PRESIDENT IS MOVING AHEAD WITH MOSQUE CLOSURES, A NATIONAL CURFEW, AND A SUSPENSION OF HABEAS CORPUS UNTIL HE DEEMS THE COUNTRY SAFE.
TO THE CHEERS OF MILLIONS, PRESIDENT TRUMP ANNOUNCED THAT DURING THIS NATIONAL EMERGENCY, THE COUNTRY'S PARKS, PUBLIC ASSETS AND CABLE NEWS CHANNELS ARE BEING PLACED UNDER THE AUTHORITY OF THE TRUMP ORGANIZATION.
AND IT WAS AT THIS MOMENT
THAT MR. TRUMP
FINALLY BECAME
PRESIDENT.
Eli Valley 2017

"Pre-EXISting Condition"

story by Eric Blitz
art by J. Gonzalez-Blitz

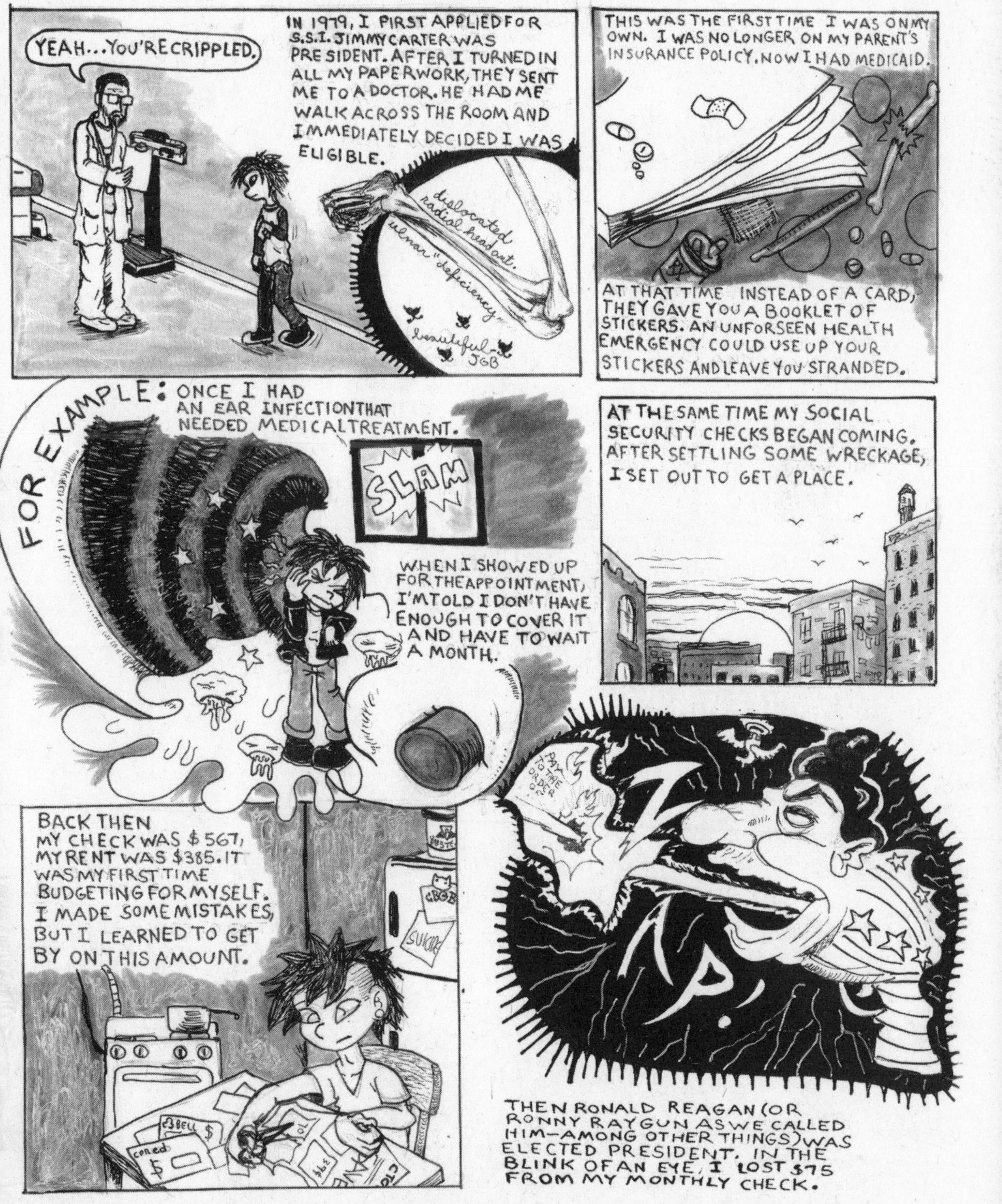

YEAH... YOU'RE CRIPPLED.
IN 1979, I FIRST APPLIED FOR S.S.I. JIMMY CARTER WAS PRESIDENT. AFTER I TURNED IN ALL MY PAPERWORK, THEY SENT ME TO A DOCTOR. HE HAD ME WALK ACROSS THE ROOM AND IMMEDIATELY DECIDED I WAS ELIGIBLE.
dislocated radial head art.
ulnar "deficiency"
beautiful-
JGB
THIS WAS THE FIRST TIME I WAS ON MY OWN. I WAS NO LONGER ON MY PARENT'S INSURANCE POLICY. NOW I HAD MEDICAID.
AT THAT TIME INSTEAD OF A CARD, THEY GAVE YOU A BOOKLET OF STICKERS. AN UNFORSEEN HEALTH EMERGENCY COULD USE UP YOUR STICKERS AND LEAVE YOU STRANDED.
FOR EXAMPLE: ONCE I HAD AN EAR INFECTION THAT NEEDED MEDICAL TREATMENT.
SLAM
WHEN I SHOWED UP FOR THE APPOINTMENT, I'M TOLD I DON'T HAVE ENOUGH TO COVER IT AND HAVE TO WAIT A MONTH.
AT THE SAME TIME MY SOCIAL SECURITY CHECKS BEGAN COMING. AFTER SETTLING SOME WRECKAGE, I SET OUT TO GET A PLACE.
BACK THEN MY CHECK WAS $567, MY RENT WAS $385. IT WAS MY FIRST TIME BUDGETING FOR MYSELF. I MADE SOME MISTAKES, BUT I LEARNED TO GET BY ON THIS AMOUNT.
PAY TO THE ORDER OF
THEN RONALD REAGAN (OR RONNY RAYGUN AS WE CALLED HIM—AMONG OTHER THINGS) WAS ELECTED PRESIDENT. IN THE BLINK OF AN EYE, I LOST $75 FROM MY MONTHLY CHECK.

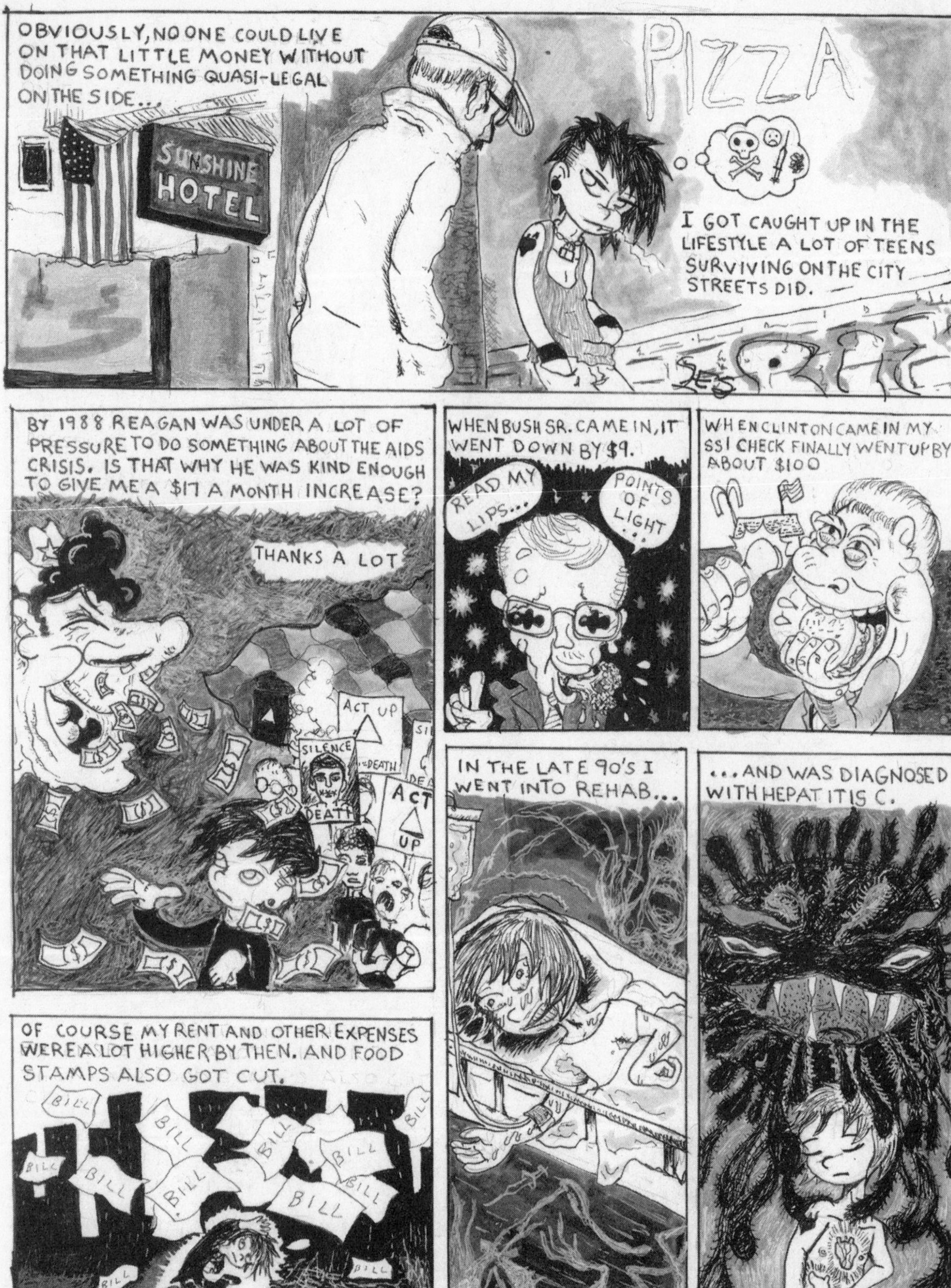

OBVIOUSLY, NO ONE COULD LIVE ON THAT LITTLE MONEY WITHOUT DOING SOMETHING QUASI-LEGAL ON THE SIDE...
SUNSHINE HOTEL
PIZZA
I GOT CAUGHT UP IN THE LIFESTYLE A LOT OF TEENS SURVIVING ON THE CITY STREETS DID.
BY 1988 REAGAN WAS UNDER A LOT OF PRESSURE TO DO SOMETHING ABOUT THE AIDS CRISIS. IS THAT WHY HE WAS KIND ENOUGH TO GIVE ME A $17 A MONTH INCREASE?
THANKS A LOT
ACT UP
SILENCE =DEATH
ACT UP
WHEN BUSH SR. CAME IN, IT WENT DOWN BY $9.
READ MY LIPS...
POINTS OF LIGHT...
WHEN CLINTON CAME IN MY SSI CHECK FINALLY WENT UP BY ABOUT $100
OF COURSE MY RENT AND OTHER EXPENSES WERE A LOT HIGHER BY THEN. AND FOOD STAMPS ALSO GOT CUT.
BILL
IN THE LATE 90'S I WENT INTO REHAB...
...AND WAS DIAGNOSED WITH HEPATITIS C.

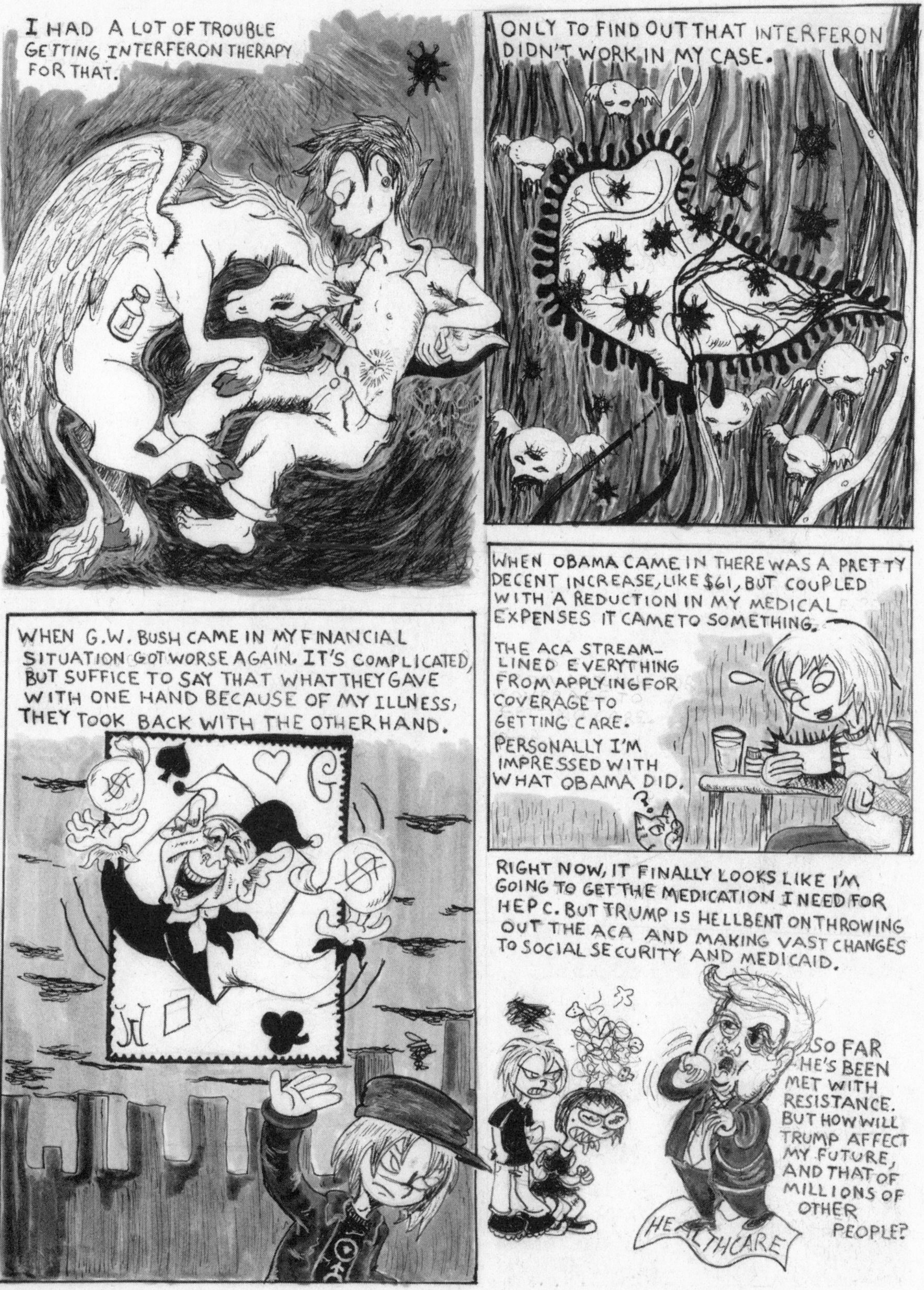
I HAD A LOT OF TROUBLE GETTING INTERFERON THERAPY FOR THAT.
ONLY TO FIND OUT THAT INTERFERON DIDN'T WORK IN MY CASE.
WHEN G.W. BUSH CAME IN MY FINANCIAL SITUATION GOT WORSE AGAIN. IT'S COMPLICATED, BUT SUFFICE TO SAY THAT WHAT THEY GAVE WITH ONE HAND BECAUSE OF MY ILLNESS, THEY TOOK BACK WITH THE OTHER HAND.
WHEN OBAMA CAME IN THERE WAS A PRETTY DECENT INCREASE, LIKE $61, BUT COUPLED WITH A REDUCTION IN MY MEDICAL EXPENSES IT CAME TO SOMETHING.
THE ACA STREAMLINED EVERYTHING FROM APPLYING FOR COVERAGE TO GETTING CARE.
PERSONALLY I'M IMPRESSED WITH WHAT OBAMA DID.
RIGHT NOW, IT FINALLY LOOKS LIKE I'M GOING TO GET THE MEDICATION I NEED FOR HEP C. BUT TRUMP IS HELLBENT ON THROWING OUT THE ACA AND MAKING VAST CHANGES TO SOCIAL SECURITY AND MEDICAID.
SO FAR HE'S BEEN MET WITH RESISTANCE. BUT HOW WILL TRUMP AFFECT MY FUTURE, AND THAT OF MILLIONS OF OTHER PEOPLE?
HEALTHCARE

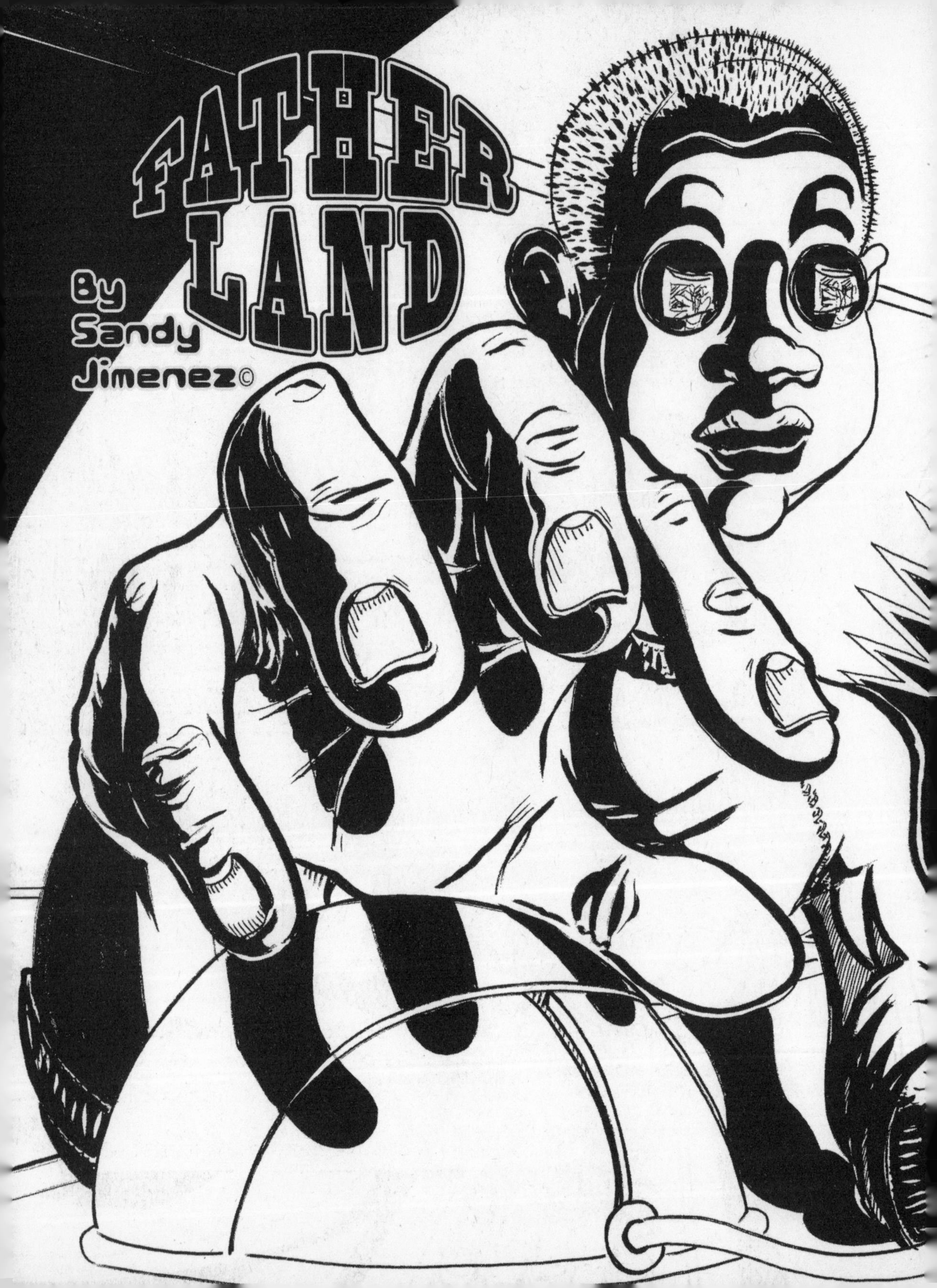
FATHER LAND
By Sandy Jimenez©

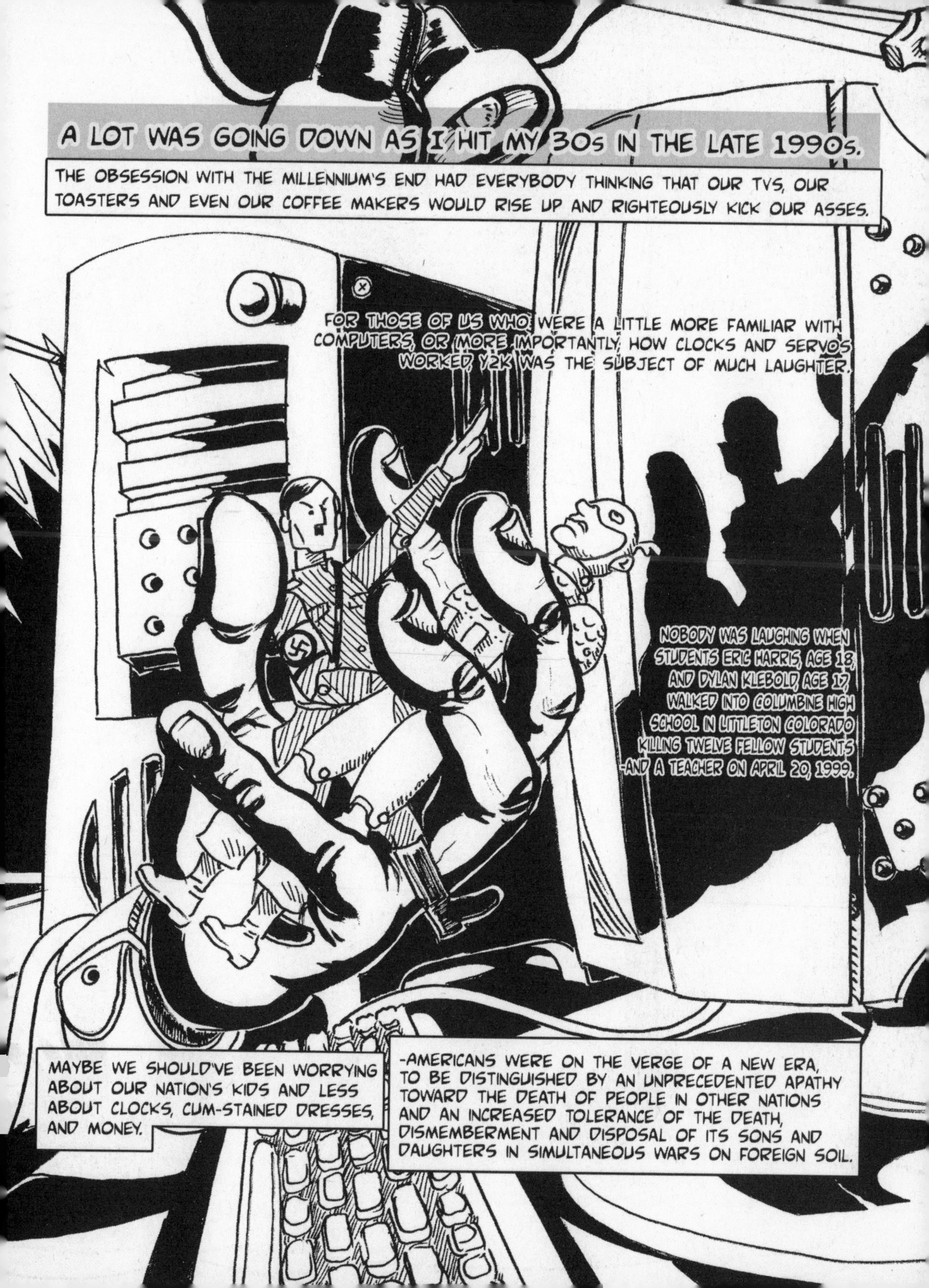
A LOT WAS GOING DOWN AS I HIT MY 30s IN THE LATE 1990s.
THE OBSESSION WITH THE MILLENNIUM'S END HAD EVERYBODY THINKING THAT OUR TVS, OUR TOASTERS AND EVEN OUR COFFEE MAKERS WOULD RISE UP AND RIGHTEOUSLY KICK OUR ASSES.
FOR THOSE OF US WHO WERE A LITTLE MORE FAMILIAR WITH COMPUTERS, OR MORE IMPORTANTLY, HOW CLOCKS AND SERVOS WORKED, Y2K WAS THE SUBJECT OF MUCH LAUGHTER.
NOBODY WAS LAUGHING WHEN STUDENTS ERIC HARRIS, AGE 18, AND DYLAN KLEBOLD, AGE 17, WALKED INTO COLUMBINE HIGH SCHOOL IN LITTLETON COLORADO KILLING TWELVE FELLOW STUDENTS -AND A TEACHER ON APRIL 20, 1999.
MAYBE WE SHOULD'VE BEEN WORRYING ABOUT OUR NATION'S KIDS AND LESS ABOUT CLOCKS, CUM-STAINED DRESSES, AND MONEY.
-AMERICANS WERE ON THE VERGE OF A NEW ERA, TO BE DISTINGUISHED BY AN UNPRECEDENTED APATHY TOWARD THE DEATH OF PEOPLE IN OTHER NATIONS AND AN INCREASED TOLERANCE OF THE DEATH, DISMEMBERMENT AND DISPOSAL OF ITS SONS AND DAUGHTERS IN SIMULTANEOUS WARS ON FOREIGN SOIL.

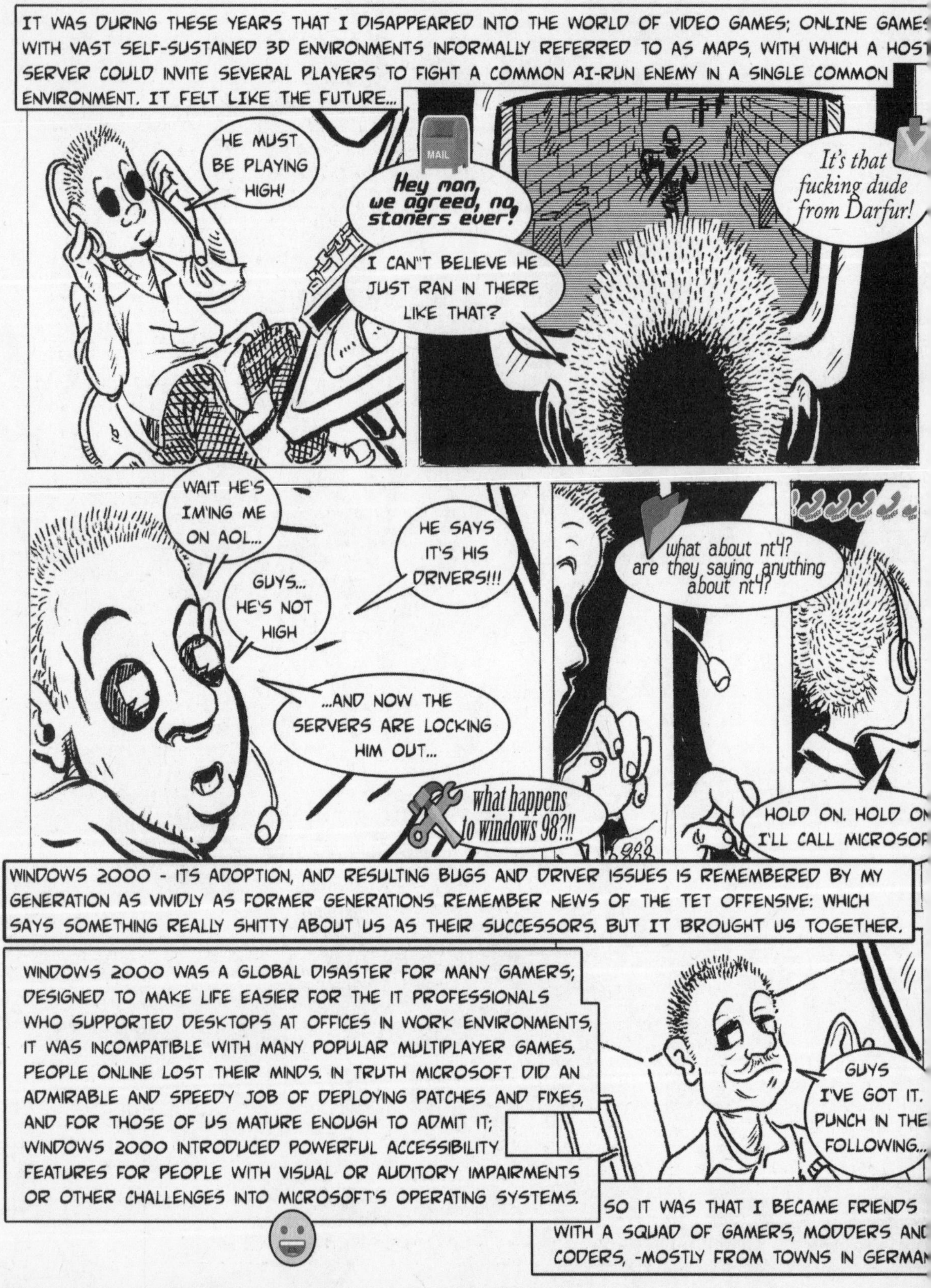
IT WAS DURING THESE YEARS THAT I DISAPPEARED INTO THE WORLD OF VIDEO GAMES; ONLINE GAMES WITH VAST SELF-SUSTAINED 3D ENVIRONMENTS INFORMALLY REFERRED TO AS MAPS, WITH WHICH A HOST SERVER COULD INVITE SEVERAL PLAYERS TO FIGHT A COMMON AI-RUN ENEMY IN A SINGLE COMMON ENVIRONMENT. IT FELT LIKE THE FUTURE...
HE MUST BE PLAYING HIGH!
MAIL
Hey man, we agreed, no stoners ever!
I CAN'T BELIEVE HE JUST RAN IN THERE LIKE THAT?
It's that fucking dude from Darfur!
WAIT HE'S IM'ING ME ON AOL...
GUYS... HE'S NOT HIGH
HE SAYS IT'S HIS DRIVERS!!!
...AND NOW THE SERVERS ARE LOCKING HIM OUT...
what happens to windows 98?!!
what about nt4? are they saying anything about nt4?
HOLD ON. HOLD ON I'LL CALL MICROSOF
WINDOWS 2000 - ITS ADOPTION, AND RESULTING BUGS AND DRIVER ISSUES IS REMEMBERED BY MY GENERATION AS VIVIDLY AS FORMER GENERATIONS REMEMBER NEWS OF THE TET OFFENSIVE; WHICH SAYS SOMETHING REALLY SHITTY ABOUT US AS THEIR SUCCESSORS. BUT IT BROUGHT US TOGETHER.
WINDOWS 2000 WAS A GLOBAL DISASTER FOR MANY GAMERS; DESIGNED TO MAKE LIFE EASIER FOR THE IT PROFESSIONALS WHO SUPPORTED DESKTOPS AT OFFICES IN WORK ENVIRONMENTS, IT WAS INCOMPATIBLE WITH MANY POPULAR MULTIPLAYER GAMES. PEOPLE ONLINE LOST THEIR MINDS. IN TRUTH MICROSOFT DID AN ADMIRABLE AND SPEEDY JOB OF DEPLOYING PATCHES AND FIXES, AND FOR THOSE OF US MATURE ENOUGH TO ADMIT IT; WINDOWS 2000 INTRODUCED POWERFUL ACCESSIBILITY FEATURES FOR PEOPLE WITH VISUAL OR AUDITORY IMPAIRMENTS OR OTHER CHALLENGES INTO MICROSOFT'S OPERATING SYSTEMS.
GUYS I'VE GOT IT. PUNCH IN THE FOLLOWING...
SO IT WAS THAT I BECAME FRIENDS WITH A SQUAD OF GAMERS, MODDERS AND CODERS, -MOSTLY FROM TOWNS IN GERMAN

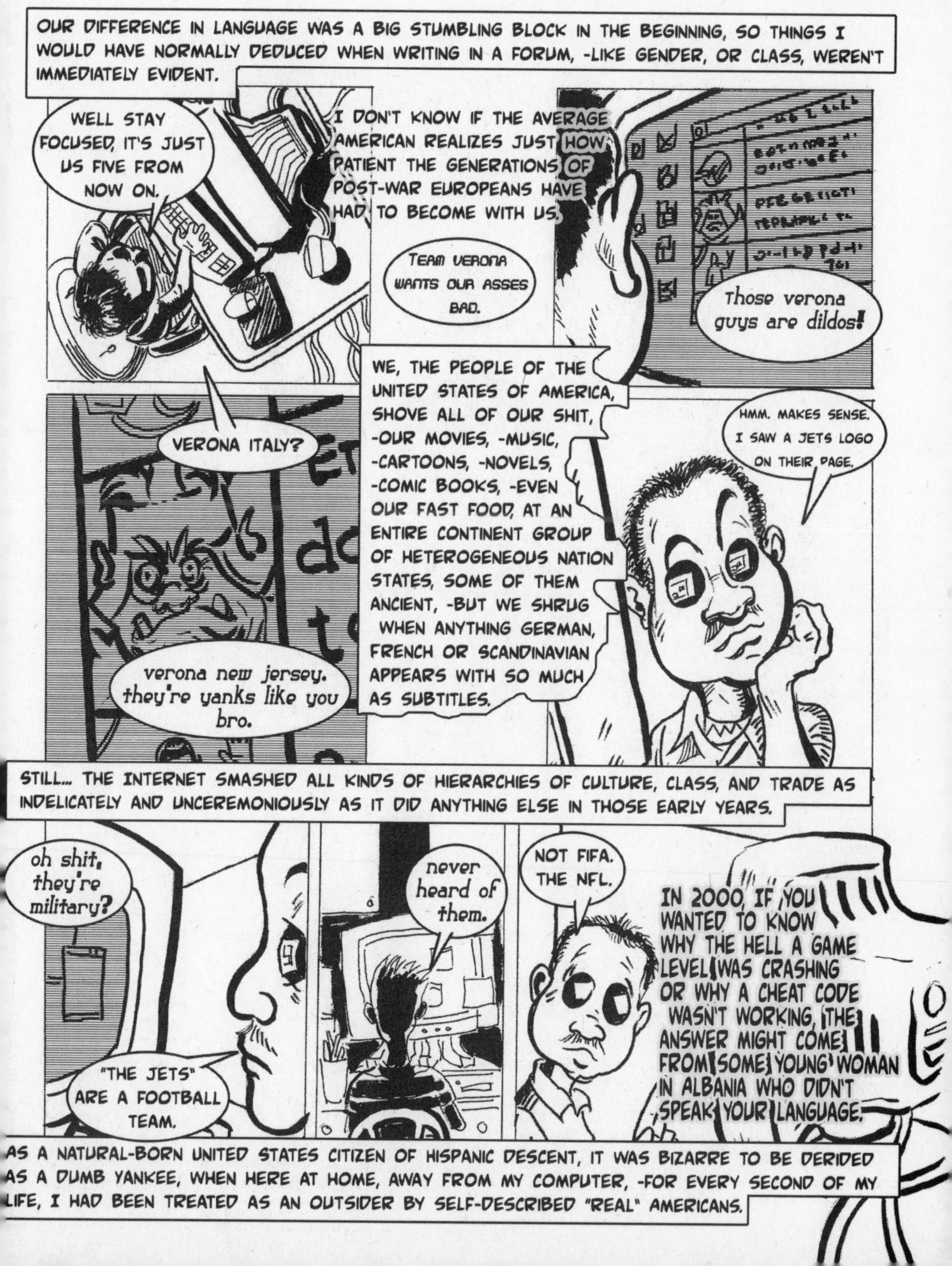
OUR DIFFERENCE IN LANGUAGE WAS A BIG STUMBLING BLOCK IN THE BEGINNING, SO THINGS I WOULD HAVE NORMALLY DEDUCED WHEN WRITING IN A FORUM, -LIKE GENDER, OR CLASS, WEREN'T IMMEDIATELY EVIDENT.
WELL STAY FOCUSED, IT'S JUST US FIVE FROM NOW ON.
I DON'T KNOW IF THE AVERAGE AMERICAN REALIZES JUST HOW PATIENT THE GENERATIONS OF POST-WAR EUROPEANS HAVE HAD TO BECOME WITH US.
TEAM VERONA WANTS OUR ASSES BAD.
Those verona guys are dildos!
WE, THE PEOPLE OF THE UNITED STATES OF AMERICA, SHOVE ALL OF OUR SHIT, -OUR MOVIES, -MUSIC, -CARTOONS, -NOVELS, -COMIC BOOKS, -EVEN OUR FAST FOOD, AT AN ENTIRE CONTINENT GROUP OF HETEROGENEOUS NATION STATES, SOME OF THEM ANCIENT, -BUT WE SHRUG WHEN ANYTHING GERMAN, FRENCH OR SCANDINAVIAN APPEARS WITH SO MUCH AS SUBTITLES.
VERONA ITALY?
verona new jersey. they're yanks like you bro.
HMM. MAKES SENSE. I SAW A JETS LOGO ON THEIR PAGE.
STILL... THE INTERNET SMASHED ALL KINDS OF HIERARCHIES OF CULTURE, CLASS, AND TRADE AS INDELICATELY AND UNCEREMONIOUSLY AS IT DID ANYTHING ELSE IN THOSE EARLY YEARS.
oh shit, they're military?
"THE JETS" ARE A FOOTBALL TEAM.
never heard of them.
NOT FIFA. THE NFL.
IN 2000, IF YOU WANTED TO KNOW WHY THE HELL A GAME LEVEL WAS CRASHING OR WHY A CHEAT CODE WASN'T WORKING, THE ANSWER MIGHT COME FROM SOME YOUNG WOMAN IN ALBANIA WHO DIDN'T SPEAK YOUR LANGUAGE.
AS A NATURAL-BORN UNITED STATES CITIZEN OF HISPANIC DESCENT, IT WAS BIZARRE TO BE DERIDED AS A DUMB YANKEE, WHEN HERE AT HOME, AWAY FROM MY COMPUTER, -FOR EVERY SECOND OF MY LIFE, I HAD BEEN TREATED AS AN OUTSIDER BY SELF-DESCRIBED "REAL" AMERICANS.

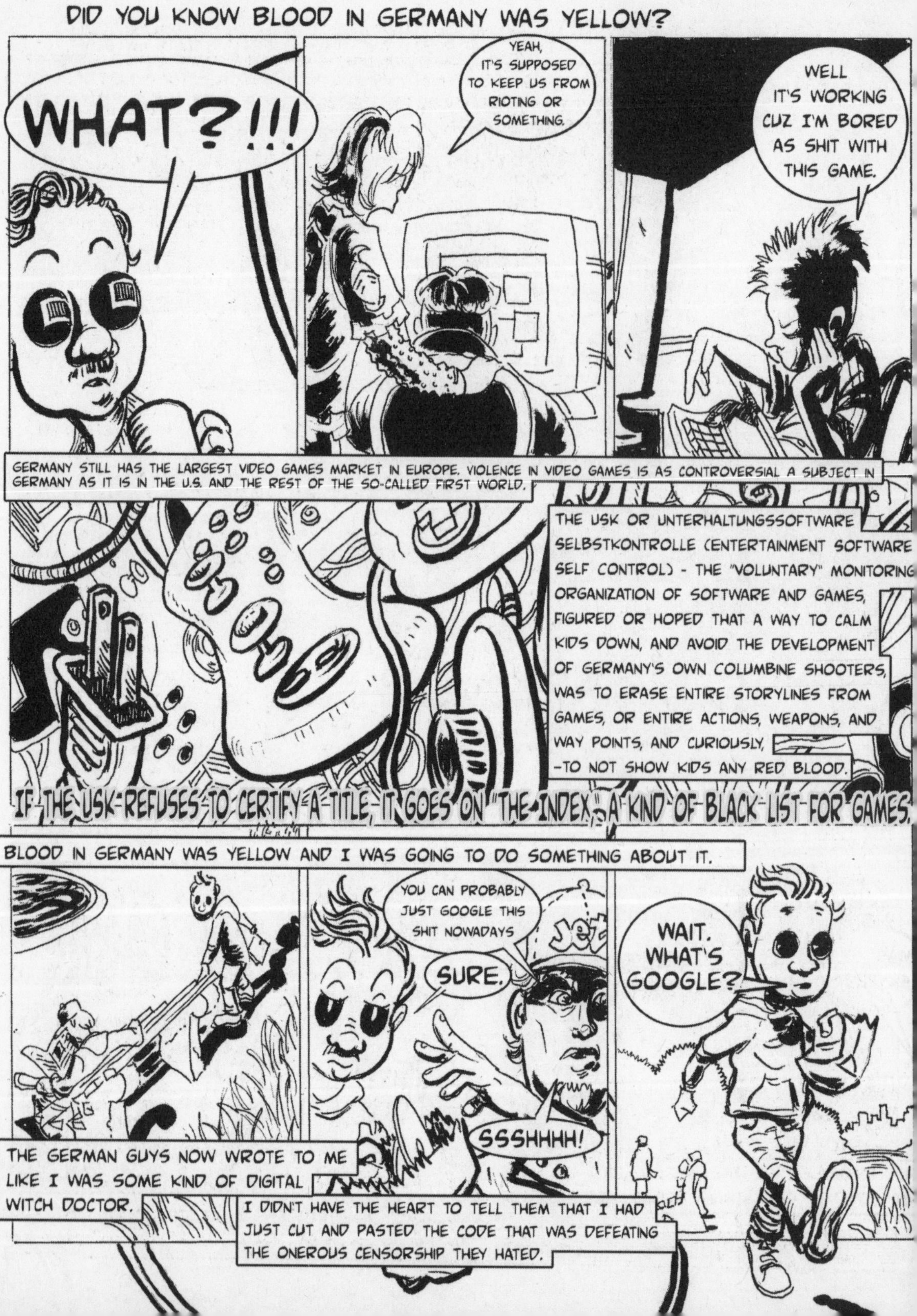
DID YOU KNOW BLOOD IN GERMANY WAS YELLOW?
WHAT?!!!
YEAH, IT'S SUPPOSED TO KEEP US FROM RIOTING OR SOMETHING.
WELL IT'S WORKING CUZ I'M BORED AS SHIT WITH THIS GAME.
GERMANY STILL HAS THE LARGEST VIDEO GAMES MARKET IN EUROPE. VIOLENCE IN VIDEO GAMES IS AS CONTROVERSIAL A SUBJECT IN GERMANY AS IT IS IN THE U.S. AND THE REST OF THE SO-CALLED FIRST WORLD.
THE USK OR UNTERHALTUNGSSOFTWARE SELBSTKONTROLLE (ENTERTAINMENT SOFTWARE SELF CONTROL) - THE "VOLUNTARY" MONITORING ORGANIZATION OF SOFTWARE AND GAMES, FIGURED OR HOPED THAT A WAY TO CALM KIDS DOWN, AND AVOID THE DEVELOPMENT OF GERMANY'S OWN COLUMBINE SHOOTERS, WAS TO ERASE ENTIRE STORYLINES FROM GAMES, OR ENTIRE ACTIONS, WEAPONS, AND WAY POINTS, AND CURIOUSLY, -TO NOT SHOW KIDS ANY RED BLOOD.
IF THE USK REFUSES TO CERTIFY A TITLE, IT GOES ON "THE INDEX," A KIND OF BLACK LIST FOR GAMES.
BLOOD IN GERMANY WAS YELLOW AND I WAS GOING TO DO SOMETHING ABOUT IT.
YOU CAN PROBABLY JUST GOOGLE THIS SHIT NOWADAYS
SURE.
WAIT. WHAT'S GOOGLE?
SSSHHHH!
THE GERMAN GUYS NOW WROTE TO ME LIKE I WAS SOME KIND OF DIGITAL WITCH DOCTOR.
I DIDN'T HAVE THE HEART TO TELL THEM THAT I HAD JUST CUT AND PASTED THE CODE THAT WAS DEFEATING THE ONEROUS CENSORSHIP THEY HATED.

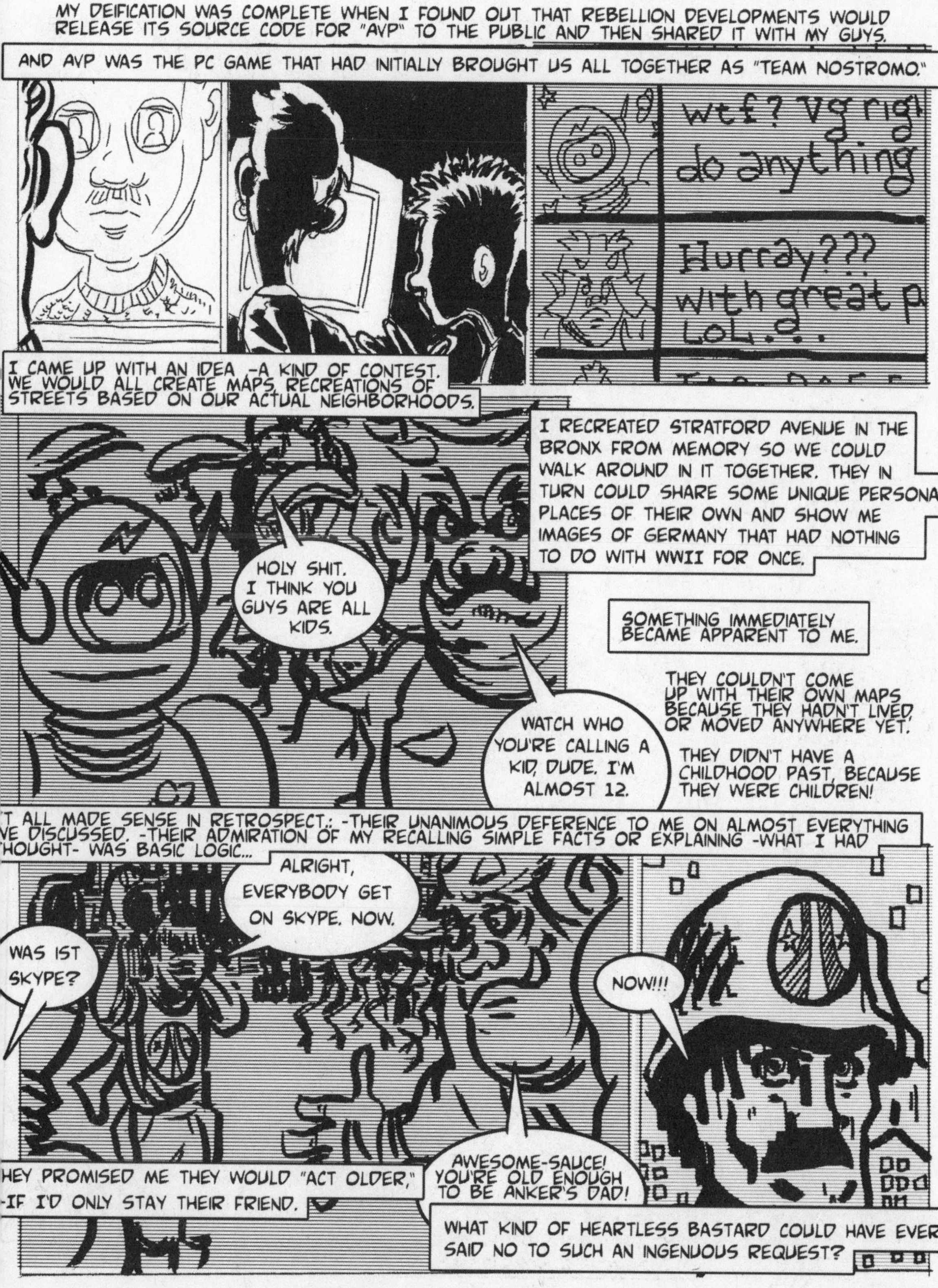
MY DEIFICATION WAS COMPLETE WHEN I FOUND OUT THAT REBELLION DEVELOPMENTS WOULD RELEASE ITS SOURCE CODE FOR "AVP" TO THE PUBLIC AND THEN SHARED IT WITH MY GUYS.
AND AVP WAS THE PC GAME THAT HAD INITIALLY BROUGHT US ALL TOGETHER AS "TEAM NOSTROMO."
do anything
Hurray???
I CAME UP WITH AN IDEA -A KIND OF CONTEST. WE WOULD ALL CREATE MAPS, RECREATIONS OF STREETS BASED ON OUR ACTUAL NEIGHBORHOODS.
I RECREATED STRATFORD AVENUE IN THE BRONX FROM MEMORY SO WE COULD WALK AROUND IN IT TOGETHER. THEY IN TURN COULD SHARE SOME UNIQUE PERSONAL PLACES OF THEIR OWN AND SHOW ME IMAGES OF GERMANY THAT HAD NOTHING TO DO WITH WWII FOR ONCE.
HOLY SHIT. I THINK YOU GUYS ARE ALL KIDS.
SOMETHING IMMEDIATELY BECAME APPARENT TO ME.
THEY COULDN'T COME UP WITH THEIR OWN MAPS BECAUSE THEY HADN'T LIVED OR MOVED ANYWHERE YET.
THEY DIDN'T HAVE A CHILDHOOD PAST, BECAUSE THEY WERE CHILDREN!
WATCH WHO YOU'RE CALLING A KID, DUDE. I'M ALMOST 12.
IT ALL MADE SENSE IN RETROSPECT.: -THEIR UNANIMOUS DEFERENCE TO ME ON ALMOST EVERYTHING WE DISCUSSED. -THEIR ADMIRATION OF MY RECALLING SIMPLE FACTS OR EXPLAINING -WHAT I HAD THOUGHT- WAS BASIC LOGIC...
ALRIGHT, EVERYBODY GET ON SKYPE. NOW.
WAS IST SKYPE?
NOW!!!
THEY PROMISED ME THEY WOULD "ACT OLDER," -IF I'D ONLY STAY THEIR FRIEND.
AWESOME-SAUCE! YOU'RE OLD ENOUGH TO BE ANKER'S DAD!
WHAT KIND OF HEARTLESS BASTARD COULD HAVE EVER SAID NO TO SUCH AN INGENUOUS REQUEST?

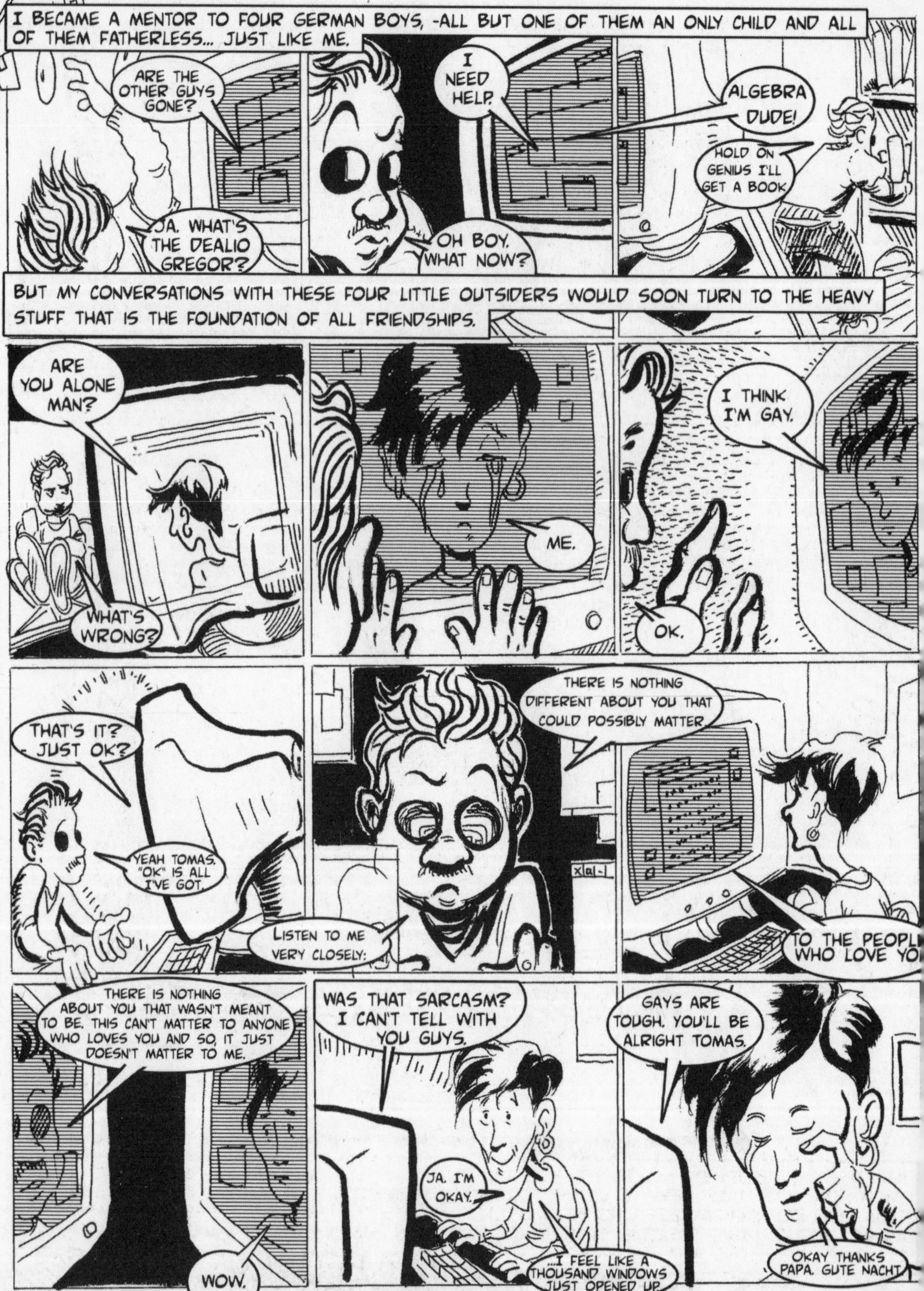
I BECAME A MENTOR TO FOUR GERMAN BOYS, -ALL BUT ONE OF THEM AN ONLY CHILD AND ALL OF THEM FATHERLESS... JUST LIKE ME.
ARE THE OTHER GUYS GONE?
JA. WHAT'S THE DEALIO GREGOR?
I NEED HELP.
OH BOY. WHAT NOW?
ALGEBRA DUDE!
HOLD ON GENIUS I'LL GET A BOOK
BUT MY CONVERSATIONS WITH THESE FOUR LITTLE OUTSIDERS WOULD SOON TURN TO THE HEAVY STUFF THAT IS THE FOUNDATION OF ALL FRIENDSHIPS.
ARE YOU ALONE MAN?
WHAT'S WRONG?
ME.
I THINK I'M GAY.
OK.
THAT'S IT? - JUST OK?
YEAH TOMAS. "OK" IS ALL I'VE GOT.
THERE IS NOTHING DIFFERENT ABOUT YOU THAT COULD POSSIBLY MATTER.
LISTEN TO ME VERY CLOSELY:
TO THE PEOPL WHO LOVE YO
THERE IS NOTHING ABOUT YOU THAT WASN'T MEANT TO BE. THIS CAN'T MATTER TO ANYONE WHO LOVES YOU AND SO, IT JUST DOESN'T MATTER TO ME.
WOW.
WAS THAT SARCASM? I CAN'T TELL WITH YOU GUYS.
JA. I'M OKAY.
...I FEEL LIKE A THOUSAND WINDOWS JUST OPENED UP.
GAYS ARE TOUGH. YOU'LL BE ALRIGHT TOMAS.
OKAY THANKS PAPA. GUTE NACHT.

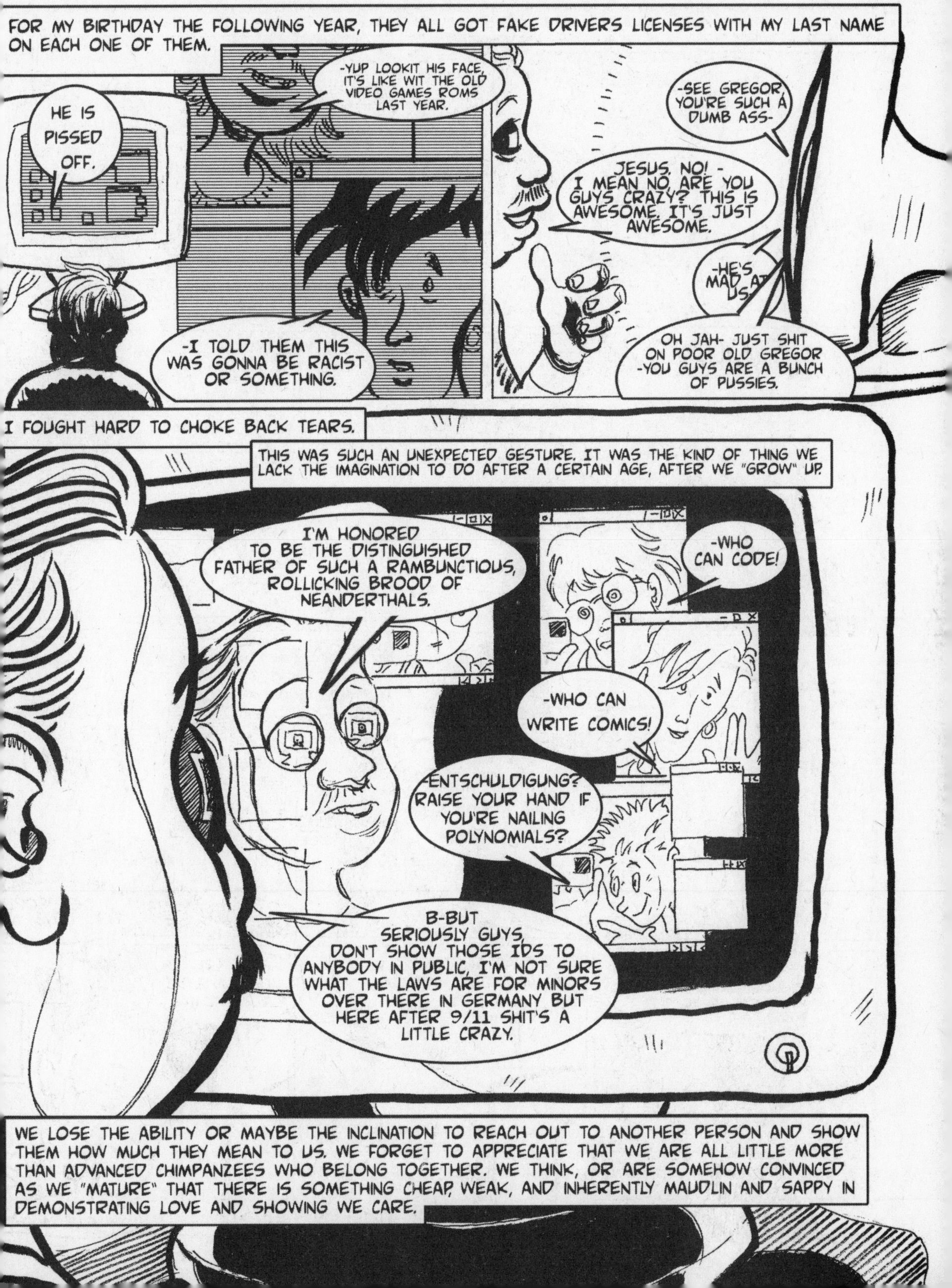

FOR MY BIRTHDAY THE FOLLOWING YEAR, THEY ALL GOT FAKE DRIVERS LICENSES WITH MY LAST NAME ON EACH ONE OF THEM.
HE IS PISSED OFF.
-YUP LOOKIT HIS FACE, IT'S LIKE WIT THE OLD VIDEO GAMES ROMS LAST YEAR.
-I TOLD THEM THIS WAS GONNA BE RACIST OR SOMETHING.
-SEE GREGOR, YOU'RE SUCH A DUMB ASS-
JESUS, NO! - I MEAN NO, ARE YOU GUYS CRAZY? THIS IS AWESOME, IT'S JUST AWESOME.
-HE'S MAD AT US.
OH JAH- JUST SHIT ON POOR OLD GREGOR -YOU GUYS ARE A BUNCH OF PUSSIES.
I FOUGHT HARD TO CHOKE BACK TEARS.
THIS WAS SUCH AN UNEXPECTED GESTURE. IT WAS THE KIND OF THING WE LACK THE IMAGINATION TO DO AFTER A CERTAIN AGE, AFTER WE "GROW" UP.
I'M HONORED TO BE THE DISTINGUISHED FATHER OF SUCH A RAMBUNCTIOUS, ROLLICKING BROOD OF NEANDERTHALS.
-WHO CAN CODE!
-WHO CAN WRITE COMICS!
-ENTSCHULDIGUNG? RAISE YOUR HAND IF YOU'RE NAILING POLYNOMIALS?
B-BUT SERIOUSLY GUYS, DON'T SHOW THOSE IDS TO ANYBODY IN PUBLIC, I'M NOT SURE WHAT THE LAWS ARE FOR MINORS OVER THERE IN GERMANY BUT HERE AFTER 9/11 SHIT'S A LITTLE CRAZY.
WE LOSE THE ABILITY OR MAYBE THE INCLINATION TO REACH OUT TO ANOTHER PERSON AND SHOW THEM HOW MUCH THEY MEAN TO US. WE FORGET TO APPRECIATE THAT WE ARE ALL LITTLE MORE THAN ADVANCED CHIMPANZEES WHO BELONG TOGETHER. WE THINK, OR ARE SOMEHOW CONVINCED AS WE "MATURE" THAT THERE IS SOMETHING CHEAP, WEAK, AND INHERENTLY MAUDLIN AND SAPPY IN DEMONSTRATING LOVE AND SHOWING WE CARE.

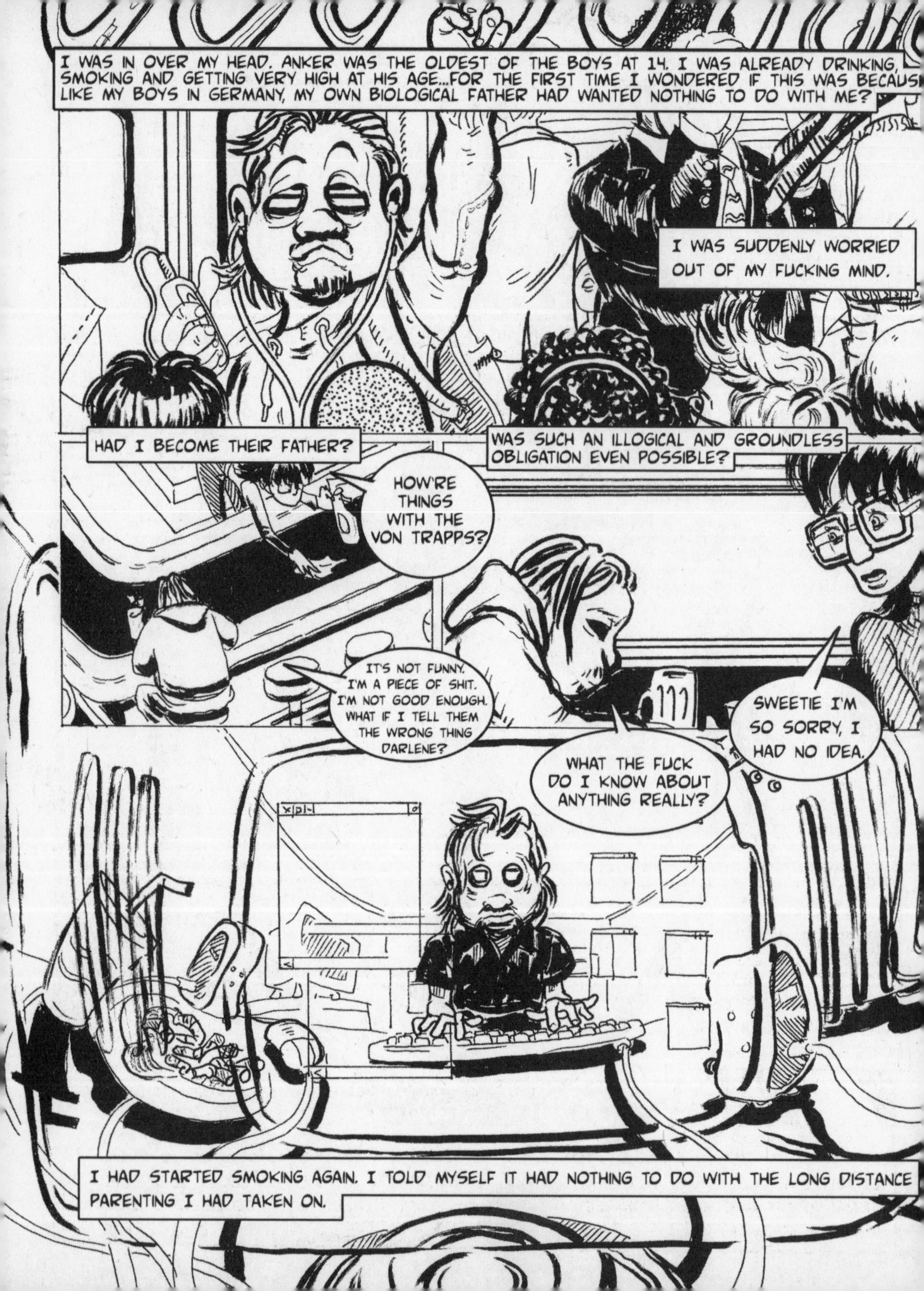
I WAS IN OVER MY HEAD. ANKER WAS THE OLDEST OF THE BOYS AT 14. I WAS ALREADY DRINKING, SMOKING AND GETTING VERY HIGH AT HIS AGE...FOR THE FIRST TIME I WONDERED IF THIS WAS BECAUS LIKE MY BOYS IN GERMANY, MY OWN BIOLOGICAL FATHER HAD WANTED NOTHING TO DO WITH ME?
I WAS SUDDENLY WORRIED OUT OF MY FUCKING MIND.
HAD I BECOME THEIR FATHER?
WAS SUCH AN ILLOGICAL AND GROUNDLESS OBLIGATION EVEN POSSIBLE?
HOW'RE THINGS WITH THE VON TRAPPS?
IT'S NOT FUNNY. I'M A PIECE OF SHIT. I'M NOT GOOD ENOUGH. WHAT IF I TELL THEM THE WRONG THING DARLENE?
WHAT THE FUCK DO I KNOW ABOUT ANYTHING REALLY?
SWEETIE I'M SO SORRY, I HAD NO IDEA.
I HAD STARTED SMOKING AGAIN. I TOLD MYSELF IT HAD NOTHING TO DO WITH THE LONG DISTANCE PARENTING I HAD TAKEN ON.

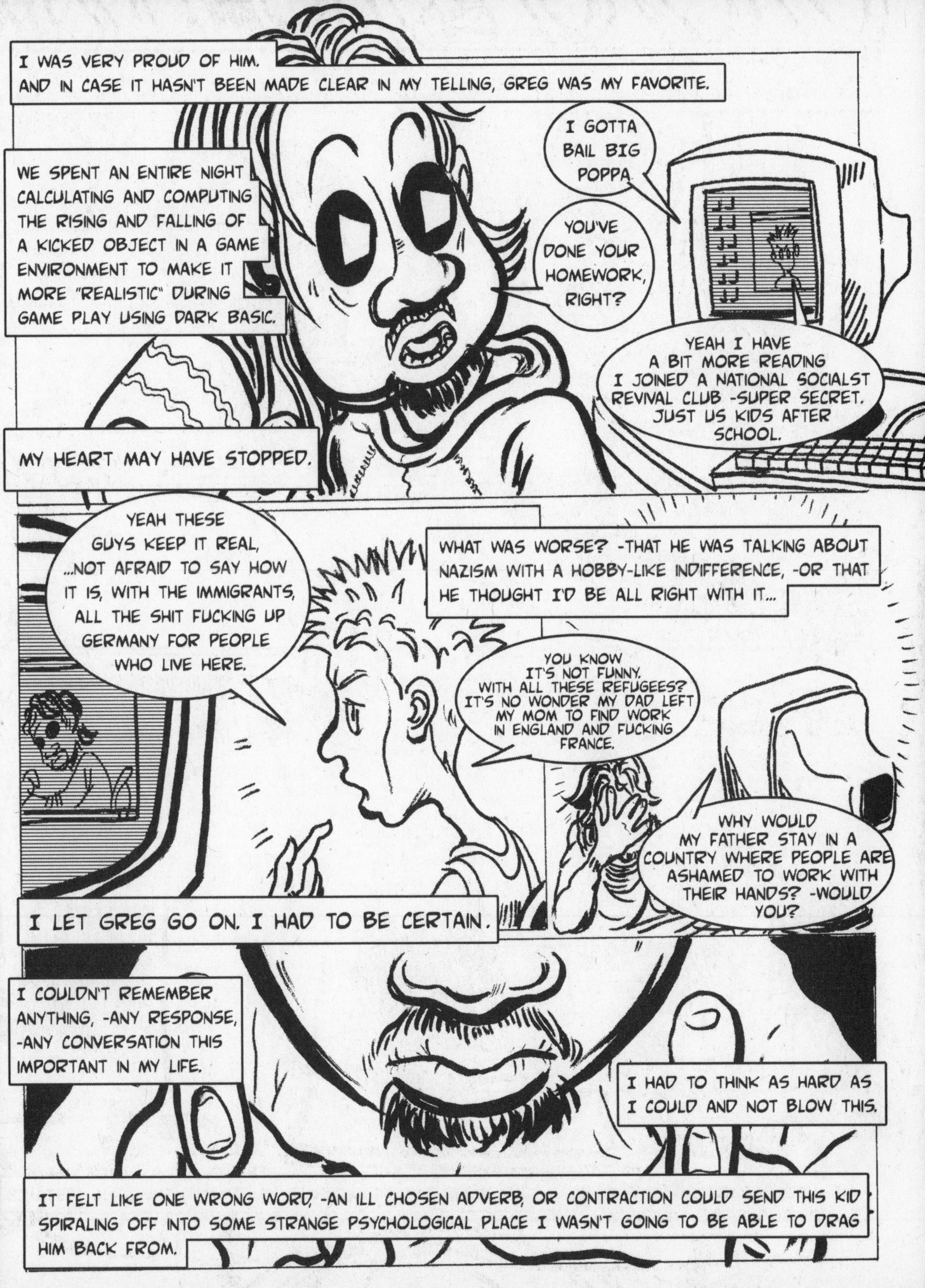
I WAS VERY PROUD OF HIM.
AND IN CASE IT HASN'T BEEN MADE CLEAR IN MY TELLING, GREG WAS MY FAVORITE.
WE SPENT AN ENTIRE NIGHT CALCULATING AND COMPUTING THE RISING AND FALLING OF A KICKED OBJECT IN A GAME ENVIRONMENT TO MAKE IT MORE "REALISTIC" DURING GAME PLAY USING DARK BASIC.
I GOTTA BAIL BIG POPPA
YOU'VE DONE YOUR HOMEWORK, RIGHT?
YEAH I HAVE A BIT MORE READING I JOINED A NATIONAL SOCIALST REVIVAL CLUB -SUPER SECRET. JUST US KIDS AFTER SCHOOL.
MY HEART MAY HAVE STOPPED.
YEAH THESE GUYS KEEP IT REAL, ...NOT AFRAID TO SAY HOW IT IS, WITH THE IMMIGRANTS, ALL THE SHIT FUCKING UP GERMANY FOR PEOPLE WHO LIVE HERE.
WHAT WAS WORSE? -THAT HE WAS TALKING ABOUT NAZISM WITH A HOBBY-LIKE INDIFFERENCE, -OR THAT HE THOUGHT I'D BE ALL RIGHT WITH IT...
YOU KNOW IT'S NOT FUNNY. WITH ALL THESE REFUGEES? IT'S NO WONDER MY DAD LEFT MY MOM TO FIND WORK IN ENGLAND AND FUCKING FRANCE.
WHY WOULD MY FATHER STAY IN A COUNTRY WHERE PEOPLE ARE ASHAMED TO WORK WITH THEIR HANDS? -WOULD YOU?
I LET GREG GO ON. I HAD TO BE CERTAIN.
I COULDN'T REMEMBER ANYTHING, -ANY RESPONSE, -ANY CONVERSATION THIS IMPORTANT IN MY LIFE.
I HAD TO THINK AS HARD AS I COULD AND NOT BLOW THIS.
IT FELT LIKE ONE WRONG WORD, -AN ILL CHOSEN ADVERB, OR CONTRACTION COULD SEND THIS KID SPIRALING OFF INTO SOME STRANGE PSYCHOLOGICAL PLACE I WASN'T GOING TO BE ABLE TO DRAG HIM BACK FROM.

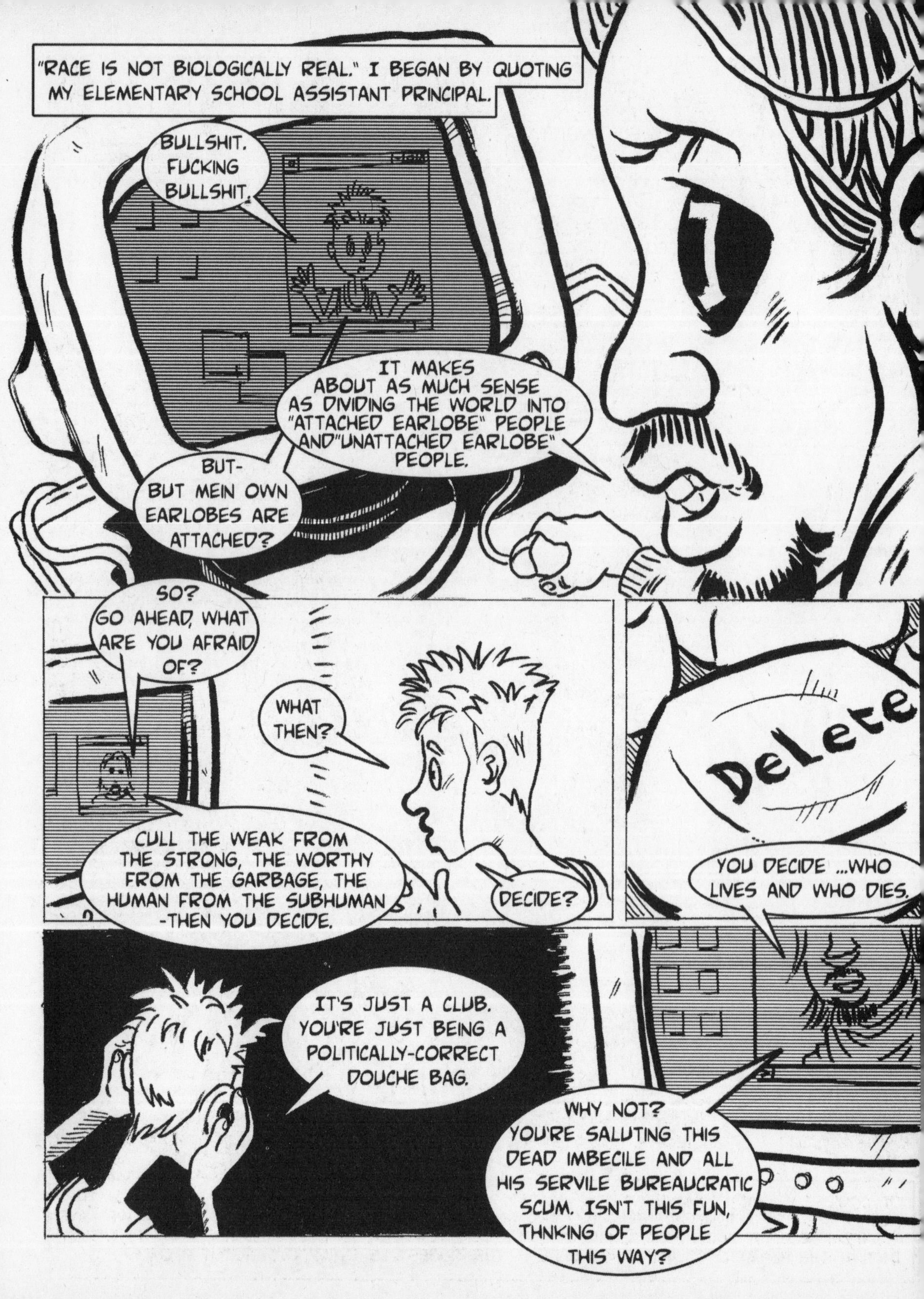
"RACE IS NOT BIOLOGICALLY REAL." I BEGAN BY QUOTING MY ELEMENTARY SCHOOL ASSISTANT PRINCIPAL.
BULLSHIT. FUCKING BULLSHIT.
IT MAKES ABOUT AS MUCH SENSE AS DIVIDING THE WORLD INTO "ATTACHED EARLOBE" PEOPLE AND "UNATTACHED EARLOBE" PEOPLE.
BUT- BUT MEIN OWN EARLOBES ARE ATTACHED?
SO? GO AHEAD, WHAT ARE YOU AFRAID OF?
WHAT THEN?
CULL THE WEAK FROM THE STRONG, THE WORTHY FROM THE GARBAGE, THE HUMAN FROM THE SUBHUMAN -THEN YOU DECIDE.
DECIDE?
Delete
YOU DECIDE ...WHO LIVES AND WHO DIES.
IT'S JUST A CLUB. YOU'RE JUST BEING A POLITICALLY-CORRECT DOUCHE BAG.
WHY NOT? YOU'RE SALUTING THIS DEAD IMBECILE AND ALL HIS SERVILE BUREAUCRATIC SCUM. ISN'T THIS FUN, THNKING OF PEOPLE THIS WAY?

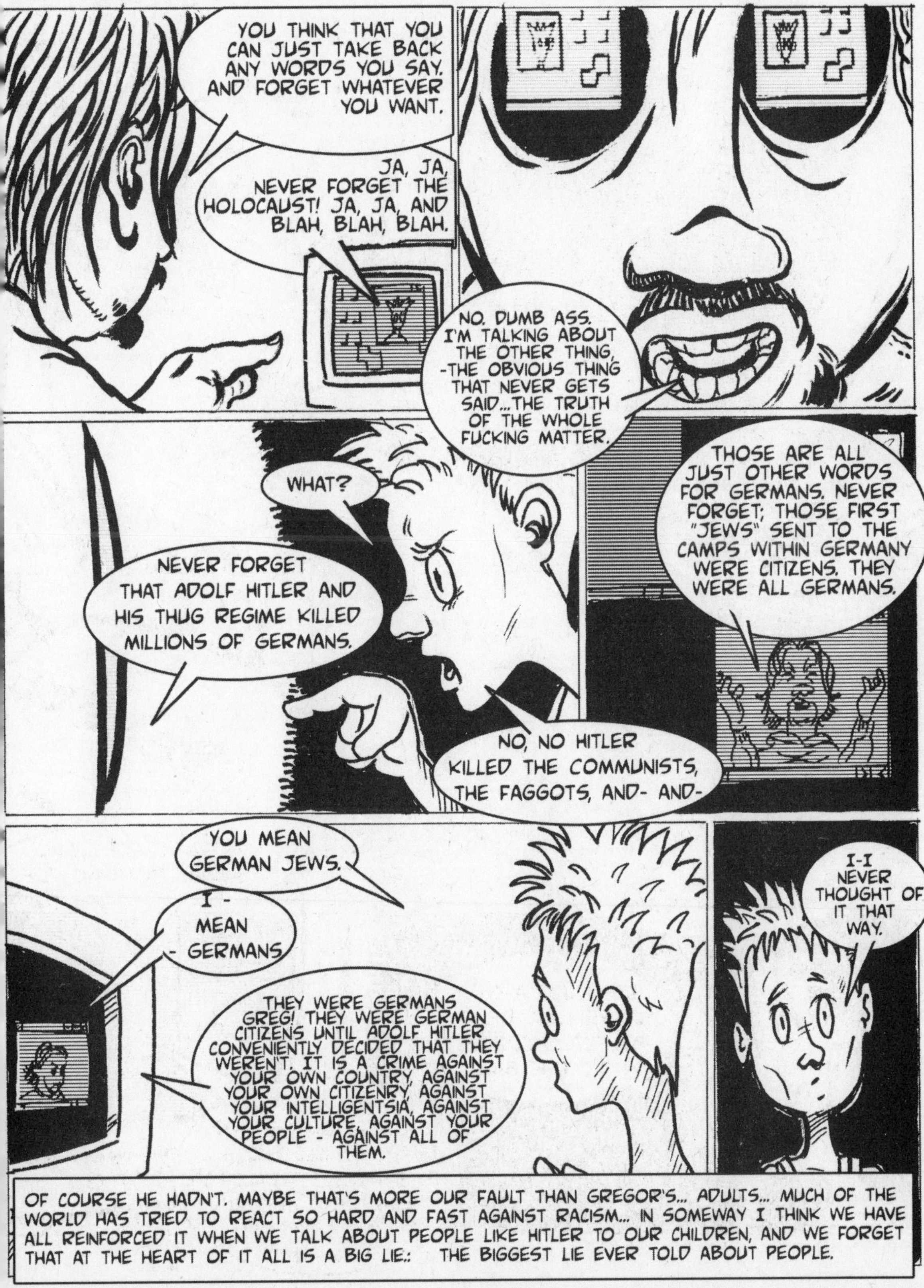
YOU THINK THAT YOU CAN JUST TAKE BACK ANY WORDS YOU SAY. AND FORGET WHATEVER YOU WANT.
JA, JA, NEVER FORGET THE HOLOCAUST! JA, JA, AND BLAH, BLAH, BLAH.
NO. DUMB ASS. I'M TALKING ABOUT THE OTHER THING, -THE OBVIOUS THING THAT NEVER GETS SAID...THE TRUTH OF THE WHOLE FUCKING MATTER.
WHAT?
NEVER FORGET THAT ADOLF HITLER AND HIS THUG REGIME KILLED MILLIONS OF GERMANS.
NO, NO HITLER KILLED THE COMMUNISTS, THE FAGGOTS, AND- AND-
THOSE ARE ALL JUST OTHER WORDS FOR GERMANS. NEVER FORGET; THOSE FIRST "JEWS" SENT TO THE CAMPS WITHIN GERMANY WERE CITIZENS. THEY WERE ALL GERMANS.
YOU MEAN GERMAN JEWS.
I - MEAN - GERMANS
THEY WERE GERMANS GREG! THEY WERE GERMAN CITIZENS UNTIL ADOLF HITLER CONVENIENTLY DECIDED THAT THEY WEREN'T. IT IS A CRIME AGAINST YOUR OWN COUNTRY, AGAINST YOUR OWN CITIZENRY, AGAINST YOUR INTELLIGENTSIA, AGAINST YOUR CULTURE, AGAINST YOUR PEOPLE - AGAINST ALL OF THEM.
I-I NEVER THOUGHT OF IT THAT WAY.
OF COURSE HE HADN'T. MAYBE THAT'S MORE OUR FAULT THAN GREGOR'S... ADULTS... MUCH OF THE WORLD HAS TRIED TO REACT SO HARD AND FAST AGAINST RACISM... IN SOMEWAY I THINK WE HAVE ALL REINFORCED IT WHEN WE TALK ABOUT PEOPLE LIKE HITLER TO OUR CHILDREN, AND WE FORGET THAT AT THE HEART OF IT ALL IS A BIG LIE.: THE BIGGEST LIE EVER TOLD ABOUT PEOPLE.

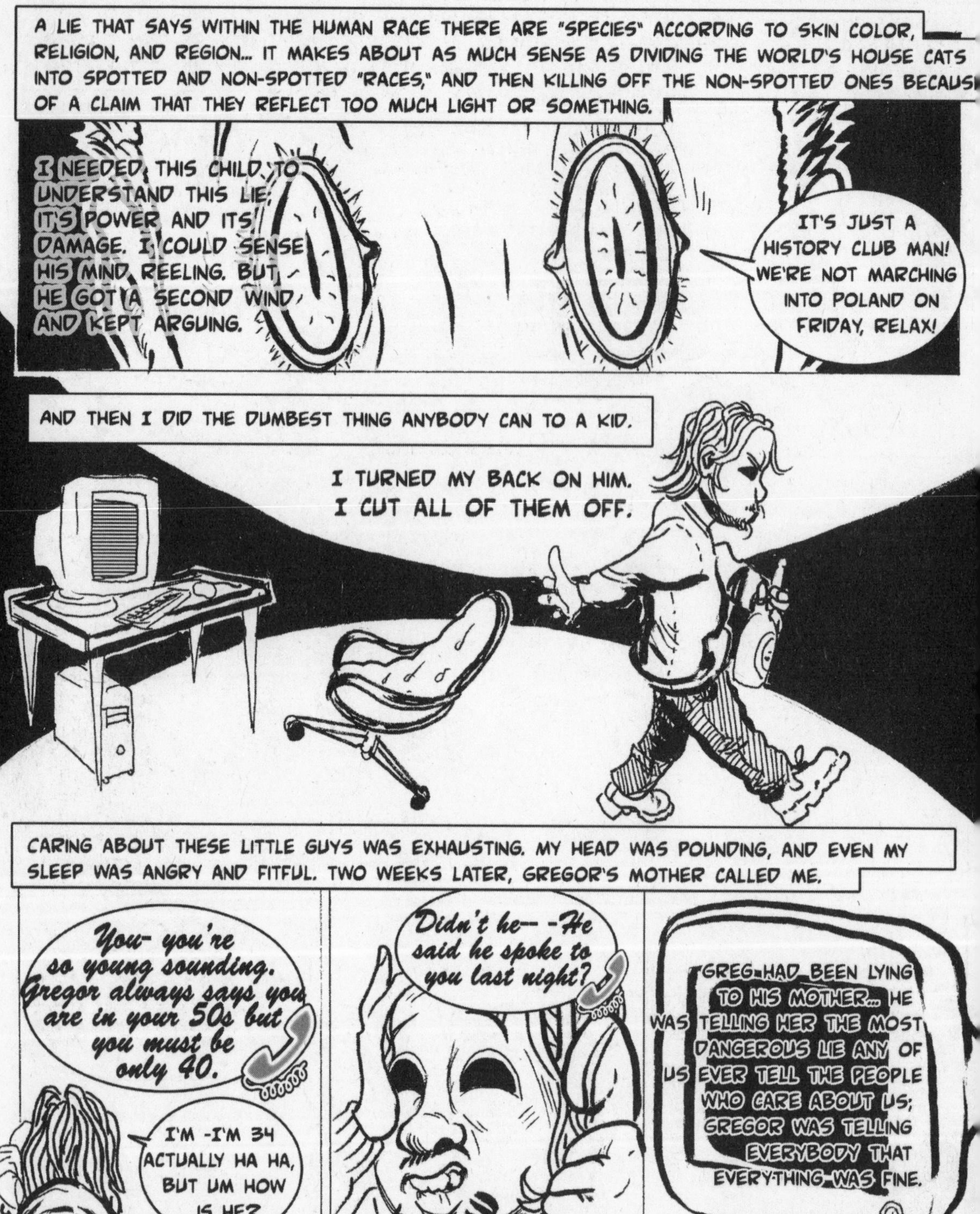
A LIE THAT SAYS WITHIN THE HUMAN RACE THERE ARE "SPECIES" ACCORDING TO SKIN COLOR, RELIGION, AND REGION... IT MAKES ABOUT AS MUCH SENSE AS DIVIDING THE WORLD'S HOUSE CATS INTO SPOTTED AND NON-SPOTTED "RACES," AND THEN KILLING OFF THE NON-SPOTTED ONES BECAUS OF A CLAIM THAT THEY REFLECT TOO MUCH LIGHT OR SOMETHING.
I NEEDED THIS CHILD TO UNDERSTAND THIS LIE: IT'S POWER AND ITS DAMAGE. I COULD SENSE HIS MIND REELING. BUT HE GOT A SECOND WIND AND KEPT ARGUING.
IT'S JUST A HISTORY CLUB MAN! WE'RE NOT MARCHING INTO POLAND ON FRIDAY, RELAX!
AND THEN I DID THE DUMBEST THING ANYBODY CAN TO A KID.
I TURNED MY BACK ON HIM. I CUT ALL OF THEM OFF.
CARING ABOUT THESE LITTLE GUYS WAS EXHAUSTING. MY HEAD WAS POUNDING, AND EVEN MY SLEEP WAS ANGRY AND FITFUL. TWO WEEKS LATER, GREGOR'S MOTHER CALLED ME.
You- you're so young sounding. Gregor always says you are in your 50s but you must be only 40.
I'M -I'M 34 ACTUALLY HA HA, BUT UM HOW IS HE?
Didn't he-- -He said he spoke to you last night?
GREG HAD BEEN LYING TO HIS MOTHER... HE WAS TELLING HER THE MOST DANGEROUS LIE ANY OF US EVER TELL THE PEOPLE WHO CARE ABOUT US; GREGOR WAS TELLING EVERYBODY THAT EVERYTHING WAS FINE.
GREGOR'S MOTHER HAD ONLY CALLED ME TO THANK ME. SHE HAD INITIALY FEARED I WAS SOME "ONLIN PERVERT;" SHE TOLD ME HIS GRADES IN ALL SUBJECTS, ESPECIALLY MATH, WERE NOW VERY GOOD, AN THAT MY INFLUENCE IN GREG'S LIFE HAD BEEN EXTREMELY POSITIVE... NO MENTION OF NAZISM.

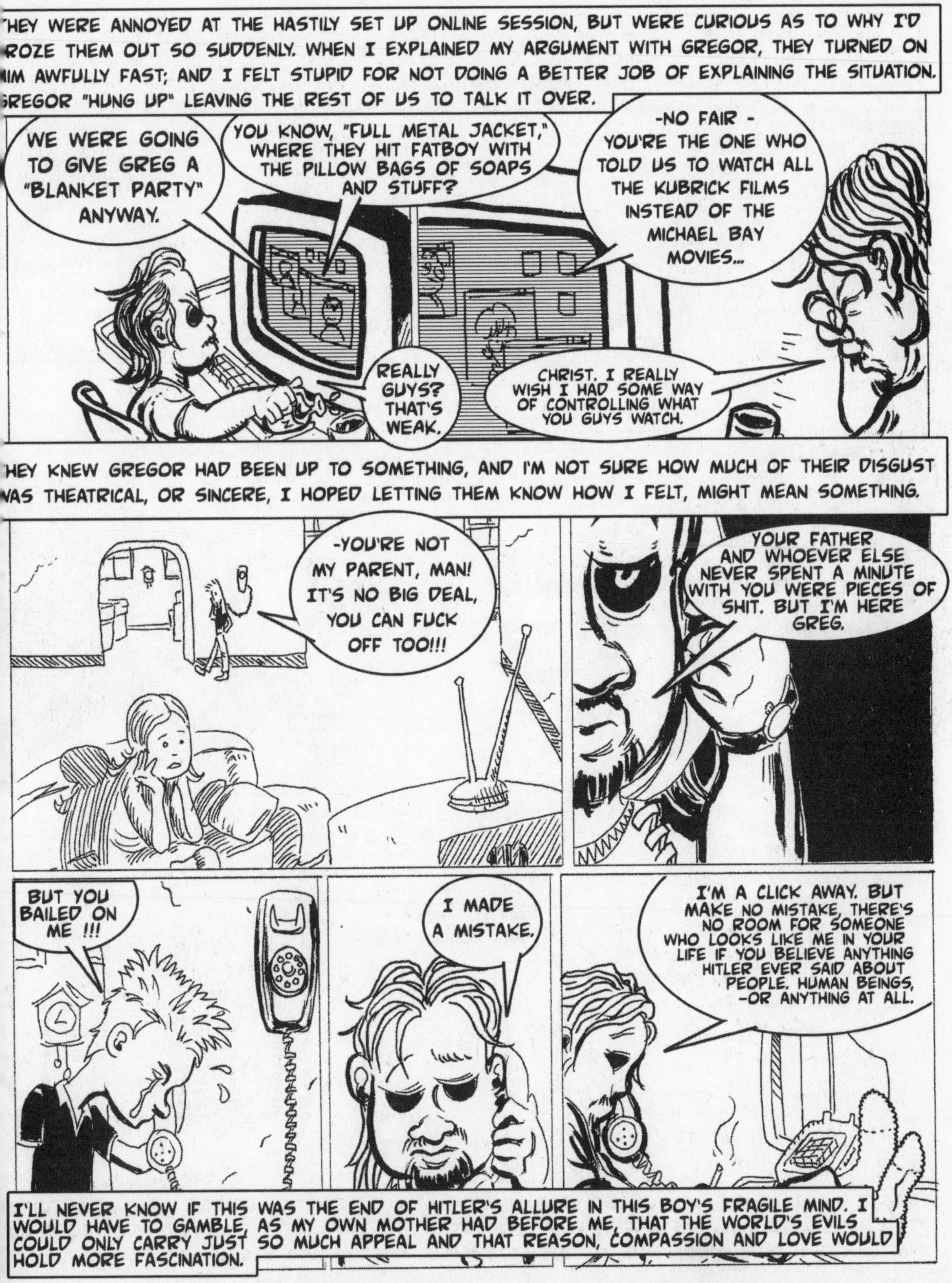

HEY WERE ANNOYED AT THE HASTILY SET UP ONLINE SESSION, BUT WERE CURIOUS AS TO WHY I'D ROZE THEM OUT SO SUDDENLY. WHEN I EXPLAINED MY ARGUMENT WITH GREGOR, THEY TURNED ON IM AWFULLY FAST; AND I FELT STUPID FOR NOT DOING A BETTER JOB OF EXPLAINING THE SITUATION. REGOR "HUNG UP" LEAVING THE REST OF US TO TALK IT OVER.
WE WERE GOING TO GIVE GREG A "BLANKET PARTY" ANYWAY.
YOU KNOW, "FULL METAL JACKET," WHERE THEY HIT FATBOY WITH THE PILLOW BAGS OF SOAPS AND STUFF?
-NO FAIR - YOU'RE THE ONE WHO TOLD US TO WATCH ALL THE KUBRICK FILMS INSTEAD OF THE MICHAEL BAY MOVIES...
REALLY GUYS? THAT'S WEAK.
CHRIST. I REALLY WISH I HAD SOME WAY OF CONTROLLING WHAT YOU GUYS WATCH.
HEY KNEW GREGOR HAD BEEN UP TO SOMETHING, AND I'M NOT SURE HOW MUCH OF THEIR DISGUST AS THEATRICAL, OR SINCERE, I HOPED LETTING THEM KNOW HOW I FELT, MIGHT MEAN SOMETHING.
-YOU'RE NOT MY PARENT, MAN! IT'S NO BIG DEAL, YOU CAN FUCK OFF TOO!!!
YOUR FATHER AND WHOEVER ELSE NEVER SPENT A MINUTE WITH YOU WERE PIECES OF SHIT. BUT I'M HERE GREG.
BUT YOU BAILED ON ME !!!
I MADE A MISTAKE.
I'M A CLICK AWAY. BUT MAKE NO MISTAKE, THERE'S NO ROOM FOR SOMEONE WHO LOOKS LIKE ME IN YOUR LIFE IF YOU BELIEVE ANYTHING HITLER EVER SAID ABOUT PEOPLE. HUMAN BEINGS, -OR ANYTHING AT ALL.
I'LL NEVER KNOW IF THIS WAS THE END OF HITLER'S ALLURE IN THIS BOY'S FRAGILE MIND. I WOULD HAVE TO GAMBLE, AS MY OWN MOTHER HAD BEFORE ME, THAT THE WORLD'S EVILS COULD ONLY CARRY JUST SO MUCH APPEAL AND THAT REASON, COMPASSION AND LOVE WOULD HOLD MORE FASCINATION.

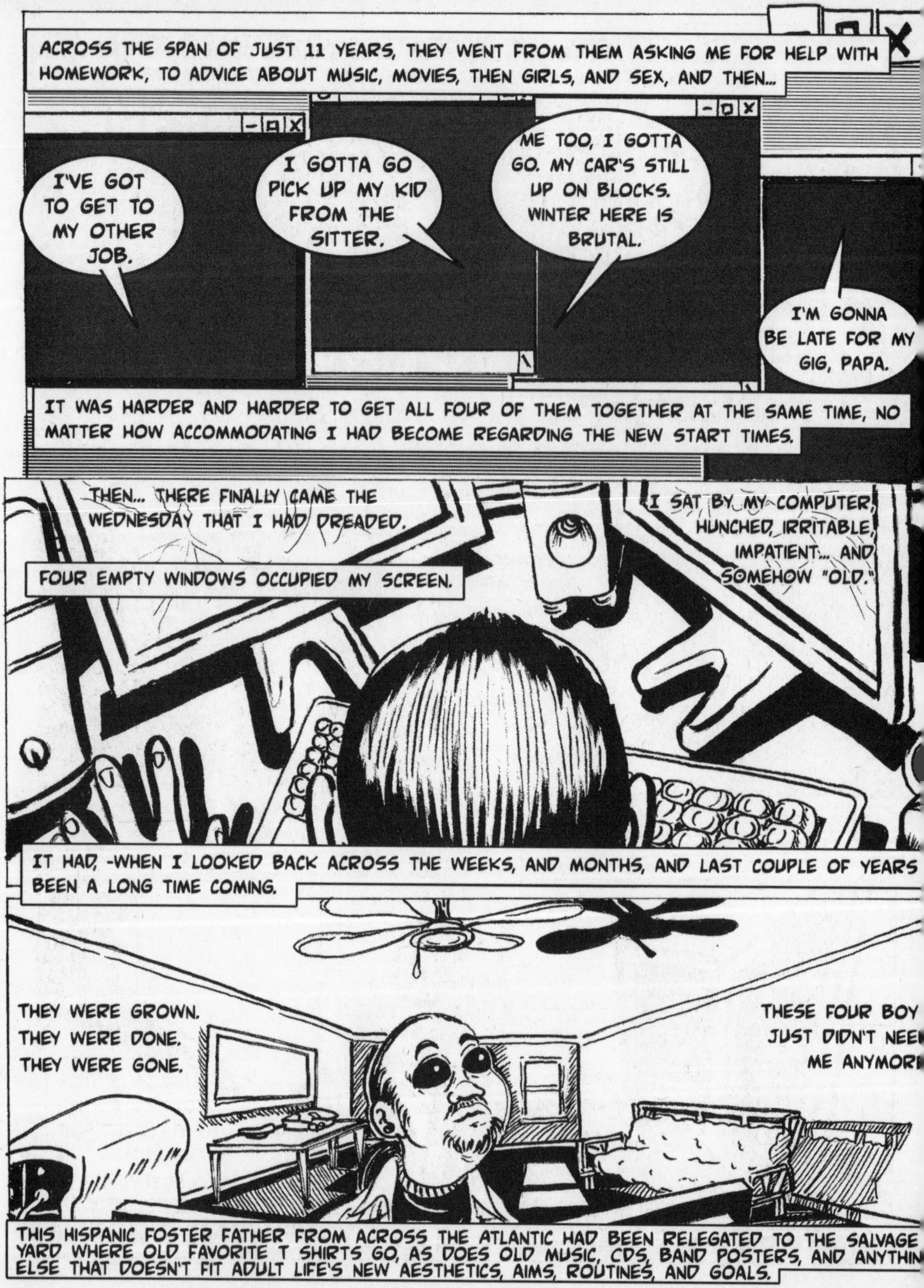
ACROSS THE SPAN OF JUST 11 YEARS, THEY WENT FROM THEM ASKING ME FOR HELP WITH HOMEWORK, TO ADVICE ABOUT MUSIC, MOVIES, THEN GIRLS, AND SEX, AND THEN...
I'VE GOT TO GET TO MY OTHER JOB.
I GOTTA GO PICK UP MY KID FROM THE SITTER.
ME TOO, I GOTTA GO. MY CAR'S STILL UP ON BLOCKS. WINTER HERE IS BRUTAL.
I'M GONNA BE LATE FOR MY GIG, PAPA.
IT WAS HARDER AND HARDER TO GET ALL FOUR OF THEM TOGETHER AT THE SAME TIME, NO MATTER HOW ACCOMMODATING I HAD BECOME REGARDING THE NEW START TIMES.
THEN... THERE FINALLY CAME THE WEDNESDAY THAT I HAD DREADED.
I SAT BY MY COMPUTER, HUNCHED, IRRITABLE, IMPATIENT... AND SOMEHOW "OLD."
FOUR EMPTY WINDOWS OCCUPIED MY SCREEN.
IT HAD, -WHEN I LOOKED BACK ACROSS THE WEEKS, AND MONTHS, AND LAST COUPLE OF YEARS BEEN A LONG TIME COMING.
THEY WERE GROWN.
THEY WERE DONE.
THEY WERE GONE.
THESE FOUR BOY
JUST DIDN'T NEE
ME ANYMOR
THIS HISPANIC FOSTER FATHER FROM ACROSS THE ATLANTIC HAD BEEN RELEGATED TO THE SALVAGE YARD WHERE OLD FAVORITE T SHIRTS GO, AS DOES OLD MUSIC, CDS, BAND POSTERS, AND ANYTHIN ELSE THAT DOESN'T FIT ADULT LIFE'S NEW AESTHETICS, AIMS, ROUTINES, AND GOALS.

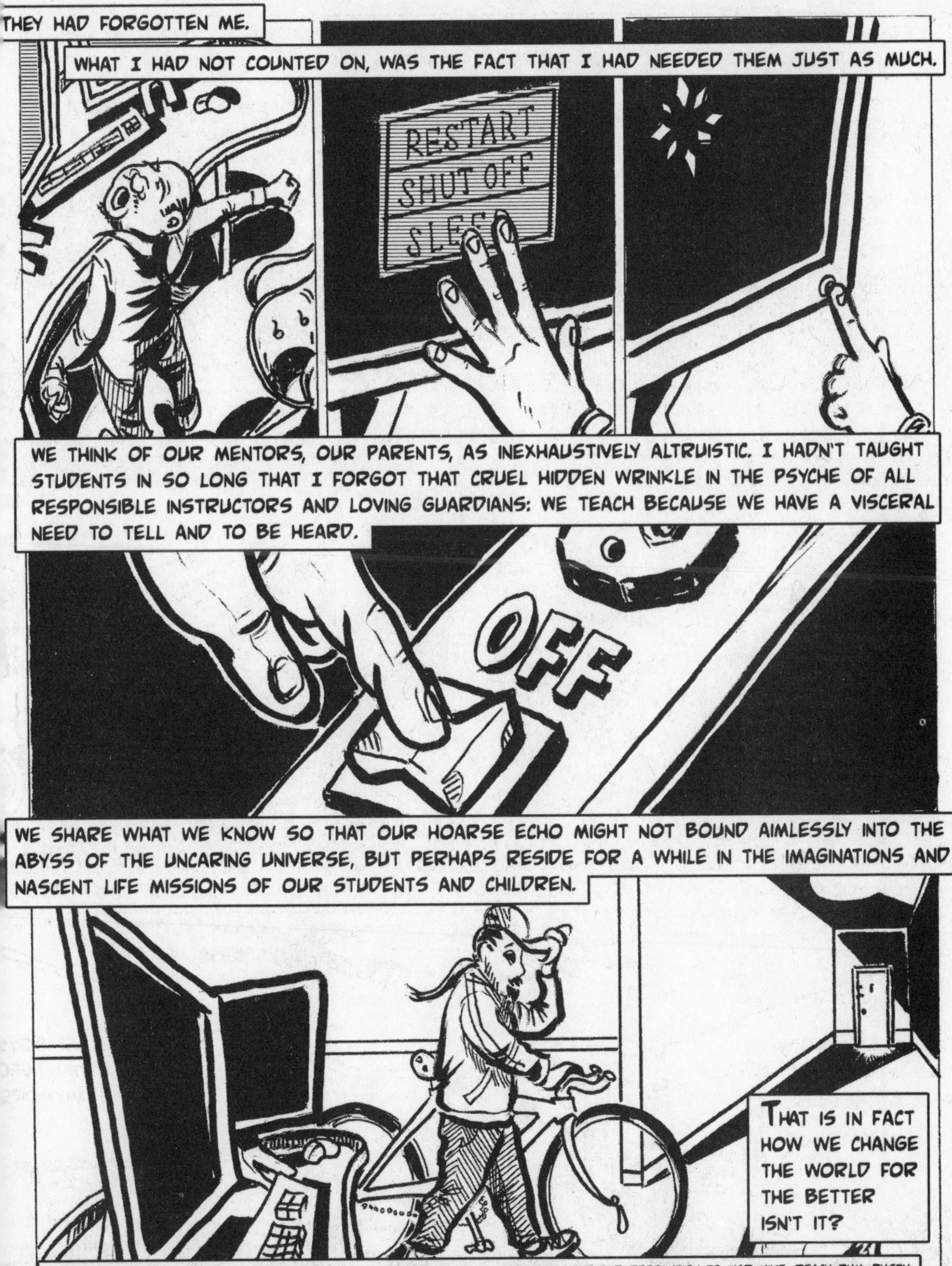

THEY HAD FORGOTTEN ME.
WHAT I HAD NOT COUNTED ON, WAS THE FACT THAT I HAD NEEDED THEM JUST AS MUCH.
RESTART
SHUT OFF
WE THINK OF OUR MENTORS, OUR PARENTS, AS INEXHAUSTIVELY ALTRUISTIC. I HADN'T TAUGHT STUDENTS IN SO LONG THAT I FORGOT THAT CRUEL HIDDEN WRINKLE IN THE PSYCHE OF ALL RESPONSIBLE INSTRUCTORS AND LOVING GUARDIANS: WE TEACH BECAUSE WE HAVE A VISCERAL NEED TO TELL AND TO BE HEARD.
OFF
WE SHARE WHAT WE KNOW SO THAT OUR HOARSE ECHO MIGHT NOT BOUND AIMLESSLY INTO THE ABYSS OF THE UNCARING UNIVERSE, BUT PERHAPS RESIDE FOR A WHILE IN THE IMAGINATIONS AND NASCENT LIFE MISSIONS OF OUR STUDENTS AND CHILDREN.
THAT IS IN FACT HOW WE CHANGE THE WORLD FOR THE BETTER ISN'T IT?
FOR MY BOYS, ANKER, CHRISTIAN, GREG, HEINZ, PAUL, THOMAS, AND WIL. -- AND WITH LOVE AND RESOLUTION TO MAD MIKE, BEACH BUM, DUSTY, EMPEROR, AL OSORIO, HOLTE ENDER, INFIDEL753, RONSINK66, ISISITRIX, JACK JODELL, LEE BAMBER, YUYU NINJA GAIDEN, MANIFESTO JOE, SEPP, (O)CT(O)PUS ... LESLY PARSLEY, TOM DEGAN, RATIONAL NATION USA, THE RUDE PUNDIT, GWENDOLYN, SINTAURO, TOMCAT, YELLOW DOG, AND MYCUE23.

<END/>

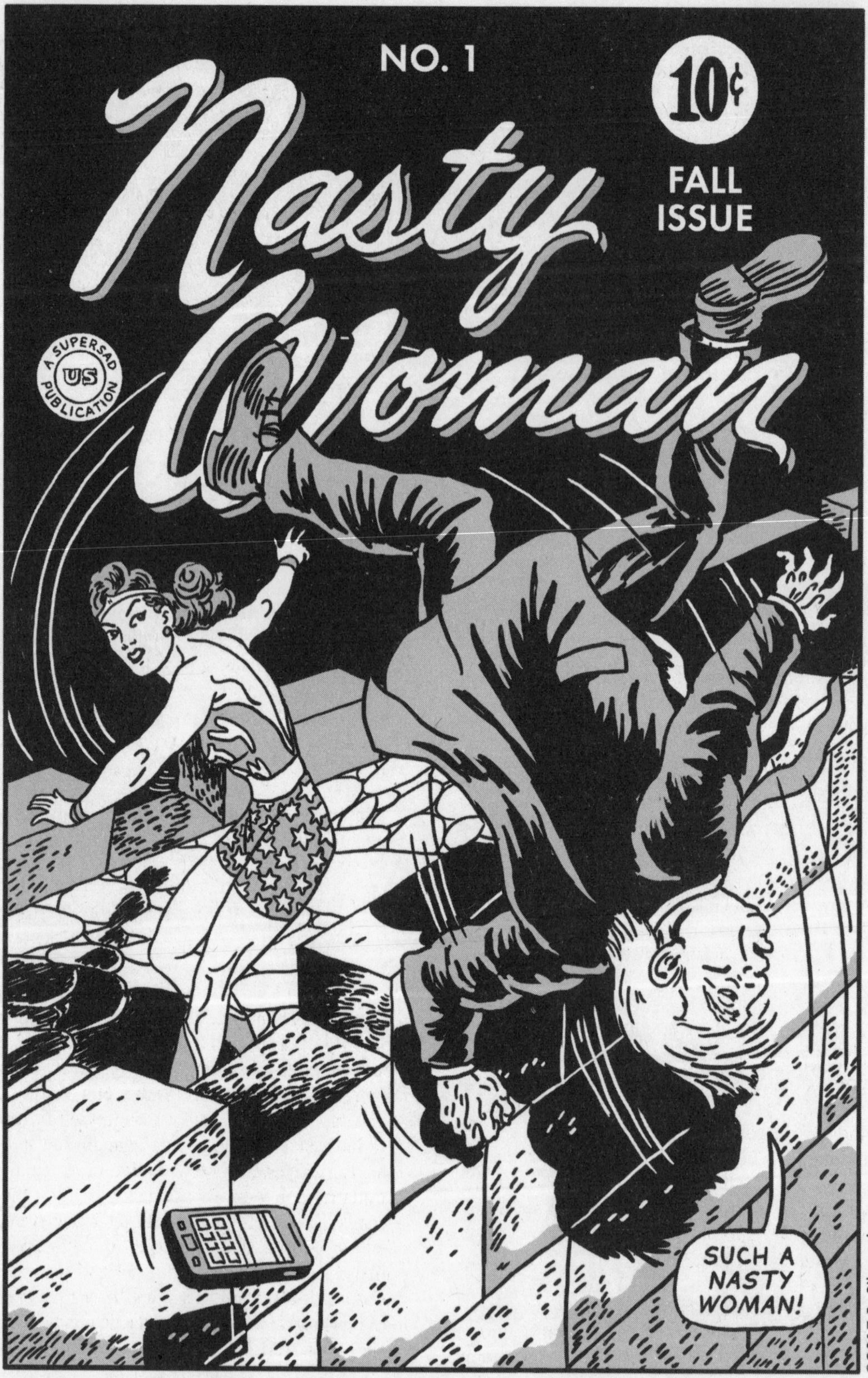

NO. 1
10¢
Nasty Woman
FALL ISSUE
A SUPERSAD US PUBLICATION
SUCH A NASTY WOMAN!

WHAT DO WE WANT TO SAY?
HOW DO WE WANT TO SAY IT?
Lucy R. Lippard

Lucy Lippard is a world renowned art critic and has written 21 books on contemporary art.

I doubt if any of us WW3 fans need much more information or analysis about what is going down in this country as we march toward fascism with a dangerous clown and his uncaring billionaire accomplices in the lead. The question for those of us in the cultural realm is not should we make art/ write/ perform/ demonstrate and so forth (of course we should), but what's the most effective way to do it? And who are we doing it for?

The outrage is palpable. Since the campaign/ election artists have created an extraordinary number of pointed images and satires and parodies and protests and on-line campaigns. Even the list of issues confronting us is too long to contemplate. It's frustrating and bewildering. Where to start?

I've been collecting resistant images since the November debacle. We know all too well how to preach to the choir. An on-line comment on Nov. 9: "Will it change anything? Nah. But it will show the world we don't support this. And it will feel good to stand together." It did. All those great marches and cartoons were the first shock of reaction. Trumpbashing was fun, from piñiatas to Barbara Kruger's *Loser*. However, the naked Trump sculpture in New York and inflated golden pigs obscuring the Trump Tower sign in Chicago, and my favorite – fake official signs marking sites of internment camps to come -- may tickle liberals and lefties, but they are hardly guaranteed to change the minds of his base. Responses to humor are dependent on the audience. So enough with the comb-over, the tiny hands, the cheeto tan, even the lovely pink pussy hats. For the second phase, it's not enough merely to blow off steam or mock our misled opponents.

We need to stop obsessing about the celebrity and get on the issues. We need to keep on being clever but work with serious, long-term campaigns.

(We can have fun doing that too?) It's time to get down to brass tacks, focus our energies on the repercussions of the stream of contemptible right wing policies – not just reacting, but pro-acting. We could stop generalizing, get specific about what's happening in people's daily lives. (Trump's very first executive order attacked people's hard-earned housing, then there's the anti-health-care bill.) Talk to more people whose lives are being affected and tell their stories in wild art. Abandon the clichés. Think positive. It's a subtle balancing point between being comprehensible and not talking down. Irony that misses its mark is dangerous. Jim Hightower (a real populist) urges us to "champion big and bold new ideas." How? Beats me… All this finger-wagging is talking to myself as much as to you.

As a cultural activist since the late 1960s, having protested Nixon and Reagan and Bushes, I've seen some powerful images and actions. Did anything we did produce change? OK, what? I've always said art can't change the world alone but with the right allies it can make a dent. Artists can produce jolts, Eureka moments, shake us up. IMAGINACTION was a slogan of the Alliance for Cultural Democracy in the '80s. Maybe the most important contributions from the bygone days were (still are) those old standbys: consciousness raising and collaboration. In the '60s, a couple of generations of artists and writers (myself included) were shocked or nudged into realizing that artists are as responsible for the society we live in as teachers or construction workers are. (Slowly, over the decades, art schools too began to get it, and eventually, even museums.) Social change, social energies, political issues and art are not oil and water, despite the commercial artworld's attempts to demote even the most imaginative activism to "didactic propaganda," "sociology, not art," etc.

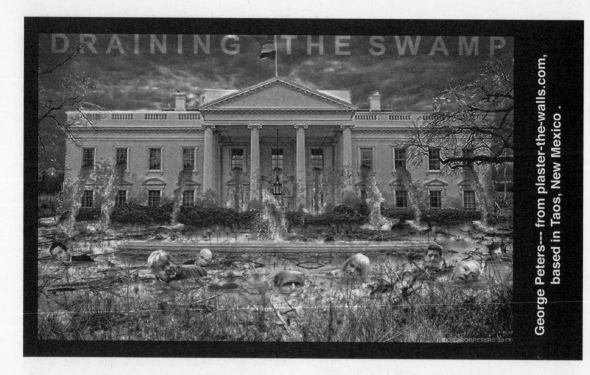

DRAINING THE SWAMP

George Peters--- from plaster-the-walls.com, based in Taos, New Mexico .

From my experience, a few hours of collective brainstorming on images and strategies can come up with wonders. Social media have upped the ante for "intersectional activism." Collaboration is key to learning how to open minds. Maybe no issue-oriented art should ever be made without working with those it affects. A favorite poster says "Nothing About Us Without Us is For Us." And when artists' contributions are ignored by the Left politicos (it happens), hang in and try again. Failure can be a great teacher.

The curator of the current Venice Biennale said recently: "Art is the place where you can re-invent the world." It is? Is the world interested? And how do we take it to the heartland, where it might actually matter? Are we collaborating with artists who live in the battlegrounds? A vast number of groups and collectives from the 1960s to the present have pioneered and re-discovered ways to bring art into the lives of those beyond the artworld. Images and stories have always seemed the most effective outreach tools. Images that tell unknown stories and images that spark well-known stories can both be powerful. It makes me tearful just to see portraits of Trayvon Martin, Tamir Rice, Sandra Bland, Marina Alexander, Jordan Edwards ....

How do we infiltrate the feckless, factless right wing news outlets and reach, at least, the doubting fringes of Trump's base? What can artists do to help get rid of the Electoral College and money in politics, slow down climate change? The Yes Men, among many others, show the way. Indivisible is doing important work but the involvement of artists might liven up even electoral politics, even education? There's been a lot of recent coverage on artworkers' notions about how to change the art world and the world. Suggestions range from free museums and art education, art fairs supporting young galleries, a resurrection of the Artists' Rights and Sales agreement, to taking over the entire Democratic Party. W.A.G.E. (Working Artists and the Greater Economy) is considering unionization "to demonstrate solidarity with the working class." An activist artist (woman) friend says "there are only two things worth doing: making information available in a way that people can hear; and contributing to work that makes the basic necessities available to all of us (food, shelter, clean water,etc...)" Education beyond schools seems crucial. "A democracy cannot survive without informed citizens," says Henry Giroux. The citizen artist is doubly responsible for offering work beyond the clichés of unproven "community," beyond the negative and the reactive.

One internationally successful artist, acknowledging that "we in the cultural sector have failed to adequately address" the frustrations of "those who feel unheard," recommends self-criticism: "It is clear that we have to reinvent the cultural sector from within, further developing its potential to become an agent for social change." (Nice work if you can get it.). A leader of Hands Off Our Revolution declares, "We will not go quietly."

Right after the election, a revered cultural policy wonk wrote: "When I think about what we need now, the words that come to mind will be unsurprising: empathy, imagination, love in the service of justice, healing that goes to the broken heart of America." Similarly, another commentator writes, "We already know what you hate. Tell us what you love." I have to admit I'm feeling a lot of empathy but not too much love at the moment. I'm all for the energy that comes with anger. May it last as long as the outrages last. A Women's March sign: "Love Didn't Trump Hate, Time to Smash the State!" But let's look at building instead of smashing. Channel the anger, stop blocking traffic so people can't get to work, stop destroying property that deprives people of necessities. It may feel good at the moment, but it's counter-productive. Impeach Trump has a nice ring but it will be useless if Pence and Ryan take over. Can art counter apathy? 47% of eligible voters did not vote. Trump lost the popular vote by millions. Rumor has it that only 3.5% of a population can overthrow a government.

Maybe it's my octogenarian status, but the stakes seem higher now than ever before. Clearly we need to RESIST but there's still a lot of work to do to fully understand our contexts, our audiences, our challenges, our strengths and our weaknesses. If we are indeed entering "a golden era of activism," what's the artist's role? What are we willing to risk? Can we conceive a future that others will want to live? I'm personally still trying to figure it out.

Help!

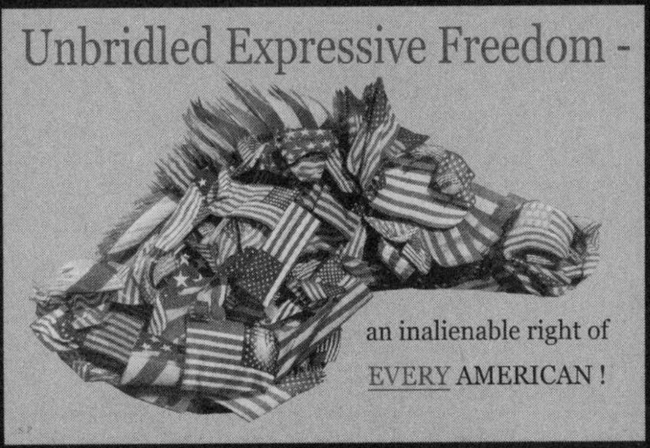
Unbridled Expressive Freedom -
an inalienable right of
EVERY AMERICAN !

Stephen Parlato-- from plaster-the-walls.com, based in Taos, New Mexico .

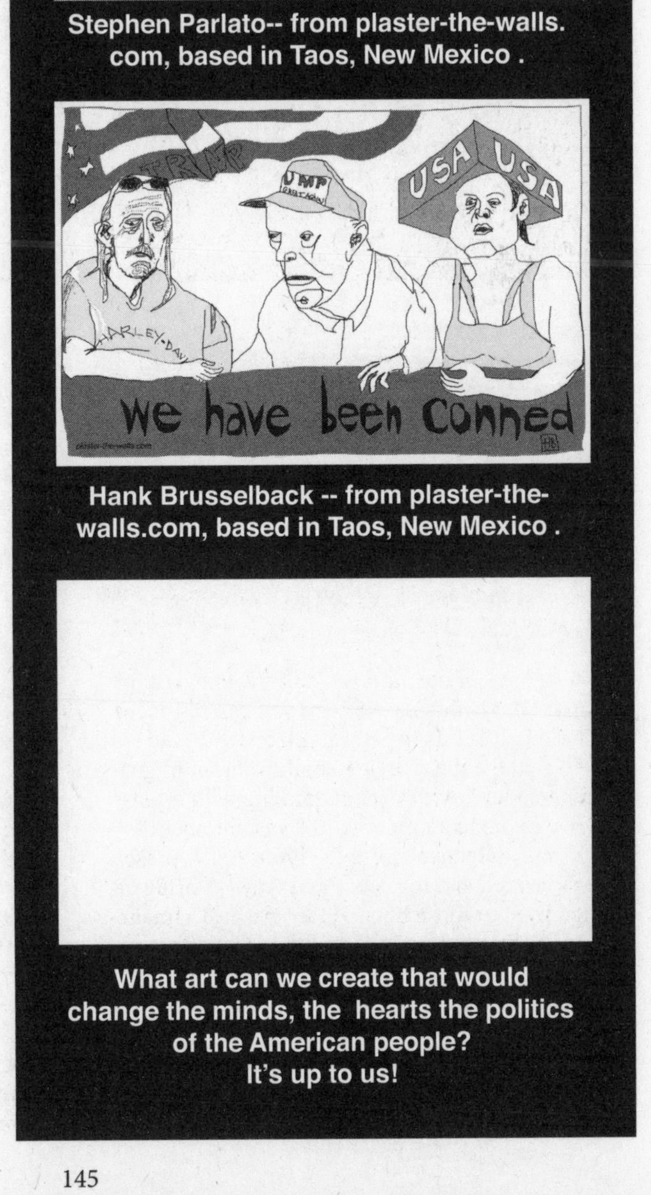
USA USA
we have been conned

Hank Brusselback -- from plaster-the-walls.com, based in Taos, New Mexico .

What art can we create that would change the minds, the hearts the politics of the American people?
It's up to us!

'MERICA'S GREATEST COMICS!

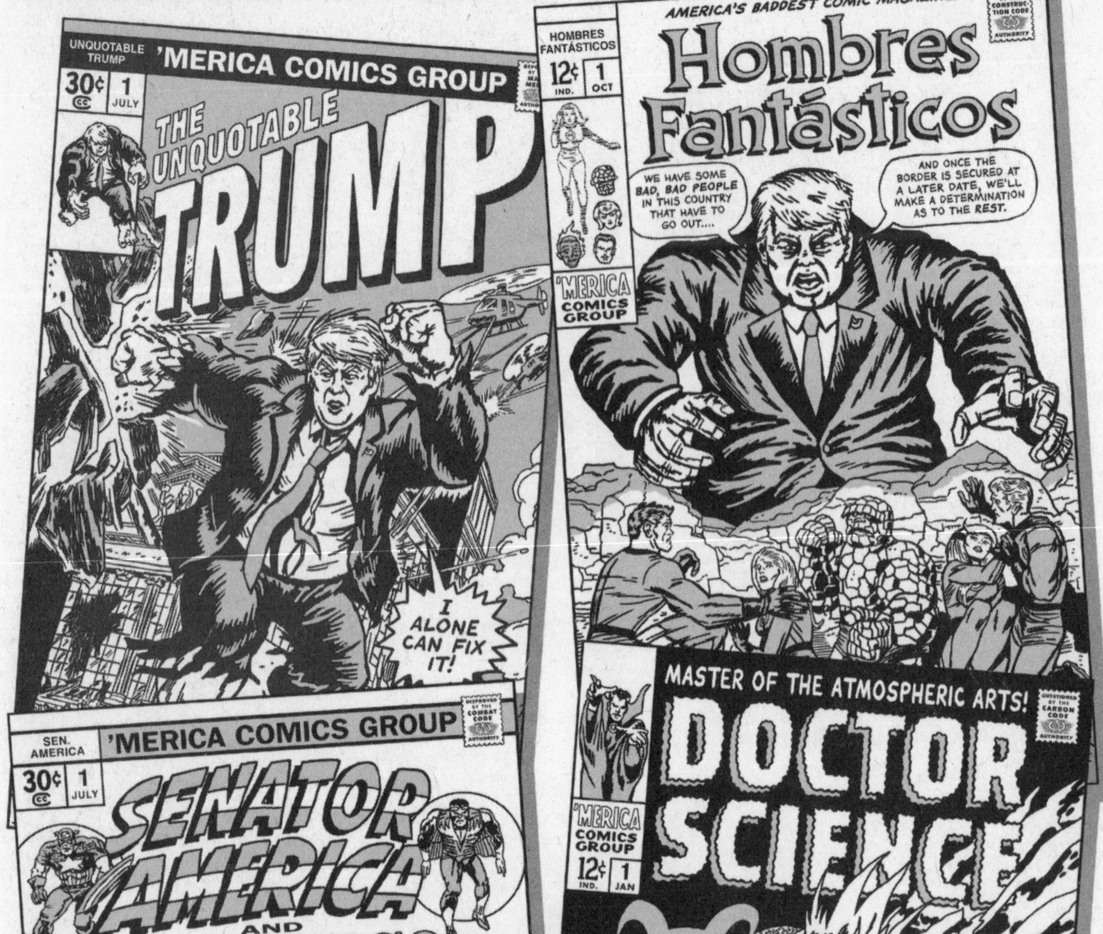

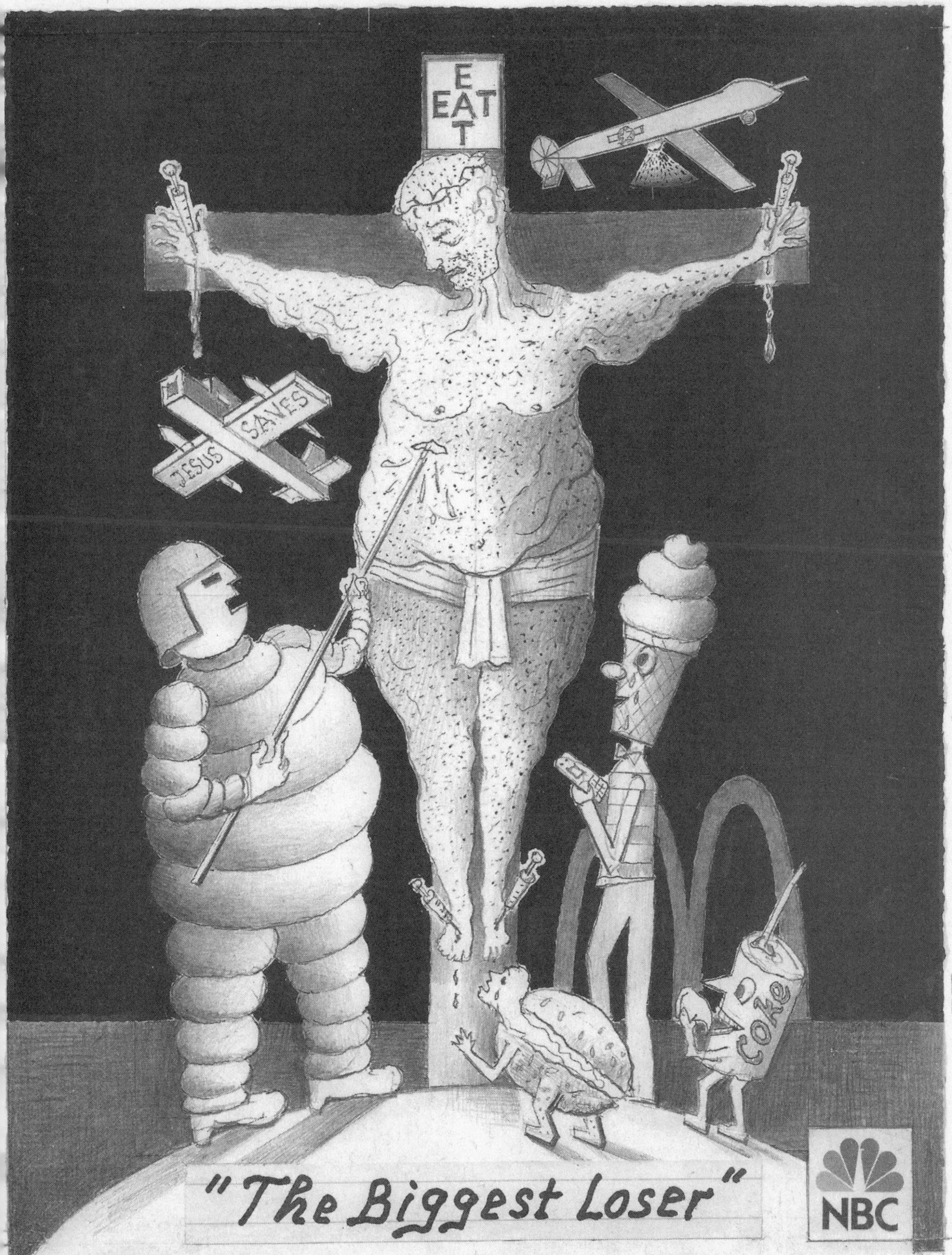
E
EAT
T
JESUS SAVES
Coke
"The Biggest Loser"
NBC

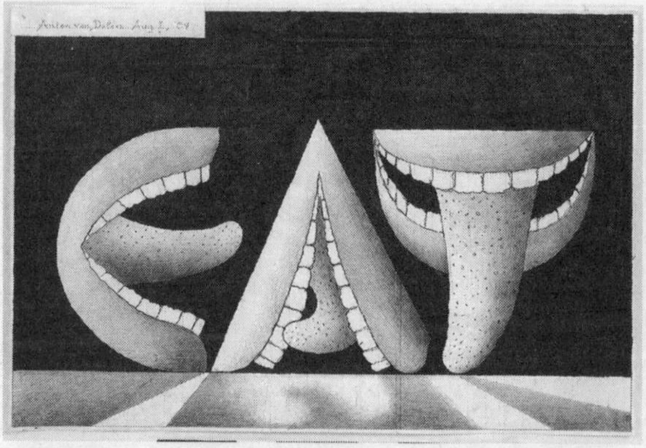

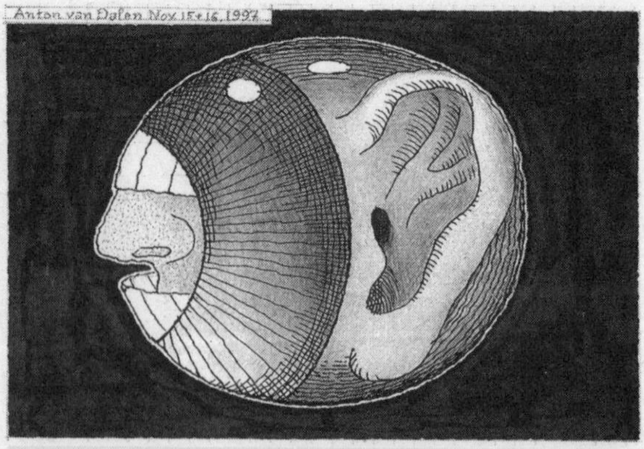
Anton van Dalen Nov 15+16 1997

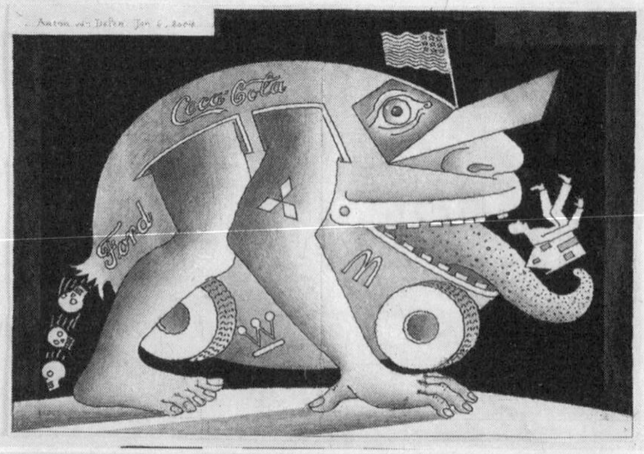
Coca-Cola
Ford

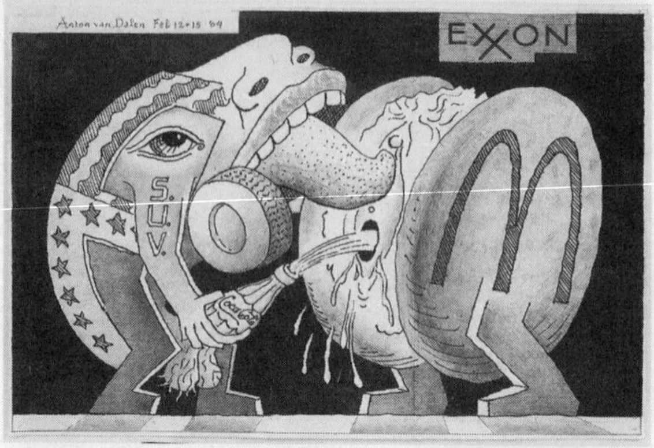
EXXON
S.U.V.

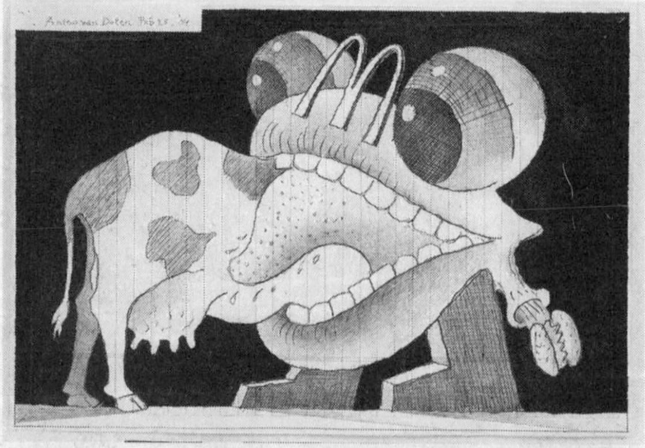

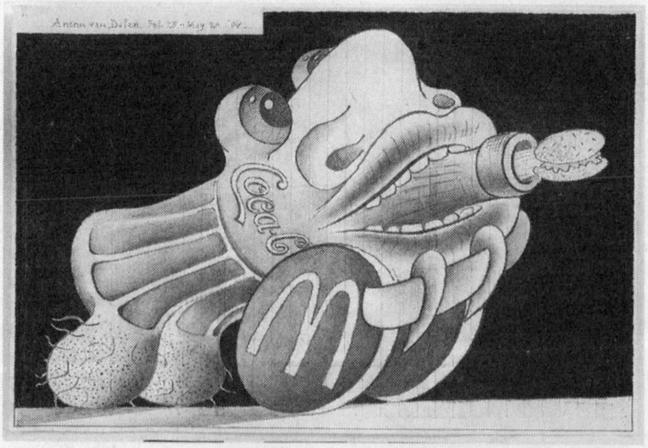
Coca-Cola

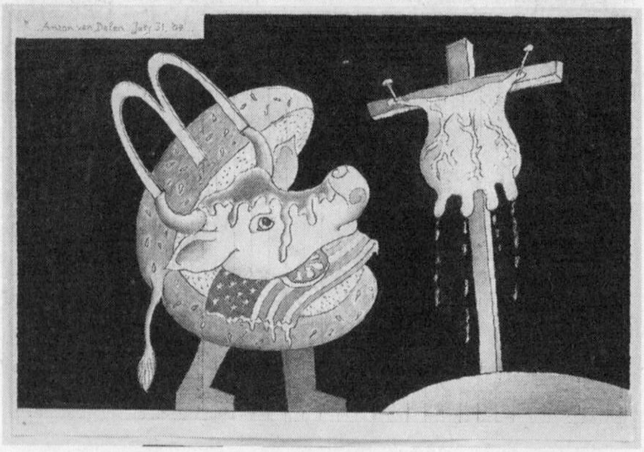

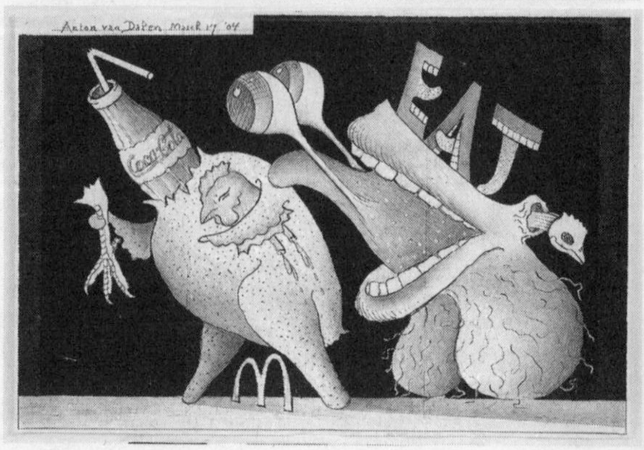
Anton van Dalen March 17 '04
Coca-Cola
EAT

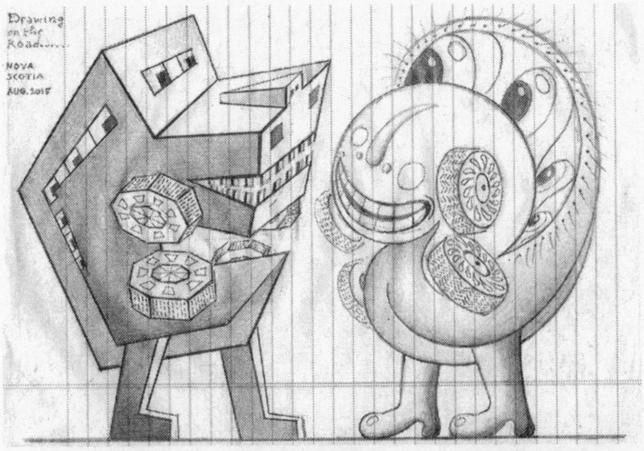
Drawing on the Road.....
NOVA SCOTIA AUG. 2015

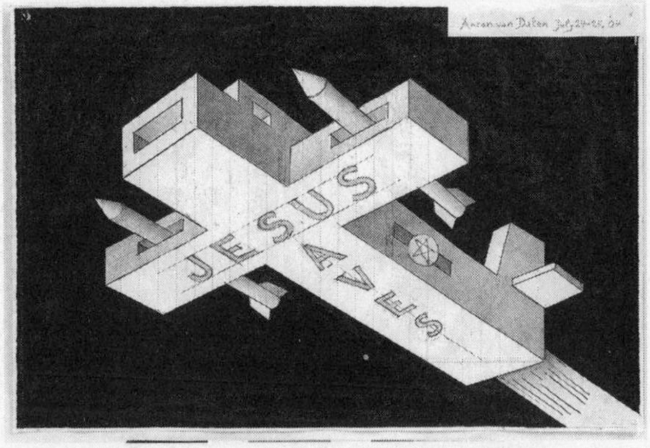
JESUS

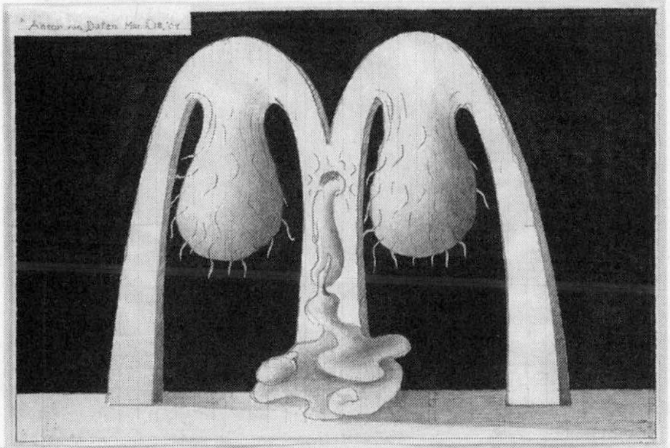

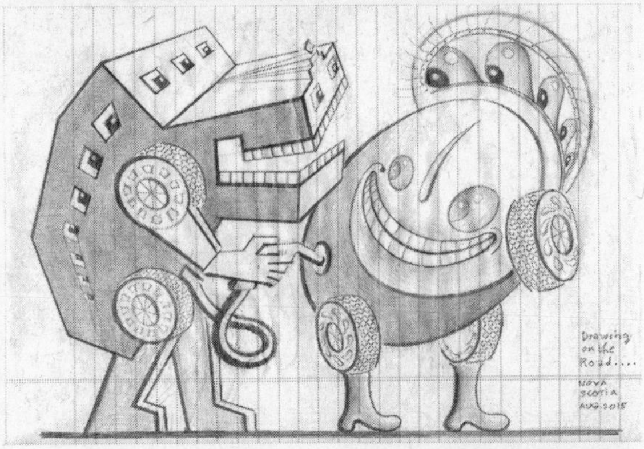
Drawing on the Road....
NOVA SCOTIA AUG. 2015

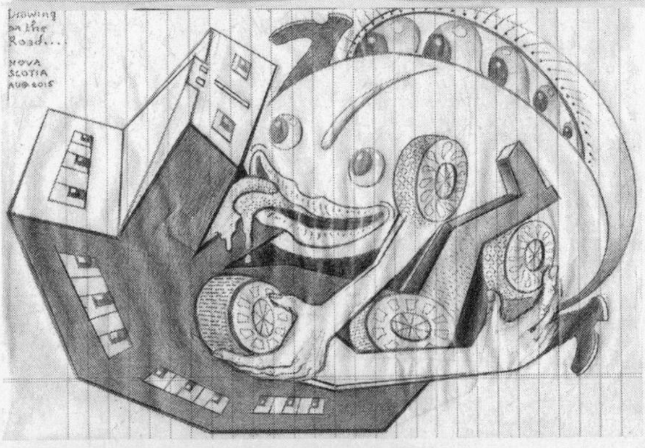
Drawing on the Road...
NOVA SCOTIA AUG. 2015

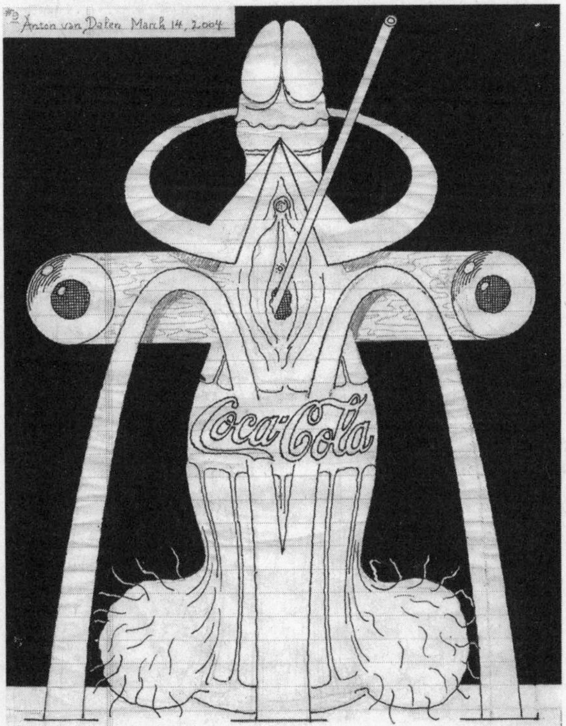
Anton van Dalen March 14, 2004
Coca-Cola

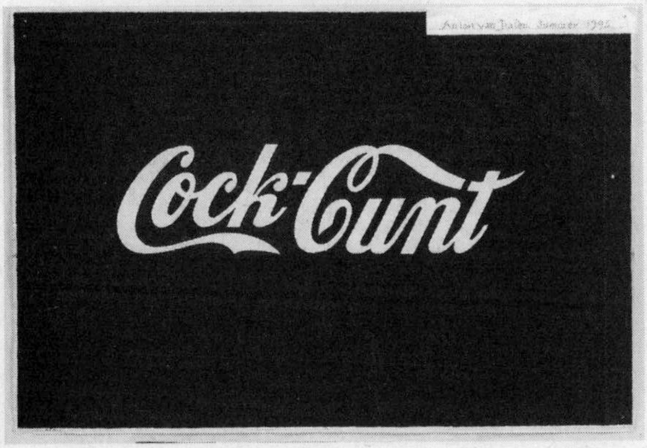
Cock-Cunt

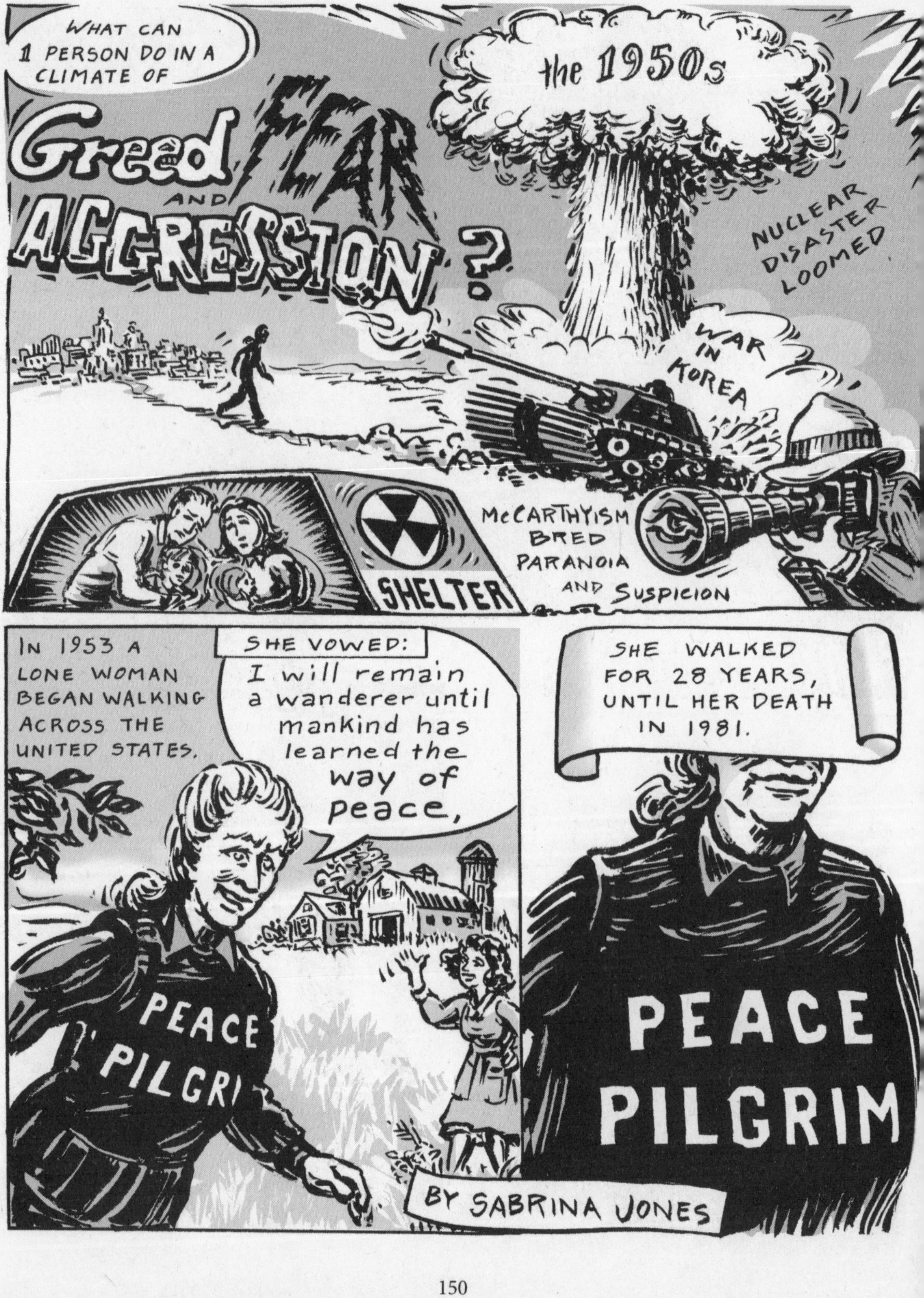
WHAT CAN 1 PERSON DO IN A CLIMATE OF
Greed FEAR AND AGGRESSION?
the 1950s
NUCLEAR DISASTER LOOMED
WAR IN KOREA
SHELTER
McCARTHYISM BRED PARANOIA AND SUSPICION
IN 1953 A LONE WOMAN BEGAN WALKING ACROSS THE UNITED STATES.
SHE VOWED:
I will remain a wanderer until mankind has learned the way of peace,
PEACE PILGRI
SHE WALKED FOR 28 YEARS, UNTIL HER DEATH IN 1981.
PEACE PILGRIM
BY SABRINA JONES

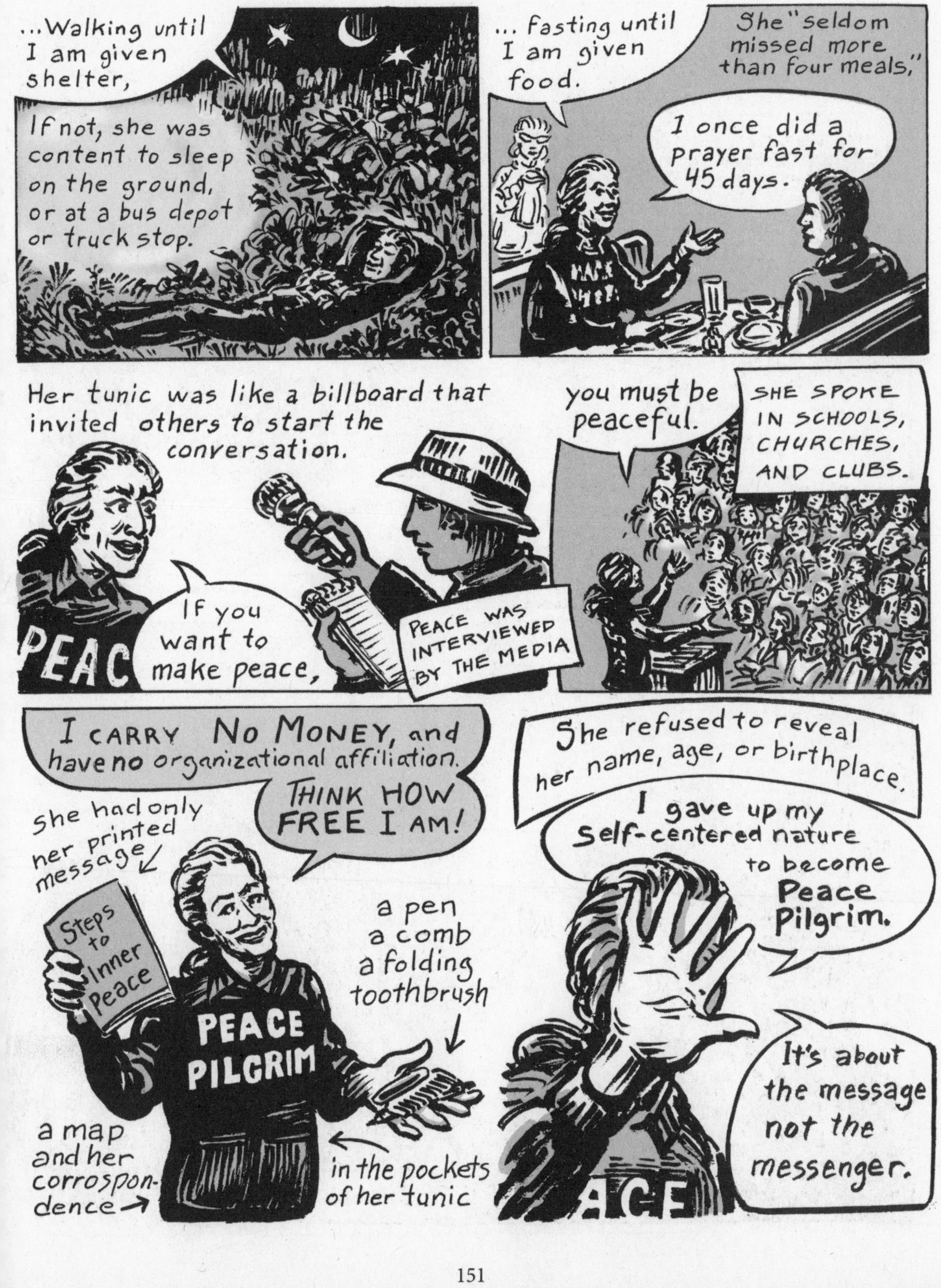
...Walking until I am given shelter,
If not, she was content to sleep on the ground, or at a bus depot or truck stop.
... fasting until I am given food.
She "seldom missed more than four meals,"
I once did a prayer fast for 45 days.
Her tunic was like a billboard that invited others to start the conversation.
PEAC
If you want to make peace,
PEACE WAS INTERVIEWED BY THE MEDIA
you must be peaceful.
SHE SPOKE IN SCHOOLS, CHURCHES, AND CLUBS.
I CARRY NO MONEY, and have no organizational affiliation.
THINK HOW FREE I AM!
She had only her printed message
Steps to Inner Peace
PEACE PILGRIM
a pen
a comb
a folding toothbrush
a map and her corrospondence
in the pockets of her tunic
She refused to reveal her name, age, or birthplace.
I gave up my self-centered nature to become Peace Pilgrim.
It's about the message not the messenger.
ACE

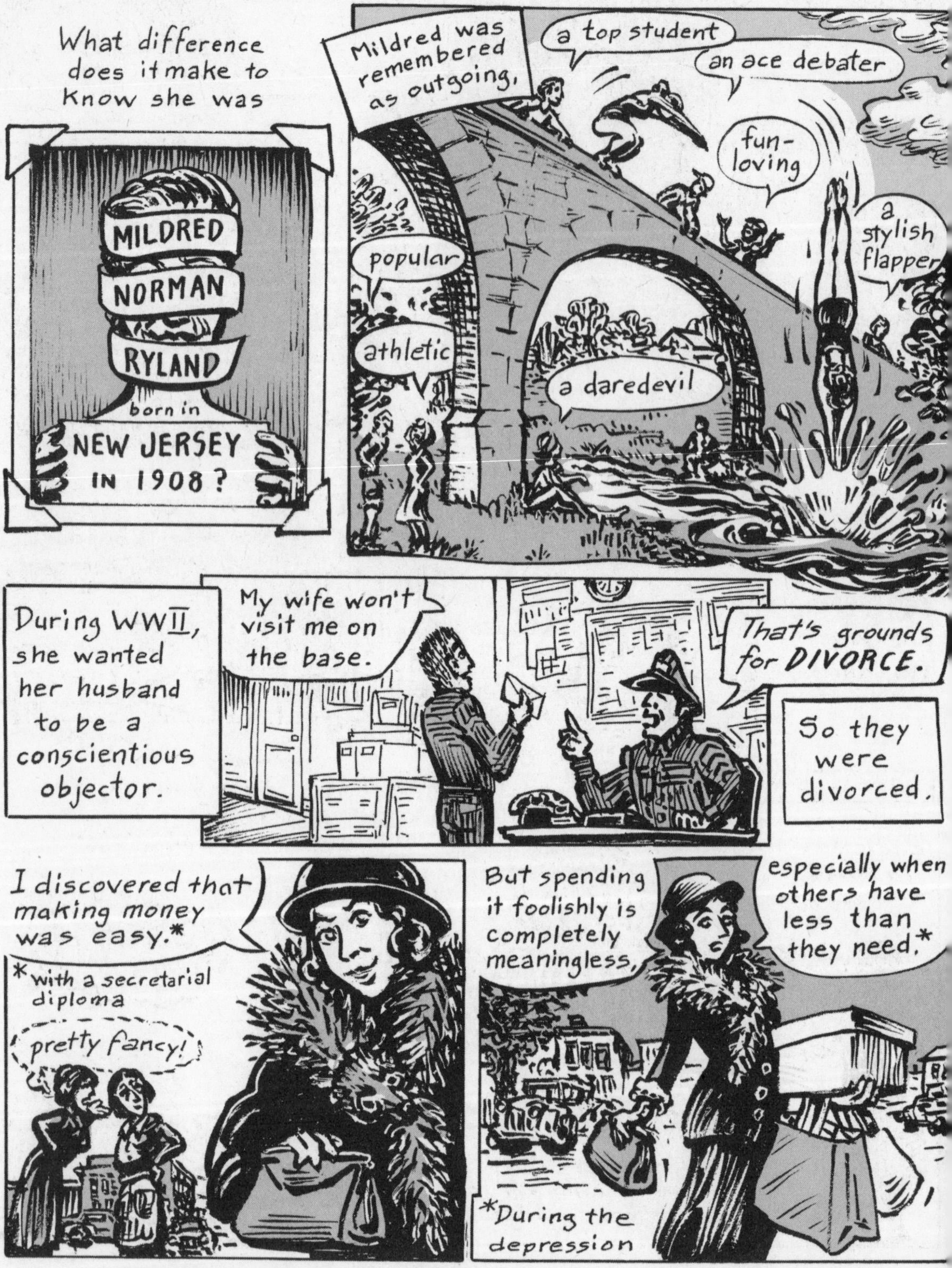

What difference does it make to know she was
MILDRED
NORMAN
RYLAND
born in
NEW JERSEY IN 1908?
Mildred was remembered as outgoing,
a top student
an ace debater
fun-loving
a stylish flapper
popular
athletic
a daredevil
During WWII, she wanted her husband to be a conscientious objector.
My wife won't visit me on the base.
That's grounds for DIVORCE.
So they were divorced.
I discovered that making money was easy.*
*with a secretarial diploma
pretty fancy!
But spending it foolishly is completely meaningless,
especially when others have less than they need.*
*During the depression

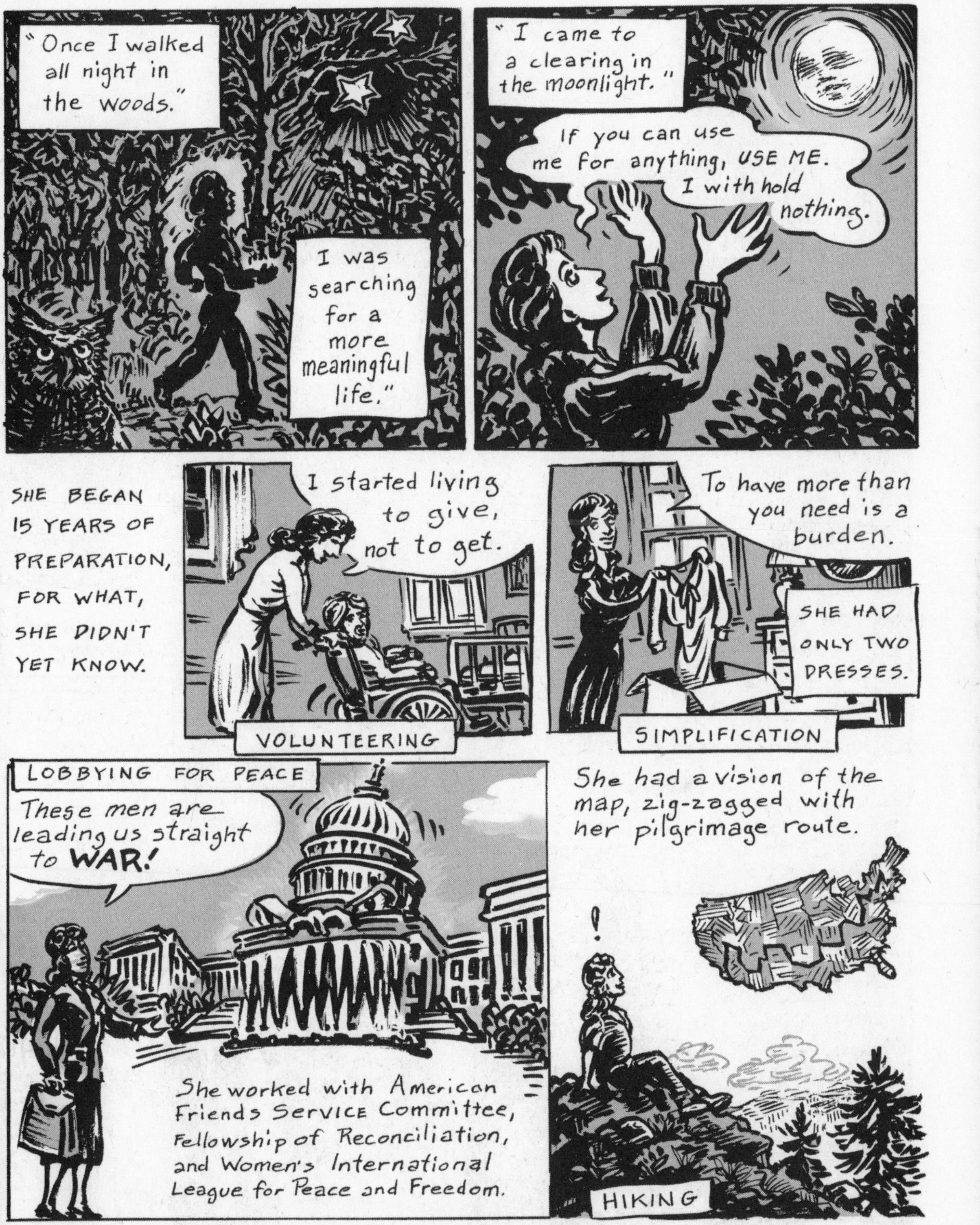
"Once I walked all night in the woods."
I was searching for a more meaningful life."
"I came to a clearing in the moonlight."
If you can use me for anything, USE ME. I with hold nothing.
SHE BEGAN 15 YEARS OF PREPARATION, FOR WHAT, SHE DIDN'T YET KNOW.
I started living to give, not to get.
VOLUNTEERING
To have more than you need is a burden.
SHE HAD ONLY TWO DRESSES.
SIMPLIFICATION
LOBBYING FOR PEACE
These men are leading us straight to WAR!
She worked with American Friends Service Committee, Fellowship of Reconciliation, and Women's International League for Peace and Freedom.
She had a vision of the map, zig-zagged with her pilgrimage route.
!
HIKING

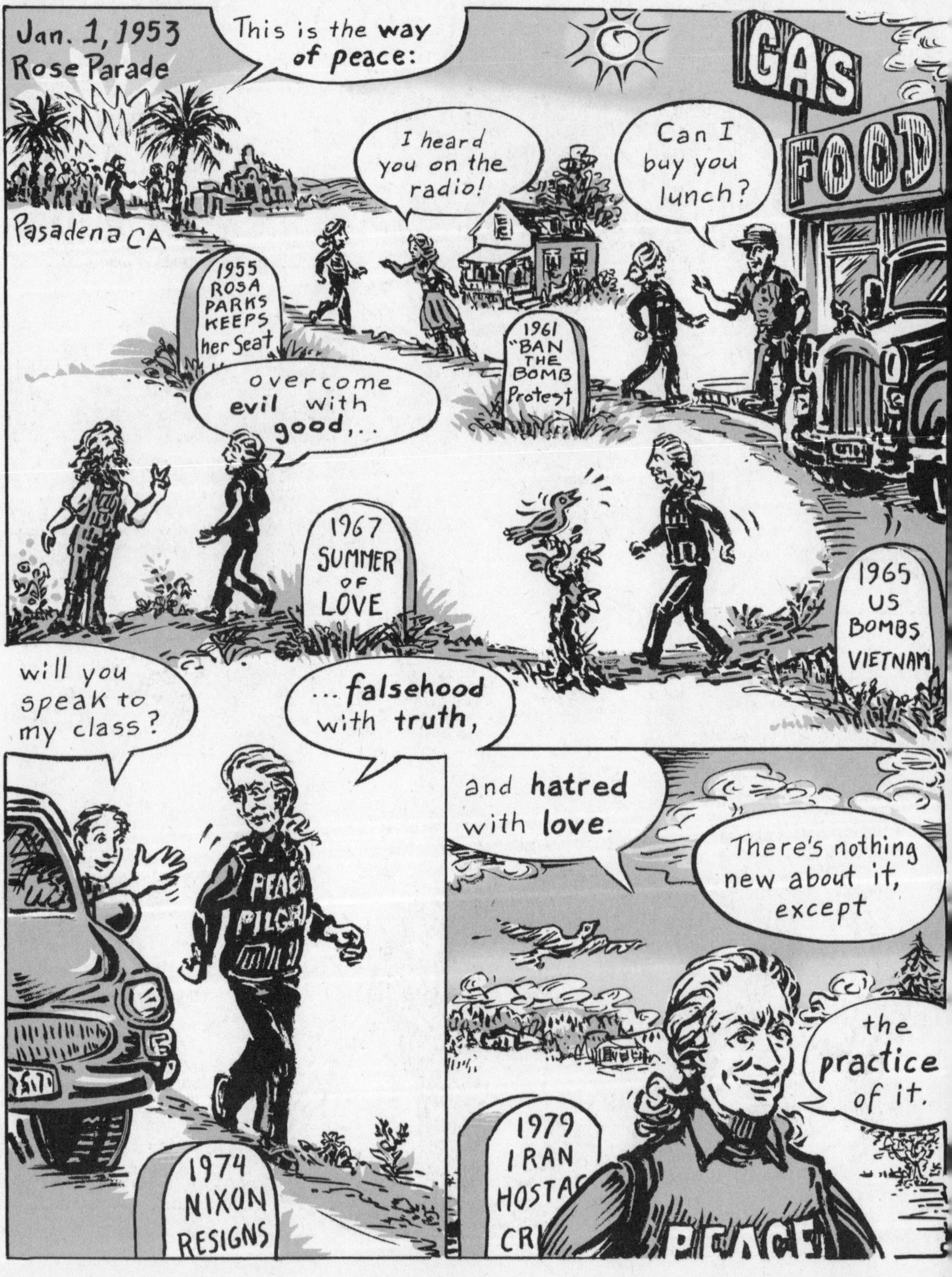
Jan. 1, 1953
Rose Parade
This is the way of peace:
Pasadena CA
I heard you on the radio!
Can I buy you lunch?
GAS
FOOD
1955 ROSA PARKS KEEPS her Seat
1961 "BAN THE BOMB Protest
overcome evil with good,..
1967 SUMMER OF LOVE
1965 US BOMBS VIETNAM
will you speak to my class?
...falsehood with truth,
and hatred with love.
There's nothing new about it, except
the practice of it.
1974 NIXON RESIGNS
1979 IRAN HOSTA
CR
PEACE

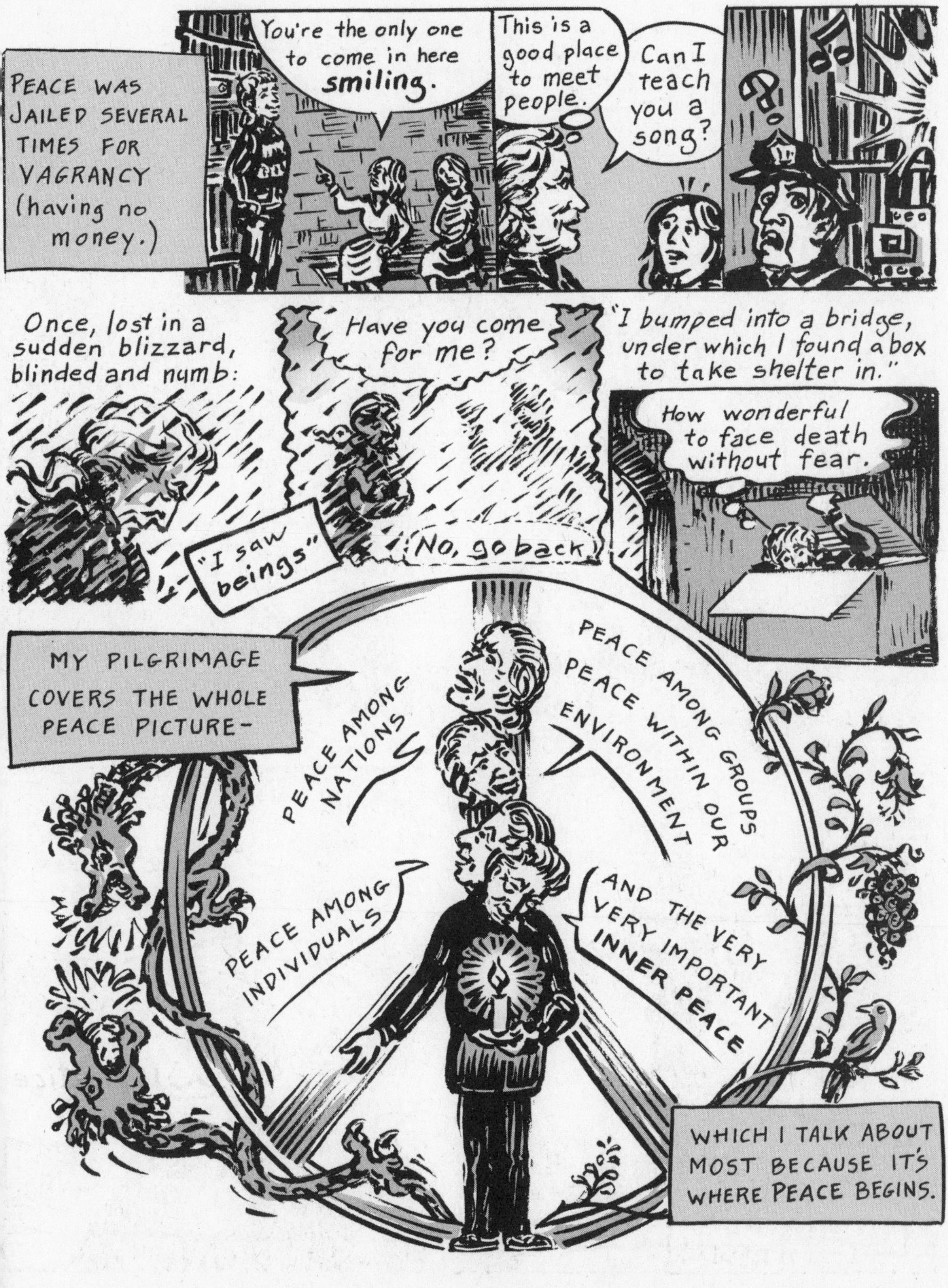

PEACE WAS JAILED SEVERAL TIMES FOR VAGRANCY (having no money.)
You're the only one to come in here smiling.
This is a good place to meet people.
Can I teach you a song?
Once, lost in a sudden blizzard, blinded and numb:
"I saw beings"
Have you come for me?
No, go back
"I bumped into a bridge, under which I found a box to take shelter in."
How wonderful to face death without fear.
MY PILGRIMAGE COVERS THE WHOLE PEACE PICTURE-
PEACE AMONG NATIONS
PEACE AMONG GROUPS
PEACE WITHIN OUR ENVIRONMENT
PEACE AMONG INDIVIDUALS
AND THE VERY VERY IMPORTANT INNER PEACE
WHICH I TALK ABOUT MOST BECAUSE IT'S WHERE PEACE BEGINS.

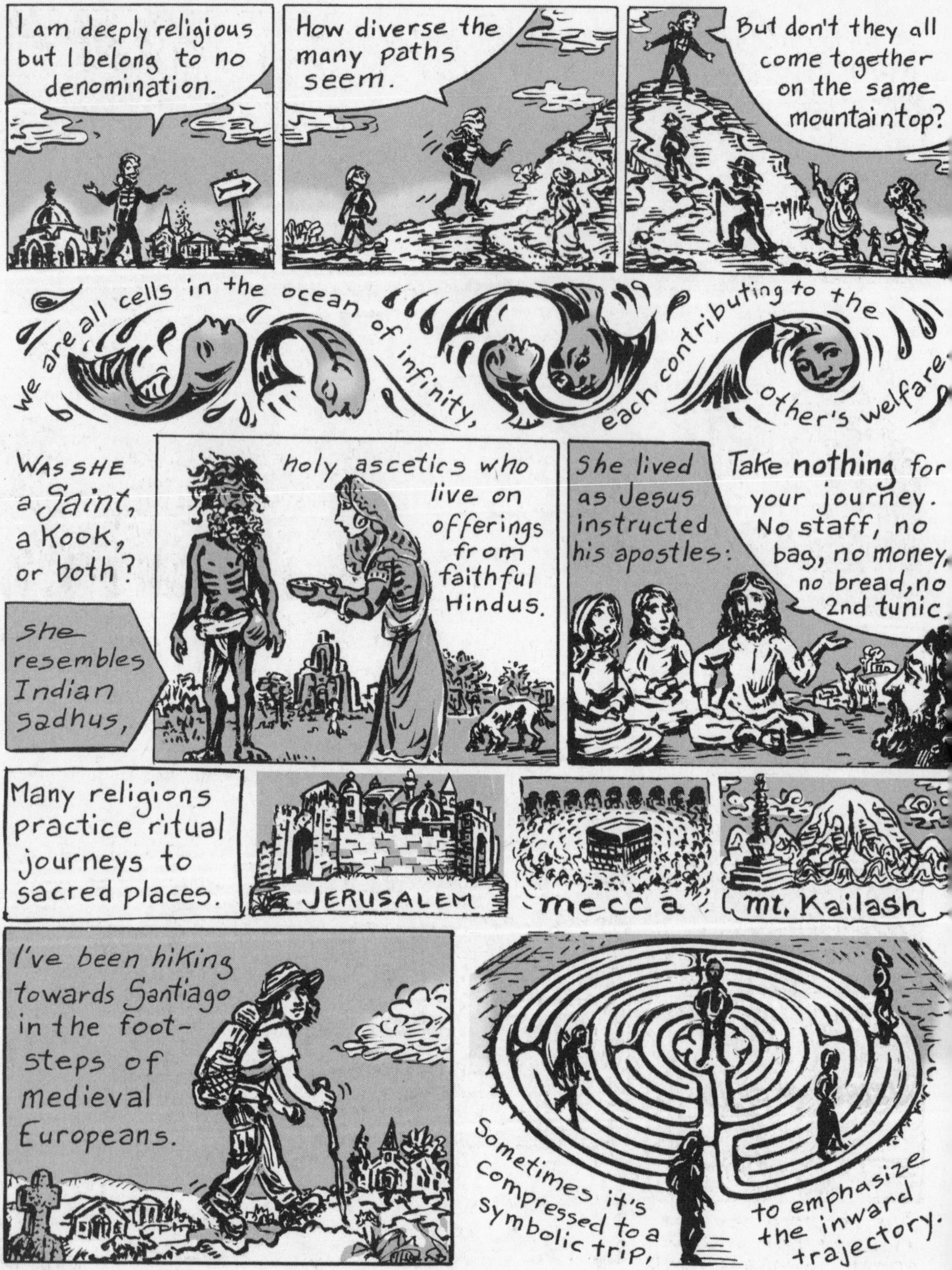
I am deeply religious but I belong to no denomination.
How diverse the many paths seem.
But don't they all come together on the same mountaintop?
We are all cells in the ocean of infinity, each contributing to the other's welfare.
WAS SHE a Saint, a Kook, or both?
She resembles Indian sadhus,
holy ascetics who live on offerings from faithful Hindus.
She lived as Jesus instructed his apostles:
Take nothing for your journey. No staff, no bag, no money, no bread, no 2nd tunic.
Many religions practice ritual journeys to sacred places.
JERUSALEM
mecca
mt. Kailash
I've been hiking towards Santiago in the foot-steps of medieval Europeans.
Sometimes it's compressed to a symbolic trip,
to emphasize the inward trajectory.

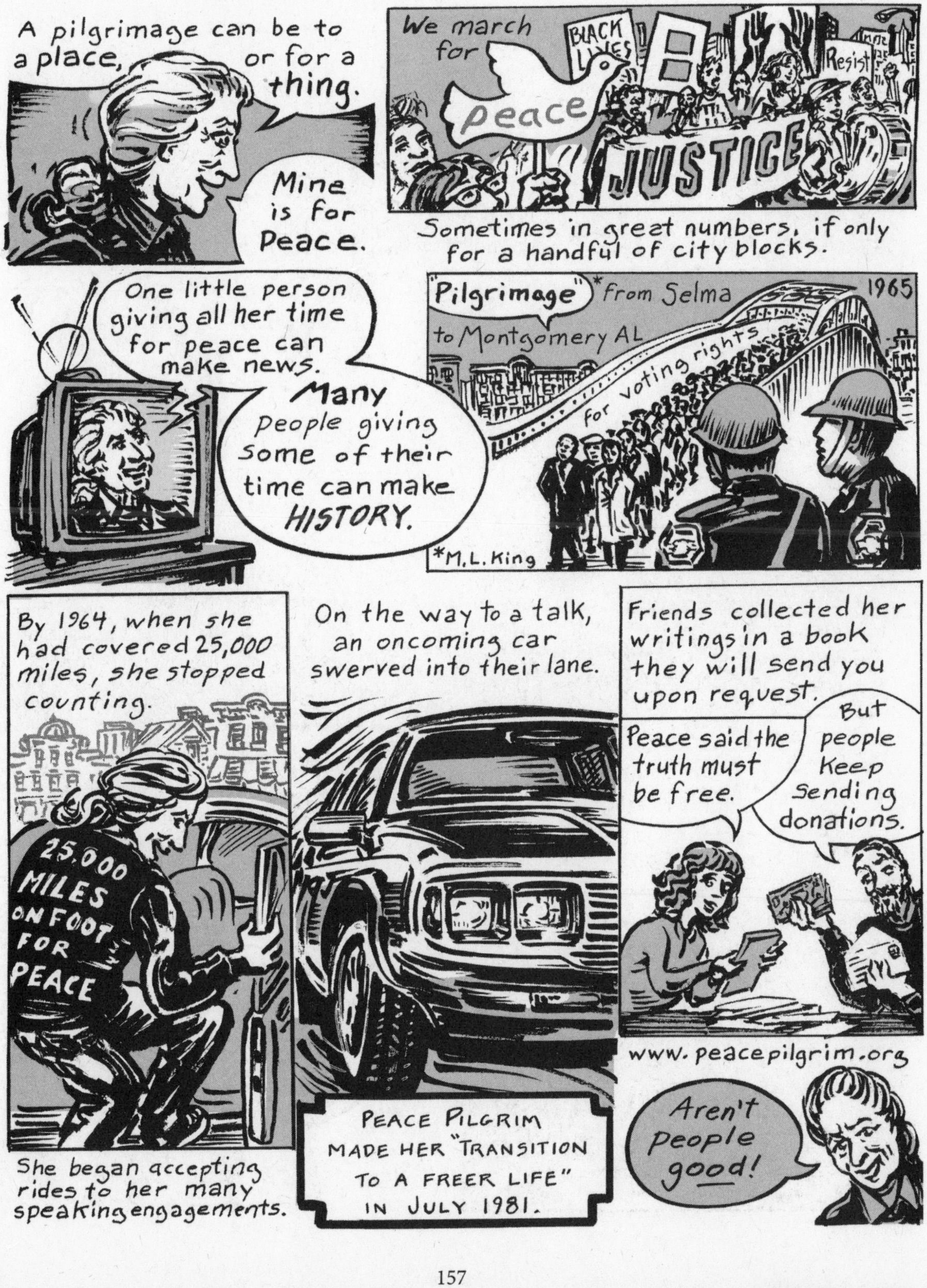
A pilgrimage can be to a place, or for a thing.
Mine is for Peace.
We march for
peace
BLACK LIVES
Resist
JUSTICE
Sometimes in great numbers, if only for a handful of city blocks.
One little person giving all her time for peace can make news.
Many people giving some of their time can make HISTORY.
"Pilgrimage"* from Selma to Montgomery AL
1965
for voting rights
*M.L. King
By 1964, when she had covered 25,000 miles, she stopped counting.
25,000 MILES ON FOOT FOR PEACE
She began accepting rides to her many speaking engagements.
On the way to a talk, an oncoming car swerved into their lane.
PEACE PILGRIM MADE HER "TRANSITION TO A FREER LIFE" IN JULY 1981.
Friends collected her writings in a book they will send you upon request.
Peace said the truth must be free.
But people keep sending donations.
www.peacepilgrim.org
Aren't people good!

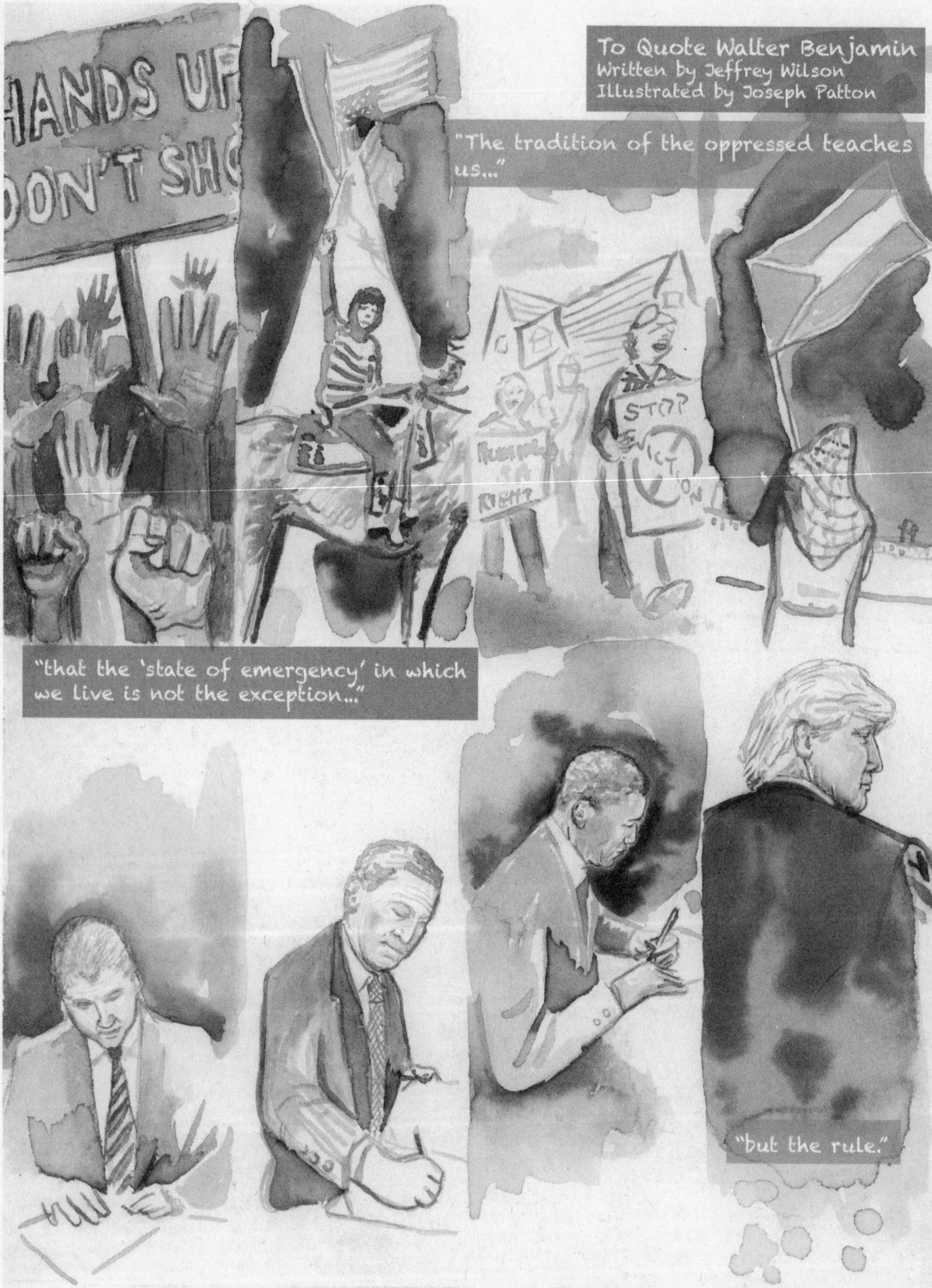
HANDS UP
DON'T SHO
To Quote Walter Benjamin
Written by Jeffrey Wilson
Illustrated by Joseph Patton
"The tradition of the oppressed teaches us..."
STOP
"that the 'state of emergency' in which we live is not the exception..."
"but the rule."

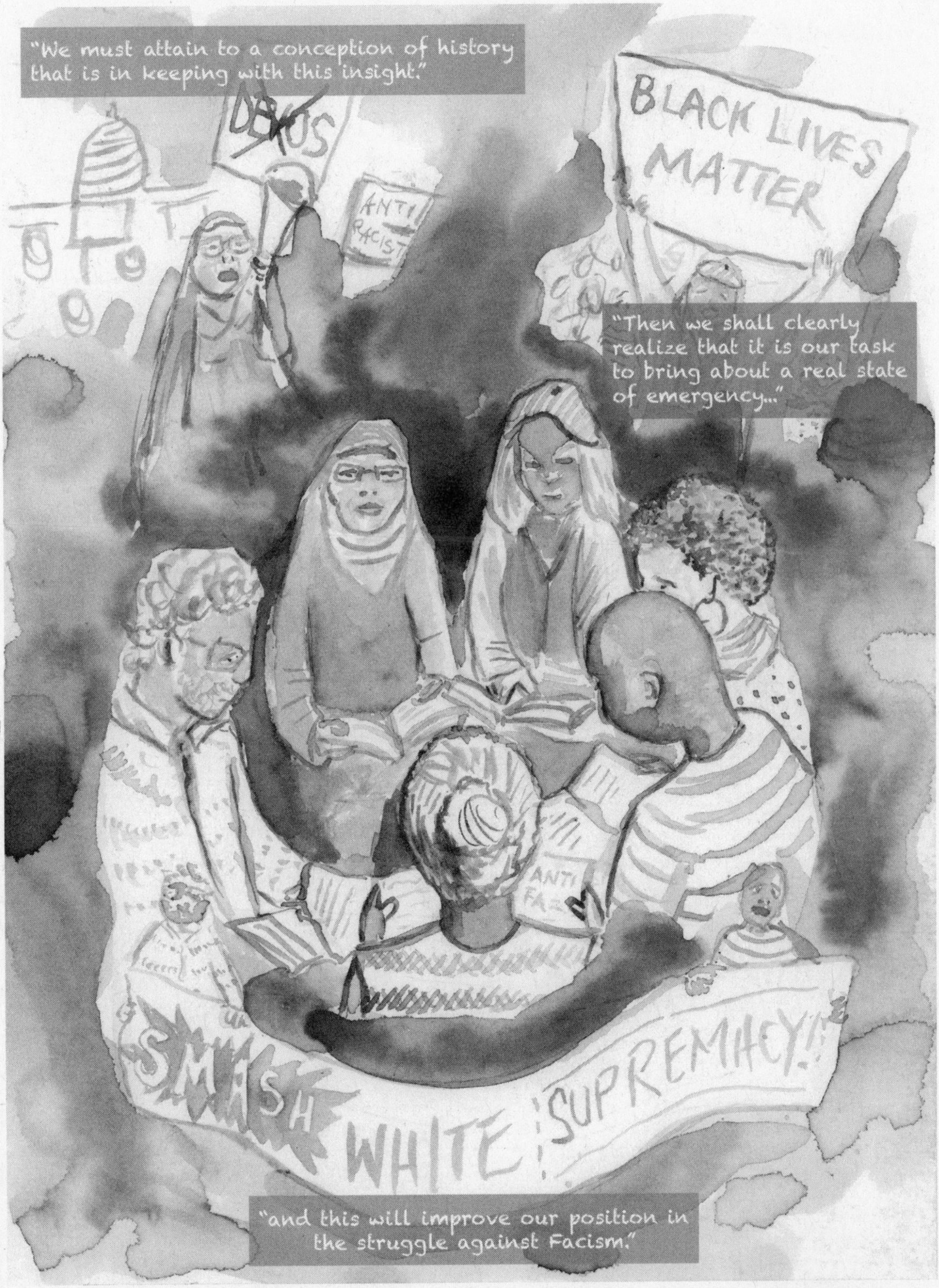
"We must attain to a conception of history that is in keeping with this insight."
BLACK LIVES MATTER
ANTI RACIST
"Then we shall clearly realize that it is our task to bring about a real state of emergency..."
ANTI FA
SMASH WHITE SUPREMACY!!
"and this will improve our position in the struggle against Facism."

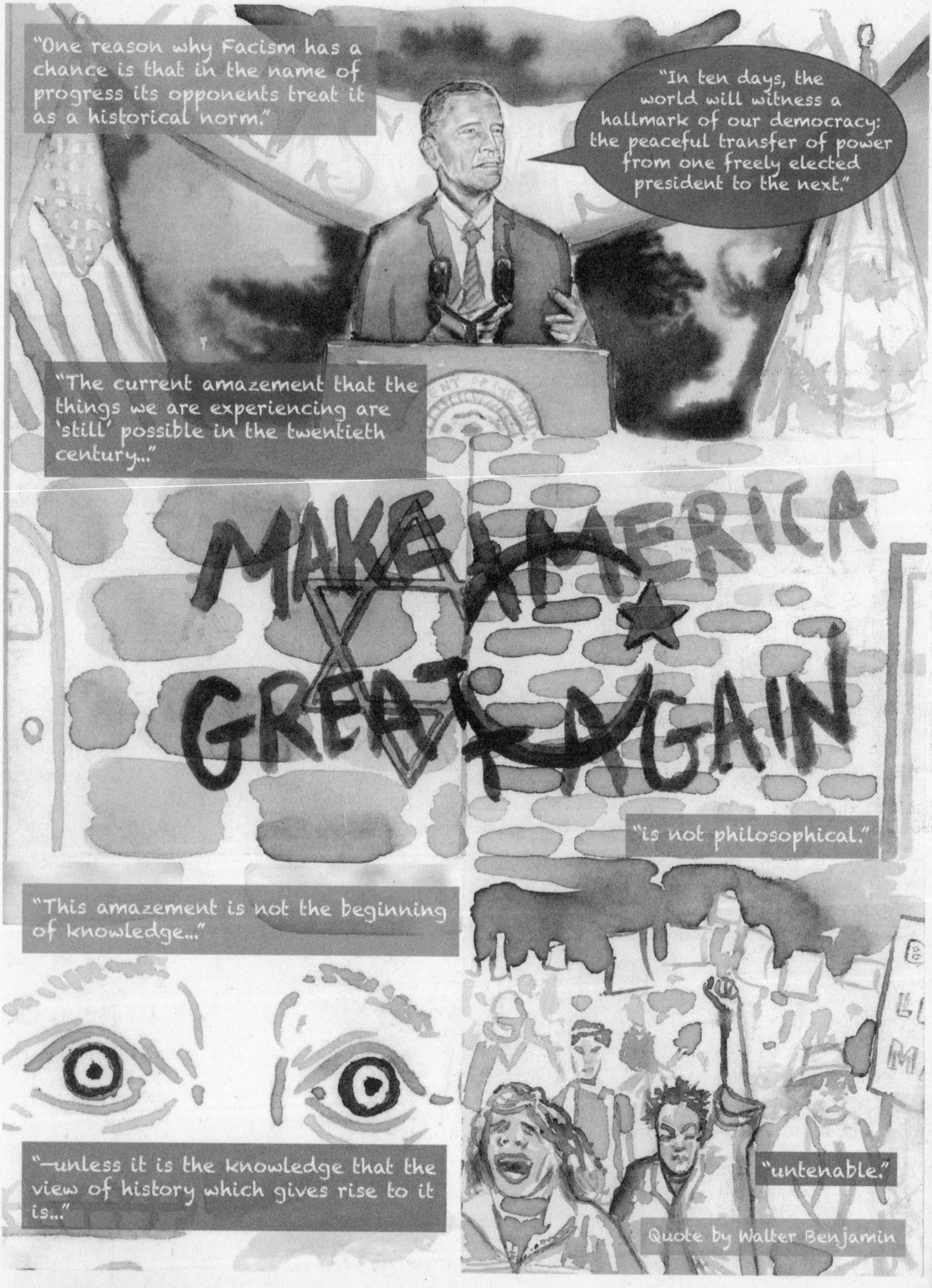
"One reason why Facism has a chance is that in the name of progress its opponents treat it as a historical norm."
"In ten days, the world will witness a hallmark of our democracy: the peaceful transfer of power from one freely elected president to the next."
"The current amazement that the things we are experiencing are 'still' possible in the twentieth century..."
MAKE AMERICA GREAT AGAIN
"is not philosophical."
"This amazement is not the beginning of knowledge..."
"—unless it is the knowledge that the view of history which gives rise to it is..."
"untenable."
Quote by Walter Benjamin